DATE DUE

~~NO 20 97~~		
~~MY 19 '08~~		

DEMCO 38-296

LISTENING TO AMERICA

LISTENING TO
AMERICA

*Twenty-five Years in the Life of a Nation,
as Heard on National Public Radio* ◆ ◆ ◆

Edited by LINDA WERTHEIMER

 Houghton Mifflin Company BOSTON NEW YORK 1995

National Public Radio,® NPR,® All Things Considered,® Morning Edition,®
Performance Today,® Weekend Edition,® Horizons,® and Talk of the Nation®
are service marks of NPR, registered with the U.S. Patent and Trademark Office.

Library of Congress Cataloging-in-Publication Data
Listening to America : twenty-five years in the life of a nation : as
   heard on National Public Radio / edited by Linda Wertheimer.
     p.   cm.
   Includes index.
   ISBN 0-395-70697-1
   1. National Public Radio (U.S.)   2. United States — History — 1969–
3.   Radio journalism — United States — History.   I. Wertheimer, Linda.
II. National Public Radio (U.S.)
HE8697.95.U6L57   1995
384.54'06'573 — dc20   95-8004
                        CIP

Printed in the United States of America

MP   10   9   8   7   6   5   4   3   2   1

Book design by Melodie Wertelet

For Sidney L. Brown
1932–1994

CONTENTS

Contents

Contents

FOREWORD

NPR NEWS MISSION STATEMENT
"NPR News employs the highest standards of journalism, the creative elements of audio, and the most intelligent use of language. Each day we analyze significant ideas and events, challenge conventional wisdom, and make the complex coherent. We believe in presenting a diversity of human stories that define and enlighten our era, recognizing the information we provide is vital to democracy."

For twenty-five years now, National Public Radio has filled a special niche in the American media marketplace, keeping alive the original promise of public broadcasting — to help the creative spirit to flourish and to help Americans hear more vividly and understand more deeply. During a time of challenges and uncertainty, it is comforting to know the network that began a quarter century ago with high standards, lofty hopes, and a shoestring budget has fulfilled its mandate, despite the odds.

National Public Radio began as an afterthought to the 1967 Public Broadcasting Act, which was designed primarily for public television. Only 104 public radio stations carried the first NPR program, *All Things Considered*, when it made its debut in 1971. The audience was barely measurable then, perhaps a few hundred thousand.

Today, nearly sixteen million Americans listen to 520 NPR member stations each week. Many additional listeners tune in around the world to hear NPR programs on stations abroad or direct from satellites. The network that began with one ninety-minute news broadcast each weekday evening now provides many times that amount of live news programming each morning and evening, seven days a week, with additional programs and newscasts around the clock.

The initials NPR have become a recognizable brand name, drawing a loyal audience of listeners who set their radios — clock, kitchen, and car — to their local NPR member stations, which they also support with their dollars. At NPR, not a day goes by without letters or electronic mail messages from listeners writing about the role and value of public radio in their lives. Many describe how they stayed in the driveway to hear the end of a particularly engaging report, or how an NPR story led to a stimulating conversation later at a party or in a restaurant.

Despite its popularity, NPR has also had its critics. Perhaps because we are a news source that seeks to expand the spectrum of views and news, NPR has been charged with liberal bias and elitism almost from the very beginning.

NPR News is fiercely independent, no matter which political party happens to be in power. As Bill Siemering, the man who created *All Things Considered,* has written recently: "We have no agenda; we report accurately; we are fair and balanced; we tell the truth." That, he adds, is enough to make some people uncomfortable.

With more than thirty hours of original news reporting each week on some of the most controversial topics in American society, including sensitive cultural or scientific subjects that some people would prefer not to hear, NPR inevitably makes some listeners unhappy or even angry. We surely have made mistakes, but our high standards and our daily editorial process underscore our commitment to solid, fact-based radio journalism. During the course of a week, we provide many points of view in essays and commentaries by both liberals and conservatives. "I simply do not believe that it is possible to do a proper, independent, and worthy journalistic job, and at the same time be loved by everybody," Richard Salant, the late president of CBS News and an NPR board member, wrote many years ago. Certainly NPR does not expect to be loved by everybody, but we do believe we are respected for the quality work we do.

The NPR audience is a true cross section of America, from farmers and taxicab drivers to teachers and CEOs. According to surveys, one in every three listeners is in a professional or managerial occupation. Nearly half of the public radio audience lives in households with incomes below $40,000. Just over half of the audience has a high school diploma, while almost a third has a college degree. One of the main characteristics of the NPR audience is that it enjoys learning and seeks to continue its education.

Politically, self-described conservatives make up the largest portion of the NPR audience, just over a third, while liberals make up just under a third, and the rest identify themselves as middle of the road. In short, the NPR audience is middle-class America — those who volunteer more, participate in school more, go to church more, read more, and are more likely to own a computer, listen to music, and subscribe to newspapers.

✦

All Things Considered was one of the first genuine newsmagazines in broadcasting when it began twenty-five years ago. There are now nearly a dozen newsmagazines on television. But despite attempts by others to copy our approach, NPR is still different, both more substantive and more fulfilling. In analyzing what makes NPR distinctive, I believe there are six general reasons why our brand of public radio journalism has succeeded. *Listening to America* is full of examples.

1. Time for in-depth reporting. NPR listeners get a comprehensive look at the world's news, every day, and whatever time of day the news is breaking. And they get the history, context, and analysis citizens need to make sense of issues, ideas, and events. NPR devotes extra airtime to our reports to make them more than headline summaries. Oversimplification is a disease of modern broadcasting. But NPR programs are meaningful because they have *time* to convey meaning. A two-hour NPR newsmagazine, such as *Morning Edition*, has almost two full hours of news and features. The average report on NPR is four to five minutes long. Taped interviews can be as long as needed for a coherent conversation, and taped remarks can express a complete thought. *All Things Considered* routinely carries longer documentary reports, such as the award-winning "Good-bye, Saigon."

2. Good writing and editing. Writing for the ear is everything in radio. A strong narrative line carries a good story and makes for compelling listening. News reports and features on NPR newsmagazines are written and edited and often rewritten and reedited, giving the programs a lucid, literate sound. It is clear to the audience that language is used carefully. When it is not, we get bags of letters. What counts most when NPR hires a new reporter or seeks a new host for a national program is what he or she knows and how well he or she writes. Although many NPR reporters and hosts have become "stars," we are not in the business of creating a personality cult around a fresh face or hairdo. NPR asks a different question: What does this reporter have to say and how well can he or she say it?

3. Content and standards. Entertainment values influence much of the media today. Bill Kovach, curator of the Nieman Foundation at Harvard, has pointed out that entertainment values lead to sensationalism, hype, brevity, conflict, immediacy, and oversimplification. Public radio, by comparison, puts content at the center of its value system. NPR has been described as radio with soul; we care about society and democracy. We assume the audience is intelligent and that they care, too, about making our diverse and democratic polity function better. NPR reporting can also be entertaining, but there is a seriousness of purpose in most of what we do — in talking about the decision to give up the Panama Canal, about trying to free U.S. embassy hostages, or about alleviating the threat of nuclear war. Public radio listeners do not expect to hear tabloid-type stories on the air. And NPR seldom goes live from the latest murder trial. We have been happy to let others sensationalize. A major media survey recently gave credit to NPR as the leading institution setting standards in American journalism. That aspect of NPR News is perhaps one of the greatest legacies of these twenty-five years.

4. Authentic voices and the human experience. Talking with all kinds of people, the ordinary and the powerful, is one of the things NPR does best: Bob Edwards talking with Red Barber, or Cokie Roberts chatting with voters in Bogue's Cafe in Alabama. We have also found our own authentic voices and made them commentators. Some of the most original, included in this book, are from Kim Williams in Montana, Andrei Codrescu in Louisiana, and Bailey White in Georgia. News by its very nature cannot all be good. But NPR programs are leavened with positive stories and profiles of remarkable people who are portrayed with their human frailties, as well as their courage and indomitable persistence.

The first NPR mission and goals statement, written in 1970, says the network will speak in many voices and dialects and "will regard individual differences with respect and joy rather than derision and hate; it will celebrate the human experience as infinitely varied rather than vacuous and banal; it will encourage a sense of active participation, rather than apathetic helplessness."

5. The advantages of radio. Television is certainly the dominant medium in America today, but as a medium for ideas, discussing important issues or suggesting solutions, radio cannot be beat. Great writing coupled with imaginative use of sound production can be more powerful than a picture. When skillfully done, a radio piece can trigger our imaginations and create vivid, long-lasting impressions and images. Some of NPR's best radio documentaries are here: Alex Chadwick's report on Czechoslovakia's Velvet Revolution is one such piece, and so is Noah Adams's report on the Reverend Jim Jones and the tragedy of Jonestown.

6. Public service. Perhaps NPR's greatest distinction springs from its basic purpose. NPR still seeks to educate at the highest level of understanding, providing important information that a democracy needs to survive. Public radio addresses "listeners as citizens and individuals, not as consumers. We create programming to serve the public and we aspire to see our audience grow. But we do not view our audience as a marketable commodity," according to our new guide on journalistic standards. In other words, NPR programming is not viewed as a profit center, and our style of radio journalism is not designed primarily to bring a mass audience to hear an advertiser's message.

✦

Today Americans are bombarded by a glut of information. Yet out of this glut there is perhaps less real knowledge and precious little wisdom. NPR has made its reputation as a community of the airwaves, where people can turn for accurate information and a constructive dialogue, leading toward greater knowledge and wisdom.

Although *Listening to America* is a printed record of twenty-five years of radio, the lively voices of NPR come through loud and clear. This is not the stuff of stodgy studios; these are real people captured in the act of consideration and creativity. Whether the subject is Watergate, an election, or urban life, by listening to NPR the nation can hear itself, and know better what it is and what it is becoming.

Choosing a few representative radio reports from the thousands broadcast each year was a task of unusual difficulty. Linda Wertheimer, one of the leading NPR voices and a member of the NPR family from the very beginning, has done a superb job. This book provides a vivid history of the major news events from the past two and a half tumultuous decades — from Nixon's trip to China to Nixon's death, from the fall of Saigon to the fall of the Soviet empire. *Listening to America* also includes some classic NPR moments, such as an illuminating report on chewing Wintogreen Life Savers in the dark.

In a letter to the Carnegie Commission in 1967, E. B. White wrote that public broadcasting "should address itself to the ideal of excellence, not the idea of acceptability." White went on to describe public broadcasting in terms that an NPR listener both twenty-five years ago and today would recognize: "It should arouse our dreams, satisfy our hunger for beauty, take us on journeys, enable us to participate in events, present great drama and music, explore the sea and the sky and the woods and the hills. It should be our Lyceum and Chautauqua, our Minsky's and our Camelot. It should restate and clarify the social dilemma and the political pickle."

The fine stories in these pages, as striking as the day they were broadcast, are a measure of just how well National Public Radio has lived up to White's admonition during this past quarter century. The reports also encompass a history of NPR, a reminder of the people who made and make this network successful. Here are the scripts, the tape-editing triumphs, the fresh approaches to storytelling which have been the hallmark of NPR from the beginning.

Listening to America is also a tribute to the well-known names and the behind-the-scenes staff who help create and sustain the network. We are a more diverse staff now and we produce better programs than we did in the early years, but our aim has remained essentially the same. Scott Simon returned to NPR after a year in network television, saying, "The chance to do work worth believing in that may be of value to others is what brings me back to this extraordinary institution in American life."

This, then, is a record of our first twenty-five years. With its dedicated and talented staff and its member stations across the country, may NPR continue to fulfill its mission and mandate for listeners in America and around the world for at least another twenty-five.

— Bill Buzenberg
Vice President, News
WASHINGTON, D.C.
JANUARY 1995

INTRODUCTION

In the early days of *All Things Considered*, I was the director. Every night at five, I gave the signal, the music started, the host of the program spoke, and ninety minutes of news and interviews, features, analysis, commentary, reviews, music, and occasional bits of nonsense went on the air. It was the very beginning of a conversation with this country, a daily recounting of what had happened and a discussion of what might be important. In the years that followed, I moved on to covering Congress and politics, finally returning to host *All Things Considered*, but I have never forgotten the terror of directing the early programs. I remember mistakes, dead air, missing tapes, and moments of panic as if they happened yesterday. However, I don't remember the words I said to start NPR's first news program rolling. The engineer who turned it all on every night is now vice president for distribution. I asked Pete Lowenstein if he remembered if I said something significant when I gave that signal to start. "Not really," Pete answered. "You generally said 'Now.' We were all looking at the clock. We all knew it was time."

Because I was there when the first program went on the air, it has been a special privilege to revisit all those years and to write about them for this book. And the process has been extraordinary: I have found myself back in good and bad old days, hearing voices I haven't heard for years, listening to the evolution of NPR News over the air, out of the archives. We began choosing material to include in this book by making a list of the major news stories of each year since NPR began broadcasting *All Things Considered* in the spring of 1971. (I write "we" because much of this search was conducted by Erin Clune and Tom Shepard, who helped assemble pieces for the book.) Our idea was to hear again accounts of the important events of the last quarter century, the way NPR listeners heard them. Next, we asked everyone we could think of to share their memories of stories they heard on our programs, stories that stayed in their minds over the years. We asked producers and reporters to think about their own best work and to make lists of special pieces we ought to consider. There were difficulties. News, by its nature, grows stale within hours. We had to sift through daily reporting, looking for the account that would bring us back to another time, creating its own context. We found that the work reporters and listeners remember often has a great deal to do with sound: birds, crowds, car doors, explosions, demonstrations, and of course, music. Even in news stories, sounds conjure up images and memories. We hear the emotion in the voices on the radio, and we often make judgments about people from the sound of their voices. In transcribing and then reading some of our work, I found that pure radio won't always stay on the page of a book. We sometimes had to substitute pieces that were affecting to read for vivid and moving pieces that had to be heard. We also had to edit the transcripts, straighten out spoken sentences, sometimes eliminate sections of sound, to make them easier to read.

Then too, the small budgets of the early years meant NPR had to invent ways to cover international stories without sending our own reporters. The same was true for political coverage. We rarely boarded a campaign plane for the first five years because we could not afford it. In reviewing those years, I found that some of our improvisations worked and others didn't.

In compiling reports from the later years, we had different challenges. After *Morning Edition* joined the roster in 1979, and we rounded out the week with Saturday and Sunday editions of *All Things Considered* and added *Weekend Edition, Saturday* and *Sunday*, we had impossible riches from which to choose. As we brought more reporters on board, our coverage moved to another level. *Talk of the Nation* brought still more voices to our air. Of the thousands of pieces we might have included, this selection is small. Of all the voices our listeners associate with NPR, only a few are in this book. While it is wonderful to have such a range of possibilities, we found the process of elimination very difficult.

✦

In 1970, the year NPR was created, a small group of public radio station managers agreed to join forces and fund a news operation. It would be based in Washington, where most news organizations maintained their largest bureaus, and it would produce a nightly news program. The group chose one of their number, Bill Siemering, from Minnesota, to create the new program and to invent the sound of the new network. It was his idea that we consider a wide range of subjects to be news, that covering culture should be as important as covering a campaign. Bill Siemering laid down the basic tenets of our belief in those early months. He decided that all kinds of people should speak on the radio, that owning a big bass voice would not be a prerequisite for presenting the news. He wanted to hear reporting that does not necessarily originate in national capitals, from people bringing a variety of experience to covering the news. Bill Siemering also wanted something that was not, and is not, available in very many places on the radio dial. He wanted quietness. He wanted calm conversation, analysis, and explication. Over the course of the first year, while Siemering thought and planned, others worked on wiring together a system that would make it all possible. In the early days, it was not technically complicated to string radio stations together, but it was almost impossible to make the system work well.

The stations north and east of Washington were connected by a loop of telephone lines. Another loop roped in public radio stations in the Midwest. The quality of this "network" was meant to be the best the telephone company could provide, but it varied from day to day. Stations around the back of each circle heard a scratchy signal down a bad phone line most nights, and there were many times when a local operator pulled a plug and took an entire set of radio stations off the air. Eventually, we threw a long loop "overhead" to pick up the public stations on the West Coast, but it was some time before we had many listeners in the Mountain West or the South, because of the difficulty of making the connections.

In the mid-1970s, two technical advances made enormous progress finally possible: broadcast satellites and FM radios in cars. With satellite transmission, our sound was clean, clear, and accessible. At that point, sound production became a signature of NPR. Our producers collaborated with engineers to create subtle mixes of sounds and voices. It became possible to hear sounds that are very difficult to reproduce, to use noises to conjure up pictures in listeners' minds. And with FM car radios, we joined the national commute and became a companion to millions of Americans. Before the satellite, we were a private party, with a committed but small band of listeners. After we began broadcasting from space, we rose with FM radio to gather an enormous audience for our morning and evening news programs.

We are now moving into our second and third generation of listeners. Young people often tell me that they sat in the back of the car, kicking the front seat and demanding that the radio station be changed as they were ferried to school. Now, they tell me, *they* are the parents telling their children to pay attention to the news on NPR. Our largest audiences now are in the biggest cities, especially those with long commutes. Public radio stations in places like Boston and Los Angeles have helped us become an important part of their communities. But we have added many other stations where there are not so many sources of information, smaller stations that struggle to serve towns like Carlsbad, New Mexico, where I grew up. NPR is available almost everywhere in this country now. Truckers tell us that there are very few stretches of American highway where our stations do not reach. Farmers listen on FM radios in tractors as they roll across the fields. We are working now to make our programs available overseas and we are planning for the next technical leap into the future.

◆

The most frequent question I'm asked about NPR is: Are we are having fun? People generally go on to observe that it sounds as though we are. There are many reasons for that, starting with the basic premise of gathering news, the fascinating process of finding out what is happening. With hours of live news programs every day, we have a very broad definition of news, and the opportunities to explore are extraordinary. From the very earliest days, we have broadcast important events and our reporters have been in the room watching everything from the Watergate hearings to the opening session of the 104th Congress.

But the number-one reason that NPR is a wonderful place is the people who work here. From the very earliest days, when there were only a few of us, we had leaders who believed in giving people plenty of room to work out their ideas. We had Bill Siemering's vision of what NPR might be and Cleve Matthews's calm conviction that no matter what disasters happened during the afternoon, we would have a radio program every night at five. From our first president, Don Quayle, who was present at the creation, through Lee Frischknecht, Frank Mankiewicz, Doug Bennet, and now Delano Lewis, we have been fortunate to have the leadership we needed to grow in good times and make our way safely through other times; we have had people who were prepared to step between those of us covering the news and whoever happened to be shooting at us. And we have needed them. At every level, administrators and managers have been committed to the same enterprise, to make us better.

In the very beginning we had Susan Stamberg clearing a path for the rest of us, inventing her own kind of radio and ensuring that women would play an unprecedented role on the new network. Susan was the first woman to anchor a national nightly news program. Nina Totenberg, Cokie Roberts, and I came along the path, taking assignments never before given to women. It is difficult to overstate Susan's personal impact on the way NPR sounds now. I think of her as the mother of our curiosity. In a similar way, Bob Edwards's calm assurance on *Morning Edition* sets a standard for the way NPR sounds. In the late seventies, he and Susan hosted *All Things Considered* together. I also think that Robert Siegel represents something we reach for, range and intelligence. His ability to switch easily from the most serious telephone conversation with a foreign leader to a frankly goofy contest is one of the reasons people listen to NPR. Scott Simon has inspired young imitators at stations all over the country; although the "small Scotts" generally can't match his style and intensity, he has convinced them that wonderful writing is the reason people remember what they hear. Noah Adams is the quiet voice down at the end of the table reminding us to get out of capitals and talk to people. He has also created a kind of writing for radio that recognizes the way people listen to words, and he constantly experiments with it. Many of us have worked together for almost twenty years, which is rare in the news business, and there are plenty of people coming along.

The opportunities that NPR has offered to women, to people of color, to very young people, to people who refuse to retire, to all sorts of voices and commentators have been unique in broadcasting. We sound, I'm told by listeners I meet, like regular people, and those same listeners feel they have a relationship with us which goes beyond disembodied voices delivering the news. Is it fun? Yes. It's also exciting and satisfying to work with the people at NPR to produce the best programs we can manage to put together before we go on the air. We have won every important broadcasting award, many of them several times. We win awards because of those lists of names you hear at the end of our programs. They are the managers who give us direction; editors who keep us clear and accurate; producers and directors who take hours of interviews, sounds, and music and, as we say, "make it sing"; and techs who help make the results remarkable. Our programs are a true collaboration. There are frustrations, we have to move quickly, and we almost always feel we could have used a little more time. But, speaking personally, I get to spend every evening with Robert Siegel and Noah Adams; Nina and Cokie and I spend much of our working lives and much more of our private lives together. It *is* wonderful fun.

My greatest regret in putting together this book is that so much is left out, particularly the hard work of daily journalism, the details of developing news which are so important to gather and report, but which have a short shelf life. It is the most important thing we do, but a book that concentrates on the biggest events does not reflect that daily mastery of the details of our national life which keeps people turning on the radio to hear why interest rates or the stock market or the political fortunes of a particular party are up or down.

I am grateful to the staff of NPR's tape library for helping us to locate pieces, for retrieving old tape from the National Archives, and for guiding us through the rundowns of the earliest years. Katherine Plumb, Beth Howard, Elizabeth Sullivan, Tom Tuszynski, Sheila Plotnick, Gary Dwor-Frecaut, and our head librarian, Rob Robinson, were always helpful and patient. The staff of the National Archives, which keeps NPR's early programs, shipped crates of tapes to us as we shopped for pieces to include. Tom Connors of the National Public Broadcasting Archives provided research, photographs, and letters from listeners. Kee Malesky and our reference library staff helped check facts and spelling. (We exhausted our sources for checking the hundreds of names that appear and were not able to confirm the most obscure.)

With the help of Michael Beacom and Erika Harding in the tape center, we transferred fragile old tapes to cassettes. Jan Verrey and Katie Schneider then transcribed those cassettes. Ori Hoffer and JoAnn Murray bridged us from one computer system to another so that we could read the later scripts and write about them on the same machine. Dave Driemeyer, who runs our computer operation, lent us his own equipment, to make the process easier. And Rick Jarrett and Max Cacas, the news department's computer specialists, bailed us out of frequent difficulties. Many of our reporters and producers took extra time to offer suggestions and lists, or to provide background on stories they'd covered. We are especially grateful to Art Silverman, Margaret Low Smith, Robert Siegel, Noah Adams, John Ydstie, Ann Cooper, Ira Flatow, Mike Waters, Susan Stamberg, Cokie Roberts, Mike Shuster, John McChesney, and Deb Amos. Ira Glass, who is one of our best producers, remembered many other people's best work. Neal Conan helped a great deal with coverage of the Gulf War, David Molpus and Marty Kurcias shared trip diaries, and a number of people gave us photographs. Bill Craven, Necola Deskins-Staples, and Mary Morgan of our Public Information Department also searched for pictures and identified programs that won awards.

I have continued to work for most of the time that it has taken to produce this book, and I owe a great deal to the executive producer of

All Things Considered, Ellen Weiss, who believes in giving us all opportunities. My working two jobs meant that Tom Shepard and Erin Clune did a great deal of the work of finding the pieces we chose from for this collection. I found I valued their judgment, not only about which pieces to group together, but on which events really do remain interesting history for readers in the nineties. I am also grateful for the fine editing hand of John Sterling of Houghton Mifflin and for the personal attention he gave to this project. He convinced us that people who listen to NPR will also want to read about it and has given us enthusiastic encouragement all the way along. And thanks to Jayne Yaffe, who restored spelling and punctuation to a radio writer's work and helped us make the transition from transcript to manuscript.

I am endlessly grateful to my husband, Fred Wertheimer, for making many things possible. It was Fred who first heard of a public radio network about to be born and sent me over to apply for a job. Through all the years since, he has always encouraged me to take the next step, to take risks, to do more than I thought I could do.

LISTENING TO AMERICA

1971

A *ll Things Considered* went on the air on May 3, when Americans took part in May Day demonstrations against the war in Southeast Asia. By 1971, U.S. troops were being pulled out of Vietnam, but bombing raids were escalating again and so were protests. That year, national opinion polls on the war were shifting, and distrust of the government was spreading. But as it unfolded, May Day fell somewhere between a call to action and a rite of spring.

It was a perfect May morning, scented with spring flowers and tear gas; thousands of demonstrators from around the country were in Washington threatening to shut down the city. As a practical matter, they never had a chance. They were disorganized and outmaneuvered, and the force arrayed against them was far beyond what was needed. In fact, the government's response to that day of demonstration was its own shock to our national system.

In the ghoulish tradition of the news business, our small staff was tremendously excited that our first broadcast would air on one of the biggest news days of that spring. We sent reporters out with tape recorders and instructions to capture the feel and texture of the day, to talk to the people who were involved, to put our listeners on those streets. At five o'clock we weren't quite ready to go when Robert Conley spoke the sentence which began it all: "From National Public Radio in Washington, I'm Robert Conley with *All Things Considered.*"

We've changed the ritual in the twenty-five years since, but we haven't changed it much. Then, as now, a scrap of music followed, and a list of what was coming. But then Conley introduced our first effort to take our listeners with us, to the Mall, to the bridges across the Potomac, to the White House, and to the Capitol, as the protesters surged through the city.

Robert Conley was a veteran of the *New York Times* and NBC, a gangling man with blue eyes and a frill of white hair topping a high forehead. He had a beautiful voice, only one of his considerable gifts for spinning stories. Much of what he said was not scripted at all. You will notice that he's stretching, vamping, waiting for that first piece of tape to come flying into the studio.

All Things Considered, MAY 3

CONLEY: In the top of the day's news — the crush, catcalls, flux, and flow of the demonstrations in Washington against the war in Southeast Asia.

As a result of those demonstrations today, somewhere between sixty-five hundred and seven thousand protesters have been picked up by the police. They have been picked up and put into buses and hired trucks and taken to a makeshift compound near the RFK Stadium. That's the home of the Washington Senators and the Washington Redskins, named after the late Senator Robert F. Kennedy.

The day started out almost before dawn and went on in flux and ebb and flow until about noontime. The demonstrators sometimes moved out into the streets, stood in front of cars. They shoved parked cars into the street. They dumped trash cans, they set them afire. They spread, among other things, nails and puddles of oil, on the pavement. They ripped up paving blocks from the sidewalks, threw them at passing cars. At various intersections you could see glass all over the street. A truck filled with paper was set on fire at one other road crossing.

While all of this was going on, flying squads of police, zigzagging on motor scooters, moved in and out of the city with tear gas, night-sticks — those are the heavy sticks that are weighted with a lead core in the center — and tried by charges and feints to break up the demonstrators.

Some of the demonstrators cut fuel lines on buses. They abandoned cars. Some motorists said that as they were stuck in the morning rush-hour traffic, people came running up, pulled open the hood of the car, and yanked out the distributor cap so the engine couldn't run anymore.

But federal authorities kept traffic moving across the four main bridges over the Potomac River. Those bridges were supposed to have been one of the main targets in this morning's demonstrations against the war.

As part of that federal power, there were roughly twenty-two hundred marines and army paratroopers. They moved into the city from nearby staging areas in Virginia and Maryland. Helicopters, for example, dipped down onto the grounds of the Washington Monument, carrying marines. The troops, whether marines or army, came into town in battle dress, with camouflaged helmets, sheathed bayonets, and rifles. With all of that power against the demonstrators, by mid-morning, Attorney General John Mitchell was able to say, "The city's open, traffic's flowing, and the government's functioning."

Great batches of the Capitol's roughly 318,000 government workers, however, set off much earlier from home than normally and showed up at work hours early, so they avoided a great deal of this. The Civil Service Commission, which is the main body overseeing the activities of all the federal government workers, said the attendance at government offices was overwhelmingly normal.

Beyond that, at the White House, Mrs. Nixon was able to give a luncheon for congressional wives without any audible or visible disturbance while that was going on. And late in the day, the Federal Bureau of Investigation picked up Rennie Davis, one of the organizers of the demonstration. They've accused Rennie Davis of conspiracy and interference with federal workers.

For many demonstrators, the mobile street tactics, the civil disobedience, are an expected spring event. But before today, many other young people have not been willing to oppose the state with their bodies. For these young Americans, today was a major test of their commitment to the ethical code of the young and the angry. It was their freedom ride, their Selma march, their May Day.

✦ ✦ At that point, our listeners heard sirens, voices chanting "Stop the war, stop the war," and the slapping noise of helicopters. Jeff Kamen was the reporter. Kamen had long bushy hair and a beard, generally wore overalls, and drove an old hearse. He was, and is, intense and combative. All his descriptions were recorded at the time they happened, at the demonstration.

KAMEN: One, two, three army helicopters flying surveillance over the small section of Washington's complicated highway system. A line of young people has just come across the highway. Traffic is stopped. Here come the police. One demonstrator knocked down by a motor-scooter policeman . . . Anger now . . . anger of the young people.
DEMONSTRATOR: Come on, people.
KAMEN: The demonstrators just told a motorcycle sergeant that one of his men did knock one of the demonstrators down.
POLICEMAN: All right, let me get an ambulance down here for you. Motor 3 on the Southwest Freeway, have one injured down here.

Could you send me an ambulance, please? It's right at Maine Avenue.

DEMONSTRATOR: . . . when he hit the kid he went right through the line.

POLICEMAN: . . . got past me and almost knocked me down . . . in the blue . . .

SECOND DEMONSTRATOR: Yeah, but it's a policeman we're talking about.

THIRD DEMONSTRATOR: Policeman on a motorcycle hit him, not a . . . not a citizen, man . . .

FOURTH DEMONSTRATOR: Right there, the man over there. Right there.

KAMEN: Sergeant, excuse me, Jeff Kamen, National Public Radio. Is that a technique where the men actually try to drive their bikes right into the demonstrators?

POLICEMAN: No, it's no technique. We're trying to go down the road, and the people get in front. What are you going to do? You don't stop on a dime.

KAMEN: What happened, officer?

POLICEMAN: . . . bricks they don't count.

KAMEN: Somebody threw a brick at you, officer?

POLICEMAN: Yes, sir.

KAMEN: Right here, as you were driving through?

POLICEMAN: Right.

KAMEN: One of the motorcycle police officers says someone threw a brick at him. I was here at the time. I didn't see anything thrown. Army helicopters coming in low, keeping constant surveillance, keeping the various command posts, military police, and obviously presidential staff advised as to what's going on.

One helicopter now is in real low, military police helicopter, up on the rise of this highway section. Young people are holding an American flag upside down. A handful of police officers has succeeded in clearing at least half of this roadway. Traffic is flowing again.

A Washington, D.C., bus has just arrived. Police officers wearing white riot helmets come out of the bus. They snap on their helmets. Integrated police team. The demonstrators are fleeing. The police officers are carrying or wearing their tear gas masks. The tactic this morning, obviously, is to keep the demonstrators on the run.

✦ ✦ And then the scene shifts to the grounds of the Pentagon, where very few demonstrators succeeded in getting close. Our reporter Steven Banker interviewed one who had arrived in a kayak.

BANKER: Is this your boat?

DEMONSTRATOR: Yes.

BANKER: Would you describe it.

DEMONSTRATOR: It's a one-man kayak.

BANKER: It must be pretty hard to get here if you're the only demonstrator in front of the Pentagon and you had to come by kayak.

DEMONSTRATOR: No, I'm sure I could have driven a whole lot easier.

BANKER: This man is wearing an orange Mae West. Is that what you have on?

DEMONSTRATOR: Just a life preserver.

BANKER: A life preserver and a white crash helmet. And he carried a green kayak from the Potomac River onto the grounds of the Pentagon. What are you going to do now?

DEMONSTRATOR: Go back to the Potomac River. Maybe paddle across and go through the reflecting pool, then back upstream.

BANKER: But surely you must have expected to meet a lot of other people here.

DEMONSTRATOR: Yes, I did. I'm kind of disappointed.

✦✦ Steven Banker reported that about thirty people eventually made it to the Pentagon and were arrested and taken away. Jeff Kamen, by this time on Pennsylvania Avenue, talked to a young man who was trying to elude the police.

DEMONSTRATOR: All the pigs came running out and just spraying mace and grabbing people and they just got them all over to the side and it was over as fast as it started.

KAMEN: Were they careful about who they maced?

DEMONSTRATOR: No, no, there was a priest up there I saw. There were — there were some straight-looking people, you know. They were just — I mean, they were macing them in the back, you know, which I can't dig. You know, they were already running and they were chasing them with the mace in their hair and in their ears and the back of their neck. And there's — you know, they were running away, not towards.

KAMEN: And they maced them in the back?

DEMONSTRATOR: Yeah, I mean, it was — they all were being maced in the back. The march never went forward. It was always being backed down here as a retreat. And instantly it was, like, stopped and turned around and the whole time they were just macing them in the back.

✦ ✦ Kamen described the arrests of demonstrators, and observed, "Today in the nation's capital, it is a crime to be young and have long hair." Jim Russell, an NPR reporter who did not have long hair, was watching the same kind of thing from the grounds of the Lincoln Memorial. As he speaks, you can hear a surging, shouting crowd behind him.

RUSSELL: Groups of demonstrators have attempted to stop traffic. They have not succeeded. They've stopped traffic only momentarily. And police moved in with such a show of force that the demonstrators were forced away. The police have been making very free use of tear gas, and at one point I saw two policemen pinning down a young man and one policeman was punching him. I couldn't see if he was punching him in the face or the stomach, but I did see him repeatedly punch the young man. And then he was led away to be arrested.

✦ ✦ Along the way, we heard from people who seemed to be enjoying the day, in great good humor, even about the effects of tear gas. Others sound bewildered, as if the demonstration was not what they had expected. Still others seem outraged.

DEMONSTRATOR: My eyes are burning a little bit. My skin burns. I always react this way to gas.

SECOND DEMONSTRATOR: I'm fine, but we're gonna shut the fucking city if it takes all day.

KAMEN: Are they going to stop you today?

THIRD DEMONSTRATOR: It's — it's just, you know, it's just so disorganized. You know, like I was hoping that we could just, you know, go in en masse somewhere and just sit down and then just, you know, be peacefully arrested. But I don't know, they just — they just, you know, the scare tactics are working, I'm afraid.

FOURTH DEMONSTRATOR: I just don't know how much more running we can do and how much more gassing we can take. I really think that we can achieve our tactic by taking a long time to get arrested, without resisting, with being nonviolent.

FIFTH DEMONSTRATOR: I was at Washington Square, and when the cop busted me they put me in the car. I was peaceful. Then when they got me in the car, they said, "You're stupid, kid," and he whacked me with the billy club in the car. Eleven stitches.

SIXTH DEMONSTRATOR: The cops jump off the bus, and said, "We going to kill you all, you all damn people." Because like we told them . . . like we didn't want any trouble. He hollerin', "You're going to get trouble." First he try to run over me with the car. After he get out the car, he going to start beating on me.

There's no room for nonviolence. The only way you're going to beat this doggone man is to use tactics that he use. After spending thirteen months in Vietnam and coming back here and getting my ass kicked . . . I don't need it.

SEVENTH DEMONSTRATOR: This is the very thing, you know, you're protesting about, man. They're doing the very thing that, you know, you're trying to end. They're coming and just beating heads. It's done all over the world, and they're doing it at home. They don't really care, you know, who they do it to, as long as they maintain the status quo or whatever, you know.

EIGHTH DEMONSTRATOR: Yeah, the cop that busted me said, "How old are you?" I said, "Nineteen." He said, "How come you're not in the army?" I said . . . you know, I didn't say anything. I didn't . . . you know. He said, "You're chicken," and he started hitting me.

NINTH DEMONSTRATOR: We were standing down on the corner and a busload of police came up and they seemed to be really pouring out of the bus, and I didn't know what to do, so like, you know, I ran like hell and, like, I was running along. Someone clubbed me in the stomach, but, like, my coat protected me. And then I was running through a parking lot and someone threw a club at me.

◆ ◆ ◆ ◆ ◆ ◆ ◆ ◆ ◆

That young woman told our reporter that the club hit her in the head. A portion of her hair had been shaved, so the wound could be stitched. She said she was not discouraged. Asked how she felt, she said, "Mad."

As I listen to the tape of that first day's broadcast, it sounds rough. Listeners had no way of knowing who was speaking, reporters and the people they talked to were almost all nameless. In some cases, we didn't say where the conversations were taking place, or where the events we listened to happened. That first day's broadcast sounds indulgent in some places, overlong in others. We wouldn't do it that way now, and yet, we would. For all its unedited, sprawling, confusing quality, we did what Robert Conley said we would on that very first day. We put our listeners out there, in the middle of everything. We served up sound and texture, shouts and sirens. Even the confusion is a reflection of that

day. We asked all kinds of people, kids and cops and passing bureaucrats, to tell us what it meant, what they saw, and what they thought
about it. We are still doing that.

Demonstrations continued throughout 1971, as opposition to the
war began to spread beyond young people and students, to people who
seemed to surprise themselves by what they were doing.

Just about a month later, Doug Terry was covering still another
kind of protest against the war in Vietnam. This time a couple of
thousand lawyers came to the Capitol to meet with members of Congress and attend a rally on the Capitol grounds. Doug talked about the
protest-by-appointment, making his own views about the war fairly
clear.

All Things Considered, JUNE 8

TERRY: Frankly, I don't know if the lobbying will have any effect at all
on the congressmen and senators. Certainly they don't need to know
that the war has done bad things to South Vietnam. Certainly they
don't need to be told that increasing numbers of Americans want us out
by the end of the year. Certainly they don't need to be told that the war
has brought about great dissension at home and is spurring the drive for
a revolution in America.

What do they need to know? The lawyers are here under the
assumption, partly at least, that the congressmen need to know that
good, upstanding, clean-cut, all-around Americans want the army
home by the end of the year, as well as those bad, low-standing, dirty
hippies and peace freaks. That's true, at least partly. For there is no
question that the longhairs have less standing, because of what they are,
than the professional men who lobbied today.

The group is a varied one, in Washington for varied reasons. Some
— one sixty years old — told me that their children have played an
important role.

LAWYER: I happen to have a number of teenaged children. I think
discussions with them and trying to reason out why we're in this war
was one of the main reasons that I became active. And then my wife
became very interested. Then gradually they won me over. I think it
was the daughters and their strong position. One has become very
militant. She made two trips to Washington this year with the students'
mobilization force to protest the war. Just listening to them, I think,
this influenced me greatly.

SECOND LAWYER: I just think that the destruction and killing that our country is doing over in Southeast Asia is so horrible and so inexcusable, to say nothing — and I do not mean to put one ahead of the other — but the killing and maiming of our young men at the behest of our president without congressional authority is so contrary to the principles of our government.

THIRD LAWYER: Though I've expressed my opinion many times on the war, I've really done very little about it, like, I suspect, a great many people. And this is really the first action that I've ever taken in my own little way by trying to do something to stop this involvement. But I have been somewhat influenced, probably greatly influenced, by my children. I have ten children, most of whom are still quite young, but my three or four oldest have had quite an influence on me.

TERRY: The rally was attended by about two thousand persons. It was addressed by a number of congressmen and senators, including those who are thinking about seeking the presidential nomination. Republican Congressman Paul McCloskey of California:

MCCLOSKEY: We're on the threshold here in these chambers — in both the House and in the Senate — of reaching the majority of 218 in the House and 51 in the Senate to exercise our constitutional responsibilities to determine when and where this country fights a war. And I think that when you meet those men and women with whom you will discuss the matter, in trying to persuade them to change their minds, it's not a matter so much of threat as one of reasonable presentation of logic and reasons that now is the time for the Congress to vote to end this war.

TERRY: Senator Birch Bayh of Indiana:

BAYH: The time has come to recognize that the shortest distance between war and peace is a straight line. A straight line out of Vietnam. I cannot believe and I do not believe that most of our countrymen believe that a plan for peace necessitates bombing four countries, invading two in order to get out of one. This will not do the job.

TERRY: Former Congressman Allard Lowenstein of New York:

LOWENSTEIN: You need to help those men in there to change their colleagues by showing them precisely what the fact is: that if you vote to continue the war, you are not voting in the interests of the country. And what sometimes seems even more important to show elected officials: you are not voting in the interests of keeping yourself in office.

TERRY: And so it went, speeches that sound very much like the usual, but this time with a bit more urgency. The lobbying efforts will continue throughout this week. Next week the Vietnam Veterans Against the War are said to be planning another full week of activities. Some congressmen feel the effort to be highly meaningful. If the lobbyists can convince the congressmen that continuing the war means a possible loss of an election or more support next time around, it could have a significant effect.

✦ ✦ ✦ ✦ ✦ ✦ ✦ ✦ ✦ ✦

I n September, there was a tiny demonstration in front of the White House which was more powerful, in some ways, than the larger, noisier rallies. It was the beginning of a movement, the first stirrings of a group that still has political power, all these years later. The League of Families of Prisoners of War and Missing in Action in Southeast Asia was organized in the spring of 1970 and had supported President Nixon in his efforts to retrieve the men held by North Vietnam. But by the summer of 1971, some of the families had grown dissatisfied with the government's efforts and had decided to take the extraordinary step of demonstrating against the president's policy in front of the White House. Jim Russell was our reporter.

All Things Considered, SEPTEMBER 28

RUSSELL: The fifteen women and one man who demonstrated here in front of the White House today are part of a splinter group, which calls itself Families for Immediate Release. The splinter group was formed in May and claims it has about three hundred relatives who support its stance. These people believe, according to the group's founder, that the administration is using the prisoner issue to buy time for the South Vietnamese government.

The women today walked in a small circle, they were conservatively dressed and carried hand-painted placards. "BRING THEM HOME," "SET A DATE FOR RELEASE OF ALL POWS," and "MY SON, IS HE DEAD OR ALIVE?" I talked first with Barbara Mullen of California. She is the wife of Major William Mullen, who has been missing ever since his airplane was shot down over Laos five and a half years ago.

MULLEN: Well, I guess we're here to ask our president to negotiate realistically for the return of our men. There has been a peace proposal offered in Paris, and we feel that it has been quite ignored by our government. And, of course, that peace proposal says that we must set a withdrawal date in order to get those prisoners back. So far Vietnamization does not allow for a withdrawal date being set because our government continues to say that we must go on defending South Vietnam until they're ready to stand alone. Well, what does that mean? It's such an open-end thing.

RUSSELL: One aspect which made today's demonstration different from most that we see here in Washington is that many of these women, the mothers and wives of American servicemen, had never demonstrated for anything before. In fact, some of the women felt very ill at ease as they marched in front of the black iron fence which surrounds the White House.

MULLEN: I think it's a very, very difficult move. I think that if you ask people in — all these people here today, you'd find out it's the first time most of us have ever done anything like this, the first time I've ever been in any kind of a demonstration.

My husband left six and a half years ago for Vietnam and I've tried to wait and have confidence that my government, when the time came, would negotiate for the return of our men. And I kept waiting, and saying, "When will the time come? The war is going on, but Nixon's going to end it, he's going to end it, he said he would." And yet the time goes on.

And then it became more and more certain that the prisoner release was going to be tied to this withdrawal date. All right. We're getting out, but we're not getting any prisoners back. We haven't tied it together. We haven't gotten an agreement. Every month that goes by, we've got less troops over there, which makes the position of the prisoners more and more precarious.

RUSSELL: Would your husband understand what you're doing today?

MULLEN: My husband would certainly understand that I'm fighting for his life. I — I don't know how I could face him, if he came back, and he said, "Well, what did you do? Let me sit there for ten years and not even ask the president, not even ask him to negotiate for my return?"

RUSSELL: Mrs. Gerald Gartley has a son, a navy lieutenant, who has been a prisoner of the North Vietnamese for three years now.

GARTLEY: We feel that the American public believe that the war is over. Our own friends ask us, "When do you expect your son home?" They do not know the tragic fact that the present policy is for no total withdrawal, but for a residual force. And as long as that residual force is there, our sons and husbands will never come home.

RUSSELL: Is this the first demonstration you've ever been in?

GARTLEY: I hesitate ever to say that I'm in a demonstration, is how I feel about it. I would — I just can't use the word "demonstration" without some powerful feeling of revulsion coming over me. To me, to do what I'm doing this afternoon is the ultimate that I can do for my son. It is really going the last mile.

RUSSELL: Finally, I talked with Mr. and Mrs. Sam Beecher, Jr., of Indiana. Their son has been missing in action for more than four years. Mrs. Beecher is the state coordinator of the League of Families in Indiana, but she and her husband feel the time has now come to exert more pressure on the administration, and they are not ashamed to come to Washington to demonstrate at the White House.

MRS. BEECHER: Ordinarily, I do not participate in this sort of thing, but I feel this is so worthy and so — the focus needs to be directed this way so much, that I felt this enough to do it.

MR. BEECHER: Curious as it may seem, I don't feel at all peculiar about this. I think this is something that, if our son knew about it, that he would heartily endorse. And consequently we feel that this is where we should be.

MRS. BEECHER: Also, I'd like to say I think the time has come for ceasing the platitudes and the generalities and getting down to specifics. This is a personal matter and we have something personal at stake and so that's why we're here. And I don't feel a bit embarrassed or uncomfortable about it. Because I think, after all, I was led to believe this is a democracy.

RUSSELL: Yesterday, as the League of Families opened its convention here in Washington, Joe McCain, the son of Admiral John McCain, warned administration officials to come up with results on the prisoner issue. And McCain added that the families of these men may even embarrass the administration.

Today's demonstration was small, but its tone of displeasure with the president was very clear. But as Mr. Nixon himself has said, demonstrations in and of themselves rarely change minds at 1600 Pennsylvania Avenue.

✦ ✦ ✦ ✦ ✦ ✦ ✦ ✦ ✦ ✦

I remember that demonstration, and the strong sense that people like Mrs. Gerald Gartley had of crossing some kind of Rubicon by carrying a sign and demonstrating in Washington. Mark Gartley came home a hero. It took him awhile to understand what his mother had done. Joe McCain's father came home and went into politics. John McCain is now the senior senator from Arizona. The Beechers' son Quentin was declared missing, presumed dead. Barbara Mullen wrote to us that she believes her husband may have been among a group of prisoners she says were abandoned in Laos in 1973. Her book about her continuing fight to find out what happened is called *Every Effort.*

In the fall of 1971, Red China was admitted to the United Nations, and Nationalist China, which we then called "China," gave up its seat. Robert Conley, who covered the UN for the *New York Times,* returned to cover the vote and write about it for us.

All Things Considered, OCTOBER 26

CONLEY: The flagpole's bare now, a mute testimony to the enormous upheaval in world alignments that have taken place here at the United Nations, bare for the first time in the history of this world body.

That flagpole, one of 131 that curve in graceful procession outside this pale slab of a building that is the United Nations headquarters, no longer carries the fluttering flag of Nationalist China, a red rectangle with a blue quadrant on which is set a white sunburst radiating in twelve points. In its own way, that bare aluminum pole, glinting here in a setting New York sun, is the final confirmation that the Nationalist Chinese from Taiwan now are banished from the United Nations, no longer able to participate in its activities in any way.

Already the United Nations itself is scrambling to catch up with the rush of events here, in anticipation of the arrival of a delegation from the People's Republic of China, to lay claim to China's seat in the United Nations, in the vaulted hall of the General Assembly, that international parliament that now lies empty before me, and on the smaller but more powerful Security Council. In fact, so rapidly did the rush of events occur here that the United Nations is out shopping in New York today, trying to buy somewhere the massive red revolutionary banner of the People's Republic of China, red with five gold stars in the upper left-hand corner. The United Nations simply didn't have a Peking flag in the house, even as a contingency. So the United Nations Secretariat has had to go to its flag maker here in New York and press to have a Peking flag run off.

All of this rush came quickly on last night's decision by the General Assembly to take away China's credentials from the Chinese Nationalists from Taiwan and offer them to Peking. At 12:28 A.M. eastern time this morning, little more than an hour after the assembly acted, a Teletype machine here at the United Nations whirred into activity, transmitting a message to Peking from United Nations Secretary-General U Thant. "Accept, sir, the assurances of my highest consideration," the message read, as it informed Peking of the General Assembly's decision.

Two hours later, at three-thirty eastern time this morning in New York, or four-thirty in the afternoon Tuesday in Peking, came back the confirmation of receipt, and official acknowledgment from Peking's acting foreign minister, Ji Peng-fei, thereby establishing a direct link between the People's Republic of China and the United Nations. Indeed, at a later reception in Peking itself, Mr. Ji, the acting foreign minister, said that the People's Republic of China already is considering sending a delegation directly to the United Nations, but without indicating when. There always is the chance too that an interim delegation could be dispatched to New York immediately, whether in a matter of days or weeks, from Peking's nearest outpost on the North American continent, her embassy in Ottawa, the Canadian capital.

So, with all of this activity, the question still remained in the corridors of the United Nations, How did this all happen? How did the flood tide of votes, visibly and vocally emotional votes, how did they run against Taiwan and against the United States by a ratio of more than two to one, in that final tally of seventy-six to thirty-five in favor of Peking, with seventeen countries sitting on the sidelines through abstentions? Was the flood tide for Peking in the end a defeat for the United States? The final tally might look that way, but there's a deeper factor, as well, that is forever present in the rips and tugs of international affairs.

For twenty-two years, the United States has been the principal supporter of the Nationalist Chinese on Taiwan — politically, economically, and militarily — and so it remained last night, all the way down to the final wire. The United States, whatever the final vote said, seemed to be, and even more importantly was seen to be, the defender and friend of Taiwan. Put it this way, as a number of delegates here did: The United States did not of her own abandon Taiwan. The United Nations did. And in international affairs, that is a vital difference. With that in mind, I'm reminded of the political boss in Pennsylvania years ago — a Republican, I believe — who decided to back a losing candidate in an election. "You'll wreck the party," that long-gone leader was told. "Yes, I will," he admitted, "and we'll own the wreckage, won't we?"

✦ ✦ ✦ ✦ ✦ ✦ ✦ ✦ ✦ ✦

S usan Stamberg is still the voice many people hear when they think of NPR. She had a great deal to do with creating our sound and developing our attitude. She has always believed that the news is improved by getting personal, and that serious stories often need a chaser. Some of the playful notes you hear on our programs can be traced directly to Susan's sensibility. This was her take on China.

All Things Considered, OCTOBER 26

STAMBERG: Political implications aside, there is one point about the decision to admit Red China to the UN that hasn't been discussed yet. And that point is that from now on there won't be any discussion about the decision to admit Red China to the UN! In fact, an awful lot of institutions and people who've depended on it will be amazed to discover they don't have "Should we admit Red China to the UN?" to kick around anymore. Seventh-grade debate societies, for instance, are now out one prime topic of proing and conning. University professors will have to drop out entire units of courses, and they'll also have to rework their course notes. Some for the first time since 1949. Blind dates, if there still are such things, have become even more terror-filled overnight. Before Monday night, when a nervous mismatched couple ran out of rain, sun, and snow to talk about, there was always Red China. And dinner parties, when they began to lag, could always be saved by the hostess chirping brightly, "Red China and the UN, anyone?" Then she could relax, knowing that between the soup and coffee, people might not notice they had nothing in common. And anyway, the soufflé had collapsed.

This sudden lack in our collective unconscious probably won't be taken into consideration by any of the diplomats and political pundits, but I think it's a good idea for all of us to be thinking of a subject to take the place of the one we've just lost. And I have a suggestion. This topic will keep us talking about the very same part of the world, and it's related to the question we've just lost. It involves a group of people who've never really been part of the China scene through most of their history, who never really participated in Chiang Kai-shek's control of their country, who have been where they are from the beginning, been there as a majority — over eighty percent of the population, long before China got red, and Chiang Kai-shek sailed over from the mainland. Here's the topic: Should we admit Taiwan to the UN?

✦ ✦ ✦ ✦ ✦ ✦ ✦ ✦ ✦ ✦

W e struggled, in those early years, to find a voice for our radio program. We wanted it to be different from the sonorous ones making the authoritative statements we associated with the television networks. We wanted to hear from more people, sample a wider variety of views, and somehow keep our voice small and intimate, a voice in the car on the ride home, on the radio in the kitchen. We tried all sorts of things in that first year, including things that served as a kind of antidote to the news of war and protest. Here's one we all liked very much at the time. It was Mike Waters's idea. He wrote and produced it, mixed bits of kettledrums underneath, and took the role of the archangel. Robert Conley was anchoring that day and introduced the piece, but some of the performers were tourists at the Tidal Basin in Washington, real people, really looking at a sunset.

All Things Considered, DECEMBER 28

CONLEY: At this point, we'd hoped to have a review of a play, but there aren't many productions around Washington this week. Instead, by far, the most impressive piece of dramatic pageantry that we've seen in some time occurred yesterday evening in the western sky, just before nightfall. In burning orange that changed to softer hues, the sun in all its majesty descended, attended by a company of clouds. The discipline of the pageant suggested that the same cast had been performing together since the beginning of the run. But that's not the case.

The clouds, for one, stay with the company only a short time before moving on. Perhaps that's the reason why each performance appears so fresh. Most of us, in fact, can only imagine the kind of tension that exists in that company of performers, some thoroughly seasoned, some relatively new.

DIRECTOR: Thirty seconds, Archangel.

ARCHANGEL: OK, clouds, may we get in formation, please? Remember this evening you're going to be doing the mountains.

CLOUD: Archangel, will there be anybody new watching this evening?

ARCHANGEL: There'll be a few new people and there'll be some people who haven't watched for a while. There'll be a student in Brockport. There'll be a salesman who's caught in a traffic jam in East Aurora, and there'll be a —

DIRECTOR: Fifteen seconds, Archangel.

CLOUD: Archangel, when will I be able to do a solo again?

ARCHANGEL: Well, perhaps next week. Now, remember, this evening the formation is the mountains, not the whipped cream, but the mountains. And it's very important you stay together.

DIRECTOR: Five seconds, Archangel.

ARCHANGEL: All right, clouds, stand by.

DIRECTOR: Cue the clouds.

ARCHANGEL: All right, clouds, you're on.

BOY: It looks beautiful, the orange and the red that's mixed together. It makes it look crazy. You can't miss it when you look off or anything. It's cool.

WOMAN: It's just such a great, great way of bringing on darkness to me. It's such a feeling of splendor. I'm the sun, I gave you a great day. Whatever you did with it, the day is over. Nighttime is taking over. And you feel a certain amount of thankfulness, like, wow, you were great and on top of it all you're giving us a show, you know, at the end and you feel like saying "Thank God" or "Thank the sun."

MAN: It looks like a strip of cloud spreading out the sun into two parts and it's pretty. It's got a rainbow, something like a rainbow color, both sides of the sun. I think the cloud helps make it all more beautiful, more pretty, and the two planes right there, quite a sight with the radiant early sunset. I think that's pretty.

Well, if I'm caught in a traffic jam at sundown, I just enjoy looking at the sunset. I just look at it and relax, wait for your time to move, take it easy, makes you feel ready to go home from a hard day's work. The sort of thing that makes you think of going home and taking your shoes off and putting your slippers on and turning the radio on and enjoying life.

CONLEY: The sunset appearing nightly in the western sky. Its author is also responsible for the sunrise and the lightning storm.

1972

Nineteen seventy-two was the year of the Watergate burglary, the first in a chain of events which forced the only presidential resignation in our history. It was also an election year. After a primary season laced with what we later learned to call "dirty tricks," Americans were asked to choose between a sitting president who had promised peace for years and Senator George McGovern of South Dakota, a candidate whose supporters demanded peace now. President Nixon won forty-nine states and, twenty-one months later, resigned in disgrace. Looking back, 1972 seems to have set a bitter pattern for our present politics. We were unhappy with our choices on election day and very soon after, we were disappointed by our president.

One of the many curious echoes from that time is the president's State of the Union message before a joint session of Congress. President Nixon talked about the plans for reform which he had presented to the House and Senate. We broadcast an excerpt from that speech on *All Things Considered* and then listened to voices from around the country, people talking about the state of their own lives.

All Things Considered, JANUARY 20

NIXON: One year ago, standing in this place, I laid before the opening session of this Congress six great goals. One of these was welfare reform. That proposal has been before the Congress now for nearly two and a half years. My proposals on revenue sharing, government reorganization, health care, and the environment have now been before the Congress for nearly a year. Many of the other major proposals that I have referred to have been here that long or longer.

Now, 1971, we can say was a year of consideration of these measures. Now let us join in making 1972 a year of action on them, action by the Congress for the nation and for the people of America.

✦ ✦ ✦ ✦ ✦ ✦ ✦ ✦ ✦

In his piece on the president's State of the Union message, NPR's Rich Adams said that the president chided the Congress for its failure to act on his reform measures. We didn't use the word "gridlock" in 1972, although apparently the concept was part of the president's plan of attack for the election year.

President Nixon's plans to reform welfare and health care sound very like the ideas raised in the debate that took place a little more than twenty years later. The president also talked about his plan to visit the Soviet Union and his decision to travel to the People's Republic of China. It is difficult to recapture how unnatural that seemed. President Nixon had long been an advocate of isolating China. Containing Chinese communism was, after all, one reason why the United States was at war in Vietnam. "I go there with no illusions," the president said that night. "But peace depends on the ability of great powers to live together on the same planet, despite their differences."

In introducing the personal versions of the state of the Union which followed, Mike Waters said that we had "been ranging far and wide over the country" during the previous week, collecting interviews for a "sampler in sound." Our notions of far and wide were apparently limited; we went as far north as Maine, but only as far south as North Carolina, and the westernmost state he mentions is Wisconsin.

All Things Considered, JANUARY 20

MAN: Well, I actually think that the Union is in pretty bad shape, as far as my opinion about it, for the simple reason that different things that are going on here in the nation that makes it — you know — make it pretty rough. So I actually think it's in pretty foul shape.

SECOND MAN: My life's fantastic. It is. I've got enough money to keep me going and I'm doing something that I like and that's it. And I don't agree with a lot of things that happen around me, but as far as my own life is concerned, I agree with everything. So I don't worry about anything. I don't.

THIRD MAN: I'm a Chicano. And even the whites are upset about this country, especially the students. But my hang-up is, I'm becoming aware of this Chicano thing, this Mexican thing. And I'm getting uptight about discrimination and the war and all this stuff and I'm rationalizing in my own mind the things that I've gone through, different aspects of it.

OK, I was in the service, I was in Vietnam, right? OK, I went over there. When I went over there I was gung ho and all for this America thing. And I come back, I've been in school, I've started to be exposed to a lot of different things. I mean, it isn't outright discrimination, you know. The store clerks snubbing you. I work in the store. The people you're serving, maybe they don't like being served by a Mexican. And this is stuff that you can't really explain. You just feel it, you know. You can tell when something like this goes on.

And in this country that I supposedly fought for, right, this kind of thing happens and it isn't right in my own mind. I can't see it. And you asked about Nixon, well, you know, I can blame Nixon and I can't because this is a accumulation of things over a long period of time. And I just feel bitter and I'm getting more bitter as time goes on.

FOURTH MAN: They ain't got enough schools. They claim they ain't got enough schools so they're trying to mix the white with the colored, and things like that ain't going to work. Because people just ain't going to let it be.

Everybody wants, you know, to mix, but it ain't going to work. They're going to have problems. Since Kennedy passed that bill, you know, "every person have their rights," it seems like they have more trouble since then than they've had before they even started that. Everybody got along good. Seemed like the colored people ain't satisfied and they just move in and take over.

WOMAN: Perhaps you could call this the romantic period of the twentieth century, yet it doesn't really pay to be too sensitive. I've come to find out you can only be sensitive in certain things and you have to be very, very strong in others.

SECOND WOMAN: I don't feel that the country is going to get better, I think there'll be some kind of a revolution.

THIRD WOMAN: I don't believe our nation is going to experience any drastic changes. I think it's too big. I think it has too many parts to move rapidly. And I think that the only way to have any real significant changes in our nation and in our lives is for the change to begin on an individual level.

We so often hear the cry for peace, but I don't see how a nation can have peace when each individual has not made peace with himself.

FIFTH MAN: Morally, it's not what the nation was founded on. It was founded on the basis of what God laid down in his word, but that is no longer what our nation's founded on. Now it's founded on more what man — what his rights is instead of what God's rights is.

SIXTH MAN: Well, I can't see as the nation is any different from what it had been for the last fifteen or twenty years. We elect the people who serve in these high offices and they promise before they take the offices what they're going to do. But they're all alike and it's all the same thing and, really, I can't see much different in the state of the Union.

✦ ✦ ✦ ✦ ✦ ✦ ✦ ✦ ✦ ✦

A few weeks later, President Nixon left for China. He took a large group of reporters with him, as well as a full complement of officials, aides, and influential people. In those days before live television could flash around the world, we all waited with great excitement for our first sense of Red China.

The president's plan to go to China in the first weeks of an election year was the first of a set of dazzling decisions that disarmed his opponents. The China trip emphasized that none of the other candidates had his experience or his nerve in the conduct of foreign policy. The president also created a concept that entered the political language. The notion that the strong anticommunist Nixon was the only American president who could reestablish relations with Red China was much discussed. "Nixon to China" became shorthand for trusting antagonists more than allies to make common cause.

Because NPR could not afford to send him along with the president, Robert Conley watched the departure for China with all of us.

All Things Considered, FEBRUARY 17

CONLEY: They were there on the South Lawn of the White House in the raw chill of a gray morning. Lots of schoolchildren with flags; government workers; passersby, and the knowing, the senators and the members of the House, the advisers and the Cabinet.

All there for the fateful beginning so few thought would have been possible such few short months ago. An American president, Richard Nixon, about to depart on a remarkable journey to what used to be thought of as America's most forbidding enemy, the People's Republic of China, the land of eight hundred million, so long thought of as Red China, a term that Washington used to pronounce with the bite of an exclamation point.

They were there, several hundred of them, to see the president off, a president, who once more asked them and the country not to expect too much from his week's visit to mainland China, not to expect, in effect, that he'd bring back in his attaché case the miraculous solution to all the world's ills.

NIXON: I ask you all to remember a statement I made last July 15 when I announced this trip. And that statement was, as you will recall, that this would be a journey for peace.

We, of course, are under no illusions that twenty years of hostility between the People's Republic of China and the United States of America are going to be swept away by one week of talks that we will have there. But as Premier Chou En-lai said in a toast that he proposed to Dr. Kissinger and members of the advance group in October, the American people are a great people. The Chinese people are a great people. The fact that they are separated by a vast ocean and great differences in philosophy should not prevent them from finding common ground.

As we look to the future we must recognize that the government of the People's Republic of China and the government of the United States have had great differences. We will have differences in the future. But what we must do is to find a way to see that we can have differences without being enemies in war.

If we can make progress toward that goal on this trip, the world will be a much safer world and the chance particularly for all of those young children over there to grow up in a world of peace will be infinitely greater.

I would simply say in conclusion that if there was a postscript that I hope might be written with regard to this trip it would be the words on the plaque which was left on the moon by our first astronauts when they landed there: "We came in peace for all mankind." Thank you and good-bye.

CONLEY: Again, Mr. Nixon's caution, Don't expect too much, a caution that his White House aides have been pressing for weeks.

Nonetheless, Mrs. Nixon, burst out with excited anticipation of the journey, a trip that'll take her and the president halfway around the world. With a swoop of her beige mink coat, Mrs. Nixon broke into a quick, joyous jig, then turned with the president to pass through a military honor guard and enter a waiting presidential helicopter. Curling away from the White House, the helicopter slid past the Washington Monument, pale in a gauzy sky, and on to the waiting presidential jet, *Air Force One*, for the journey across the Pacific.

And one thought the president is carrying with him for his talks with the Chinese premier, Chou En-lai, and with that father figure of the Chinese revolution, Mao Tse-tung, is a thought left with him at a working dinner at the White House the other night for André Malraux of France — Malraux, the writer, philosopher, and political figure. As the dinner was ending, Malraux turned to the president, and said, "When you journey to Peking, when you meet Mao Tse-tung, Mr. President, you'll be meeting a man who's a colossus. But, Mr. President, a colossus who is dying."

✦ ✦ ✦ ✦ ✦ ✦ ✦ ✦ ✦

In 1972, the earliest primary in the nation, then as now, was in New Hampshire. Jim Russell made several trips to the state, covering the candidates and speeches. He wrote about the Republican loyalists of the Granite State and about the invasion of young people supporting antiwar candidates. The story in New Hampshire was Senator Edmund Muskie of Maine, the Democratic front-runner, whose campaign collapsed there, and Senator George McGovern of South Dakota, who didn't win but became a contender when he came in second. Here's a selection of Russell's political reporting from that year, beginning with consideration of a word we tossed around quite a bit in 1972.

All Things Considered, MARCH 6

RUSSELL: In looking at the issues of this primary in New Hampshire, journalists and politicians have sensed the presence of a phenomenon which may be more important than any of the normal issues of a presidential campaign. It is most difficult to articulate this phenomenon. Its name seems to be just beyond the tip of the tongue, but the symptoms of the malaise are clear enough. General unhappiness, a sense that life should be better in America, a sense of isolation, and a fear that the individual has lost control of his own life.

Now, certainly some of this malaise, this ill feeling, has its roots in the traditional issues: the Vietnam War, the prisoners of war, the economy, national defense, pollution, unemployment, civil rights, and so on. But after all has been said and done, after speeches on all of these issues by the candidates, there seems that a residue is left, a residue of discontent. Syndicated political columnist David Broder of the *Washington Post* has also found evidence of this malaise, of the turned-off feeling that some people have toward politics this year. Broder and a team of reporters conducted in-depth voter surveys in New Hampshire, and the phenomenon of malaise popped up.

BRODER: Well, I think you've put your finger on the strongest theme that came through, which was the "they're all politicians" theme, that none of them are really going to make any great difference in the things that concern us. There is a good deal of that kind of cynicism about the whole thing, and it may be that it will be reflected in a rather small vote. I don't know, that's a surmise on my part.

I think it would be a mistake to say the New Hampshire voters are not concerned about the problems or about the primary, but my feeling was that Democrats have not yet found anyone who appears to them as the man most likely to deal effectively with the problems that they have. I would think that the strongest figure in the state by far is President Nixon, not only among the Republicans that we talked to but among a number of Democrats who say that they're going to write in President Nixon, or, even if they're going to vote for Democrats in the primary, plan to support Mr. Nixon in November. His strength was quite impressive.

✦ ✦ ✦ ✦ ✦ ✦ ✦ ✦ ✦

A week before the New Hampshire primary, Jim Russell went to Daniel Webster's birthplace, the tiny town of Salisbury, to talk to voters about their perceptions of the candidates and the election. Aggie Shaw was the town clerk. She told Jim that the town would vote Republican, but she disagreed with Broder on how people felt about President Nixon.

All Things Considered, MARCH 7

SHAW: The general feeling of the people I have talked to is "Nixon, no." I think they figure he's going to get it anyhow, but they wish he wouldn't. It may not sound very nice, but they don't trust him! They think he's a wheeler-dealer. I haven't heard any great enthusiasm for any candidate. That may shock you, but I really haven't heard them.
RUSSELL: Aggie had told me that the state of the economy was very much on the minds of the voters, so I asked her if the voters of Salisbury blame President Nixon for the nation's economic woes.
SHAW: They do not say that, but you know yourself you have to blame someone when things are bad and they feel that instead of rushing all over the world, straighten things out here first.

✦ ✦ ✦ ✦ ✦ ✦ ✦ ✦ ✦

A round the middle of June, we reported the story that, although it had no effect on the outcome of the 1972 election, changed our country and our regard for politicians for at least a generation. On June 19 we were not yet calling it the Watergate burglary, and you will note that Susan Stamberg's attempt to name it did not stick. She introduced one serious and one not-so-serious conversation about the break-in at Democratic National Committee offices at the Watergate.

All Things Considered, JUNE 19

STAMBERG: This is certainly a day of intriguing cloak-and-dagger words in the news. First "hijackers" and now "spying" or what the chairman of the Democratic National Committee has called "political espionage," the attempt to bug his party's headquarters in Washington over the weekend, otherwise referred to as the Caper of the Bungled Bugging.

The incident raises a number of serious questions about the credibility of politicians and political groups. Rich Adams raised some of these questions in a conversation today with Richard Strout of the *Christian Science Monitor.*

ADAMS: Mr. Strout, to someone who is already somewhat skeptical of the political process and is perhaps about willing to give up on organized politics, what effect do you think this kind of cloak-and-dagger activity would have on him?

STROUT: Well, I think this deepens the feeling of suspicion, of being unable to believe what's going on here, a credibility factor. This is a raw and flagrant example that captures the headlines, but it's only the latest in a series of them. And I think there's a feeling of frustration and bitterness and cynicism all over the country about Washington, where queer things of this sort can happen.

ADAMS: Let's turn back to our imaginary cynic again, who, sitting there watching all of this, must be asking himself, If this is what politicians do to each other, what might they do to the country?

STROUT: Well, I think you put your finger on a very important thing. I think that the real issue now is the credibility of Mr. Nixon and his administration, just as it was in the days of Lyndon Johnson.

I don't know what the average listener or reader or viewer can say when a group of five men, one of whom is employed by the Republican National Committee, is arrested at gunpoint in the offices of the

Democratic Committee, and they have on them sophisticated electronic and photographic apparatus and they have some sixty-five hundred dollars' worth of new hundred-dollar bills that are serially consecutive.

ADAMS: What effect, if any, do you think this whole thing will have on the political scene?

STROUT: I don't know. I would say that it would be argued for a long time. I think that what the professional politicians suspect and are rather fearful of is that there is some great new undercurrent and emotional swell going on in the United States that has produced such men as McGovern and George Wallace and given them very large votes in the primaries. There's a great new turnout of youngsters who are coming in. And I think there is a feeling of cynicism about the incumbents, and there may be a turn-the-rascals-out movement. It's too early to know that.

ADAMS: Do you think it might also produce a turning away from the established political process, just throwing up the hands, and saying, "I don't want to deal with either of these parties"?

STROUT: Well, that's a very broad question. I would hope not. There was some talk about that in sixty-eight, but it didn't seem to be so. I think that both on the Republican and Democrat side there's a feeling that it's possible to deal with these matters with the normal procedure.

But we seem to be losing part of the normal procedure in the decline of the presidential press conference. I think that was part of, almost, you might say, our form of government, to be able to go and periodically ask the president, "How about it?" and to be reassured. Sort of get an idea of where he stood on these things.

Then there's been another change in our form of government. I think the diminution of power of Congress is one of the most graphic and dramatic things that's happened in the past fifty years, that Congress is treated with some contempt by the executive and it just doesn't seem to be able to act.

ADAMS: So overall you've drawn a pretty ugly picture of the whole process.

STROUT: Well, I don't know that I draw an ugly picture of the process. I think that the public is able to step in and remedy this and find out who — well, I was going to say, who's on their side and who isn't. But where a war goes on that apparently the public doesn't want, that Congress repeatedly has shown that it doesn't want, and yet the thing keeps on going and we don't seem to be able to stop it, well, then you have a feeling of discomfort and disillusion and cynicism. And you are likely to get a cumulative unrest and perhaps even anger.

✦ ✦ ✦ ✦ ✦ ✦ ✦ ✦ ✦

The late Richard Strout of the *Christian Science Monitor* took the long view of White House scandals. His first presidential news conference was in the administration of Warren G. Harding. He told me that he and a number of other reporters were shown into the Oval Office to gather around the president's desk and ask questions. President Harding planned to play golf after their conversation, Mr. Strout said, and he greeted the reporters, saying, "Boys, go easy on me."

Jim Russell completed our initial coverage of the Watergate weekend with an interview on how best to bug an office or a telephone. He visited a small business in downtown Washington called the Spy Shop. Its proprietor, Clyde Wallace, who claimed a wide background in "intelligence," explained state-of-the-art surveillance in 1972, showed Jim ballpoint pens that concealed transmitters, and offered advice.

All Things Considered, JUNE 19

WALLACE: Our problem with a lot of people is that when a bug is discovered, they become emotionally upset. They can't stay calm enough to think the thing out. They make a lot of noise when they go out to find it. They start screaming and shouting about it. They think their phones are bugged. They call somebody on the same phone that they think is bugged. So they alert the people that are doing the bugging.

We recommend that when someone suspects that they're being bugged that they carry on business as usual, but feed wrong information from that suspect area. Go outside someplace and call in someone that is competent enough to inspect the place.

RUSSELL: If a bug is found, Wallace says you should call in the FBI. He admits that his years in the business have made him cautious. He periodically checks his own home for bugs and has equipment attached to his telephone to detect phone bugs.

Before leaving Wallace, I had to ask him one question about this weekend's attempted bugging of the Democratic National headquarters. Wallace spoke scornfully of the weekend incident.

WALLACE: This whole thing is ridiculous. No responsible Republican would have ordered such a thing done. I think this was strictly a bunch of amateurs that wanted to build themselves up, maybe in the Republican group. They were opportunists and quite amateur.

RUSSELL: Wallace said that although he and his team would not have done that kind of bugging job, if they had wanted to, they could have done it.

WALLACE: I am certain that if we really did want to do it, well, it would have been done and nobody would have known the difference.

RUSSELL: That's sort of the way it goes, isn't it? The ones you hear about are the ones that don't work.

WALLACE: That's right. The ones you hear about are the ones where the amateurs were involved. You very seldom hear about where the experts were involved.

RUSSELL: Do you have any bugs in this office?

WALLACE: Yes, as a matter of fact we do. At different times we automatically record interviews such as this, so that we have an exact copy of what we said. There can never be any question.

✦ ✦ ✦ ✦ ✦ ✦ ✦ ✦ ✦

In the summer and fall of 1972, clearly we needed a respite. The Democrats were staggering out of an acrimonious convention that appeared to doom their candidate, and stories about Republican campaign payoffs, slush funds, and extorted contributions were appearing in the *Washington Post* under the bylines Bob Woodward and Carl Bernstein. And although the United States had withdrawn most of its troops from Vietnam and had no plans to send others, the war was still with us.

In August of that year, we asked our listeners for their ideas for something we called Commercials for Nicer Living. No kidding. We asked them to suggest something simple to make life nicer, which we would then produce as a radio commercial and broadcast on *All Things Considered*. A few weeks later, Commercials for Nicer Living were on the air. You'll have to imagine the softly splashing water and the soothing voice of this one, my personal favorite, submitted by Jan Saecker of Markesan, Wisconsin.

SAECKER: Take your shoes off and find some shallow water and try the safest water sport in America . . . wading. That cool, clear puddle from the latest cloudburst would be ideal. You notice how your head stays dry and your hair unmussed, how you can wear practically anything that suits your fancy.

Well, wading barefoot beats any sort of boating. No mast to rig or motors to roar in your ears. Just step right in and wade. It's quiet too. You won't disturb the fish. Relaxing for tired feet.

You'll find it's a cozy sort of sport, even when the air turns cool in the autumn. You can take a sweater along to the lake and keep the sun warm on your back. Ah, boy, feels good. Anybody asks what you're doing, just tell them you're wading for Godot. That ought to stop any smart remarks right there.

✦ ✦ ✦ ✦ ✦ ✦ ✦ ✦ ✦

The president won one of the most convincing electoral victories in American history, carrying forty-nine states. However, he did not sweep large numbers of Republicans into Congress along with him. Below the top of the ticket, the election reflected a fair amount of disagreement and dissent in some states.

At the end of the year, President Nixon launched the Christmas bombing of North Vietnam, he said, to hasten the end of the war and to force North Vietnam to sign a peace agreement with the South. In fact, an agreement was signed in early 1973. It was "Peace with honor," President Nixon said.

Robert Conley had conversations about our national state of mind at the end of the year with three journalists, Hugh Sidey of *Time* magazine, Joseph C. Harsch, editorial writer for the *Christian Science Monitor,* and Richard Dudman of the *St. Louis Post-Dispatch.* He asked the three men what the Vietnam War had done to us as a people.

SIDEY: Well, I think we start out first with the fact that you've got a whole generation, or almost two, of children who know nothing but a war, the Vietnam War. We have this thing that has been ten years long, in which children have grown to awareness, to puberty, to adolescence, and finally into young adulthood, and for some of them all of these changes in life have occurred with nothing but war.

And I think it's had a profound effect on these people, particularly the young people. I think they've become disillusioned in many ways in the public processes. They were deceived, they were lied to, as was the whole country in this time. But I think it had a profound impression on them more than anybody else, to witness a president of the United States telling them one thing and then doing another, time after time after time.

I also think that it probably disillusioned them as to the wisdom of their elders in many instances because the logic of this war has now fled. We are, even in this time, bombing massively while the very cause for that whole conflict, namely, the containment of Red China, has long ago gone out the window. So it makes no sense even in my own kind of Iowa horse sense, or it makes no sense even academically.

CONLEY: This whole matter of the Vietnam War, which has gone on these ten long years now, Joe, what do you think it's done to us as a people?

HARSCH: I do know what it's done in one respect. It has impinged on the American consciousness in an unusual way. There's never been anything like it in our history. The American people are a people who have been accustomed by their historical experience to always have their way. In every war they've fought, they've got everything they wanted.

This war is a profoundly new and different kind of experience. We've never been frustrated like this before. To be frustrated by a little tiny country on the far side of the world that doesn't even speak English, it's a sort of traumatic experience for the American people.

I think myself that probably no great country ever does reach maturity until it's suffered a very serious setback to its purposes, until it's been defeated once. And maybe it'll be a good thing for us. I hope so.

CONLEY: Picking up on that, Joe, are you suggesting that perhaps the innocence has now crumbled away and these sort of agonies of adolescence mean that we're now going into maturity?

HARSCH: Yeah, our age of innocence is certainly gone, if it ever existed. That is, we've always assumed that we were a country of superior morality. And now we find that we've been doing things, which are certainly in the eyes of most of the rest of the world highly immoral, highly improper. So here we are using enormous military power in something other than a palpably or even arguably moral cause.

DUDMAN: For one thing, it's worn down our capacity for outrage. Americans know that American planes are killing a lot of women and children, a lot of civilians. And they don't like to think about it. They don't buy the books, they don't read the papers about it, they try to forget it. Part of what went wrong with McGovern was he reminded them of it. So they took their hatred out on him because he reminded them of their own guilty consciences.

And I think when something like the Watergate scandal comes along, they don't have the capacity for outrage that they normally would have for something like that, that was comparable to Teapot Dome. But we settled into a habit of knowing that we're inflicting unspeakable pain on another people. And it's really done a lot of harm to our whole fabric of society, I think.

CONLEY: But it's not just complacency, is it? It's much more than that.

DUDMAN: It's not complacency. I think really "guilt" isn't too strong a word. I think there's an uneasy feeling that things are not the way they should be. That we're in the wrong position.

CONLEY: What evidence of this do you see of how this crops up in us as a people? You've certainly been around the country enough, not just here in Washington.

DUDMAN: Well, it's partly in a kind of feverish pleasure seeking. There's a lot of that. It's a kind of seeking of escape. You see it in adults, you see it especially in youth.

CONLEY: The reality is too painful to behold, therefore . . .

DUDMAN: I think that must be it. They try to get away from it. The kids now, instead of going in for current events and dealing with current problems, they'd rather take up offbeat Oriental religions, or instead of reading fact, they read fantasy. It's a desire to escape from an unpleasant present.

CONLEY: Do you see anything of benefit that's come out of these long years of Vietnam for us?

DUDMAN: Well, I really don't. In fact, I think the way we're getting out of the war, if we are, is probably the worst possible way. I've always felt that this involvement in Vietnam, to try to pick up after the French and hold South Vietnam as some kind of anticommunist bastion, was a mistake, a misreading of the historical possibilities.

And yet we seem to be on the verge of getting out of it as if somehow we've won, as if it's not been a mistake at all. I think that the president has not supplied the kind of leadership that would prepare America for realizing that it's made a mistake and for correcting its future course. He's talked about defeat and humiliation instead of making a mistake. He's talked about the United States maybe becoming a pitiful, helpless giant. It isn't being a pitiful, helpless giant if you see a mistake that you've made and you decide, This is a mistake, I'm not going to do this, follow this course anymore. And to talk about peace with honor, it sounds as if abandoning a mistaken course is somehow dishonorable. I don't follow that, and I think it has not conditioned — not educated the American people to learn a lesson they should have learned from this terrible experience.

CONLEY: Hugh Sidey, do you think America has gotten anything out of these long ten years of Vietnam?

SIDEY: I think we've learned that our resources are limited. Remember Lyndon Johnson, guns and butter, we could do anything. We could go anyplace, do anything, bear any burden, John Kennedy said. We can't. We're human. Our resources are limited, our will is limited. I think we've learned that about ourselves.

I must add, however, there are those historians who think it's the beginning of the end, that our society will not recover, that we neglected our domestic problems so much, we've poured so much of our will, our energy reserve, and our resources into this war, that our society is fragmented permanently and it will simply limp along and get worse. I don't subscribe to that, but there are those who say that.

CONLEY: What do you mean? While we were out scrapping in the street, the house fell apart?

SIDEY: Yes, essentially that. That we put everything in that and ignored our base of what was back here.

1973

✦ ✦ ✦ ✦ ✦ ✦ ✦ ✦ ✦

The day before President Nixon was inaugurated for his second term, the term that ended with his resignation, we broadcast a conversation with one of those New Hampshire voters who Jim Russell had met in Salisbury, Aggie Shaw. Russell asked how she'd voted. We were all surprised at Aggie Shaw's answer.

All Things Considered, JANUARY 18

SHAW: I didn't vote for anyone. I didn't think any candidate was worth a vote.

RUSSELL: Now, that's really a shocking thing to say, because being a town clerk, you're involved in, you know, politics on the grassroots level, and yet here comes a national election and you don't vote for anyone. Did you have trouble wrestling with that decision?

SHAW: Not a bit. Not a bit. Once the primaries were over and I saw who the candidates were going to be, I didn't have any trouble deciding that I didn't want any of them.

RUSSELL: Have you ever not voted before?

SHAW: Never. I've always voted.

RUSSELL: What does that mean to you? What does that tell you about your country?

SHAW: It tells me that I've lost confidence in the people that they're running to lead the country.

RUSSELL: Do you think that it is possible to elect good men to office anymore?

SHAW: Not just good men, no. Unless they have plenty of money backing them, they don't stand a chance of being elected. I personally think they should run our elections so that once they've chosen a halfway decent candidate to run, they should all get equal time, free

33

time, so to speak, on TV to present their cases and not string it out for two or three years of high-powered advertising, so to speak. Selling the candidate. That absolutely gives me the horrors. That's what they're doing, they're selling a product.

RUSSELL: Are there any answers?

SHAW: Start saying what they mean, regardless of whether people like it or not. Why don't they tell us the truth. I have much more admiration for a candidate that says something I don't like if he really means it, not back down then gradually because so many voters protest. His own personal opinion on what he's really going to do and then when he gets in, do it. Not promises, promises, promises and then when they get in . . . you mention a promise. I remember four years ago they said this. It's one thing I'll give President Nixon credit for. He is the best man to keep a secret in the whole wide world. Four years ago he had a secret plan to end the war and he's still got that secret. He's never told us that secret. He's never used it. And four years is a mighty long time for a secret plan that was going to end the war immediately.

✦ ✦ ✦ ✦ ✦ ✦ ✦ ✦ ✦

A ggie Shaw served as a lesson to all of us who were new to punditry. If you want to know where the country is headed, ask. When a lifelong Republican like Aggie Shaw gave up on President Nixon, we should have understood more clearly than we did the uneasy relationship the American people had with him. I remember that January as the month the Watergate burglary trials began, the president was inaugurated, NPR moved, and Lyndon Johnson died.

We moved our offices in January 1973 to 2025 M Street in Washington, right across the street from CBS, our most glamorous neighbor. Most of the others were auto body shops. But we had enough space and, for the first time, we had more than one studio. We moved over the weekend, not at all sure that when we pulled the switch for the next news program anything would work. When President Johnson died, I'm afraid we saw his death to be a major test of our broadcast system and our ingenuity because all our files were packed.

Our reporter George Bauer asked Russell Baker of the *New York Times*, who had covered Johnson as Senate majority leader, and Hugh Sidey, still covering the White House for *Time*, to talk about LBJ.

BAKER: Oh, well, he was a great Rabelaisian figure. He was about ten times bigger than life. My association with him began when I first came to Washington in 1954. He had just become majority leader then. And I first met him at a dinner that some friends of mine gave, and I was seated next to him at dinner. This was before his first heart attack, and at that time he was living with gusto, as they say now. He smoked his dinner and talked all through it. I don't think he ever had a mouthful of food. It was one of the most extraordinary gustatory performances I've ever seen in my life.

And I'd just come from England and been assigned to cover the Senate, and he asked me what I thought of the Senate. And like all young men who had just come from London, I said I thought it certainly didn't stack up very well against the kind of debate that you found in the House of Commons. And that upset him. "You always want talk, you people who've been to England," he said. "You want talk? I can give you talk." He says, "I've got Wayne Morse. I've got Lehman. You want a civil rights speech, I can give you Humphrey." He says, it's not talk. He says, talk doesn't mean anything. It's what gets done. It's who does it. And he made no bones about thinking that he was the man who got the results, that the talk was just window dressing for young saps like me.

BAUER: Mr. Sidey, when I say "Lyndon Johnson," what does that bring up in your mind?

SIDEY: Well, he — Mr. Baker is correct. He was bigger than life. I remember Richard Goodwin, his speechwriter. I said describe Johnson to me in a brief sentence. He said, "When he eats, he eats more. When he swears, he swears more. When he legislates, he legislates more. He's just more."

BAUER: How did he appear to you as members of the press? Did he deal effectively with the press corps? Mr. Sidey?

SIDEY: He had a love-hate relationship with the press. But I think one thing must be said for him. He understood the function of the press better than perhaps some other presidents did. He wanted to intimidate the press. He wanted to line them all up, to make them jump through the hoop, to love him, to report things as he saw. But he never in a legal fashion or through courts or other ways tried to change laws or haul people in or put reporters in jail. But he would, of course, try to snow you, try to just overwhelm you with facts.

BAUER: I'd like to ask you both what you think his greatest success and his greatest failure was as a president. Mr. Baker?

BAKER: At the moment I suppose you'd have to say that his attempts to bring the country into the twentieth century on the civil rights issue would be his greatest success. I think without doubt that's the area in which he made the most successful strides.

SIDEY: Yes, I would agree with that. Civil rights certainly was that area.

BAKER: History may reveal to what would be our amazement that his Vietnam policy was a great success. At the moment it certainly looks catastrophic.

SIDEY: It's too early to condemn him for Vietnam. In the short range it looks bad. But who knows? Maybe it will turn around one of these days and we'll look back and see that it brought a certain stability to that region that might have help set up this generation of peace that Mr. Nixon talks about.

✦ ✦ ✦ ✦ ✦ ✦ ✦ ✦ ✦ ✦

C onsidering the myths we've made of Watergate, it is difficult to remember how long it really took to roll. The *Washington Post* had been writing about the break-in and the cover-up for almost a year before the Senate hearings began. Most of the Watergate burglars pleaded guilty, so the impact of the trial was muted. In April, Robert Conley wrote that the Nixon White House began to remind him of covering the Kremlin, watching who stood where at official gatherings, trying to divine which figures were gaining power and which were going the other way. It was called Kremlinology, Conley said.

We introduced a new commentator in 1973. Had Congressman Emanuel Celler of New York not retired when he did, he might have presided over Judiciary Committee hearings on the impeachment of a president. That duty fell instead to Congressman Peter Rodino of New Jersey. Celler was eighty-five when he began writing essays for us. He had served fifty years in the House, elected in 1922. When Manny Celler considered scandals, he went right back to Teapot Dome.

All Things Considered, MAY 16

CELLER: I wonder how many of our citizens were as frightened as I was by the ways of the Watergate revelations. But for the courage of a federal judge and the persistence of some of the press, a sickening perversion of our whole political process would have become a standard of political behavior.

Not even a Reichstag fire can compare, or even compete. The lies, the perjuries, the destruction and attempted destruction of character, the moneys washed, the conspiracy of silence, reads like a handbook, "How to Secretly Capture a Country," or better yet, "Dictators without Labels."

In my fifty years in Congress, I have conducted many an investigation: Adam Clayton Powell, the New York Port Authority, the Department of Justice in the chase after mink coats and deep freezes, baseball, and all manner and kind of antitrust violations. And always, the motive of wrongdoing was greed. I was barely in Congress when the Teapot Dome scandal broke. Again, greed.

But Watergate — what pushed Watergate? A fight for power, naked, raw power. I don't believe for a moment that these men around President Nixon did it out of zeal, out of devotion to the person or the ideas of President Nixon. I've been around too long to swallow that sort of nonsense. They did what they did to preserve their own power, their own ego satisfaction. If Nixon were not reelected, what would they be? PR men, management consultants, and the like, but not in the White House.

What I can't swallow is the sentiment I hear expressed that so great was their loyalty to their president that they were ready to sacrifice their careers and moral sense for his sake. Absurd! Their loyalties and duties did not give them the privilege of playing God. However blameless the president may be, he's right in one respect — the responsibility was his. He permitted his top staff to decide what was good for him and they played their game in a war against the people to keep and enhance their own power.

It is a platitude of political life that court intrigues are not for the king's benefit. This the president should have known. The first whiff of Watergate should have put him on guard. Accepting all the president has said on the subject as factual, the question still remains, How could a seasoned politician be that naive?

Watergate may yet be a saving grace for the country. The steady ingathering of power within the White House was a dangerous exercise. The Congress proposed and the president disposed. Executive privilege was being extended to ridiculous lengths. We're moving towards a closed society. Intimidation of the press and other media of communication were an almost daily occurrence.

Maybe now there will be a chastening of the spirit, a return of respect for the people, a turn to humility, fewer tilts and fewer men on horseback. I do not deny that such chicanery went on in many elections, but always they were on a measurable scale on a local or state level. I search my memory for a comparable example to Watergate. I find none. Let public men beware of arrogance and insulations. They are daggers in the back.

✦ ✦ ✦ ✦ ✦ ✦ ✦ ✦ ✦

S usan Stamberg took note the next day that not all Americans were paying attention to Watergate with the same horrified fascination as Congressman Celler.

All Things Considered, MAY 18

STAMBERG: In an article for the *Washington Post* on the first day of Watergate hearings, Jules Witcover wrote, "If you like to watch the grass grow, you would have loved the opening session of the Senate hearings on Watergate." Well, apparently not too many television viewers liked watching the grass grow. The early Nielsen ratings showed that NBC was out in front, but the NBC research department figured something like a third less viewers were tuning in for the hearings than usually dial up daytime network television for the soap operas or the game shows.

I phoned around the networks and some local stations this morning to find out about public reaction to preempting soaps for Watergate. A press agent at NBC in New York told me that yesterday there the network received fewer phone calls than they had expected: 210 against preempting shows like *Hollywood Squares* — that's a game show — or *Another World*. It's a soap opera, but NBC refers to it rather elegantly as a "daytime serial drama." And then they said they got 10 calls thanking them for running the Watergate hearings. There were also 40 or 50 calls yesterday from people who wanted to know when the coverage would begin and end.

Sally McGraw is manager of Audience Services for the NBC TV network. She says the calls today have been about the same, maybe slightly heavier than they were yesterday, and also that viewers mostly complain that they're being deprived of their favorite programs.

MCGRAW: They're displeased because all three of the networks are covering the Watergate case. They wonder why just one network can't show it.

STAMBERG: What's your answer to that?

MCGRAW: Well, we try to explain to them that the networks do operate independently. You know, they do not really work in cooperation. And then we try mainly to reassure them that they're not going to miss any part of their stories, that we will pick up with the stories right where we left off. And this is, I think, very reassuring. A lot of people don't seem to realize this. They feel that if we skip the stories for a couple of days that we will actually skip episodes. So in most cases when we explain that to people they are certainly, you know, mollified.

STAMBERG: At the CBS TV network in New York, callers have been more upset than happy about the preemptions for Watergate. When I asked a secretary in the CBS Programming Information Department whether she'd been flooded with calls, she said, "Can't you tell by the fact that I can't talk to you anymore?" And then she hung up.

And the switchboard operator at ABC's affiliate station in Washington says that their line has just been jammed all day — so busy, in fact, that she doesn't have enough people to switch the calls over to. She tells people that the soaps aren't on because of a network decision. "I guess they think it's a public service," is the way she explains it. I had more questions, but that operator said, "Honey, I don't really have time to talk."

On Monday, at least, the switchboards should be a little bit calmer. There are no hearings on Monday so it will be back to the eternal drama of *Days of Our Lives*.

✦ ✦ ✦ ✦ ✦ ✦ ✦ ✦ ✦

National Public Radio also broadcast the Senate Watergate hearings, and our stations also heard from annoyed listeners about preempted morning concerts and missed bluegrass programs. As we struggled with this story, we kept coming back to the idea that the American people needed to talk about Watergate. We covered the news, we broadcast the hearings live, but we also went to Burtonsville, Maryland, to Paint Branch High School.

TEACHER: Who is to blame? How do you feel about the whole affair? Was — do you think President Nixon was a victim or a participant?

STUDENT: Well, firstly, I think the president had no idea of what was going on while the Watergate burglaries were going on and the illicit activities involved there. I think that, knowing Nixon, and that he is a relatively shrewd politician, I can't imagine him after, you know, it was discovered that a burglary was committed in Watergate that Nixon would not find out immediately who was involved.

SECOND STUDENT: I don't think the president was involved or knew about the Watergate. And I don't think he might have suspected a cover-up. I'm sure he suspected one, but he wasn't willing to believe that his friends that he had known for so long would do something like that.

THIRD STUDENT: President Nixon is professional enough a politician not to become involved in, or not to let his name be involved with, any of these activities. So I don't think that he had any prior knowledge of the conspiracy or the actual burglary. He probably read about it in the newspaper the morning after. But I find it hard to believe that he wasn't aware, in some respect, of the attempt to — I guess, another conspiracy — an attempt to cover up the information.

TEACHER: How do you, as a young American, regard the whole Watergate affair?

FOURTH STUDENT: I've always been kind of a skeptic as to the ethics of politicians. And Watergate just kind of reinforces it. I think that's the kind of mood a lot of Americans feel, especially young people, that government, the establishment, is, you know, not really, you know, showing all its cards. And it's not really representing the true needs of the people. Possibly the American people don't really have that much power in deciding who is in the White House. Maybe it's instead of — I mean, the people deciding — maybe the decision is made on who is the better political saboteur.

✦ ✦ ✦ ✦ ✦ ✦ ✦ ✦ ✦

John W. Dean III, counsel to the president, testified before the Senate Watergate Committee in the middle of June and accused the president of participating directly in the cover-up of the Watergate burglary. The first day he read a statement hundreds of pages long, detailed and explicit, about his own complicity, the president's role, and the involvement of Dean's White House colleagues in the handling of Watergate. A solemn young man, with his hair pasted down, Dean seemed too young to be the president's counsel, and not impressive enough to be the president's nemesis. But in the early days, before the existence of the White House tapes was revealed, Dean was the best placed and most willing witness the committee had. But was he the truth teller he seemed to be? "I realize it's almost an impossible task if it's one man against the other that I'm up against, and it's not a very pleasant situation," he said. "But I can only speak what I know to be the facts, and that's what I'm providing this committee."

Josh Darsa covered the Watergate hearings for NPR. He had worked for Edward R. Murrow at CBS and, like many of those young men, he sounded like Murrow on the air. He filed this story on the second day of Dean's testimony, the day the senators began questioning Dean.

All Things Considered, JUNE 26

DARSA: If it wasn't vivid before, today's session of the Watergate hearings conclusively illustrated the one fact in this investigation upon which hinges the future course of this committee, this administration, and history.

That fact is that John Dean at this moment is alone in presenting what he says he believes is the truth in the Watergate affair. If John Dean can be corroborated by other figures involved in Watergate, if his testimony before this committee can be cemented, if what he is saying is the truth, then the ramifications are enormous. Here's Senator Herman Talmadge of Georgia:

TALMADGE: Mr. Dean, your charges are very grave. What makes you think your credibility is greater than the president's?

DARSA: And there in Senator Talmadge's terse, to-the-point style of questioning, there it was. John Dean versus Richard Nixon at this point in time; or rather, and closer to the point, John Dean versus the president of the United States.

DEAN: I've told the truth as I've seen it.

DARSA: Senator Montoya, reflecting on the president's April 17 statement of this year, saying, "I condemn any attempts to cover up in this case, no matter who is involved."

MONTOYA: Was the president telling the truth when he made that statement?

DEAN: No, sir. By that time he knew the full implications of the case. Haldeman and Ehrlichman were still on the staff. There was considerable pressure that they remain.

DARSA: Montoya led Dean through a chronology of presidential statements about Watergate and the administration's lack of knowledge or lack of involvement in it.

DEAN: I feel the president was aware of an effort to cover up Watergate. The first time I had firsthand knowledge he was aware of this was September 15, 1972, when I met with him.

MONTOYA: How would you characterize the Watergate burglary?

DEAN: That's probably the most difficult question asked yet. I would say it was the opening act of one of America's great tragedies.

DARSA: Throughout the day's questioning, Dean's credibility was the focal point. He stuck by the voluminous, stunning story he read yesterday during six hours and 245 pages of testimony. When Montoya asked how Dean could reconcile his testimony to the committee with the denials and statements of President Nixon, Dean said, "The truth will out eventually. I strongly believe the truth always emerges. I have only one ally — the truth."

Dean said he knew that major efforts had been made in a calculated campaign to discredit him. He denied his own motivation for testifying that he was trying to obtain immunity for the obstruction of justice. He said he was motivated by the conclusion that he had reached the end of the line in the cover-up and he just did not have the constitution internally to proceed with what was going on. So I decided, he said, "to go the other way."

✦ ✦ ✦ ✦ ✦ ✦ ✦ ✦ ✦ ✦

Susan Stamberg kept the names and numbers of people she'd talked to for all sorts of reasons, and periodically called them back to see what they thought of the news we were reporting. She made these calls in July, just after former Attorney General John Mitchell made a last-ditch effort to save the president, asserting that he knew about the cover-up but had not told the president because, he said, the president would have "lowered the boom" on his aides and might have lost the election.

STAMBERG: The latest Gallup poll finds that three out of four adults don't want their sons to go into politics. The reason: too corrupt. The survey was done in the early weeks of the Watergate hearings.

But the definitive opinion poll on Watergate remains to be done, the poll the Watergate senators keep talking about. What popular judgment will be made as a result of exposing the Watergate hearings to the court of public opinion? We worked that poll a bit this morning, phoning across the country to old friends of *All Things Considered,* men and women who are typical of themselves and, just possibly, of you.

We began with Charlie White, a rancher in Manhattan, Kansas. What were his reactions to John Mitchell's testimony?

WHITE: Well, I think Mitchell is honest. I think he has tried to protect the president somewhat and is doing it justly.

STAMBERG: You voted for Richard Nixon this past fall.

WHITE: That's right.

STAMBERG: And Mitchell says he knew about the cover-up. He didn't tell the president because he was sure, in Mitchell's words, that Mr. Nixon would "lower the boom."

WHITE: Yes, I think he would have. If he would have done that during the campaign, I'm sure that it would have changed probably a lot of people's opinions and it would change the way they voted.

STAMBERG: Would it have changed the way you voted, Charlie?

WHITE: No, it wouldn't have. Because I was voting for some of the things Nixon said he was going to do, not for the things his undercover people were doing. I would have been very much disappointed, it would have bothered me, but I still would have voted for Nixon as compared to McGovern.

STAMBERG: Well, Charlie, what is it that makes you and John Mitchell assume that the rest of the American voters wouldn't have voted exactly the same way?

WHITE: Probably I misjudge the American people. But I do feel that any time there's a bandwagon to get on, a lot of people like to crawl on it. We've seen this. If it hadn't been so, why that wouldn't be all you see on television and in the newspapers.

STAMBERG: In general, though, Charlie, what do you think is going to come out of all this? We're pretty far along in these hearings — about halfway — at the halfway mark now of the list of witnesses for the Watergate phase. Do you think we're ever really going to get at the truth and know exactly what happened, who knew what when, who covered up? Or do you think we'll end up with as big a question mark as we began with?

WHITE: Maybe even more questions than what we began with.

STAMBERG: Would it take the president himself appearing before the Watergate committee?

WHITE: I'm not really sure that that would clear it up. There isn't any reason for me to believe that if he was to testify that he would tell everything that he knows.

STAMBERG: Clint Vaughn is a Democrat for Nixon. He manages a furniture store in Las Cruces, New Mexico.

VAUGHN: I think it's the biggest waste of taxpayers' money there ever was. I think there's many, many areas where they could — if they'd put that much effort into other areas, such as our drug problem, it would be money much more well spent.

STAMBERG: John Mitchell told the senators that he knew about the Watergate cover-up in 1972, that he did not tell the president because he was sure the president would, in Mitchell's words, "lower the boom," and that would come back to hurt him in the election. You voted for Mr. Nixon. If he had lowered the boom, would it have affected your vote?

VAUGHN: No, ma'am. It would not have. I respect Mr. Nixon fully and wholly, and I think he's done a — I think he's been one of the greatest presidents we've ever had. I support all of his programs and I just feel terrible, like most other Americans do right now, that this thing has come up and blackened his name to any extent. But it would not have affected my vote for Mr. Nixon, no.

STAMBERG: In other words, you still feel the president would have gotten the landslide victory?

VAUGHN: I sure do.

STAMBERG: This is Jan Saecker, a housewife and mother of three. She lives in Markesan, Wisconsin, and she was a McGovern supporter.

SAECKER: It seems to me Mr. Mitchell is holding back. I don't mean to say that he's necessarily holding back information. But he looks as if he always has his brakes on. One wonders if John Mitchell was covering up before, if he would not still be willing to cover up to a certain extent. I have the feeling that if he was willing to protect the president to such an extent before, he's probably still protecting the president.

STAMBERG: So you're not really satisfied that you're hearing the truth from John Mitchell?

SAECKER: No, I'm not.

STAMBERG: Do you think we're ever going to get at the root of all of this?

SAECKER: No, I do not, but the reason is not the willingness of people to camouflage or to tell the truth. I believe so much information was destroyed in advance that we have no chance of arriving at the whole truth.

✦ ✦ ✦ ✦ ✦ ✦ ✦ ✦ ✦

That same July day Robert Conley spoke about the White House and the president's efforts to keep going despite the Watergate hearings and the uneasiness in the country. On that day the president met with Henry Kissinger, he agreed to see Senator Sam Ervin, who headed the Watergate committee, and he appointed some federal marshals.

All Things Considered, JULY 12

CONLEY: There's a sense of weariness within the White House these days, and it's apparent the moment you step in the door — weariness, or perhaps a frazzledness, a wearing around the edges that comes from the continued assaults of the Watergate case. Or maybe "corrosiveness" is even a better way of describing the effects that Watergate is having.

Whatever it is, the White House just isn't what it used to be. It's a palpable feeling, and it crops up in a number of ways. There is, for instance, a sense that the president himself is even more isolated than he would choose to be, even though Richard Nixon is a man who prefers to work by himself, more than most men.

The latest indication comes from his daughter, Julie Nixon Eisenhower. This time she let drop a remark after a White House reception. "I'm sure," she said of her father, "I'm sure he's trying to run everything himself now." That's one aspect of the effects of Watergate.

Another crops up in the case of Melvin Laird, the former secretary of defense. Mr. Laird came into the White House with great reluctance, to help the president patch up his wounded staff, riddled by the Watergate resignations of H. R. "Bob" Haldeman, the president's former chief of staff, and John Ehrlichman, the president's former domestic adviser.

Mr. Laird, in his role as the new domestic adviser, let it be known that he wanted the president to clean out some more staff, including Ronald Ziegler, the president's press secretary. That, in the belief that the president's spokesman had been tarnished by making dodging and misleading statements about Watergate.

But Mr. Ziegler stays on. So do a number of former aides to Mr. Haldeman and Mr. Ehrlichman. And there's no evidence yet to be found at the White House that anyone is taking Mr. Laird's counsel on staff changes.

◆ ◆ ◆ ◆ ◆ ◆ ◆ ◆ ◆ ◆

Toward the end of July, the president decided to speak out. Rather than hold a news conference, he met with White House staff members in the Rose Garden. Conley covered the event and the president said something we've always remembered.

All Things Considered, JULY 20

CONLEY: Back to the White House came the president, home from the Bethesda Naval Medical Center in suburban Maryland. Recovering, but not recovered yet, from viral pneumonia. And once there, the president had the White House staff — one hundred or so — out into the Rose Garden for a pep rally, in a sense, and to display the Nixon grit once more about Watergate.

NIXON: I was rather amused by some very well intentioned people who thought that perhaps the burdens of the office, and you know, some of the rather rough assaults that any man in this office gets from time to time, brings on an illness. And that after going through such an illness, that I might get so tired that I would consider either slowing down or [*laughs*] or even, some suggested, resigning.

Well, now, just so we set that to rest, I'm going to use the phrase that my Ohio father used to use. Any suggestion that this president is ever going to slow down while he's president, or is ever going to leave this office until he continues to do the job and finishes the job he was elected to do — anyone who suggests that — that's just plain poppycock. We're going to stay on this job until we get the job done.

CONLEY: One quirk in all that was the president's own daughter, Julie Nixon Eisenhower, who revealed that the president had asked his family, if only as a talking point, whether they thought he should resign.

NIXON: No one in this great office at this time in the world's history can slow down. This office requires a president who will work right up to the hilt all the time. That's what I've been doing. That's what I'm going to continue to do, and I want all of you to do likewise.

Oh, I know, many say, but then you'll risk your health. Well, the health of a man isn't nearly as important as the health of a nation and the health of the world. I do want you to know that I feel that we have so little time in the positions that all of us hold and so much to do. And what we were elected to do, we are going to do. And let others wallow in Watergate. We're going to do our job.

CONLEY: Presidential aides were upset when Julie Nixon Eisenhower first mentioned that resignation talk — a mistake, they said. But she bounced back with the comment, What do they know? Now the latest turn: the White House says that Julie Nixon Eisenhower will be making no more public appearances for a while, nor will she be mentioning Watergate. It's rather ridiculous to be repetitious and for her to say the same things over and over, the White House decided.

✦ ✦ ✦ ✦ ✦ ✦ ✦ ✦ ✦

President Nixon remained in office for one more year. In September 1973, we felt the first of the constitutional shocks that were coming. Vice President Spiro Agnew resigned that fall and pleaded guilty to tax evasion, for not paying taxes on bribes paid to him while he was governor of Maryland and vice president. Under a new constitutional amendment, Congressman Gerald R. Ford of Michigan was appointed vice president.

Egypt attacked Israel in October, beginning the Yom Kippur War. The Arab states oil boycott tripled the price of gasoline, and lines formed at gas stations.

On November 20, the president ordered Attorney General Elliot Richardson to fire Watergate Special Prosecutor Archibald Cox, an event which came to be called the Saturday Night Massacre. Richardson refused and resigned, as did his deputy. The solicitor general, Robert Bork, fired Cox. Cox had gone to court, attempting to obtain the White House tapes, refusing to back down. But in firing him, the president lost control of the issue and, ultimately, the tapes. The House decided to hold hearings on impeachment.

Late in the year we heard from *San Francisco Chronicle* columnist Art Hoppe. He offered an explanation for Watergate.

HOPPE: Here's another unwritten chapter of history. It's from that unpublished work, *A History of America: 1950 to 1999.* The title of this unwritten chapter is "Mr. Nixon Splits."

How the president rose from the muck of Watergate to achieve true greatness can now be revealed. The key we now know is that the country had long been governed by two men. One was of course the president. The other was of course Mr. Nixon.

The president conducted foreign affairs, conferred with Dr. Kissinger, and delivered dignified presidential addresses. Mr. Nixon, on the other hand, was in charge of wiretaps, personnel, and holding press conferences to kick the press around some more.

The president had won universal admiration for his courage and wisdom in handling foreign affairs, but as Mr. Nixon's chicanery and deceit in dealing with domestic matters dragged the president down into the mire, the rift between the two men widened.

Things culminated one weekend in November, as the president read a good book in front of the fire to improve his noble mind, while Mr. Nixon sat idly watching the Redskins on television.

"Listen to this, Dick," said the president, "and I wish to quote, 'He is such an incarnate hypocrite that whatever object he pursues, he pursues crookedly. Creeping along the ground to some small end, he will always magnify every object in the way and consequently will hate and suspect everything that comes in the most innocent manner between him and it. So the crooked course will become crookeder.'"

Mr. Nixon humbly interrupted. "They shouldn't say that about us, sir. I'll attack the press again immediately."

"That's a description, Dick," said the president, "of Uriah Heep from *David Copperfield.*"

"Oh, it's nothing to do with us, then, sir?" said Mr. Nixon.

"I'm not so sure, Dick," said the president, thoughtfully. "Anyway, I've decided to come clean with every congressman, speak before every press conference, and cooperate fully with the courts. You may have accidentally destroyed the tape of my conversation with John Dean, Dick, but I'll give them my recollections of it that I dictated into my dictograph."

Mr. Nixon smiled secretively. "Gosh, I can't find them anywhere, sir."

"It's a good thing I didn't trust you, Dick," said the president. "I also wrote down my missing recollections of that missing tape in my diary."

Mr. Nixon spoke slyly. "If I'd known that, sir," he said, "I'd have used something else to start the fire."

The president grew angry. "At last I see through you, you fiend. It was you who hired those Watergate bumblers, blackmailed the milk industry, pulled off the Vesco deal."

Mr. Nixon looked fawningly at the president. "Only to assure your reelection, sir."

"It was you," cried the president, "who bugged and burglarized innocent citizens."

Mr. Nixon cringed. "Only to protect your security, sir."

"It was you," cried the president, "who advised me to defy Congress and the courts."

"Only to preserve your presidential powers, sir," said Mr. Nixon, desperately.

"No," said the president, "You were trying to ruin me, Dick. Why?"

Mr. Nixon's humble mask dissolved before the president's eyes. "Because everybody always loved and admired you," he said, "while they loathed and despised me. I couldn't stand it any longer. I had to drag you down to my level."

The president grimly rolled up his sleeves. "Well, they're not going to have Dick Nixon to kick around anymore."

The deed done, Mr. Nixon fired, the noble president lived happily ever after, dealing openly and honestly with all. As for the disgraced and sly Mr. Nixon, he last surfaced in Tijuana, where he operated a used car lot until run out of town by the Better Business Bureau.

1974

✦ ✦ ✦ ✦ ✦ ✦ ✦ ✦ ✦ ✦

O n the evening of August 8, 1974, President Richard Nixon told the nation that he would resign his office. On that long day, while the country waited, NPR turned to its listeners and asked them to phone. We did not have the technology to organize national call-in programs. Instead we created a kind of round-robin system, switching to stations around the country and listening while the local anchor took telephone calls. Mike Waters anchored the broadcast from Washington.

NPR broadcast all of the Senate Watergate hearings and the House Judiciary Committee hearings on impeachment. We rushed onto the air for marathon readings of the text of the tapes released by the White House and again when the Judiciary Committee released a fuller version. But our broadcast on the day the president resigned has stayed with me for years. I felt as if we had reached out across the country and held hands as people do at important moments. The broadcast went on for seven hours. I listened from the Capitol, and I remember being reassured by the voices calling in. The people who called in were fearful, sad, angry, relieved, and impressive.

Bob Edwards began each hour of that day with a news summary. In those days, our newscasts were not interrupted by traffic reports and contained few taped segments. On this particular day, Bob Edwards's newscast was a somber essay about a world waiting for the end of a president.

Special Coverage, AUGUST 8

EDWARDS: Today there is more than just rumor to indicate President Nixon will resign. House Minority Leader John Rhodes and an unidentified White House aide say the president summoned Vice

President Ford to the Oval Office this morning to notify Ford of his decision to step down. House Majority Leader Tip O'Neill says he's been told the resignation would become effective tomorrow. The official announcement is expected tonight at nine, eastern time, from the president himself. Mr. Nixon's speech will be heard live over most of these public radio stations.

Under the law, a president must submit his resignation in writing to the secretary of state. Henry Kissinger met this afternoon with Ford and the president at the White House. Kissinger met with the president on two occasions last night, leaving the White House in the early morning hours. It is possible that Mr. Nixon could have formally resigned at any of those meetings.

Sources say the president's announcement of resignation tonight will become effective at midday tomorrow. Others say tomorrow evening. No one is saying flatly that there will be no resignation, though some point out that it is entirely possible the president might choose to step aside temporarily, under provisions of the Twenty-fifth Amendment, while the impeachment process continues.

On Capitol Hill, Republican Senator Edward Brooke of Massachusetts introduced a sense of the Congress resolution, indicating the president should be granted immunity from all prosecution, should he resign. Brooke said he would withdraw his motion if the president does not make a confession of guilt. The resolution would not be binding and would not have the force of law.

Watergate prosecutor Leon Jaworski could still bring charges against Mr. Nixon if he chose to do so. State and local prosecutors could also bring charges, and the president would not be immune from civil action by private citizens. As for impeachment, Democratic Senator Frank Moss of Utah said Congress should proceed with its debate and possible trial, even if the president resigns.

Other leading Democrats agree. House Majority Leader Tip O'Neill, Senate Majority Leader Mike Mansfield, and Majority Whip Robert Byrd have all made statements indicating the impeachment process should continue. Senator Byrd says, "We all feel that whatever abuses of power were committed ought somehow to be laid out on the public record."

An exception among congressional leaders is House Speaker Carl Albert, who feels the impeachment process should come to an end with the publication of the final report by the House Judiciary Committee. At a press conference today, Albert said the transition of power will be smooth and orderly. And Albert says he is not bothered about the prospect of his once again becoming the man who would take over the presidency, should anything happen to Ford.

Early this afternoon, White House News Secretary Ronald Ziegler, described as looking grim and choked with emotion, made a brief statement to the White House press corps.

ZIEGLER: The president of the United States will meet various members of the bipartisan leadership of Congress here at the White House early this evening. Tonight at nine o'clock, eastern daylight time, the president of the United States will address the nation on radio and television from the Oval Office.

EDWARDS: After making his brief remarks, Ziegler walked off and let his deputies handle the rest of the briefing. Gerald Ford's press secretary announced that the vice president has canceled his scheduled twelve-day political trip to the far west. Paul Miltich described Ford's demeanor as remarkably calm, very businesslike.

Sources close to Ford say the vice president met with his senior staff members today and promised them a smooth, orderly transition to a new administration. The sources say Ford will be at his home during the president's speech and will likely have no comment afterward.

The *Chicago Sun Times* reported this morning that Ford has compiled a list of vice presidential candidates. The list included fourteen names, including that of Republican Senator Charles Percy of Illinois. Today Percy was asked if he would accept an offer to become vice president.

PERCY: I looked at that list and I can't imagine anyone on that list refusing President Ford if he becomes president. And I hope that we can assemble from across the country the greatest talent this nation has to offer, and I hope no one will refuse anything if Jerry Ford becomes president and wants to unite this country.

EDWARDS: A Pentagon spokesman says U.S. military forces are continuing normal operations and, in Jerry Friedheim's words, "There's no reason for us to do anything differently during this current government crisis." Other defense officials strongly discount the likelihood of any Russian attempt to take advantage of the U.S. political situation, emphasizing that the transfer of presidential power will be immediate, leaving no gap in authority.

Word of a possible change at the White House has made some U.S. allies nervous. A government official in Saigon says the last act in the Watergate drama is giving North Vietnam and the Vietcong just the right opportunity for an all-out offensive. That assessment comes amid reports of a communist buildup of men and arms; stepped-up attacks by the Vietcong; and a cut in U.S. aid to Saigon, voted by the House.

In the Mideast, Egypt is reportedly reexamining its policy of heavy reliance on Washington to guarantee further Israeli withdrawal from occupied Arab lands. A major newspaper in Jerusalem expressed fear that a change in the White House would threaten disengagement agreements negotiated by Secretary of State Kissinger. Both Israel and the Arab countries had hoped for an overall Mideast settlement during the Nixon presidency. As America's allies wonder about possible changes in U.S. foreign policy, they might be reassured to know that Secretary of State Kissinger will likely stay on in a Ford administration. Those were some of the dramatic events here today in Washington.

WATERS: All right, let's find out what you're thinking about today's activities. We're going to take some calls from the Southeast. Good evening, where are you calling from?

MCGOVERN: Good evening. I'm calling from Arlington, Virginia.

WATERS: May we have your name, please?

MCGOVERN: Yes, McGovern.

WATERS: And what is your reaction to the impending resignation of President Nixon?

MCGOVERN: Well, I think now, at this point, he's not being very magnanimous or trying to think of the country. I think he's like a cornered rat and just being forced out by people who are sympathetic, I guess. I mean, he's not doing it for the country or anything. He's just cornered and there is no escape for him. And I feel that he should not be getting immunity because he has fooled us long enough. I mean, not me but most of the people. He's deceived them, he's done all that he could to cause hardships to his political foes.

WATERS: Do you have positive feelings towards Vice President Ford?

MCGOVERN: Well, I think there are lots of better people than him, but I guess nobody could be as bad as the one that we have now.

WATERS: That's an interesting opinion. OK, I don't want to be abrupt, but we want to move along so we can take more calls. Thank you.

Good evening, where are you calling from, please?

CARTER: Lexington, North Carolina.

WATERS: And what's your name, sir?

CARTER: My name is Reverend Wilson Carter.

WATERS: Yes, Reverend Carter.

CARTER: Well, I guess my main feeling at this point is a kind of sense of relief that this long era of uncertainty is coming to an end. I think my most positive feeling is that the system has worked, and that gradually and slowly we've ground to a conclusion, which I think is a just one. But now that it's all over, or seems to be all over, I even find that I feel a sense of sorrow, and a sense of the personal tragedy for President Nixon, whom I have never admired.

WATERS: Reverend Carter, do you find that common among the people that you work with, as well?

CARTER: Yes, I do. I find many people down here are awfully glad that he's resigning.

WATERS: Well, I was speaking particularly to the feeling that you mentioned of having concern about the man, having concern about his feelings.

CARTER: I think perhaps more than I wish they did. I sometimes feel that people identify with the man more than with the office and with the great responsibility for the country, and therefore they overlook many of the serious wrongs that have taken place in the White House.

WATERS: Reverend Carter, thank you very much indeed. Let's go now to the Middle West, to public station WILL in Urbana, Illinois. Standing by there, Dan Simeone.

SIMEONE: We're taking calls from across the Midwest. A caller now from Osceola, Iowa. Your reaction?

WOMAN: I do not want President Nixon to be punished. I think he's been punished too many times now. I think it's just a terrible, terrible thing.

SIMEONE: You see this as a personal tragedy for him, then?

WOMAN: Absolutely. Words can't express my feelings. I think he has been persecuted. I think the Democrats are mad over the seventy-two election, and I feel that he has been persecuted way, way too much, and he is not guilty. He was voted in by a great majority of people, and these polls aren't true, because I've talked to many, many people that have never been polled and I have never been polled in my life!

SIMEONE: Well, thank you very much. We have a caller on the line from Missouri. May I have your reaction this evening?

MAN: Yeah, I think it's very definitely a breath of fresh air for the country. I just think the Watergate situation has gone on so long, and it's sort of "The king is dead, long live the king." I'm very glad we're getting someone in with Gerald Ford's capabilities.

SIMEONE: Sounds as if you've been expecting it.

MAN: Oh yeah, in fact with all the rumor that's been going around, I thought it was going to happen last night.

SIMEONE: OK, that's going to round things up here in the Midwest, Mike.

WATERS: To the western United States now, and public station WOI in Ames, Iowa, and Doug Brown.

BROWN: Here we have our first phone call from Dallas, Texas. Can I have your name, sir?

YEAGER: My name is Gene Yeager. My feeling is kind of a sense of irony, kind of tragic irony, at the whole situation. Nixon's campaign slogan, as I remember, was "Nixon's the One," and he certainly kind of proved that he was the one. It seems to me that at last the terror at the top, as the *Saturday Review* once put it, is coming to an end. And perhaps we'll have an end to a lot of the buggings and wiretaps and illegal activity that the Nixon administration has certainly done.

BROWN: Do you look for a sense of trust to be returning back to Washington, perhaps?

YEAGER: I certainly hope so. I think more than any other thing, the entire situation has focused the Washington scene in the eyes of the average voter. And it certainly can do nothing but good and give us a sense of trust, or at least a closer observation of what our elected officials are doing.

BROWN: Thank you, Mr. Yeager. We'll return to NPR in Washington.

WATERS: Susan Stamberg, who's been on vacation, is back with us. Welcome back.

STAMBERG: Thank you. I'm hot off the beaches of Delaware, literally. I just got out of the car. It's not the kind of thing you can stay on vacation for, when an important day like this happens in the country's history.

WATERS: Susan, you said something the other day, that it is the people who may be alone who particularly would like to hear other people at a time like this. We're going to hear now from some other listeners to National Public Radio. We're going now to station WBFO in Buffalo, New York, and Richard Malawista.

MALAWISTA: With me in the studio is Marcia Alvar. Our next call is from Philadelphia. Could you give us your name, please?

BOWERS: Uh, John Bowers.

MALAWISTA: And how do you feel about today's news?

BOWERS: Well, unfortunately I have not been near a radio, so I don't know if this is repetitive or not. But my main concern is the fact that we're now going to have two top officials, neither of whom were elected, when Mr. Ford picks a vice president. That concerns me more than most anything else, rather than the guilt or whatever.

For two years at least, and certainly for shaping the Republican successors in seventy-six, the people — particularly Republicans but also the country as a whole — have had no direct choice, and I think that's one of the tragedies of the whole thing.

ALVAR: Sir, are you afraid he's not going to be responsible to the people?

BOWERS: Well, I would guess that's probably not a real fear because I think it wouldn't be possible to have someone who's totally irresponsible chosen. I think it's partly a theoretical problem I have, but it's also a problem of ideology, of political ideology. I would hate to see dramatic changes wrought with Mr. Ford's vice president that could never have been done through the polls. I'm not sure I have anything specific in mind, but there's certainly the danger there.

ALVAR: Sir, thank you for your comments.

WATERS: This is NPR in Washington, where we're having a special edition of *All Things Considered* this evening, and we're going to you now for your reactions to the day's activities, to NPR member station WOI in Ames, Iowa, and Doug Brown.

BROWN: We have a call now from Corvalis, Oregon. Sir, are you there? What is your name, please?

LILL: Howard Lill, L-i-l-l.

BROWN: What would you like to say?

LILL: Well, I would just like to say that my wife and I are very depressed. We thought so much of Mr. Nixon that we both cried today. And we are in our eighties. We think that he was the best president that we ever had. And we can't understand why a thing like this Watergate or whatever they want to call it can be blown up to a point where they can retire him from office and humiliate him to the extent that they have. I think it's purely political, and I can't think any other way. I try hard to be broad-minded, but I can't help but think it's purely political. And God knows I hope that this retirement that we're expecting tonight don't go through.

BROWN: Thank you very much. We'll return to NPR in Washington.

WATERS: Right now we want to find out what opinions are in the north central region. We go to public station KSJN in St. Paul, Minnesota, and Gary Eichten.

EICHTEN: We're talking with Roger Malloy from Minneapolis. Mr. Malloy?

MALLOY: Well, I have two thoughts. I suppose there's a lot of thoughts the American people can have. One, if he is going to resign this evening, I think this is good for the American people. I think that I speak for a lot of people in saying we've had enough of Watergate and all of that.

But most importantly, I think that if nothing else that comes out of all of this two years of Watergate, the American people have got to realize now that we really need some election reform. We've got to really get behind Congress in pushing for this. And I think that probably in spite of himself, Richard Nixon will be able to go down in history as at least perpetrating election reform, if nothing else, in this term of office.

EICHTEN: Mr. Malloy, how do you feel about the prospect of having two people running our government, neither of whom have been elected by the people?

MALLOY: Well, I think that would be fine. To be very honest, I think there's nothing wrong. I think Mr. Ford's qualifications are very good, and whoever he chooses to be his new vice president, I'm sure he will choose wisely.

But I think that if nothing else Gerald Ford has going for him, he does have the support of the Congress, he has the support of the House. I think that there's going to be a lot of people that will probably get behind him, to try to make all of this come together again.

EICHTEN: OK, thank you very much for calling.

♦ ♦ At nine o'clock that evening, President Richard M. Nixon spoke to the nation from the Oval Office of the White House to say that he would resign at noon the following day and that "Vice President Ford will be sworn in as president at that hour in this office." The speech lasted sixteen minutes. The president said that in the last few days it had become clear to him that he no longer had "a strong enough political base in the Congress." That was as close as he came to acknowledging that he was about to be impeached by the House of Representatives. The president spoke instead about his accomplishments in office and about the national interest. "I have never been a quitter. To leave office before my term is completed is opposed to every instinct in my body. But as president I must put the interests of America first." After the president's speech, Mike Waters took more telephone calls.

WATERS: We're going now again to some of the people in America to find out how they feel, whether indeed they feel that the nation has been healed by the experiences of this evening. We're taking calls again from the Southeast — the District of Columbia, Maryland, and Virginia.

Good evening, where are you calling from and could you give us your name, please?

LOWRY: My name is Tom Lowry, and I'm calling from Arlington, Virginia.

WATERS: Mr. Lowry, how do you feel about the president's address this evening?

LOWRY: I found it appalling.

WATERS: In what sense?

LOWRY: In the sense that this man has evaded justice for the past two years, and it appeared tonight that this was the last and most evasive step in that course of action. He did not admit wrongdoing. He said he was resigning because of practical, political considerations, that the Congress no longer gave him sufficient support. He did not even attempt to explain why he was making the speech tonight, beyond those terms. He said he was serving the national interest, and I think it's clear he was serving his own interest.

STAMBERG: Mr. Lowry, do you in any way feel you're exhibiting the kind of vindictiveness that we just heard Congressman John Rhodes warning the nation about and saying he hoped people wouldn't show?

LOWRY: There's not an element of vindictiveness in what I feel. I feel that if that man wanted to serve the Constitution, then he would have stayed the course and allowed the trial to go on in the Senate. If he truly believed he were innocent, he would have done that. If he did not believe he was innocent, or if he did not believe he could prove his innocence, he would have alluded to it in his speech tonight. So I found his speech tonight evasive, if not deceptive.

WATERS: Thank you, Mr. Lowry. We're going to have some reaction now from the Middle West and the South. We're going to public station WOSU in Columbus, Ohio, and Don Davis.

DAVIS: We've got calls coming in from the South at this time, so we're going to go in that direction. First to Compton, Kentucky, and to Susan Chandlis.

CHANDLIS: I say it was the Checkers speech all over again, plus a phony State of the Union message. But I saw no frank admission of culpability, no honest regret or remorse of any kind. I found the whole speech altogether sickening.

DAVIS: You don't think he'll accomplish his announced goal of binding up the nation's wounds?

CHANDLIS: I think he had to say that, and he said it. But I don't think that was his intention.

DAVIS: Thank you for calling us, Susan, we're going to have to go on now to a gentleman calling from Beckley, West Virginia. Dale Damian, I believe.

DAMIAN: Yes, I'd like to say that I am glad that President Nixon has resigned, and I feel the constitutional process should go ahead and continue, and they should bring out all the facts as to whether or not he was guilty in obstructing justice.

I also think, one point I haven't heard anybody make, is to congratulate Mr. Ford or wish him the best in his future endeavors in his office.

DAVIS: Well, Mr. Damian, you just have. Back to Mike Waters at NPR.

WATERS: In our studios here, Bob Zelnick and Susan Stamberg. Susan, you have some reaction from the future president of the United States.

STAMBERG: I do. Gerald Ford, this evening, according to the Associated Press, said that the president made one of the greatest personal sacrifices for the country by resigning as president.

Mr. Ford appeared outside his home shortly after Mr. Nixon announced that he would resign. Ford says that he plans to continue Nixon's foreign policies, with Henry Kissinger remaining as secretary of state. These are Ford's words: "I want him to be my secretary of state. I'm glad to announce he will be my secretary of state."

Gerald Ford said he expects a spirit of cooperation between the new president and the Congress, and he said, "I've been very fortunate in my lifetime in public office to have a great many adversaries in the Congress, but I don't think I'll have any enemies in the Congress."

Continuing in his reaction to the president's statement, Gerald Ford said, in praising Mr. Nixon, "I think the president of the United States has made one of the greatest personal sacrifices for the country and one of the finest personal decisions, on behalf of all of us as Americans."

Having watched Nixon's foreign policy for the past five and a half years, Ford said, "Let me say without any hesitation or reservation that the policy that has achieved peace will be continued, as far as I'm concerned, as president of the United States."

Gerald Ford came out from his house in Alexandria, Virginia, something like fifteen minutes after Richard Nixon finished his televised address. He spoke for about ten minutes without notes. He emphasized his administration would pursue peace. He praised Henry Kissinger as a very great man. He said his foreign policy, developed under the Nixon administration, would be continued. And apparently spectators applauded when Henry Kissinger's name was mentioned.

WATERS: We understand that there are a number of people on Capitol Hill who have spoken at a press conference there about the new president, and Linda Wertheimer is on the line now. Linda, what's the story?

WERTHEIMER: I think the story certainly is "The king is dead, long live the king." The new president of the United States that will be sworn in tomorrow, Jerry Ford, is a very old friend and close colleague of many of the people here.

Carl Albert said he'd served twenty-five years with Jerry Ford in the House of Representatives, and that's been the experience of a great many people here on the Hill. Jerry Ford is very well liked up here. He's a very friendly sort of person. And it's always said of Jerry Ford that if you had to jump ship when he was the minority leader and he was pressing a position that he wanted his party to take, that anyone who jumped ship on Jerry Ford could always count on being warmly greeted by him the next day because he doesn't hold a grudge. He's a complete politician.

But the people on the Hill all have candidates for vice president and, of course, with the natural instincts of politicians, they are pressing those people who have stood for election and have received a good, sizable body of popular support. And of course, two of the people who come to mind from opposing sides of the spectrum are two governors of our most populous states, Reagan and Rockefeller. And then another person who is very high on the list of preferences here is Elliot Richardson, who was one of the few survivors of the Watergate experience to come out of it with all of his constituency intact.

So that's some of the speculation that's going on here.

ZELNICK: Linda, the governor of our most populous state is Ronald Reagan. The governor of our second most populous state is Malcolm Wilson, isn't it?

WERTHEIMER: That's true. Good point.

STAMBERG: Wilson who? What about Charles Percy, who's name came up in the old days, eight months back when people were speculating as to whom Richard Nixon might appoint as number-two man?

WERTHEIMER: Charles Percy said that he would be glad to serve, and he volunteered himself this morning for not only that position but any other position that Jerry Ford might ask him to fill. He feels that Republicans around the country and Democrats must rally to the president, and that includes giving their service to the new administration. Percy is willing.

STAMBERG: Thanks, Linda.

WATERS: I think this program in a way is a little bit like what I hope is occurring in the nation, in that two things which seem to be very separate are being brought together. I think in a sense we have two programs. One is here in the studio, where we ask for reaction and share some views, and the other is where we get some views from our listeners.

We're going to have reaction now from the Middle West, and for that we're going to Urbana, Illinois, public station WILL. Standing by there, Dan Simeone.

SIMEONE: We have reaction to the president's message from Leavenworth, Kansas.

WOMAN: I just feel as though I've awakened from a bad dream. The last two years have been probably the most traumatic experience I have ever experienced, and I am sixty-four years old. I've lived through two wars and a depression. The feeling that I've had toward this president — and I am a Quaker — has been one of complete horror and disbelief and fury.

SIMEONE: Then you saw the resignation as an inevitability?

WOMAN: I hoped. He should have done it a year ago. He should never have been elected.

SIMEONE: OK, thank you. We have another caller on the line. Where are you calling from, first of all?

OTTESON: I'm calling from Kansas City, Missouri. This is Ted Otteson on the line. My reaction to the president's speech is one of outrage. I think the politicians are misjudging the country, if your program is any indication. I just heard Ford talk about Nixon's great personal sacrifice, when he is, to use the term he applied to Dean, a self-confessed felon. He is resigning because he is going to be impeached!

If he gets away with this, I think there will be a tremendous reaction all over the country. Politicians seem to feel that the president's personal and family tragedy is somehow worse than other people's. What about the tens of thousands of Vietnam War draft evaders for whom he would not consider amnesty? I think if there's going to be an amnesty for Nixon, let it be general amnesty for both sides, for all sides. Let's bring the boys home from Canada and Sweden, if we're going to forgive Richard Nixon.

SIMEONE: Well, thank you very much for your comments. And, Mike, that's a wrap-up of a few of the comments from around the Midwest. Now back to National Public Radio in Washington.

WATERS: We're going to our listeners, calls from the Southeast — the District of Columbia, Maryland, and Virginia. Good evening. Would you tell us where you're calling from, please?

HINTON: I'm calling from Washington, D.C.

WATERS: May we have your name, please?

HINTON: Kathleen Hinton.

WATERS: What's your reaction to this evening?

HINTON: Well, I'm afraid I feel very disturbed. I feel a little better after listening to your guests. But after listening to the reactions of the network newsman to the president's speech, I really felt very confused.

I just feel very concerned about this streak of sentimentality which seems to rise up amongst Americans at the slightest little bit of drama. And it gives me the feeling that this man also will get off without taking real responsibility for his actions.

Listening on your program this afternoon to people in Gerald Ford's district, there seemed to be this same tendency to look at this man as if he were something really unique, without blemish, and to get on the bandwagon again. I just feel too concerned not to say something to somebody about it. I get the feeling that Congress is ready to do anything they can to avoid taking any more responsibility for this, and it concerns me very much.

✦ ✦ ✦ ✦ ✦ ✦ ✦ ✦ ✦

President Ford unconditionally pardoned former President Nixon in September, but that did not end Watergate. There were trials that fall on the cover-up, and former members of the administration went to jail for their part in it. Robert Zelnick, who had a lot to do with the hardening and sharpening of our news coverage during this critical period, covered the trials. He was weary of Watergate when he wrote this essay in late September, noting that by this time, the White House tapes were old news.

All Things Considered, OCTOBER 27

ZELNICK: To this observer, though, it's the fresh impressions that really count. For whatever reason, their tone, the pauses, the voice inflections of the speakers, the taped White House conversations we have heard, present a picture of Richard Nixon and his aides far different from that previously presented by the transcripts alone.

For one thing, Mr. Nixon himself seems far more in control of his staff than had earlier been evident. He guides each conversation, leading each speaker first here, then there, responding to certain suggestions, ignoring others, returning to subjects he wishes pursued, allowing others to die on the vine. He grasps passing references in a manner that suggests a prior familiarity, even with topics purportedly being discussed for the first time.

A staunch loyalty to his subordinates also is unmistakable on the former president's part. Apprised that he can cut his losses by inducing some of those involved in pre-break-in events to accept full blame, Mr. Nixon retreats from the idea. From reading the transcripts alone, one was never certain why.

But on tape Mr. Nixon sounds both emphatic and sincere as he recalls Dwight Eisenhower cutting Sherman Adams adrift and vows to stick by members of his own team and take the heat. Why then the subsequent firings, the appointment of a special prosecutor, and ultimately compliance with a Supreme Court decree that brought his presidency to an end? This is perhaps the great mystery of Watergate, the president who determined to stonewall it, but, who, in the end, retreated at every significant step. Again, the answer is suggested by the tapes. For while Richard Nixon indeed seemed in control of his confederates, one never sensed that he felt in control of his administration or of the government.

Mr. Nixon seems nothing so much as a fugitive from the very forces he nominally controlled. He is afraid of secretaries who may know too much, of Justice Department prosecutors whom he can legally fire at will, of runaway grand juries, of congressional committees, of citizens, who, in another context, he once compared to children.

Absent on the tapes is any sense of totalitarian objectives on the part of Richard Nixon or his top advisers. The awesome powers of the Presidency were, indeed, used frivolously, even repressively at times, but only as part of the cover-up, only to draw the covered wagons around the White House, only as protection against the darker powers that plague this band of outsiders in their own household. For Richard Nixon and his men, Watergate became a world of hobgoblins and every day was Halloween.

So the elements that coagulated to bring about the fall of Richard Nixon do emerge from the tapes. Leadership of the White House team drew Mr. Nixon inevitably into the cover-up, a fierce loyalty to his men prevented him from cutting the cancer out before it afflicted his presidency. A fear of outside forces prevented him from standing firm.

All this led, in turn, to a blurring of distinctions between what was merely embarrassing and what was criminal, what would sting and what would kill, and this merger carried over into the cover-up operations. Means both legal and illegal were employed to shield conduct that was both legal and illegal. That was the essence of the way the White House operated during Richard Nixon's Watergate ordeal. It is also the essence of the conspiracy to obstruct justice.

✦ ✦ ✦ ✦ ✦ ✦ ✦ ✦ ✦ ✦

The day after Christmas, we had this small dose of salts from Goodman Ace. He was a year older than the century when he wrote this. Goodman Ace was a radio icon, half of the Easy Aces, with his wife, Jane. Their weekly radio program originated from Chicago in the early 1930s and lasted almost twenty years. In a long career, he wrote for the *Saturday Review*, for Milton Berle and Tallulah Bankhead, and after Jane Ace died in 1974, he wrote for us. Age was a favorite subject.

All Things Considered, DECEMBER 26

ACE: The subject being discussed was age, type O, O for old. It came in a conversation with a dear friend, whom for want of a better name we will call Groucho. Come to think of it, in the many years of our cherished friendship, I have never called him by his given name, Julius. Now and then Captain Spaulding, but never Julius.

Groucho was visiting in New York and invited me to lunch. I found him in his hotel, quite happily flanked, rather enveloped, by two pretty nurses and his attractive executive manager, Miss Erin Fleming.

I asked him how he felt. He replied he was eighty-three, as if that answered my question. I told him that old age, like beauty, is in the eyes of the beholder.

Despite Groucho's late-in-life infirmities, quote "two major-minor operations," he calls it, in my mind's eye appears a crouchy Groucho in that ill-fitting frock coat, his grotesque black painted mustache, seemingly bristling with every leering leap he made at the statuesque Margaret Dumont.

That's the way I saw him that afternoon as we pondered the question of how old is old age. Why do many of the over-sixty-five's have a hang-up about admitting approaching senior citizenship, and why they don't appreciate that they are on the threshold of a new, freewheeling, and, if they play their cards right, joyous lifestyle, where the restrictive and antiquated rules of social behavior don't apply anymore?

We talked about some of the early telltale signs that indicate that you are getting up there. For instance, a person — OK, it was I — a person reads the front page of a paper and he comes to the end of a column and the line reads "Continued on page 61, column 2," and he turns to page 61 and finds a full-page ad.

So he turns back to page 1, and the same line now reads "Continued on page 51, column 2," and he turns to page 51 where he finds column 2 is a *New York Times* ad describing the special, weekly large-type edition it prints for people with limited vision.

So he turns back to page 1, and the line now reads "Continued on page 51, column 5." So he turns to page 51, column 5, and he settles back to read, but by now he has forgotten what the last line of the story was on page 1. So he turns, and so on and so on.

Do you relate to that? Yes? You are now in the early stages of becoming a member of the serene seniority set, and that is one of the countless daily challenging games you are entitled to play, only one of the thousand natural shocks that flesh is heir to. Old age is not merely bingo and shuffleboard. Enjoy the privilege of grumbling when you breakfast in a coffee shop and are irritated by the noise pollution of cold cereals happily swimming in bowls of milk on tables around you, all that ear-splitting crackling, snapping, and popping. Act your age. It is your inalienable right to tell them to pipe down. Or when someone tells you of the death of a mutual friend, and you asked how old he was and are told he was seventy, and you mutter, "So young." You are automatically a paid-up member of OA.

Groucho and I disagreed on one thing. He said old age has no birth date. It creeps slowly and inexorably up the human frame. "Not true," I replied. And I told him of the day I was in an elevator and two attractive girls got on. They smiled. I preened, and I knew I still had it. However, when we reached the ground floor, one young thing held the elevator door open for me, while the other one rushed out to hold open the heavy street door while I stepped out, a shambles of myself of the moment before. In one elevator ride I had aged twenty years.

And if you've dozed off while listening to me, don't let it bother you. In your fun-filled December years you are permitted a dozen daily dozings. Welcome to Dizzyland.

✦ ✦ ✦ ✦ ✦ ✦ ✦ ✦ ✦

Jack Benny died that night of December 26, 1974, and Susan Stamberg called Goodman Ace back the next day, to talk about Benny. He told Susan he met and fell in love with Jack Benny many years before. "More years than I care to remember, even before he was really thirty-nine."

Bob Edwards pronounced the benediction on the year that changed so many lives. There may be names here you don't recognize after twenty years. Cokie Roberts would say, "Call your parents, ask them. You probably ought to anyway."

All Things Considered, DECEMBER 31

EDWARDS: One year ago today, Richard Nixon was toughing it out. Gerald Ford had just promised he would not pardon Nixon. And Nelson Rockefeller was still smarting because he had been passed over for the number-two job. My point here is that things change and each of you could find your life dramatically altered by this time next year when we look back upon 1975.

Consider, for example, that in January of seventy-four, Steven Weed and Patricia Hearst were picking out their china pattern. TV's cuddliest couple was Sonny and Cher. Liz Taylor and Richard Burton were showing us that true love will endure. Peter Rodino was not yet a household word. We were still swooning over Sam Ervin, chuckling at Joseph Montoya, cheering Lowell Weicker, and measuring Howard Baker for a chair in the Oval Office.

A year ago today the antiwar crowd was telling us that the CIA had spied on them and the FBI had been playing dirty tricks. We called them "headline-grabbing paranoids."

Last year the world's most powerful man was Henry Kissinger. Today it's King Faisal. We used to curse Yasir Arafat. Today he gets standing ovations at the United Nations.

Does anyone remember Florida Senator Edward Gurney, vowing to get to the bottom of Watergate as a member of the Ervin committee? That was before his indictment. John Connally was being marked for the White House, but that was before his indictment.

I wonder what Philippe Petit was doing last New Year's Day. Was he thinking about walking a tightwire between the towers of the World Trade Center? Paramount was telling us *The Great Gatsby* was going to be even greater. And speaking of frauds, not all of you had heard about Evel Knievel last New Year's Day.

Little League baseball was called chauvinist for refusing to allow girls to play. Then they proved it by refusing to allow foreign children to play in the "world series."

Moses Malone, the rookie with the Utah Stars, signed a one-and-a-half-million-dollar contract. This time last year he was playing high school basketball. The sports world gave us the comeback of the year. As we went about correcting our Vietnam mistakes, one of the war's victims, Muhammad Ali, was winning back the title that had been taken away from him. Last year we all laughed at the World Football League. Well, some things never change.

We used to tell you that the most powerful man in Washington was Wilbur Mills. That was before his stripper friend took a swim. Today's journalistic frustration is that we can't tell you who is the most powerful man in Washington. We suspect it's Sonny Jurgensen. We know it's not the Joint Chiefs. All the famous names who were there last year are gone now, and the new ones, like much of Washington these days, are an anonymous group, and Pentagon staffers are grateful that the army wears nametags. Not true of their chairman, General Brown, winner of this year's Earl Butts Brotherhood Award, who promises to make the foot in the mouth part of the military uniform.

My favorite Washington fate of 1974 was that of J. D. Sawyer, former associate attorney general. Last January he was appointed to his job by his close friend, William Saxbe. Sawyer was provided thirty-eight thousand dollars a year and an enlarged redecorated office suite at a cost of more than twenty-five thousand dollars. But before he could break in his new furniture, Sawyer wrote Saxbe, there is really no role for the associate attorney general. Saxbe agreed, and Sawyer talked himself out of a cushy job.

The world's 1974 Fickle Finger of Fate trophy should undoubtedly go to Hiro Onoda, who last New Year's Day and the twenty-eight preceding New Year's Days was patrolling the Philippine jungles, wondering when Roosevelt would surrender. He returned to Japan, saw all the wonders of our modern world, and retreated to South America. Think you'll have the same dull, humdrum life in seventy-five? You might be better off if you do. Happy New Year.

1975

I n the winter of 1975 a new crowd arrived in Washington. Benefiting from a fit of "throw the rascals out," Democrats had made enormous gains in the Watergate election year, picking up nearly fifty seats in the House. There were new Democratic senators from states that generally elected Republicans. California and New York had Democratic governors. The country was ready for change. In January of that year, Elvis Presley was forty, and Fred Calland took notice. Fred wrote about music for NPR. He has a classical-FM voice and can rattle off opus and movement with the best of them, but always with a hint of mischief.

All Things Considered, JANUARY 8

CALLAND: Forty years ago today was born in Tupelo, Mississippi, someone who was to affect, influence, guide, and shape popular music all over the world, as had no one before or since. The statistics and the bio are fascinating reading of the "only in America" genre. Elvis Presley wasn't born with much in the way of musical talent in his background, and there was considerable indication that his basic shyness, attractive as it might have been, would not permit him to go far in the country music racket, as competitive as any other racket.

In retrospect, he seems, but only seems, to have been the central personality around which was to swirl all sorts of nonmusical currents, rather than the cause itself. Things like the rise of the "teen-ocracy," the rise of country music as the most financially important branch of popular American music, and the long overdue amalgamation of certain black strains into the country style, itself an amalgam of early American popular types, from the parlor ballad to the British popular dances. You name it, it's all there.

Memory brings back very clearly the horrified record salesman who tried in vain to move their middle-class shopping center customers to the so-called "better things," like the classics, like Mantovani, like even Frank Sinatra. But no. For a teenager, young married, middle-ager, for many, many people, Presley was all the rage, and no one else would do but Presley.

Well, the young, sexy, smoldering-voiced kid made it big, and is at forty, as loved and listened to as ever. The shocked listeners of the mid-fifties, when Presley made a hit, are now either reconciled to or amazed by the fact that all the fuss was indeed the ferment of something very big. For example, the Beatles, who, lest we forget, were capable of creating great songs in the earlier ragtime and pop styles, knew immediately that the nascent rock movement contained all the elements that they and a whole generation of listeners were looking for; a new personality, a new beat, frank lyrics stating an open, embracing celebration of love, lust, mating, betrayal, fun, and general joy of life.

Presley was regarded by the older generation as a scarcely definable but terrible threat to morals, civic responsibility, and so forth. But he gathered adoring fans by the millions — an entire generation, in fact. Time passes, and that generation is now in its forties. So is Elvis Presley. But there's a whole generation that would rather not think about it.

✦ ✦ ✦ ✦ ✦ ✦ ✦ ✦ ✦

F red Calland threaded five of Elvis's greatest hits through that essay, ending with "Love Me Tender." Calland's taste in music is as broad as his knowledge. That same month, he followed Elvis with Amadeus.

All Things Considered, JANUARY 27

CALLAND: He was born 219 years ago today and died 35 years later. Death at such an age of a cause not known for sure was tragic for himself, for his family. But for posterity? Mozart didn't really give a hoot. His life, his efforts, his genius, were at the disposal of his contemporaries. For posterity, it doesn't really matter how short his life was, for it was so productive, that very few music lovers can grasp the entire range of his accomplishments.

One example only. His opera *The Magic Flute,* long considered at best a charming, musically infectious eighteenth-century soap opera, and at worst, a closed joke about the bigotry of kings and clerics, has, in our time, come to be seen as one of the funniest, most profound celebrations of the joy of coming into full human consciousness, hardly an outdated subject, and containing in the priest Sarastro's music what George Bernard Shaw termed "the only music yet written that could be put in the mouth of God without blasphemy."

After two hundred years, the enigma of Mozart is still unresolved. Why such talent for musical sounds, for intellectual grasp of musical, dramatic, and literary forms? Whence such insight and compassion for his fellow human? Even his name forms a paradox: Wolfgang Amadeus, stride of the wolf, beloved by God.

He wrote in every form known to his day, and he was always greedy to know what was to come as well as what had been in his art. He wrote for every instrument he ever heard. He tried his hand at aleatoric, or chanted music. He tried computerized composition before anyone had ever heard of the beast, the computer. He would have written for the harmonica, no doubt about it, except that no one had invented it yet.

✦ ✦ ✦ ✦ ✦ ✦ ✦ ✦ ✦ ✦

In the spring of 1975, Saigon fell. Led by the newly elected Watergate Democrats, the House had voted against President Ford's request for additional help for South Vietnam. That decision signaled the end of this country's involvement, and the North Vietnamese began a major offensive. In April, they were advancing on Saigon.

This next piece is out of order. We actually broadcast it ten years after the events it describes. At the end of April 1985 we looked back on the experience of leaving Vietnam, a program we called "Good-bye, Saigon." Art Silverman produced the piece, inspired by an audiocassette recorded by a helicopter pilot.

Air Force Second Lieutenant Richard Vande Geer helped airlift the last Americans out of Saigon as the city was falling to the North Vietnamese. The cassette was a kind of letter home to a good friend, recorded in May 1975. Art made the pilot the center of the piece, but then spoke to a number of others, soldiers and diplomats, reporters and civilians, about their memories of the last day and night in Saigon. Noah Adams is the narrator. Vande Geer tells his own story. He had been on a mission in Cambodia. He had some days off and he had gone to Thailand for rest and relaxation. It was from there that he was summoned back to Saigon.

VANDE GEER: The moment I walked into the room, I told them I wanted flowers in the room and I wanted some gin. And I wanted the best body massage that Bangkok had to offer and a place and a woman for me. Now, keep in mind, I had been up about forty hours, and I was still having flashbacks of Phnom Penh.

ADAMS: Those flashbacks of Phnom Penh, he wanted to burn them out of his mind, and maybe, if he got enough sleep, drank enough gin and had that body massage, maybe he could forget about it. But it was not to be. The front desk called with a message from headquarters.

VANDE GEER: The message said that there would be a plane waiting for me at the airport at seventeen hundred to take me back. Of course it was hard to believe that there could be such injustice in the world, but be assured there is.

I really didn't have a good idea why I was being recalled. I had no clear idea as to what was going on, but we felt as though it had something to do with Saigon.

ADAMS: He was right. It was Saigon. A lot of people wanted to get out before the communists took over. Everyone had heard rumors — a bloodbath would follow. There would be acts of revenge for those who worked with the Americans.

Some Vietnamese had already left. The American military airlifted them out of the country on cargo planes. But on that last day the North Vietnamese destroyed the airport runway.

UNIDENTIFIED NEWSMAN: The ground and artillery attack on the Tan Son Nhut Airbase came at four o'clock in the morning.

ADAMS: At an airport gymnasium State Department Officer Joe McBride was at work, processing refugees.

MCBRIDE: All of a sudden, boom, boom. Background explosions and then the buildings started shattering. The phosphorus and bulbs in the ceiling were coming crashing down, including one that came down and crashed on my head, and I says, "Oh shit."

ADAMS: Peter Arnett worked for the Associated Press. He had seen more of the war in Vietnam than most reporters.

ARNETT: We were all in the Caravelle Hotel, and there was this enormous shelling and explosions from the direction of the airport. I remember opening the window, and the night sky was lit up with explosives. I went to the roof of the Caravelle Hotel and there were dozens of newsmen there.

UNIDENTIFIED NEWSMAN: And we could see black plumes of smoke coming up from Tan Son Nhut Airport.

SECOND UNIDENTIFIED NEWSMAN: You could see the muzzle flashes.

ARNETT: And in the next half hour we saw three aircraft shot down by rockets.

ADAMS: U.S. Army Captain Stewart Harrington was at the airport.

HARRINGTON: What they were doing was the North Vietnamese were telling the Americans and the South Vietnamese that Ton Son Nhut was no longer a conduit out of the Republic of South Vietnam. My reaction was that, "Well, this is it. We're going." And to me the phrase "We're going" meant that we were going to leave the Republic of Vietnam by helicopter.

ADAMS: On the morning of April 29, 1975, Jack Cahill, a reporter for the *Toronto Star*, was in Saigon, waiting for a prearranged signal to tell him the final evacuation had begun.

CAHILL: Well, we were supposed to be all waiting to hear "White Christmas" being played on a — the FM radio. That was the signal for the evacuation.

HARRINGTON: That was a part of the plan. We call it "the plan," in quotes. The plan said that we were going to signal everyone when it was time to assemble at the safe sites, and the signal that the evacuation was on and that Americans should discreetly report to these safe sites was to be the playing of Bing Crosby's "White Christmas," accompanied by the phrase that "the temperature in Saigon is 105 and rising," or something like that.

ADAMS: American Julie Forsythe was a Quaker worker in Saigon.

FORSYTHE: And only the Americans were supposed to know that, you know. Now, you can imagine how long only the Americans knew that. Maybe ten minutes. You know, we heard about it from other Vietnamese people. We didn't hear about it from the Americans.

ADAMS: Le Thi Dung, like many other Vietnamese, was frightened. She was forced into making agonizing decisions.

LE: Very early in the morning a friend of mine, a doctor, a Vietnamese doctor, he came over to my home very early, and he say, "Now we have to get out Vietnam very quickly. Otherwise we are going to be trapped in." I try to select things, but we can bring only kilos. How can we bring? My mother wanted to take the incense bowl in my father's altar. In our house we have an altar to the ancestors, and I pray for my father. I say, "We are leaving you," and I ask him to protect us in our crossing of the ocean, but I feel so guilty because I know that from that day on we will no longer be Vietnamese, you see.

ADAMS: Many Vietnamese made the painful decision to give up their country that morning. On this last day of the war, helicopter pilot Vande Geer was on the aircraft carrier *Midway*, waiting with other American helicopter pilots for orders to begin the evacuation.

VANDE GEER: A Vietnamese Huey flew out toward sea and found the carrier, and the man who got out of this aircraft was quoted as saying approximately a week earlier that any South Vietnamese that left the country were cowards and that everybody should remain in South Vietnam and fight to the bitter end.

This man was General Ky. Now I really don't have any personal feelings about the war over here. I really don't care one way or the other, but I did find myself feeling that I wish he had been shot down.

ADAMS: But Vande Geer soon had to put thoughts of a flamboyant Nguyen Cao Ky out of his mind. The orders had finally come down. Vande Geer and the other helicopter pilots climbed into their aircraft and headed off towards Saigon, forty minutes away by air. Late in the morning, Canadian reporter Jack Cahill was still doing his job covering the news. As he did, Vietnamese on motorbikes and on foot, carrying suitcases, made him sense it was time to go.

CAHILL: But it was all terribly confusing. Nobody ever heard "White Christmas" or anything being played, and nobody knew really where to go, what to do. But anyway, I filed my story, walked back to the hotel, and everybody had gone.

ADAMS: In Saigon, TV cameraman Barry Fox was standing with other reporters next to an evacuation bus. The bus was lost. It had been circling around the city for hours. It ended up at the Saigon riverfront.

FOX: It was at that point that I suddenly realized that the air was full of helicopters, and I looked up and there were just dozens of helicopters flying over the port.

So we got on the bus, and that — at that time — created panic amongst the Vietnamese who were at the port when we got there. They saw the bus leaving. They wanted to get on the bus. They were trying to climb in the windows of the bus, and people were hanging onto the outside, and the driver drove away. We slowed down to go by the gate, and a woman carrying a baby jumps on. The bus doesn't stop, and nobody's stopping them . . .

There's an air of hysteria, and she loses her grip on her baby, and the baby falls off the bus, and then she jumps off the bus, and the bus, as far as I could gather, ran over the baby.

ADAMS: Fear made people do terrible things on that last day, but along with hysteria, there were acts of courage. State Department Officer Joe McBride saw a little of both. His job was to drive people from points around the city to evacuation pickup spots. McBride remembers it was almost impossible to organize an orderly departure because the evacuees were afraid of being left behind. However, McBride recalls one exception.

MCBRIDE: There was a big Vietnamese that had a — he was in civilian clothes. A big, tall Vietnamese. Spoke good English. Came up to me as I was trying to organize things, and said, "Maybe I can help you." And he said, "What are your priorities?"

And I laid out my priorities as best I could. And he said, "Fine. Fine. I'll take care of it." I came back four or five times after that guy started organizing things, and he would generally have a group of people lined up and organized and I'd take them.

I'd turn to him, and I'd say, "Look, I am running out of gas. I am running out of time. The choppers are leaving. This is going to be the last run." And I asked the guy, "Where is your family?" And, "It's you and your family now . . ."

And he said, "We can't do it." And I said, "What do you mean?" He says, "I've got twenty-four people in my family. There's no way we can do it in one — just one run."

And I said, "I'm, you know, they're telling me I've got to go home." And the guy just said, "Well, it's been nice working with you." He extended his hand, shook mine, and said, "See you around. Thanks for trying."

VANDE GEER: I made three sorties into Saigon. No, four sorties. I am sorry. I could tell you about — how real the fear was that I felt. The VC [Vietcong] had commandeered Air America Hueys, and they were flying them around, which simply made a very interesting chess game.

ADAMS: As the day wore on, it became clear that promises would have to be broken. Promises to Vietnamese who had worked for the Americans that they would get out on this final day. There were delays in helicopter lifts. The plan was falling apart. The North Vietnamese were surrounding the city.

A young Vietnamese woman, Chung Wan Linh, worked for the South Vietnamese government. An American friend was supposed to tell her when it was time to evacuate. She waited but didn't hear from him.

LINH: For me that was the last blow. So I decided that I have to go to the embassy. Well, I try to make my way to the marine, and I asked one of the marine, I said, "Could I go in the embassy?" and the marine said,

"There's no one in embassy except people who have been accepted to go there to wait for the helicopters. Do you have a pass?" And I said, "No, I don't," and so the marine said, "In that case, I am sorry."

FOX: People had brought their possessions and their bundles and whatever was important to them, and were trying to carry them through the crowd.

UNIDENTIFIED MAN: I had my wife standing with my two children, and I try to get in through the gate, but they give us a warning that anyone try to break in they going to shoot to death.

LINH: I saw all the newsmen with their equipment and so on, and that also gave me a feel that in fact the situation was desperate. Otherwise newspeople would not leave.

FOX: It was just solid Vietnamese, shoulder to shoulder, pushing, shouting.

MCBRIDE: I got to the side gate, and I wanted to get over. Obviously they couldn't open that gate, and the marines said, "No, sir, I can't let you over." I said, "Why not?" And he says, "If you do, they'll start coming, and then I'll have to shoot. I don't want to have to shoot them, sir. Please don't come over."

FOX: I could see from what was going on around me that the embassy was getting worried as to how it was going to survive the onslaught of all these people. They had absolute knowledge that there was no way the helicopters were going to get all these people out of the compound.

MCBRIDE: And I circulated through the crowd, walking gently, pushing through, "Excuse me. Don't worry. There's plenty of helicopters for everybody." All this in Vietnamese, of course. "We're not going to abandon. Don't worry." I just didn't want panic to start.

And quietly gathered about twenty-five or thirty Americans who were out there with their dependents, and at that point the two marines came over the gate, and they must have been six foot two, six foot five. They were big, big men, wearing their flak jackets and the helmets.

The marines kept pushing the crowd back. Every time we'd let somebody else through, particularly a Vietnamese with an American. People waving papers and, you know, testimonies why they had to get out. Stories. And we were doing everything we could do to keep the panic down and assuring everybody constantly.

And every once in a while the marines will lock and load their rifles, you know, with the bolts to make a snapping sound, scaring people back, and I'm thinking, God these guys are cool, because all it would have taken is one panicked person with a grenade, one person going out of their mind with a knife.

ADAMS: Originally the U.S. Embassy was not among the general evacuation points at all. It was to be reserved as the way out for the ambassador and his staff. However, by late afternoon it had become an irresistible last hope for Vietnamese wanting to leave.

More than six thousand of them had gotten out by way of a safe corner of the city's Tan Son Nhut Airport and other spots. With nightfall the helicopters had stopped going to those places but were still coming to the embassy compound. The thousand who had found their way inside the walls considered themselves lucky.

HARRINGTON: Repeatedly we told these folks, "If you'll all cooperate, we'll all go, but these choppers cannot take your suitcases. Please throw them all away."

I mean, these people were good. They threw away everything. The only people we had problems with, ironically, were Americans. And a number of Americans in the crowd, before we got rid of them all, argued that, you know, "This is my ride" or, you know, "I'll write my congressman," and groused about it. But the Vietnamese were good. They were docile and cooperative, once we got them under control.

VAN DE GEER: We thought that they were going to call off the operation when it became dark because we never expected them to send us into such a bad situation to begin with, even if it was daytime. But as you probably know, they continued the mission on until nearly five o'clock in the morning. The night sorties were the worst because we flew lights-out. The tracers kept everybody on edge. To see a city burning gives one a strange feeling of insecurity.

ADAMS: At the embassy, Americans had been delaying their own departures as long as they could, to keep the helicopters coming for the Vietnamese. But Washington was ordering them to get out. The CIA's Frank Snepp.

SNEPP: The halls were overrun with humanity because the evacuation was going off the roof. At this point, there were helicopters going off the roof, and the embassy had become a labyrinth of humanity. People were hungry. They had animals tucked under their arms. They had — they were screaming for water, and we pushed our way through them, as we made our way up the stairwell towards the helicopter path. I felt such shame because we were leaving before the Vietnamese in the embassy.

MCBRIDE: I was ready to leave. I had done what could be done. [Sighs.] In any case, whoever was loading said, "We need a couple. Joe, how about you? You're ready."

It was all red inside. The chopper was all red. It was like the nightlights that they would use on a submarine or something. And there was a very high-pitched whine that I'd never heard before, an incredible turbine kind of whining sound. And the back gate was down enough that when the helicopter lifted off and we were heading out over Saigon, it was dark, and you could see fires in the city. You could see fires in a lot of places.

ADAMS: It was now a little after five in the morning Saigon time, April 30, 1975. The helicopters were coming further apart, but a final six of them were due in. That would be enough to handle the remaining 420 Vietnamese citizens waiting in the embassy courtyard. Waiting with them were Captain Stewart Harrington, Colonel John Madison, and another army officer. Captain Harrington describes what happened next.

HARRINGTON: The senior marine on the scene was a Major Jim Keene, and Keene came out of the embassy, went up to Colonel Madison, and said, "Sir, the evacuation's over. It's Americans only."

And Colonel Madison looked at Keene. I was standing right there. And he said, "No way. We have these 420 people here and we were promised that there'd be the six more lifts that we need, and we're not leaving until the — until they're gone."

And Keene said, "Can't do it." He said, "It's a presidential order, and I am not going to risk the safety of my men any longer." His men were around the perimeter of the embassy.

Madison said, "I'll take it up with the ambassador." And Keene went, "You can't, sir. He just left," and he pointed to a CH-46 that was leaving and had just taken off, was about fifty feet in the air above the roof of the embassy.

Good soldier that he was, Colonel Madison made that call. He said, "OK, Stew, you stay here with the radio with these people and play like everything's normal and we'll slip into the embassy and get up to the roof, and you make it to the roof when you can."

So I went to the trunk deck of a car that had its headlights on, pointed, and where the people were all, you know, I am sitting here and the people were five feet away, the first row.

And I sat there with this radio, talking to helicopters that weren't there, and the people kept saying, "Is the helicopter coming?" And I would tell them, "Don't worry. A big helicopter's coming, don't worry, don't worry," and I did that for five or ten minutes, until I thought I'd given them enough time.

So I put the radio down, and I said to the Vietnamese nearest to me, "I got to take a leak." And I slipped over into the bushes and then I, whish, made a quick move, and into the door of the embassy and charged up the stairs.

ADAMS: Captain Harrington ran up to the embassy roof, climbed aboard a partially filled helicopter, and left. Now, after sixteen years of fighting, the American presence in the Republic of South Vietnam was down to eleven marines. There was a long wait for another helicopter. The marines thought they had been forgotten. When it did come, they knew they had to make a run for it. The question was, Could they get to the roof before the Vietnamese? Sergeant Terry Bennington:

BENNINGTON: Well, we backed in slowly initially and when they realized what we were doing, they started for us and we headed for the door. And I think we beat them with maybe a second to spare, and we got the door shut and got it barred. And of course that wasn't going to hold them that long, and we knew that. So everybody got up onto the roof at that time and then we barred the doors on the roof and there were still, you know, it didn't take long for the Vietnamese to get through the door and come up that ladder well.

So we took CS gas and we took red smoke and green smoke and any other smoke we could get our hands on, and it did work. Once we threw the red smoke and the CS gas and everything, they started running. Unfortunately the turbines started to suck the CS gas inside of the chopper. So we kind of gassed ourselves there, too. But the chopper pilot finally looked back and I think he saw what was happening and he got us out of there pretty quick. He definitely got us out of there pretty quick.

ADAMS: The president's press secretary, Ron Nesson:

NESSON: The evacuation has now been completed. The president commends the personnel of the armed forces who accomplished it, as well as Ambassador Graham Martin and the staff of his mission who served so well under difficult conditions. This action closes a chapter in the American experience.

LINH: When I saw the last helicopter leave the top of the U.S. Embassy, I felt I was not really angry but hurt, like, you know, you trust your really good friend. You think that you have been having a good friend. You work together for so long and when you are in danger or in hardship, even, you know, instead of helping you, they turn their back away.

VANDE GEER: We pulled out, meaning the special operation unit, close to two thousand people. We couldn't pull out anymore because it was beyond human endurance to go anymore.

I am back now. I got back today. I am in bits and pieces fairly incoherent only because it's been such a fast pace. I have no word on when I will be withdrawn. I haven't had a chance to feel it out really. And I'll just have to wait and see.

ADAMS: But Air Force Second Lieutenant Richard Vande Geer had one more helicopter rescue after he made this tape. When the Cambodians seized the SS *Mayagüez* in May of 1975, Vande Geer was again called into action. He was airlifting a squadron of marines when a rocket hit his helicopter.

At the Vietnam Veterans Memorial in Washington, where the names of the dead are listed chronologically, Richard Vande Geer's name is last.

VANDE GEER: Again, Dick, I apologize for the very poor way that I have explained to you what has been happening. I don't think it will be too terribly long before we are together again. I wish you peace, and I have a great deal of faith that the future has to be ours. Adios, my friend.

✦ ✦ ✦ ✦ ✦ ✦ ✦ ✦ ✦

One American who did not leave on that terrible day and night was Peter Arnett of the Associated Press. He stayed for another twenty-five days. Years later, he did the same thing again, staying in Baghdad after most Americans left, and reporting on the Gulf War for CNN from an extraordinary vantage point. When he did leave Saigon in 1975, he went to Hong Kong, and from there spoke by telephone with Susan Stamberg. He described how South Vietnamese citizens reacted on the day the North Vietnamese tanks entered Saigon.

All Things Considered, MAY 27

ARNETT: Well, about fifty of them poured into our office. The AP office is on the fifth floor of a downtown building. And as the tanks came in, about fifty jumped into our office seeking sanctuary. They were absolutely desperate. They were absolutely convinced they would die.

The Vietnamese, many Vietnamese I knew, had not been able to get out of the city. They went to ground. They went and hid in their homes. They hid under beds. In fact, our whole Vietnamese staff sort of went into hiding for the first few hours.

On the streets, the occupation was so rapid that the people of

Saigon didn't know what was happening. The communist soldiers in their pith helmets and baggy pants were amongst them almost instantaneously. Events moved very quickly. The Americans left on April 29 and all during that night. The last American helicopter came in at eight o'clock in the morning. At ten o'clock in the morning President Minh had surrendered.

Now, there had been no fighting in Saigon at the time he surrendered. So the people of Saigon, those who hadn't been listening to the radio, didn't realize what was happening. Now, the surrender was at ten o'clock. By eleven-fifteen, the tanks and the trucks were coming in. So many people were just wandering around the streets. And suddenly you had tanks and you had soldiers with flags. Of course, the flag was everywhere, the communist flag, the blue and green with the yellow star. That flag was flying everywhere, and the population of Saigon looked absolutely surprised.

I was out watching the tanks come in, and the trucks, and there were a lot of people open-mouthed. But the people of Saigon were rather stoic and many things had happened to them in the last twenty years. They stood and looked. And when they realized that there was not going to be any immediate shooting, or any killing, they sort of went about their own way.

And that happened on the first day, and by evening of the occupation, there were thousands on the streets, thousands of South Vietnamese on their motorcycles, walking around and talking to some of the soldiers, and it seemed a very natural thing to have happened.

STAMBERG: I wonder if finally you can describe your own reaction to that sight.

ARNETT: Well, I'd been covering the war since 1962 when I'd first gone to Saigon. I stayed in the Caravelle Hotel, and I, and other Americans, the few advisers in Vietnam at the time, some of them lived in the Caravelle Hotel. And often in the afternoon they'd whip out of the hotel in uniform with pistols and guns, and throughout the years I'd been there — I stayed there for eight years straight — and Tu Du, the main street of the city in the central square, seemed to be sort of a foreign enclave. It had become an American enclave. The bars had American names and the shops had American signs. It became very American to me. It was very Western, anyway, the Continental Hotel, and all that sort of thing.

And I sort of — and all I'd known of the city was that it was a Western city at that time. It was an American city. Well, it was. I was dumbfounded when I did run out of our office building at around eleven-thirty that morning and saw the first North Vietnamese truck come down Tu Du Street with the flag waving and the soldiers leaning forward in their pith helmets with their guns, sort of holding them casually, looking up at the tall buildings in surprise and as the population looked in surprise.

To tell you the truth, it was just — it was an overwhelming sensation I had, and my knees gave way. I'd been predicting this sort of thing for years. I felt that it was inevitable the communist side would win. But on seeing it, I — I was just overwhelmed with emotion. I tried to get up five flights of stairs to the office. The elevator had gone down. And I made the first four and I literally crawled the last group of steps, and I crawled into the office, and I shouted out, "By God, they're here," and I tried to write a bulletin.

On reflection a little later, on just sitting down and perspiring, it forcefully hit me that the years, for twenty years, the United States, in particular, and the West, in general, had been supplying weapons, had been putting in a tremendous effort to prevent this event from happening. And that the worst thing that could have happened to the world from American eyes, from American policy, for quite a long time, was that the communists would take Saigon, the communists would take Vietnam. This was the worst conceivable thing. And fifty-five thousand Americans died to prevent that from happening. You know, half a million South Vietnamese died to prevent that from happening, plus Koreans, South Koreans, New Zealanders, and Australians.

And yet when the trucks came in, the tanks came in, it seemed the most natural thing in the world. And the next twenty-five days I was there, it continued to be a very natural occupation and I wondered at the beginning and throughout, why all this intense emotionalism about the Vietnam War? What happened, it was so natural, that the earlier period and all the years, it seemed to me just an incredible waste.

1976

The year 1976 was draped in bunting. We celebrated the bicentennial of the American Revolution steadily for six months, moving by midsummer into a presidential election campaign, which spun out the patriotic speeches a few months longer. We nominated candidates who came from the center, who seemed to embody the possibilities open to ordinary people in this country. Jimmy Carter, the former governor of Georgia, who won, offered us a government as "good and as loving as the American people are." Gerald Ford, who had never been elected vice president or president, contributed the best campaign song I've ever heard, perfect for the bicentennial year. It began, "I'm feeling good about America." We had many meditations on the meaning of our anniversary during 1976. Gerry Pratt, a commentator from Portland, Oregon, got in early.

All Things Considered, JANUARY 8

PRATT: There's a birthday party going on. The nation's two hundred years old, and people are putting on those historic uniforms, and politicians all over the land are paying their lip service to the politics of Jefferson and Adams.

There was even a freedom train came to our town with a dozen railroad cars filled with what the papers said were copies of original memorabilia, including Lincoln's hat and the Liberty Bell. It was like a rolling version of "This Is Your Life, America," with an automated sidewalk that swept you through two hundred years of baseball, invention, and war. In something over thirty minutes you saw the whole thing. It was the biggest thing to hit our town since food stamps, which were somehow missing from the memorabilia on the train, along with other milestones that have added lines of character to this nation's image.

But the real beauty of the thing is that the bicentennial buffs have opened the door on a whole new birthday routine. Just imagine now if on your birthday, instead of the office staff surprising you with a candle cupcake, they roll back the years and trace the great moments of your life.

What a reflection! There was a time of timidly falling in and out of step with those protest marchers that one day, watching out for some neatly dressed young dude taking pictures from the sidelines because the word was out that they were keeping track of everyone in the parade.

But in between, there were glories of being alive and involved. There was the magic of a Eugene McCarthy, soft-spoken, penetrating, taking the state that year over the Kennedy charisma, and over the Kennedy dough, as well. And there was the other Kennedy, himself, young and promising, leaning over the fence in Astoria, saying hello.

I suppose there are other moments that will not be included in the bicentennial celebration: the Japanese internment camps for some Americans, and MacArthur and Eisenhower with the troops breaking up the depression riots in Washington, D.C. Those didn't have quite the same place in our memorabilia as the generals do at Bataan or on the beaches of Normandy.

It's as if we had to confess who we voted for in the ignominious elections and recall the times we sat in less than noble pose and listened to bigots and insecure racists and sometimes, in a strange visceral poison, were swept up with some of it ourselves.

No, America, two hundred years of birthdays is not all that smooth sailing, is it? There have been holes in the road and tough turns in getting here. It's not too unlike the thoughts you have after forty-eight years of birthdays, when that oh-so-young secretary brings on the cupcake complete with candle, and says, "Happy birthday."

✦ ✦ ✦ ✦ ✦ ✦ ✦ ✦ ✦

In January 1976, China's premier Chou En-lai died of cancer. He brought the revolution, as Bob Edwards said that day, from the caves of Hunan Province to Beijing. While Mao Tse-tung was the philosophical leader of China's revolution, Chou En-lai was the man who managed the government and foreign policy, breaking with the Soviet Union, campaigning for China's seat at the United Nations, inviting Henry Kissinger and then President Nixon to visit. Bob Edwards spoke to the security analyst Morton Halperin, who served in the Nixon adminstration, about American reaction to the death of Chou En-lai.

HALPERIN: The most significant thing, I think, was that there seemed to be universal agreement in the United States that he was a great national leader. It's difficult, really, to recall the great bitterness about the Chinese during the fifties and well into the sixties in which we viewed them as a bunch of gangsters who had taken over our beloved China and subverted it into a Marxist country.

Remember in 1954 John Foster Dulles, who was then the secretary of state, refused to shake hands with Chou En-lai for fear that somebody would take a picture of it and that picture would be used in the United States to embarrass him. And even into the sixties Kennedy and then Johnson were afraid to move on China for fear that they would get blamed for dealing with this awful traitorous regime. All that was gone, and mostly what you had is admiration for him as a great leader of a large nation.

EDWARDS: It was certainly quite a turnaround. A good deal of that change has to do with our relations with the Soviet Union, doesn't it? I mean, we've come to see good relations with China as a form of leverage on the Soviet Union?

HALPERIN: In fact, I think probably Nixon's greatest contribution to American foreign policy may well come to be seen as his ability to sell the notion of good relations with China as, in effect, an anti-Soviet move, one that was designed to improve our bargaining posture with the Russians.

And, of course, the Chinese are the only people in the world more skeptical of détente than the critics within the United States. They keep warning us that détente with the Russians is the road to disaster, and that we shouldn't trust the Russians at all.

And this, of course, really is very ironic when you come to think of the fact that when Mao first came to power with Chou En-lai and others, we really saw him as a puppet of the Soviet Union. And we talked about and really believed that somehow Marxism was an unnatural ideology that had been imposed on the Chinese, and which would some day be thrown off. For the first ten years of that regime, we really acted as if we believed that China would reemerge as a liberal, democratic society. And we really failed to grasp and to accept the fact that this was a genuine nationalist revolution, which the Russians in many ways feared as much as we did.

EDWARDS: We saw it as one big monolithic world communist conspiracy. Do you think we've learned better?

HALPERIN: Well, I think as far as China we have. We now clearly understand that the Chinese are the enemies of the Russians. It's hard not to if you've ever talked to them or listened to their propaganda.

But it seems to me that to an incredible degree we've been very slow about learning that lesson anywhere else. For a very long time we persisted in talking about the revolution in Indochina, of Ho Chi Minh, as if he too was somehow a puppet of the Russians. For a long time we tended to see Castro, and to some extent we still do, as a tool of the Russians, who when he does something is doing it because the Soviets have ordered him to do it.

And as with the case of the Chinese, we may well have contributed to driving these countries to closer relations with the Russians than they really wanted. But that myth really dies very hard in the United States.

✦ ✦ ✦ ✦ ✦ ✦ ✦ ✦ ✦

P atty Hearst went on trial in the spring of 1976. The granddaughter of William Randolph Hearst, the publisher, she was a college student in February 1974 when she was kidnapped and held for ransom by the Symbionese Liberation Army. Scott Simon described her this way: "Patty Hearst was one of the signifying figures of America in the 1970s, a kidnap victim who joined her captors, the heiress who denounced her parents, renounced privilege, and became a guerrilla soldier. The revolutionary who was arrested then condemned those she called comrades."

Her parents paid millions to get her back. She'd been abused by her kidnappers, but she'd apparently decided to join them. The SLA sent her family a recording in which she even renounced her name and when we next saw Patty Hearst, she was in battle dress, carrying a gun, helping to rob a bank. We sent our reporter Donovan Reynolds to talk to spectators at the trial of this kidnap victim turned bank robber.

All Things Considered, FEBRUARY 19

MAN: Legally, I think that she's — she may be very well guilty of the bank robbery, but the issue isn't anymore whether or not she committed the bank robbery, you know. It's whether or not she had a gun at her head. And if her lawyer can convince the jury of that, she walks away. And I think he's done that without going any farther than talking to her on the stand. Right now there's reasonable doubt, and she's the first witness.

SECOND MAN: How does she explain the fact that she sprayed the sporting goods store?

FIRST MAN: Well, she certainly didn't kill anyone at the sporting goods store, and she had an ample opportunity —

SECOND MAN: No, but it has to do with where her head was at at the time.

FIRST MAN: Well, those were, at the time, the only friends she knew. At that point she had been called a common criminal by the attorney general of the United States.

SECOND MAN: The tapes speak for themselves. She came out and she made statements about the tremendous devotion she had to all her comrades. And now she's calling them every name in the book.

WOMAN: It's an important trial, especially, I think, for the defense if he tries to get the brainwashing defense. It's something that I think will be new, because coercion has always existed as a defense, but this is very new and I wonder how it will turn out.

SECOND WOMAN: What I'm waiting for is when she's forty years old and has kids, and all the statements she's going to make then. So I feel like we're going to always know what Patty Hearst is doing. You know, Jackie Onassis or something. And so I feel like I'm growing up with her, man, you know, and so [laughs] when she's, you know, in grief or something, I don't know, I just think it'll be very interesting.

THIRD WOMAN: The only thing I really know for sure is that if she hadn't of been kidnapped, she wouldn't be in this position right now. She wouldn't be on trial right now. She'd probably be married and have a kid and be living a normal life, you know. A rich, normal life.

✦ ✦ ✦ ✦ ✦ ✦ ✦ ✦ ✦

Which is what finally happened. Everyone Reynolds spoke to that day expected an acquittal, but Patty Hearst, a.k.a. Tania, was convicted and went to jail. After two and a half years President Carter commuted her sentence. When Hearst's story was made into a movie in 1988, Scott Simon spoke with her, and I've included the interview here. She describes the circumstances that led her to join the SLA.

HEARST: By that point I had been locked in the closet for nearly two months. People say, "Well, were you raped?" And it was, like, only mentally, emotionally, physically. I would have believed anything. I believed I was going to be killed by them if I didn't join, and in fact I am sure that's the case.

SIMON: You were submitted to physical punishment if not outright torture.

HEARST: Absolutely. They used classic methods of Chinese thought reform, and, you know, by using what is called the three d's, which is debility, dependency, and dread. You know, after they debilitate the person by locking them in a closet and depriving them of food and exercise and light and subjecting them to loud noise, then you're dependent on them for everything, including your life. And then you're dreading the fact that they're going to kill you at any second for no particular reason except that you're no longer useful.

SIMON: Patricia Hearst Shaw says the extensive coverage of her kidnapping strengthened the SLA's own lies and self-delusions about their strength and numbers. In fact there were only those seven who had kidnapped Patty Hearst: the leader, who called himself Field Marshal Cinque; another man and three women; and her principal tormentors, a couple named William and Emily Harris.

HEARST: They staged very elaborate ruses for me. A member of another cell coming to the house, or Cinque was going to a war council meeting, or somebody from a medical unit or a supply unit was coming over.

SIMON: So you thought there was this vast national network out there that, if you did escape, would track you down and kill you anyway?

HEARST: Well, yes. And they assured me that it was only my ignorance that prevented me from knowing more about the size and strength of the SLA.

SIMON: To prove her allegiance to the group and make Patty Hearst also wanted by police, the SLA robbed a branch of the Hibernia State Bank in San Francisco and made certain Patty Hearst was photographed by automatic security cameras.

HEARST: The reenactment, as portrayed in the film, is really quite remarkable. The director, who was Paul Schrader, decided that image was so strong in everyone's mind that rather than challenging anyone's memory of it, he did it in that freeze-frame motion, exactly the same as the bank camera showed. You know, the same jerky bank-camera movements.

SIMON: A few weeks later, let us note, you were the getaway driver for William and Emily Harris? You were sitting there in the car, and they went into Mel's Sporting Goods. William Harris shoplifted a bandolier, something to carry ammunition. And you looked out and you saw the two of them wrestling with security guards, looking to you for help.

HEARST: Yes. In the van they had a machine gun, a semi-automatic weapon, a shotgun. This is how they went shopping. So at this point I had been trained extensively in what to do in this kind of a situation. So when I did look up, I saw Bill Harris being held on the ground and looking over at the van, and Emily Harris being held by two men, and, you know, they're looking and looking, and at that point I just clicked and did exactly what I had been taught to do for all those weeks, and I just picked up first the automatic weapon. I tried to fire it, and it jumped out of my hands, and I grabbed it again, and they came running back to the van, and it really wasn't until they were in the van and driving away, and I'm rolling all around the back because there were no seats, that it finally hit me: What had I done?

SIMON: That's why you didn't just drive away from them and escape or shoot at them?

HEARST: Well, yeah, I guess that's what they do too, you know, men who go off to boot camp. They don't want them thinking about what they're supposed to do if something happens because they'll get killed.

SIMON: Inevitably the questions are raised that over the time you spent with the Symbionese Liberation Army, there were, as you note, many moments when you were left totally alone in one apartment or another. You could have escaped.

HEARST: Absolutely. Certainly there were many opportunities where if I had been in control of my faculties, yes, I could have escaped. But I was so well in their control at that point that I felt that I had nowhere to go and really couldn't escape.

SIMON: When you were taken into custody and raised your fist, defiantly, is how the gesture was read, and when you were asked to list an occupation —

HEARST: OK, well, when I was arrested, they'd asked for an occupation, and I just, you know, didn't have one. And they insisted on an occupation and so at that point, I said, "Urban guerrilla." And so now I have this, you know, perfectly embarrassing thing that everybody remembers.

SIMON: But, Mrs. Shaw, can you see where those vivid images and anecdotes seem to undercut the believability of your story?

HEARST: Absolutely. And it did for years. That was a big problem. Although I am not sure how well it could have been refuted at that time because it was all so immediate and people had such incredibly strong feelings about it.

SIMON: In the mid-1970s there was a poster of some note featuring a grainy black-and-white photograph of Patty Hearst in a black beret holding a submachine gun in her arms like a bouquet of prom-night roses, and she stood in front of the seven-headed serpent symbol of the Symbionese Liberation Army. "Tania, we love you," read the poster.

For many who followed her story, the intrigue and wonderment about whatever happened to Patty Hearst persisted, less because it was incredible but because it was absolutely believable that during the worst years of the war in Vietnam and urban racial violence an American heiress would renounce her wealth and declare herself a violent revolutionary. The woman in the poster named Tania is now thirty-four years old and lives with her husband, Bernard Shaw, and their son in Westport, Connecticut. She attends society parties, is active in raising money to find a cure for AIDS, and says that perhaps her kidnapping in 1974 more powerfully confirmed her into picking up the life of an American heiress.

✦ ✦ ✦ ✦ ✦ ✦ ✦ ✦ ✦

Susan Stamberg and I have generally disagreed about politics. I almost always find it fascinating; she very rarely does. When, in the spring of 1976, it seemed likely that Governor Jimmy Carter of Georgia would be the Democratic nominee, what interested Susan was his smile. I feel constrained to add that upon hearing this interview again, I realized that it did teach us something about our future president. The interview begins with the sound of a ringing telephone.

All Things Considered, MAY 5

STAMBERG: Dr. Sanderson, please.

SANDERSON: Yes.

STAMBERG: Hello, my name is Susan Stamberg. I'm calling you from National Public Radio in Washington, and I'm recording this conversation. I understand that you are Jimmy Carter's dentist, and we figure that he is smiling harder today than he ever has after he won all those primaries, and that you, as his dentist, really do deserve some credit for those famous teeth that he's showing.

SANDERSON: I wish I could take the credit, but I'm afraid Mother Nature will have to take all that credit. He's just got a beautiful set of teeth.

STAMBERG: Are they all real?

SANDERSON: They're all his own.

STAMBERG: So many people are talking about his teeth these days. Do you think, does that amuse you, or what?

SANDERSON: Yes, it does. It certainly has been something to talk about in the news media.

STAMBERG: You know, there are a couple of jokes that are cropping up about his teeth. I guess that happens when anybody's got a prominent feature on their face and then they in turn become a prominent person. Have you heard any of the jokes?

SANDERSON: No, not really, but I've — I have had several patients tell me that they've heard things, you know, said on the Johnny Carson show and places like that.

STAMBERG: Well, Johnny Carson said the answer was "2001." And the question was, "How many teeth does Jimmy Carter have?"

SANDERSON: Well, he's always smiling. He's got more to smile about, I guess, than anybody else right now.

STAMBERG: I guess. Would you say that Jimmy Carter was a good patient? You know, so many people get frightened when it comes time to go to the dentist.

SANDERSON: He's very conscientious, and he's — you couldn't ask any more from your patient.

STAMBERG: Is that right? He keeps his appointments? He shows up?

SANDERSON: He's on time and comes three times a year.

STAMBERG: Is that what you would advise all Americans to do?

SANDERSON: Oh, I think twice is enough, but he's that conscientious.

STAMBERG: Dentists always tell you that they can tell everything about you and the way you live your life simply by looking into your mouth.

SANDERSON: I don't think that's true. I hope not.

STAMBERG: Why? You don't want to know that much?

SANDERSON: I don't want my dentist to know that about me.

STAMBERG: Do you know that we're talking about a mouth now that may become one of the most famous in the world?

SANDERSON: Well, I think it already is.

STAMBERG: Yeah. And also which may become a matter of national security?

SANDERSON: Well, I don't know about that, but he's certainly got a nice set of teeth.

✦ ✦ ✦ ✦ ✦ ✦ ✦ ✦ ✦

Another revolutionary heard from in our bicentennial broadcasts: John Henry Faulk was a good old boy from Texas, whose folksy storytelling generally had a political edge. He had his own national radio program in the fifties, when, accused of having communist ties, he was blacklisted and fired. Faulk sued his accusers for libel and won. *Fear on Trial,* his book about the experience of being blacklisted, was a best-seller and was made into a movie.

All Things Considered, JULY 3

FAULK: Howdy, folks. This is John Henry Faulk, sitting on my place down here in Madison County, Texas, reflecting on this bicentennial year, and particularly on the Fourth of July, 1976.

Old Pea Vine Jeffrey is a neighbor of mine from Morris County, came over to see me the other day and we were talking about the Fourth of July. Pea Vine made an interesting observation. He said, "Folks will be out all over the country now having big picnics and big speeches and they'll be waving flags and talking big about this country and how far we've come in the last two hundred years."

And I said, "That's right, Pea Vine." And then he backed off and looked up at the sky, and said, "You know, Johnny, those old boys that got together, they weren't so old. Many of 'em were just young men with ideals and principles that they were willing to die for.

"They framed the Declaration of Independence there. Old Thomas Jefferson sitting there writing it. Nobody wanted to correct it much, they tell me, when he got through writing it, because he got it all said in the Declaration of Independence, what this society that they were talking about was going to be all about. And remember where at the end of it they pledged their lives, their fortunes, and their sacred honor? They meant business, and they proved to old King George and Lord North in the next several years just how much business they did mean. They was deadly serious about that.

"They were all traitors to the king. They were all revolutionaries, fighting a revolutionary war. A price on their heads. Old King George and his troops could have got a hold of 'em, they'd have made them wish they never had thought of the notion of independence. And today, in the United States, I just can't quite reconcile myself to how far we've come, from those ideals and principles.

"Just look up there at Washington, D.C. You never hear a man discussing those principles and ideals no more. You hear 'em talking more like old Lord North talked. And the beating of our breast and saying we're the biggest and the best in the world, same thing that old King George and Lord North was a-saying two hundred years ago. Here we are now. Our leadership is now proclaiming that kind of claptrap and nonsense.

"As a matter of fact, if they was to have a big celebration up there in Washington, D.C., on the Fourth of July, government sponsored, the likelihood is that they'd have the FBI and the CIA checking out everybody that come, and not a single one of the men who signed the Declaration of Independence could pass their loyalty test. Did you ever stop to think about that? That's how far we've come from the ideals and the principles that brought this here society into being.

"Why, they'd all be declared troublemakers, traitors. Have a big dossier done on each one of them, a-sitting in the files of the FBI. We ain't paid off in very good coin, have we, the sacrifices that was made that we could come about as a free people?"

✦ ✦ ✦ ✦ ✦ ✦ ✦ ✦ ✦

S usan Stamberg called around on the fifth of July to see how the bicentennial had been for a variety of people. She also talked to Marvin Kitman, who reviewed the television coverage. Despite all the anticipation of the great day, most people seemed to take the anniversary in stride.

All Things Considered, JULY 5

STAMBERG: How did the bicentennial make it as a television extravaganza? CBS did sixteen straight hours, with Walter Cronkite holding the anchor. At NBC John Chancellor and David Brinkley jumped to about a hundred different places around the country. And ABC had a token few hours.

Marvin Kitman reviews television for *Newsday* and *The New Leader* magazine. Marvin, what did you think?

KITMAN: Well, I thought that the TV coverage did not move right along like your average bicentennial minute. What I particularly found disappointing with the media event was the fact that there were no disasters. I mean, they didn't have anything there. They didn't show you anybody getting a flat tire, somebody running out of money at a street fair. There were none of those traffic jams lasting three days that we had been led to believe would happen.

STAMBERG: And you know what else they told us? In your neck of the woods, your New Jersey, they were sure the people would fall, break the railings that guard the Palisades, watching those tall ships, and they'd go plunging into the river there. That didn't happen either.

KITMAN: Right, and also the tall buildings we have, you know, were supposed to fall over when everybody rushed to the side with their martini glasses and field glasses to look at the ships. There wasn't a single building that fell over.

STAMBERG: You were disappointed?

KITMAN: Yes. I mean, they didn't have any raping. There was no pillaging or plundering or overturning cars. And I kept wondering where I got these high expectations from, and it's basically from television. For weeks the local news shows in this area had been warning everybody about all the terrible things that were going to happen. And, I mean, it was the television coverage that kept all those extra people away who were going to cause all the trouble.

STAMBERG: Now, what kinds of conclusions do you draw from that?

KITMAN: Well, one thing is that we don't have the same kind of people today as we had two hundred years ago. If there had been local television in 1776, there would never have been a Concord or a Lexington. The Minutemen would have stayed home. I really felt sorry for CBS and NBC. They had all those cameras and crews all over the country waiting for some disaster to happen. They were ready for the big one, the overthrow of the government itself, a revolution, which I think would have been a much more meaningful bicentennial event than something like the tall ships.

I kept looking at all those ships on television. And they're things of beauty. And I personally have never seen a tall ship I didn't like. But I haven't been able to figure out why tall ships are part of a bicentennial celebration in the first place. I mean, they could have had a parade of old IRT subway cars or trolleys or Fifth Avenue double-decker buses. I mean, they would have looked beautiful also.

STAMBERG: How do you think President Ford did?

KITMAN: I thought that he was very weak. He did not fall off the aircraft carrier, as we had been led to expect. He did not break the bell when he rang it. I thought he was kind of a bit player in the whole thing. I can't imagine that the former president — what's his name?

STAMBERG: Richard Nixon.

KITMAN: Richard Nixon, yeah, now, he would have really taken charge of the thing, the show. He would have denounced people left and right. He would have been much better, I have a feeling.

[Phone rings.]

HENDERSON: Hello.

STAMBERG: Could I talk with Jack Henderson, please?

HENDERSON: You're talking to him.

STAMBERG: Hi, Jack. It's Susan Stamberg in Washington. How are ya?

HENDERSON: OK.

STAMBERG: Jack, you're a high school student in Buffalo, Missouri. And I told you I was going to call you today to find out what you did yesterday. What did you do?

HENDERSON: Well, we had a family reunion, my mother's side of the family. We talked over old times and ate watermelon and fried chicken and set off a few fireworks. And then last night we all drove down and saw a stock theater group do a bicentennial production. It was really entertaining. It was about three hours long and it was a wonderful show. It was inspiring. I mean, it sounds kind of corny to hear me say that, but it really was. I enjoyed it.

STAMBERG: Do you ever get self-conscious about patriotic feelings? You know, you said, maybe it sounds a little corny. Do you ever sort of watch yourself that way, and think, Oh gosh?

HENDERSON: I'll tell you, it seems that way a lot. I mean, it seems people are embarrassed anymore to stand up when the flag goes by in a parade, or something like that. And I think we needed a celebration like this in our country, maybe to pep up the patriotic feelings.

STAMBERG: This is Jan Saecker in Markesan, Wisconsin. I wanted to talk about what you did yesterday.

SAECKER: Well, by twilight the lake was mirror-still last night with a quarter moon hung up in one corner, something like a lantern. And hundreds of people had anchored their boats out, ready to watch the fireworks. There they were with their lights on, for all the world, like so many candles on the surface of a dark cake. And from the shore I wanted to watch the fireworks, but I found myself watching the people, instead, shining on the lake with their watch lights. I thought that was very appropriate.

STAMBERG: What a lovely image that is. You're making me just see it. Were you in a boat, too, or on the shore?

SAECKER: I was on the shore. I was playing piano in the restaurant. And every now and then, between songs, I'd go to see the fireworks.

STAMBERG: Did you mind having to work?

SAECKER: Not at all. It was fun. To me, when there's something important going on, I like to watch the people. It was very quiet the evening that President Nixon resigned, and it was like that last night. It seemed that they were all thinking. And several people told me that they had been really moved, touched by the bicentennial. They were unashamedly stirred by patriotic feelings. That surprised me.

◆ ◆ About a week after the bicentennial celebrations, we announced the results of a poll of our listeners on what we should include in a time capsule for the tricentennial. Twenty-five items were selected, based on letters we received. A Watergate souvenir got the most votes. One gentleman from Carbondale, Illinois, suggested an "Elect Nixon" button and an "Impeach Nixon" button. Listeners suggested guideposts to American culture: a Sears Roebuck catalogue and a *TV Guide*, newspapers from July Fourth and Beatles records.

To represent the civil rights movement, a copy of Martin Luther King's "I Have a Dream" speech. Also, something from the Vietnam War, the women's movement, and the moon landing. There were items intended to be nostalgic: cash, coins, credit cards, and thirteen-cent stamps. Drugs were included, illegal ones as well as birth control pills and Valium. And things that mean a lot to Americans: blue jeans, guns, Frisbees, and computers.

For the future, there were seed packets, "something from a nuclear power plant, perhaps waste," and a list of predictions about life in the tricentennial year. Also, a rural mailbox, which would become the capsule. Susan Stamberg promised we would lock it in a closet in our offices at 2025 M Street and send a key to a child born on July 4, 2076. We've moved, Dear Child, but the capsule is with us.

✦ ✦ ✦ ✦ ✦ ✦ ✦ ✦ ✦ ✦

O ur coverage of the presidential campaign of 1976 was one of our better attempts to make a virtue of necessity. Lacking funds to fly with the candidates, we spent the fall on the ground with voters. One of the places we picked to stand for the national campaign was Dallas. President Ford opened the state fair, Carter volunteers were there too, and Robert Krulwich was with them.

All Things Considered, OCTOBER 11

KRULWICH: It's hard to tell how many people are actively involved in the national campaign here. This weekend at Carter headquarters, forty-three people showed up to hand out leaflets at the state fair. But when we talked to one of them, it turns out they weren't all real Carter supporters.

CARTER VOLUNTEER: Well, I'm working the campaign on the Carter side this weekend to fill hours for a paper at the end of my government class.

KRULWICH: Look around this room and tell me how many people you see who are doing what you're doing?

CARTER VOLUNTEER: I'd say at least half.

KRULWICH: Privately you support the president?

CARTER VOLUNTEER: Yes.

KRULWICH: Ford headquarters, a suite of rooms on the ground floor of a small office building here, also had about twenty volunteers working on signs and conducting a telephone survey. A good many were kids, below voting age, delivered to the headquarters by their parents. And the students were there too.

Where are you from?

FORD VOLUNTEER: Ursuline Academy.

KRULWICH: Is your campus paying a lot of attention to this election?

FORD VOLUNTEER: Well, yes, especially the seniors who are taking government, because they're having to work so many hours in someone's campaign, like calling people and working here. There are some seniors around here that I think maybe are doing it just sort of because they have to, but a lot of them are really interested in it.

KRULWICH: The mood among campaigners is very mellow. The Carter people like their candidate, but don't love him. Many would have preferred Governor Jerry Brown of California or Hubert Humphrey. And that's even truer on the Republican side, where Ronald

Reagan was the real hero. So, since no one feels too strongly about the nominees they've got, this campaign is not very fierce. In fact, it's kind of friendly.

CARTER VOLUNTEER: You know, in seventy-two and in other elections, in sixty-eight, you know, you had this division. People were really mad and angry. But I noticed today at breakfast, we were sitting down with Wallace people, you know, from my precinct, and that's the first time I talked to Ted Joyce in six years.

KRULWICH: Three Carter workers in the front seat of a car on their way to the fair this weekend:

SECOND CARTER VOLUNTEER: This is a fun campaign. It's a lot of fun.

THIRD CARTER VOLUNTEER: I'm happy about everything except my congressman, Dale Milford.

[*Laughter.*]

I would like to trade him off for just anything. I'd even trade him for a few Republicans that I know of.

[*Laughter.*]

KRULWICH: Does anybody miss the excitement of sixty-eight, seventy-two?

SECOND CARTER VOLUNTEER: No.

FIRST CARTER VOLUNTEER: Well, I don't know about that. It's kind of like, you know, when your house burns down and you find out really who your friends are. That was in seventy-two. But, you know, it's kind of like, I'm a Catholic and I believe in repentance and, so, hell, you know, we'll just invite them all back and forgive them.

KRULWICH: But you don't have the emotional issues that you had in sixty-eight and seventy-two?

SECOND CARTER VOLUNTEER: No. See, most of us came up in politics through the Vietnam War and the civil rights issues. OK, most of the people in my age group who work in politics either got involved in civil rights or Vietnam. And those were such horrible and emotional and scary issues that you get a very combative sense. And this year there are not those kind of issues, and I think that that makes it all more of a good time and come to the fair and pass out little hats and have fun.

1977

♦ ♦ ♦ ♦ ♦ ♦ ♦ ♦ ♦

R adio ladies marked a milestone in the spring of 1977, the year of
the final *Mary Tyler Moore Show*. Susan Stamberg explained why,
with help from Bob Edwards.

All Things Considered, MARCH 18

STAMBERG: Mary sprightly. Mary perky. Mary lightly. Mary quirky.
But no more Mary Saturday nightly. Tomorrow is the last *Mary Tyler
Moore Show*. After seven years, the lovable bunch at the Minneapolis
newsroom is calling it quits. Tomorrow's episode has all of them
getting fired, except for anchorman Ted Baxter, who has a proclivity
for introducing himself as "Ted Baxter, anchorman."

The new owner of WJM-TV wants his news show to be rated
number one and figures the only way to do this is to fire all the people
who know what they're doing and keep the only one who doesn't. Too
many of us in this business understand that decision only too well. It
could have had a neater ending. Ted could have gotten smart, for
instance, or Mary married. Or Sue Ann Nivins, the naughty "Happy
Homemaker," could have gotten nice. But all of that might have been
too unrealistic. Better to fire them and keep Ted.

The Mary Tyler Moore Show has become an addiction for most news
broadcasters. I was a closet viewer myself, until about five years ago
when my then producer (don't ask about the circumstances that led to
his leaving) confessed he watched more religiously than he attended
church. And that gave me license to admit my habit, only to discover
that all of us were hooked, seeing ourselves in that show more vividly
and more uncomfortably than in anything else on television. We've all
been there and been them. We've all had days when we wore Ted
Baxter's shoes or Sue Ann's or Lou Grant's. The only one we hadn't
been was Mary Richards herself, but that changed two and a half
months ago when Diane Diamond joined us.

So the show goes on, in our newsroom, if not on the small screen. Meanwhile, what's the legacy? Well, Mary was the first TV comedy heroine to be single, working, and an obvious nonvirgin, and she never got struck by lightning. Ted was the first to show the world that behind the TV anchorman's facade of pearly teeth and empty pomp lurked a core of pearly teeth and empty pomp. Rhoda and Phyllis proved you could leave one neighborhood, join another, and still get viewers. All it took was a radical change in your basic nature.

And all of them together showed that Minneapolis just might be a town to take seriously. Not a bad legacy. For sheer fun, for too often uncomfortable reminders of the realities of broadcast journalism, for lessons in womanliness and friendship and consideration, thanks to them all. May we someday meet again in that great newsroom in the sky.

EDWARDS: And when all of us are gone, Ted Baxter will still be here.

✦ ✦ ✦ ✦ ✦ ✦ ✦ ✦ ✦

President Carter began his term in office by getting out of his car. Instead of riding in the armored limousine provided for his inaugural parade back down Pennsylvania Avenue from the Capitol to the White House, he walked. The president spent the first part of that year doing things his way, with varying degrees of success. Among other things, he proposed a tax rebate to stimulate the economy. It could not be too big because that might stimulate inflation. The administration economists settled on fifty dollars. Susan Stamberg and Bob Edwards try not to spend it all in one place.

All Things Considered, APRIL 14

STAMBERG: Do you feel like a little kid who's been offered a chocolate bar before the spinach, but then her mother changes her mind, knowing that there's not going to be that fifty dollars or more arriving in your mailbox? Well, just to rub it in, or to make you not feel so bad, we've put together a little list of things fifty dollars can buy these days in these United States. It's not a very long list, but here goes.

EDWARDS: Fifty dollars will buy you a seventy-one-mile metered taxi ride from the middle of Manhattan to Hillsdale, New Jersey.

STAMBERG: Fifty dollars will buy you six marriage licenses in Murfreesboro, Tennessee.

EDWARDS: One hundred and fifty McDonald's hamburgers, the plain ones.

STAMBERG: Three hundred and eighty-five thirteen-cent stamps, a fifty-minute hour with a psychiatrist, five pocket calculators, seven record albums, or two and a half bags of groceries.

EDWARDS: For fifty you can be part of a Miracle Morning at Elizabeth Arden's.

STAMBERG: And that is body massage, facial, makeup, haircut, set, and shampoo, plus a manicure.

EDWARDS: And a partridge in a pear tree. Or ten six-pound bags of chicken feed.

STAMBERG: Or eight copies of the King James Bible.

EDWARDS: Twenty-eight six-packs of Pabst Blue Ribbon beer.

STAMBERG: Seventy-seven gallons of gasoline.

EDWARDS: A twelve-and-a-half-minute telephone call to New Delhi, India.

STAMBERG: Three pair of denim jeans, but they cost more prefaded.

EDWARDS: For fifty dollars you can spend four nights at the YWCA in Omaha.

STAMBERG: A one-year subscription to *Time* and *Newsweek* magazines.

EDWARDS: You get about ten pounds of coffee for fifty dollars.

STAMBERG: You could fly first-class from Kansas City to Des Moines for fifty dollars, but then you couldn't get back.

EDWARDS: Fifty dollars will buy you one share of stock in General Electric.

STAMBERG: Four shoes made in Taiwan, but only three American ones. (We haven't really checked on that one. We just threw it in to be funny.)

EDWARDS: But here's what the fifty dollars won't buy for you, even if you had gotten it. Fifty dollars won't insulate your house against another bad winter.

STAMBERG: It won't overhaul the motor of your old car to keep it running for another five years.

EDWARDS: It won't pay your taxes, your rent, or your mortgage.

STAMBERG: On the other hand, fifty dollars would about cover the services for one week of the NPR Research Department, one Mr. Rob Robinson, who helped us to put this list together.

✦ ✦ ✦ ✦ ✦ ✦ ✦ ✦ ✦ ✦

The rebate was dropped, in part, because it was not a significant amount of money to most Americans. The new president's new ways of doing things, his efforts to reorganize government, his habit of acting unilaterally, and his ideas about redoing budgets and energy policy all made life difficult for the new Speaker of the House, Thomas P. O'Neill of Massachusetts. An old-fashioned pol, Tip thought that the Democratic Speaker had to pass the Democratic president's programs, and because he was good at it he managed some difficult victories for President Carter.

Every generation of Capitol Hill regulars has its benchmark Speaker, and Tip O'Neill is mine. Those who came before are history, those who come after are upstarts. Except for one obviously mendacious moment, this is a pretty good picture of Tip. We broadcast it to mark his first one hundred days.

All Things Considered, APRIL 14

WERTHEIMER: Tip O'Neill, the Speaker of the House. He's one of the biggest men in the House, tall and broad with a huge head of snow-white hair. He wears rumpled suits, speaks with a Boston accent, and if you were to look down on the floor from the galleries for the first time, you could probably pick him out. He looks as if he owns the place.

But it wasn't always so. O'Neill came out of the Eleventh Ward in Cambridge, Massachusetts, totally Democratic, mostly Irish, the ward that John Fitzgerald Kennedy swept in his first political venture to win a House seat. O'Neill took a more conventional road to the Massachusetts legislature, where he rose to become Speaker, and then to the Congress when Kennedy ran for the Senate. But for O'Neill, the change was not an elevation.

O'NEILL: You just cannot imagine, from 1948 to 1952 I was the Speaker of the Massachusetts legislature. It's the most powerful Speakership in America, to the extent that the Speaker names the chairmen of all committees and assigns all the members to all committees on both sides of the aisles. And the Speaker's office had a tremendous amount of patronage. There was complete, one hundred percent discipline, terse and tough, but always united.

And then Jack Kennedy decided to run for the United States Senate. I ran, came down here, and lo and behold, the Republicans had captured the House. Eisenhower was the president. Joe Martin was the

Speaker. I served on the committee of Merchant Marines and Fisheries. Coming from the land of the mighty to obscurity so quickly was really a frightening episode.

WERTHEIMER: But like the natural leader most House members quickly tell you he is, O'Neill recovered his balance. He caught the eye of the strongest Speaker of modern times, the powerful Sam Rayburn of Texas. And Rayburn called O'Neill to ask him to serve on the Rules Committee, the committee that schedules legislation for the floor, the leadership's court of last resort. The Rules Committee was Tip's first step towards leadership and his progress was typical of the House, slow, measured, but not as slow as some, as you will hear. Anyhow, it all started with that phone call from Speaker Rayburn.

O'NEILL: I was absolutely astounded because at that time I was only the second man in the history of this country who had been offered a place on the Rules Committee in the second term. That was usually for members who had been here many, many years.

He said, "Hey, I want one pledge out of you that you will follow party as far as voting bills out of the committee is concerned. And then you can reserve your rights and vote otherwise when it gets on the floor."

And I served eighteen years on the Rules Committee and, very interestingly, we were reminiscing about the last four or five Democratic chairmen of the Rules Committee. Right now we have Jim Delaney of New York. At the age of seventy-six, he's the youngest Democrat to have held that office in like probably thirty-five or forty years. Previous to him was Ray Madden, who was in his eighties. Previous to that was Colmer from Mississippi, who was eighty-one before he attained the chairmanship. Previous to that was Judge Smith, who was well in his eighties. And previous to that was old Al Sabath, who was chairman when he was ninety-one years old, which reminds me of a story.

Al Sabath died late, I think in fifty-two or fifty-three, I forget now. And he had been chairman of the committee on Rules for some time. And the oldest member to get elected to the House was a fellow by the name of Bowler from Chicago. He was eighty-three or eighty-four years old.

One day Eddie Boland walked up to him, and says, "Congressman Bowler, history says you're the oldest man that's ever been elected here. How is it at the age of eighty-four you'd like to come to Congress?"

"Well," he said, "fifty-one years ago I was a member of the Chicago City Council with Al Sabath. And the party dictated who was going to go to Congress, and we both had the same seniority and we flipped a coin and I lost. And Sabath went to Congress and they had promised me that I would be the next congressman. So," he said, "fifty-one years later Sabath died. It was my turn."

WERTHEIMER: O'Neill's turn came when Speaker Carl Albert named him the party whip, putting him on the escalator which leads to the Speakership. Speaker John McCormack of Massachusetts also took an interest in O'Neill.

But despite his long service to the established leaders of the House, Tip O'Neill practices a modern brand of politics. He's moved out front on some of the key reforms that have made the House what it is today. He helped to bring about the recorded teller vote, making it easy to put members on record on key votes on amendments. Recorded votes were rare in the House before the reform. The reform made passage of an amendment to end the war in Vietnam possible. Again, O'Neill was in the lead on that issue.

He supported a change in the rules to make committee chairmen stand for reelection every two years, which brought down three chairmen and effectively ended the reign of the autocratic barons of the House. He was the first member of the leadership to say publicly that President Nixon would have to leave office. But O'Neill is at something of a loss to explain his sense for changing winds.

O'NEILL: Well, it's the type of politics that I was brought up in. I'm considered to be part of the establishment, and I've been in public office a long time, following the discipline of party politics.

The majority of things that are done in public life with all the openness that we now have in government are kind of done behind the scenes. Now, what do I mean by that? I like to go to the committee and talk it over with the members one by one, tell them what my amendment is, what it does, and try to win them and their confidence that way, rather than oppose them on the floor of the House by offering an amendment because defeating a fellow that's carrying a bill in a wide open scrapping of an amendment, it's abrasive. It sets a pattern that's wrong. Playing by the rules of the game as is expected. And I'm never afraid of change.

If I've been voting one way and my research now shows me that I've been wrong, I have no qualms about changing my mind or my vote if I think that the times need it, but only if it's in the best interest of the Congress or the country or my area, but never with the idea of the next election.

WERTHEIMER: There are contradictions in O'Neill. He believes in playing by the rules and in changing his mind. He believes in open government, but he likes to work behind the scenes.

The Rayburn protégé draws much of his strength from the younger members of the House. He says he wants to be a strong Speaker, but he recognizes that he leads a House full of independent people, many of whom ran against the institution and its establishment in the first place. The days of strong Speakers like Cannon, Longworth, and Rayburn are over. So for O'Neill, his first step in establishing the pattern of his own version of strong leadership was to share some of his power.

When the Policy Committee met early this year to select committee positions for the new members, O'Neill voted as one member of the committee and did not try to steer the process. He's taken all the Democratic leaders into his inner circle. Under O'Neill, the circle of those holding power is larger than it's ever been before. But it has O'Neill at its center and he's watchful of power bases in other areas.

o'neill: Speaker Carl Albert was extremely kind to me and he consulted me on everything, but for the most part the two of us were making the decisions. And I've broadened that now to include the majority whip and the deputy whip and the chairman of the caucus, Tom Foley. And we met every day faithfully and discussed programs, and the Policy Committee meets, you know, twice and three times a month or even more, and the whip organization. And we hope we're making them a part of the organization and a part of the decision making of the House. That's the only thing that I can see that's new around here.

✦ ✦ ✦ ✦ ✦ ✦ ✦ ✦ ✦ ✦

A nother moment of transition was marked by sports columnist Robert Lipsyte, who appeared regularly on our programs for a number of years. Bill Bradley of New Jersey is now in his second term in the Senate, but in April 1977 he was ending a ten-year career in professional basketball.

All Things Considered, APRIL 21

lipsyte: The prolonged adolescence of Bill Bradley is over. He finished his tenth, his last, his most frustrating season as a professional basketball player. His team, the New York Knicks, played poorly and did not make the playoffs, and Bradley was a substitute.

With customary tact, I asked Bill the other day, "How does it feel to go out a loser?" As he has for the ten years I've known him, Bradley examined the question in the fine, cool chambers of his mind before answering. "I guess the idea is to retire on top as a hero. Bill Russell did it and so did Jimmy Brown. But that's trying to perpetuate an image of invincibility that is not a correct reflection of quality or of being human."

Bradley continued, "I've played games this season when people yelled, 'You're too old.' But that doesn't detract from the previous nine years, nor does fear of hearing those yells detract from the possibility of enjoying those games."

Bradley came to the Knicks in the fall of 1967 on the wings of hyperbole, the perfect boy to save the game. He had been a nonscholarship student at Princeton. His banker father paid his way, and he had not only led Princeton to basketball glory, but according to John McPhee, his *New Yorker* magazine biographer, he raised the moral climate of Princeton. Bradley then went to Oxford for two years on a Rhodes scholarship, and when he arrived at pro basketball in the fall of 1967 the management of the Knicks appeared grateful he was stopping by on his way to eight certain years in the White House.

Bradley was never an overpowering individual player. But his contribution to the game, both physically and culturally, was enormous. As a man who ran even without the ball, he became a critical part of the Knicks magical 1969–1970 championship season. In college he'd been a team by himself. In the pros he became a shining example of collective play.

Because Bradley was white, handsome, articulate, somewhat eccentric in dress and behavior for a pro athlete, no endorsements, no petmobile for Bradley, upper middle class and, at six feet five inches, not too tall. His presence authenticated the values and pleasures of this game for all those whose interests transcended hard-core sports fandom: corporate ticket buyers, the advertising and media communities, and women.

For ten years Bill Bradley had a very good run. He earned several million dollars, traveled throughout the world for pleasure, collected interesting people, produced a play, wrote a very good book called *Life on the Run*, developed expertise in several areas, including investment banking, made some political allies, and continued to parry the big question from family and friends, "But what are you going to do when you grow up?"

Bradley will be thirty-four years old this summer, the first since childhood that will not hold the promise of hoops. In his book, he wrote about the Faustian bargain: "In return for the pleasures and glory a professional athlete eventually must live all one's days never able to recapture the feeling of intensified youth."

And now that intensified youth is over. Or is it? Bradley has political ambitions, at least the Congress, and the highs and lows and celebrity of big-league politics may not be all that different from the hardwood floor. Bill Bradley, who I will surely vote for, may just be getting an option to extend that Faustian bargain.

◆ ◆ ◆ ◆ ◆ ◆ ◆ ◆ ◆ ◆

When Steve Biko died, probably murdered by prison officials in South Africa, he was the leader of the black consciousness movement, which Jackie Judd said, quoting Biko, was attempting "the cultural and political revival of an oppressed people." Donald Woods, a South African newspaperman and political ally of Biko's, believed him to be the most important black man in South Africa. Jackie interviewed Woods when his book, called *Biko*, was published in 1978. I've placed the interview in this chapter, because Biko was killed in 1977. Woods talked about Biko as a leader of his people.

All Things Considered, MAY 28, 1978

WOODS: In Steve Biko's case, it was a mixture of the genuineness of the man. He was a reserved, rather shy man in a way. Well, no, I wouldn't use the word "shy." He was reserved without being shy, but possibly "diffident" is the word. And he had unusually high gifts of eloquence. He could articulate thoughts very well. He had great courage, which we saw him exercise on a number of occasions. And he had insights which I think are given to few people.

JUDD: He became a leader among South Africa's black population despite being banned by the government. How did he do that?

WOODS: Well, it was a remarkable achievement for him to have become a nationally acknowledged leader in spite of his ban. The ban prohibited him from addressing meetings, from being quoted, from speaking to more than one person at a time. And yet he built up a national following because of his thoughts, largely by word of mouth. People could see him one at a time, and of course, some of his writings did circulate secretly.

JUDD: But it seems from your book and what you've just said that his personal attributes were compelling, in addition to his ideas. Did the black population of South Africa know those traits that you were just speaking of?

WOODS: No, I would say that very few of them would have known that side of him, because very few of them, comparatively speaking, would have been in personal touch with him. And this makes it again all the more remarkable, his achievement in developing such a following. Had the man been able to address audiences all over the country, had he been able to communicate as freely as he would have liked, I believe he would have had an immense following.

You know, to me the great tragedy of South Africa, and I used to write about this in my syndicated column, was that the white people of South Africa couldn't personally talk to or hear from a man such as Steve Biko. Make no mistake, Steve was tough. I think there is a tendency to portray him as a kind of passive saint. And I think he was anything but that.

His methods happened to be nonviolent in the sense that he was busy, certainly at that phase of his political leadership, to get blacks out of the psychological feelings of inferiority, which the apartheid laws had visited on them for decades. But I would not rule out Steve as sanctioning violence at a later stage of the struggle if he saw that nonviolent pressures were not having the effect. I mean, no one can really say that. The man is dead. But I would not have been surprised had he later turned to violence. He was a very tough man, indeed, and I think it is sort of a mistake to sort of assume that he was passive.

JUDD: I was going to ask you about that, about the inclination to strike back at the people who are oppressing you, and why that didn't happen in Steve Biko's lifetime. He was a person who had something to say to many, many people, and he wasn't allowed to say it.

WOODS: He wasn't allowed to, but ironically I don't think he felt the frustration you might imagine he would because he was in some way managing to communicate with the audience he was addressing to begin with. The first audience he was concerned with was the young blacks. And he was getting through to them. At a later stage he would have wanted, I think, to address himself to the whites. But his priority was with the attitudes of the young blacks.

JUDD: Steve Biko once said, and this was a quote in your book, "I have no personal ambitions. I have hopes. My hope is to engage in doing justice in the South Africa of the future." You said earlier that there might be a tendency to portray Steve Biko as some sort of saint. When you hear a politician, and I think Biko could be called a politician, saying something like this, it has an air of unbelievability to it.

WOODS: Yes, except if you knew the man, you would see. I honestly have never come across anyone who had fewer hang-ups. Personal ambition is a form of hang-up, isn't it? And I think that he was a person who had a surer center than anyone else I've met. He had no need of props of any kind.

✦ ✦ ✦ ✦ ✦ ✦ ✦ ✦ ✦

G roucho Marx died near the end of the summer, at the age of eighty-six. We announced his death with a thirty-second scene with Margaret Dumont, the one in which he suggests she should leave in a taxi, or in a huff, or in a minute and a huff. Fred Calland compared Mr. Marx to Mr. Dante, Mr. Shakespeare, Mr. Eliot, and Mr. Joyce, and we listened to a few bars of Groucho singing "I only came to say I must be going." Then we turned to Goodman Ace, a good friend.

All Things Considered, AUGUST 20

ACE: Groucho Marx was one of our precious few, one-of-a-kind men. In the almost fifty years I've spent in his company or in our weekly telephone chats, I was constantly amazed by not only his improvisational wit, but by his serious and articulate awareness of world affairs.

However, in public, to Groucho all the world was a stage and all its men and women merely players, contestants on his *You Bet Your Life* TV program, off whom he could bounce what all the obits I've read so far have unfairly referred to as insult gags.

Not true. It was his love for people and their reactions to his left-field quick quips that entranced him. To him, for instance, it was no insult when we stood on the street before his hotel in New York, when a society matron toddled over, and asked him, "Are you Groucho Marx?" He meant no putdown when he replied, "That's funny. I was just going to ask you that."

Or a few moments later in the elevator going up to his room, a young priest shook his hand and said, "On behalf of my mother, I would like to thank you for all the pleasure you've given her on television. My mother will be happy to know I told you." And Groucho smilingly looked up at him and said, "I didn't know you fellows were allowed to have mothers."

I asked him after we got into the room why he couldn't have said thank you before he did his gag to soften what might be thought a putdown. But he replied, "Nobody ever listens to what you say. They laugh and walk away and wonder if they had heard you correctly."

He demonstrated that a few moments later when we sat in his room and a friend called to invite him over for a home-cooked meal. After some haggling he accepted. The woman who called made the mistake of asking if he liked roast beef. "If it goes home early." And the woman replied, I could hear her clear across the room, "Oh, we know you like to leave early, Groucho. Any time you want to go, it's all right with us." He quietly hung up and pointed to the phone to prove that what he said, that people don't listen, was true.

But for me, it is no time to list the thousands of nonsequiturs that have been credited to Groucho. For me, this is the time to recall that I believe my friend foresaw the inevitable. Whenever we phoned each other during the past year or year and a half, he invited me to come visit him in California. His own words were always the same. "Aren't you coming to see me before I die?" In anguish, I tearfully confess now that I didn't quite make it.

✦ ✦ ✦ ✦ ✦ ✦ ✦ ✦ ✦

Periodically, those of us who talk on the radio take advantage of the platform we work on every day to say something personal. We don't do it often. In November 1977, I said something about the abortion debate. The occasion was a decision to fund temporarily the Departments of Labor and Health, Education and Welfare for thirty days while the abortion debate went on. The funding bill had been held up for five months.

All Things Considered, NOVEMBER 4

WERTHEIMER: Abortion is not a subject that was politically discussed even a few years ago, but it's been the subject of a long and heated national debate for the past few years.

And since June, twenty-seven members of the House and Senate, all men, average age sixty-one, have been talking about abortion in the House-Senate conference on the appropriation bill for the Departments of Labor and Health, Education and Welfare, a sixty-one-billion-dollar bill which carries a rider, a provision added in the

House, banning federal funding for abortion with certain exceptions.

The exceptions have been the basis for the prolonged discussion over the summer and fall. The conferees agreed to permit abortions in cases where the pregnancy endangered the life of the mother. But beyond that, they and the Houses they represent have not been able to agree.

They disagree on the question of permitting abortion in cases where the mother's health might be damaged, of permitting abortions in cases where the baby, if it were born, would have a genetic disease or defect, like Tay-Sachs disease or Down syndrome. They disagree on whether federal funding could be used for abortions in cases of rape or incest. And for months, twenty-seven men have met and argued about what to do.

The discussion has been a difficult one for all the participants, those who oppose abortion and those who don't, and it has demonstrated every day of the discussion the difficulty of settling through legislation a socially sensitive and medically technical question. Watching and participating in the abortion discussions requires a strong stomach. Phrases like "back room butcher" are among the mildest.

It's become apparent that the men who make the decisions have in some cases an imperfect understanding of female sexuality and physiology, an imperfect understanding that permits comments like one made by a male Senate staff member who asked a female colleague, "Is ovulation the same as orgasm?" and permits comments like one made by a member of the House, who looked at the measure currently on the table and told the conference that it went too far in permitting federally funded abortions. He observed that "Under this bill, anyone in this room could get an abortion," gesturing towards a table of all male colleagues.

The long discussions appear to have brutalized the members, who have had to sit for weeks talking about painful examples of defective children slowly dying of incurable genetic diseases, about bungled abortions, and about the right to life.

And members have made harsh jokes, talking about whether abortions in the case of rape would be permitted for teenagers who were not forcibly raped but were technically victims of statutory rape because of their age. One member observed, "It's not a question of consent. The question is whether she enjoyed it."

On the same subject, medical treatment for victims of rape or incest, one member wanted to know if that included abortion procedures like dilation and curettage. "It would," another member replied, "allow a quick scrape."

Talking of abortions in cases where the mother's health would be damaged, one member told his colleagues the language before them was too liberal. "We don't want a woman who wakes up with a hangnail to be able to get an abortion," he said.

The discussions have often been too much for the members who take part in them. When the conferees in the House refused to accept a more liberal provision on abortion for victims of rape or incest, arguing that it should be forced rape, one congressman pointed out that abortions in the case of statutory rape would permit pregnant teenage children to have abortions. And he called for votes on permitting abortions for children seventeen and younger. When that was rejected, he tried sixteen and fifteen and fourteen and thirteen, and then the conferees rebelled. "You're trying to make us look bad," one shouted. "Are you going to take it down to age one?"

And the discussions in the conference and in the six times abortion has been debated in the House and Senate have been more than some of the civilians, whose job it is to watch debates, can bear. I'm thinking of a staff member who logs debates in the House and has arranged with her colleagues that when abortion is discussed, someone else takes her place.

Senator Edward Brooke of Massachusetts, who's led the fight to permit certain abortions under federally funded Medicare programs, told reporters that the irony of middle-aged men sitting in a room and determining what poor women may do with their bodies has not escaped them. But the majority of members in the House are willing to make that decision, while a majority of the Senate feel that a flat ban on abortions other than lifesaving ones is wrong. The decision the Senate made today does not change anything. It merely delays for another thirty days the time when this debate begins again.

+ + + + + + + + +

At the end of the year, President Carter went overseas. Although he had run promising to concentrate on domestic issues, as generally happens with presidents he found operating on the world stage more pleasant and even potentially more productive than dealing with Congress. President Carter had negotiated a treaty with Panama and was working on a Middle East peace conference with some success, but when he visited Poland he ran afoul of an interpreter who turned him into a comic figure. It was so horrible and so hilarious that Susan Stamberg called Marshall Brickman, a TV comedy writer, for a reality check. Here comes that ringing telephone.

All Things Considered, DECEMBER 30

STAMBERG: Hello.

BRICKMAN: Hello.

STAMBERG: Are you Marshall Brickman?

BRICKMAN: I am.

STAMBERG: This is Susan Stamberg at National Public Radio. You know why we called you?

BRICKMAN: Tell me.

STAMBERG: Well, you heard about the story about President Carter landing in Warsaw and making his opening remarks. And apparently what he got was a translator who didn't know his job terribly well. Because the president said, in English, "I have come to learn your opinions and understand your desires for the future." And the translator translated that as "I desire the Poles carnally."

BRICKMAN: It's probably a better foreign policy.

STAMBERG: Now this first person, who will be nameless, this first translator has been replaced. I guess they don't know how to take a joke over there. And the second guy's come in. His name is Jerzy Koricki, I think. He's thirty-six. He's slim and bespectacled and what he said was "I'm really scared."

BRICKMAN: Was that the translation of something the president had said?

STAMBERG: No, I think in that case —

BRICKMAN: It was his own comment?

STAMBERG: Mr. Koricki is speaking for himself.

BRICKMAN: What might have happened is that Carter wrote the speech, and then he wrote on the top, "Have somebody polish this." And that they read it as "Have somebody Polish this."

STAMBERG: If you were writing this scene, as you've written so many, say, for Woody Allen, or some of the funny stories for *The New Yorker* magazine, could you improve it in any way?

BRICKMAN: Yes, I think it's too broad. It's not believable. People wouldn't believe it as a comedy. They wouldn't believe that it could really happen, you see. So what you'd have to do is make it a little more realistic. I would get someone who looked a little more like a president, and I probably wouldn't have it take place in Poland because, you know, of the obvious problems. But I certainly couldn't make it any funnier.

STAMBERG: Now here is one more bumbling that happened. Mr. Carter said, "The Polish constitution was one of three great efforts in the historic struggle for human rights." And the translator had Carter telling them that the Polish constitution was a subject of ridicule.

BRICKMAN: Gee, he's going to have a lot of trouble getting room service tonight.

STAMBERG: Well, I don't know. He's been allowed to leave, though.

BRICKMAN: Listen, I have to go because there are two guys in trench coats at my front door.

STAMBERG: I won't keep you any longer.

BRICKMAN: And they say that they want to talk to me about the phone calls that I've been getting.

1978

In 1978 National Public Radio and I made a modest amount of history. We broadcast the Panama Canal Treaty debates, live from the chamber of the Senate. It had never been done. Gary Henderson, our engineer, and I sat in the corner of the gallery overlooking the Senate and did the play-by-play. Robert Siegel, in a studio at NPR, was our color commentator.

Each day, we carried long hours of Senate debate, and when the Senate paused, as it often does, for quorum calls and eventually for votes, we switched back to NPR for analysis. In those pre-C-SPAN days, only those civilians who were sitting in the chamber could hear the Senate debate. Our audience was fascinated and horrified, in about equal parts, to hear for themselves how the self-styled "world's greatest deliberative body" actually sounds. Broadcast coverage of debates had not yet altered the style of the Senate. Although senators have never been shy, they were not then the strutters they have become, making outrageous speeches, hoping to be picked up by the nightly news.

I remember with great affection the late Senator James Allen of Alabama. He was a tall courtly man who habitually addressed me as "little lady," remembering not to do it only when I called him "big senator." Robert Siegel thought that Senator Allen sounded a bit like a ram's horn when he declaimed on the Senate floor, especially when he drawled the name of Panama's head of state, General Omar Torrijos. The general, we were told, listened to the radio as well, relayed by the Pan-American Union. At times, he would be so infuriated by the debate that he would smash his radio against the wall, or throw it out the window. Moments later, he would shout to his aide for another radio.

Many senators strongly resisted President Carter's decision to return the canal to Panama. They felt that giving Panama control over the canal was completely unnecessary, that we had strong interests in using it if, as, and how we liked. But more than that, they thought giving up the canal was weak. The historian David McCullough, whose book *The Path Between the Seas* was a best-seller that year, told Robert Siegel that memories of Vietnam were hanging over the debate.

All Things Considered, FEBRUARY 22

MCCULLOUGH: It's as though the specter of Vietnam is in the room all the time in the Senate and in the hearing rooms before the debates began. And people don't have to even use the word and it's there. And the truth, of course, is that we lost a war in Vietnam, a very costly war, in more ways than just money, obviously.

SIEGEL: To a country so small that no one thought it was possible.

MCCULLOUGH: That's right. And in the jungle and in a place where France went first, just as in Panama. And it's interesting how nations respond to defeat and humiliation. When France was destroyed so overwhelmingly, so quickly in the Franco-Prussian War, for example, their response was to — we will go to Panama and we will win a great victory against nature. We will show the world that the grandeur of France still exists.

SIEGEL: We will build a canal.

MCCULLOUGH: We will build a canal for all the world to see and use and benefit by. And of course then they failed again. So for us now to talk about giving up something that's such a model of American success, which was really such a grand American success story, has very real psychological, emotional effects. It doesn't matter which side of the argument you're on.

And then, of course, we're very gun-shy about consequences for misjudgment. I think it's the kind of judgment that got us into Vietnam that we're concerned about, much more than, say, are we going to literally have to go and fight a Vietnam-like war in Panama.

The Suez Canal has been a battleground for a long time. It's been the cause of the location for bloody wars. The Panama Canal has never been. If there was such a thing as Pax Brittania at one time, we've had Pax Americana in Panama.

So for those people who are reluctant to see us withdraw from Panama or to change the status quo in Panama, to set up a new kind of relationship there, there is the sense that, Why should we do that, when everything has been really so comparatively tranquil there, compared to, say, Suez, the other great crossroads of ocean traffic?

The arguments are contradictory, just as the history is contradictory, just as people are contradictory. I think also, if I may try and use an analogy that works, I think that it's really unrealistic to accuse those who talk of possible future troubles in Panama of a violent nature, to accuse them of caving in to intimidation. Because those people who talk or think about such consequences aren't being realistic. It would be a little bit, it seems to me, like arguing that if you were in a ship and there was a weak spot in the hull and you suggest to others on the ship that maybe it would be a good idea to correct that situation, that someone might say, "No, you're being intimidated by the ocean."

✦ ✦ ✦ ✦ ✦ ✦ ✦ ✦ ✦

In May, the town of Tchula, Mississippi, celebrated Hartman Turnbow Day, to honor a seventy-three-year-old cotton farmer who had led an effort to register thousands of black voters in his part of the state. Hartman Turnbow's grandfather was a slave, owned by the Turnbow family. "That's where we got the Turnbow name," he told David Molpus, who visited Turnbow at his farm, part of which was the original Turnbow plantation.

All Things Considered, JUNE 13

TURNBOW: White folks raised me. I was raised right out there at Lexington. Old man B. S. Bell run the Rexall Drugstore and then had a plantation over here in the Delta. They was rich white folks.

I started workin' for them when I was nine years old, and I worked for them till I got twenty. Married and left 'em. And I never did have no trouble with 'em. They loved me and I loved them. Well, I thought just as much of Mrs. Bell as I did my mama. She had Mr. Nichols's little boy. She had her son's boy, little Benny. They would come to her lap and get down on their knees and she would carry 'em over to their lesson.

And then when they get through, I'd be milking my cows and straining my milk and then I'd come and get my books and I'd get right down to her lap on my knees with my books, just like they did, and she carried me over to my lessons, and she didn't make no difference.

See, in them days, I didn't want nothin' but just that little money they was payin' me and that food they was feedin' me, and the next I wanted was to do what they said. And I did that. I said, "Yes, ma'am" and known by all of them and meant that.

MOLPUS: What was law and justice like back then?

TURNBOW: [*Laughs.*] I wanna tell you that. I wanna tell you what law and justice was in just a few words.

You heard that story about "A heart's a heart and a figure's a figure. Everything for the white man and none for the nigger." That was about the law. There wasn't no law, not for no Negro. You know, the Negroes didn't know what law was. There wasn't no law. It was just there but what the white man said. That was that and that was law in plantation days.

MOLPUS: And even when, let's say, one black got in a fight and stabbed another black, what would happen?

TURNBOW: Oh, if one Negro killed another one, he didn't never stop plowin'. He'd just work on in the field and his boss man go to court and get up there in court, and say, "That's my nigger. He's a good nigger." And that's all to it. That's all to it. I knowed too many times Negroes killed one another and didn't even go to court. The boss went.

MOLPUS: Let's talk about the civil rights movement, when all this atmosphere began to change. When you first came in contact with civil rights workers and people talking about registering to vote here in this part of the Delta, in Mississippi, what were your thoughts? How did you react to that?

TURNBOW: Well, when they came around to talking about registering and voting, I never had did it and I never had seed it did and I never had knowed any Negroes to do it and I just didn't believe it could be did, when I first heard of it.

But later we let a fellow talk to us about registering and votin', to be a first-class citizen, and I asked him, was he drunk. He said, no, he wasn't drunk. "That's your personal rights. You're supposed to register and vote."

I say, "Man, you want to get a lot of Negroes killed up?" He said, "The federal government will help you." I said, "The federal government ain't never helped nobody." He said, "Well, cause you ain't never done nothin' for the federal government to help you."

So I said, "Come back again." So he come back to Holmes County again and that was in 1963. And we decided we would try it.

So then about twenty of us went to Lexington to register to vote. Oh, we met the sheriff out there in Lexington and he blowed his top. He looked at us, twenty of us standing up there. He put one hand on his pistol and the other one on his black jacket, and hollered, "All right. Who'll be first?"

Well, of those twenty of us, twenty of 'em commenced to looking at one another right fast. I seen this guy run. I stepped out of the line, told him, "I'll be first, Mr. Smith." He said, "All right, Turnbow. Go on down 'side the curb. Go in the courthouse, the first door on the left, and do what you've got to do."

So that evening, about two more of us got registered. The next day the rest of the twenty got registered. About that next week, a bunch of 'em come down and firebombed my house, the living room, this room. Throwed two firebombs. It had just been painted and they burned it all out. Throwed a firebomb in the back bedroom and then commenced to shootin' at us. I run out there with my rifle and I commenced to shootin' at them, so they soon cleared away. And so the next morning, about eight o'clock, the sheriff come, put me in jail, charged me with arson.

MOLPUS: The sheriff put you in jail?

TURNBOW: Sure, put me in jail.

MOLPUS: Why did he think you were guilty of arson? Why would he? What did he say? Why would you shoot up and burn your house?

TURNBOW: Well, that's what I wanted to know. He said I did it for publicity. And I was convicted for arson in the preliminary court.

When the time come to hear the case again in the federal court in Jackson, why they had dropped the charges because they know that wasn't going to stand up in federal court.

MOLPUS: You lived through those earlier sharecropper plantation days, the struggles of the civil rights movement, and now today, where blacks can register and vote without being intimidated. But economically, blacks are still in very poor shape in Mississippi. How do you compare today's Mississippi for blacks to what it was then?

TURNBOW: The white people in Mississippi today, they're looking for a new way to overcome and put the Negro back where he was. It looks like the white people ain't giving Negroes jobs, as much as they could. They just absolutely ain't trying to work no more. But the white man can't do Negroes like he used to do and get away with it.

MOLPUS: Well, blacks in Mississippi more and more have black candidates to vote for. You've got a black mayor in Tchula, a black member of the legislature from this area, Mr. Clark. You've got two black candidates for the Senate this time, Mr. Kirksey and Charles Evers. Tell me about black politicians in Mississippi and how well they're doing.

TURNBOW: Of course, you know this. I don't have to tell you that. Any time you come up with black politicians you has a world of white peoples against it. They don't want that. And then we has a world of brainwashed Negroes. We call 'em Uncle Toms. They've got to die and you've got to have the burying of 'em. And get them out of the way and then let everybody be educated.

And then politics and everything will level out and these educated Negroes and educated white folks, you'll see. You's a younger man than me and they're going to get along together and ain't going to have all these fights and stuff like they're having now.

MOLPUS: You told me in the beginning that you did leave Mississippi for a few years. Do you ever regret that you came back?

TURNBOW: No, and never will. [*Laughs.*] No. I'm going to die here. I'm going to die here. I'm living well.

✦ ✦ ✦ ✦ ✦ ✦ ✦ ✦ ✦

After months of discussion, President Carter successfully concluded his historic negotiation between Egypt and Israel, with the Camp David Accords. Israel returned land to Egypt, and Egypt took the enormous step of recognizing Israel. Accounts of the final talks between President Anwar Sadat of Egypt and Prime Minister Menachem Begin of Israel tell of the American president going from one to the other, sitting on the floor of the cabins at Camp David, scribbling on a yellow legal pad, struggling to find common ground. Camp David was chosen because it is the most private presidential retreat, which is the reason some presidents like it and some don't. In anticipation of the meeting, David Ensor found out what he could about Camp David.

All Things Considered, SEPTEMBER 3

ENSOR: Camp David was built during the depression by the Civilian Conservation Corps. When Franklin Roosevelt chose it as a summer retreat, he called it Shangri-la. According to FDR's son, Elliott, the place at that time looked more like a marine training camp, made up of rough pine cabins with metal beds, a bathroom door that refused to shut, and bare walls, ornamented only with some of Roosevelt's favorite cartoons.

Roosevelt took Winston Churchill up there, and FDR was there on D-day. Truman didn't care much for the place; he preferred the beach. But Eisenhower loved it and renamed it after his grandson, David. The Kennedys kept their horses there when Jack was president. LBJ liked the place, but people who were there with him said it made him restless.

Camp David really came into its own under Richard Nixon. He had the cabins modernized, built a conference hall, and made, while president, nearly 120 trips to the Catoctin Mountain retreat. He went there a lot to think about how to get out of his Watergate problems. He would also lend it to aides sometimes. In his book, *Blind Ambition*, John Dean describes coming to a key decision in his life there, the decision to turn on the cover-up instead of helping it continue. I called him in Los Angeles and asked him what Camp David is like.

DEAN: Well, it certainly is rustic and out of the thrash of life, and particularly Washington life, being removed and up in the hills the way it is. It's sort of a — I guess you'd have to say it's sort of rustic chic. The buildings all appear to be log cabins. But when you get inside you find they're very nicely furnished, not elegantly, but certainly tastefully.

And the surroundings themselves being heavily wooded and paths going through the woods from one cabin to the next create very much of an out-of-the-way atmosphere, where you're likely to think more about what's happening inside your head and the like than you would be with, say, the normal thrash of being in Washington.

ENSOR: While they are on the mountaintop, the Americans, Israelis, and Egyptians will have the use of a swimming pool, bowling alleys, stables, a skeet shooting range, archery targets, saunas, a par-three golf course, a trampoline, shuffleboard, pool, Ping-Pong, and an underground bomb shelter.

There is also a cabin for showing movies. Both the Israelis and Egyptians have said they want to watch Westerns, one Israeli wag reportedly asking for *How the West Bank Was Won*. President Carter has watched *Close Encounters of the Third Kind* up there recently, more than once.

The meetings between the three leaders will probably, for the most part, take place in the president's cabin, which is called Aspen Lodge. Inside it may look the way John Ehrlichman described it in his novel: "Aspen Lodge was a place of warmth and calm. The decor was subdued. There was not a single disquieting vibration from the old wooden duck decoys, the soft-toned watercolors, the neutral drapes and upholstery. The rooms lulled and comforted. Outside the storm doors of Aspen Lodge, however, were jarring reminders of the real world, sentry posts with guards against assassination, bomb shelter entrances, two-way radios."

Another aide to President Nixon once called Camp David the nearest thing we have to a medieval castle with a moat and foot guards. President Carter hopes all that privacy, something politicians don't get much of, will produce from Begin and Sadat and their aides two uncharacteristic qualities, candor and flexibility.

There's a precedent for Camp David working that kind of magic. When Eisenhower hosted Nikita Khrushchev there in 1959, the Soviet leader arrived full of tough talk and bluster. He was threatening to force the allies out of West Berlin. But alone with Eisenhower and a single interpreter tramping through the woods, he apparently proved surprisingly companionable and even reasonable. Eisenhower said, "We were able to have a real bull session." Jimmy Carter hopes for the same.

✦ ✦ ✦ ✦ ✦ ✦ ✦ ✦ ✦

Joe Frank has his own radio program in Los Angeles now, a curious mixture of funky philosophy and dramatic delivery. He was part of the seventies at NPR. As we all know, much of the sixties happened in the seventies.

All Things Considered, OCTOBER 22

FRANK: When I was growing up, my family used to spend its summers on Long Island. This was in the late forties. We had an apartment in Manhattan and our country home in Harbor Heights, a small community of cottages and bungalows set on a hillside overlooking Long Island Sound. I have many fond memories of that period, when things were simple and secure and I felt safe in the bosom of my family. And life was full of mystery and wonder.

When you're a child you're so alive to experience. The world dazzles you, especially the world of other living beings. Do you remember how you felt about ladybugs? I loved them. Whenever a ladybug would land on your arm or your shoulder or the back of your hand you'd be very careful not to scare it away by an abrupt movement and you'd count the spots on its back to see how old it was. Is that a myth? And somehow ladybugs knew that you'd never hurt them, that they were sacred, that they were immune from violence. After all, they were ladies and you treated them as such. And then finally, after checking you out completely, it would fly off and disappear into the shade and you'd feel a kind of pang, a sense of loss.

And frogs were a delight. They were so funny-looking with their popping eyes and green splotchy bodies. Sometimes they'd blow themselves up like balloons and you'd sneak up behind them and tap their rear ends and they'd spring way up in the air and land a few feet away. And if you lifted a frog in your hand and stroked its belly it would fall asleep. [*Snores.*] And at least once during the summer you'd come across a stray turtle. It was inevitable. It always happened. And you'd pick it up by its shell, feeling a little bit squeamish, worried that it might bite you with its ugly, prehistoric little head. And its feet would be jerking violently in the air. And you'd take it home and keep it for a pet, until finally your parents persuaded you to take it back wherever you found it. And you'd give in reluctantly, but afterwards you'd feel proud that you did the right thing.

And of course, butterflies were a treat. Whenever you'd see one land on a branch, its wings poised with their bright, beautiful colors, you'd cry out, "There's a butterfly!" What a perfect name, butterfly.

Often in the evenings, especially on the weekends when we had family out to visit, we'd gather on the back lawn and sit around the fire, unfolding summer furniture, or stretch out on blankets on the ground and sing songs from the old country. My mother played the accordion and my uncle Jules played the mandolin and someone else had a guitar, and it was all very festive and people would dance and sing and the children would sing along. And we'd also play among ourselves and try to catch fireflies in our cupped hands. And we'd roast marshmallows at the ends of twigs and then eat them, crisp and burnt on the outside and sweet and mellow on the inside.

And every summer for three weeks my grandmother would come out and visit us. She was a widow. She was very reserved and dignified, but she always brought me a box of — I don't remember what they were called, but they were tubes of light flaky dough filled with soft, melt-in-your-mouth chocolate, shaped like cigars. So there was a double pleasure. While you ate them you could also make believe you were smoking.

In the evenings during the week, my mother, my grandmother, my dog, and I would walk along a country road to meet my father on his way back home from the city where he worked. And we'd walk past farmhouses and barns and fenced-in cows and horses and past wooded areas and cornfields, my dog having a wonderful time trotting along and sniffing at things and chasing birds. And the crickets would be out in full force. And there was honeysuckle that grew beside the road at a certain place, and I'd pick a few blossoms and suck the syrup out of them.

And there was always a sense of anticipation, waiting for my father's car to appear. And then finally my father would come driving up the road in shirtsleeves, his tie loosely knotted at the collar, looking puffy-eyed and a little tired. And he'd stop and we'd all pile into the car, my dog yelping and whining, his tail slapping back and forth, lapping at my father's face with his tongue, so full of emotion. And then we'd drive back to the house and have dinner.

Almost thirty years later I found myself living in Manhattan. My senses had been dulled by traffic; pneumatic drills; sirens; TV sets from other people's apartments; constant crowding; loud music; the news of the day replete with fires, accidents, murders, robberies, natural catastrophes, scandal, and revolution. My only relationship with another species was the ongoing war I was conducting against cockroaches that infested my apartment. Every night when I came home I'd kill them in my kitchen and my bathroom.

My family was in disarray. Many of the older generation had died or moved to Florida. My own generation, my cousins, were spread all over the country now, hardly ever talked to one another, and no longer believed in the religion and had abandoned the culture in which they were brought up. Some of them were even into est and TM and other new religions.

As for myself, I worked in the music business. I produced rock concerts. Late one afternoon I was on Route 81, headed for Syracuse. The previous night I'd put on a heavy metal show in Binghamton, eight thousand kids, mostly between the ages of thirteen and eighteen, stoned and crowded into a civic center, presumably to have their minds and their hearing permanently impaired.

That night I was presenting the same show in Syracuse. The throughway was jammed with traffic, which hardly moved, so I drove off at the next exit and took a country road that seemed to parallel the highway. But it soon branched off. I followed it anyway, thinking I'd rather be moving in the wrong direction than not moving at all. The road turned to gravel. Then a few miles further down I realized I was running out of gas. I coasted downhill in neutral and only applied the accelerator when the road was level or uphill. But finally the motor died and the car rolled to a stop. I got out, looked around at cornfields bordering both sides of the road and began to walk.

It was dusk, only another hour or so of light. I felt in limbo, somewhere between being furiously upset and not caring at all. And for the first time in what seemed like ages, I was listening to the crickets and watching fireflies. And if you can believe it, I found some honey-suckle growing in the grass beside the road.

And then I saw a car coming from a great distance, and I had the strangest sensation that I could feel the presence of my mother and my grandmother and could hear my dog snuffing around somewhere in the field and that in that car was my father coming home to us from the city and that we'd all pile in and drive back to the house for dinner. And that everything that seemed to have happened since the last time he came down that road was only the crazy, disturbing dream of a child, guilty nevertheless of complicity in that dream.

But it wasn't my father. It was Maury Gwertzman, director of A and R at Capitol Records, who'd also driven off of the same exit I had in order to get away from the traffic. So I got into the back of his limousine. The occasion seemed to demand some celebration, so we opened a bottle of Dom Pérignon, put a cassette of Kiss on the tape deck, and rolled up the windows.

✦ ✦ ✦ ✦ ✦ ✦ ✦ ✦ ✦ ✦

In November, 911 people died at Jonestown, in Guyana. Small children were murdered, along with some of the older members of the People's Temple, followers of Jim Jones. The rest committed suicide, drinking Kool-Aid laced with poison. Authorities investigating the deaths found nine hundred hours of audiocassettes at Jonestown. James Reston got the tapes through a Freedom of Information suit and wrote a book about Jonestown called *Our Father Who Art in Hell.* Reston and Noah Adams designed a radio script that used those tapes, to attempt to explain why hundreds of people, members of a religious cult, agreed to die together in the jungles of Guyana. The program was called "Father Cares: The Last of Jonestown."

Jim Jones began as a powerful preacher who gathered a considerable congregation in California, based, Noah said, on a "combustible mixture of sacrilege and socialism." Jim Jones's followers believed that he was divine.

Special Coverage, MAY 24, 1981

JONES: Christianity was never based on the idea of an unknown god. I am going to cause you to know that you are what Jesus was. It is written that you're a god. I'm a god, and you're a god. And I'm a god and I'm going to stay a god until you recognize that you're a god, and when you recognize you're a god I shall go back into principle and will not appear as a personality. You are a god. But until I see all of you knowing who you are, I am going to be very much what I am, God, almighty God! [*Applause.*]

✦ ✦ In 1977, Jones claimed that twenty thousand people belonged to the People's Temple in several congregations around California. Jones was an important figure in the state, named head of San Francisco's Housing Authority. But then, people who had left his church began talking about cult practices, beatings, manipulation, and intimidation. Almost overnight, Jones left the United States with his followers and created a new community in the small South American country of Guyana. The plan was to farm in the jungle, to attempt a kind of New Jerusalem based on Jim Jones's notions of socialism. Noah Adams narrated.

ADAMS: The people of the temple worked long days in the fields, stood in long lines for food, and at night after dinner they would be assembled in front of the pavilion for the town forum meetings. Everyone, even the children, almost a thousand people, looking up at Father. He would ascend to the big wooden chair, cushioned with pillows, a small table beside him, a cup of soda pop always full. His aides stood behind him, the temple band off to one side.

And for long hours, well into the morning, he would hold forth as the leader and inquisitor and judge, father and god. He led the songs and the prayers and the trials and told them the fearful events happening out in the world they had escaped. He was their only source of information, their only dispenser of justice.

Just before their only Christmas in the jungle, Jim's mother died. She had come with them to Jonestown. The death came at a tense time. The U.S. government had stopped sending the social security checks, a mistake that was quickly corrected, but it was perceived as a threat since the seniors of the temple were bringing in about forty thousand dollars a month. The night after his mother died, Jim talked about the death. He was bitter. He blamed the people for making his mother worry, and then he talked about much more.

JONES: What did you have to get to do? I didn't do that. No, I never did it in the States, but I do it now. I buy whatever the hell I can get.

Huh? You know you can buy a telephone bill? And buy your mail. You can buy anything in the United States.

Yes, you may go to the restroom.

They'll take our money to give us information about the FBI. Don't tell me they won't because I've already got it. They take my money to give me information on who Grace Stone is talking to. And don't spare her neck.

If you're going to commit treason, you better know who you're dealing with because after we're all dead here you might go to a social party, after you try to get your little reward, your little thirty pieces of silver for selling out the greatest people on earth, and you walk in with a Judas tribe, and the wife of Judas might be one of the ladies I'd laid to make a socialist.

[*Applause.*]

JONES: And she might give you slow poison in your champagne. You don't know how clever I am. One thing you've all done is underestimate me. I made plans for treason long ago 'cause I knew I couldn't trust nothing. I knew I couldn't trust anything but communism and the principle in me. Yes, restroom.

I knew that that's what I had to depend upon and not depend upon the arm of the flesh and never put all your eggs in one basket. So, honey, I put my eggs in many places. And you figure that out if you want to.

Some of you are too naive. You don't know what I'm — what Jim Jones is all about. You can't even follow him. You haven't even smelled where he's at yet, much less followed him. You don't even know who he is and you might miss him. If you didn't have a real good look at him, you wouldn't even know who he looked like. You really haven't got next to him, but I've got all kinds of things in store.

[*Applause.*]

JONES: You who are stupid pissants and reptiles and lower than the primates. You could make a hoopie if you want, but your hoopie makes me sickie, and so you can make your hoopie while I do something that's far more significant. I got me some big plans, both here, there, and everywhere.

[*Applause.*]

JONES: Got lots of plans.

✦ ✦ Jones, in his madness, feared people from the outside world, particularly the friends and family of Jonestown residents, who wanted their relatives to return home. On several occasions, when authorities attempted to ask individuals if they wanted to leave, Jones threatened mass suicide. Guyanese authorities retreated, but family members in California kept the pressure up.

A California congressman, Leo Ryan, traveled to Jonestown with some family members in a chartered aircraft on what he perceived as a rescue mission. Jones described it to his people as an invasion. In those long nights of preaching and testifying, Jones prepared his people for suicide.

Ryan was received and entertained at Jonestown, and while he was there he was approached by people who did want to leave and he promised to take them home. Ryan and four others were shot and killed by Jones's followers at the airstrip. That was the event which brought about the final "white night" at Jonestown.

JONES: Every day I've lived since I was a child — the first time I felt guilt, when a little dog died, I wanted to commit suicide. But I've had some little dogs and cats in life that had me alone to take care of them. At that age that's all that kept me through.

Then a little bit later my mom needed me, and some poor soul down the road needed me, that was poor and minority and been treated badly. Then come along the black in the community that I always was their champion. It's always been that way. Somebody needed me. So you can do what you have to do 'cause I stay alive and do all this thinking, and I am bored and I am disgusted and I am sick with people who do so little with socialism when they have such a good example to follow.

ADAMS: Father went on and on into the night, his congregation scared and confused and worried. He needed them now even more. They responded often with shouts of praise and murmurs of amen and lined up to come to the microphone to testify to their love for him and their love for socialism, a love so pure they would do anything to prove it — commit suicide, even kill their children.

JONES: And how do you feel about you may die tonight?

WOMAN: Since I've been here I've — all I've seen is the beauty of socialism, and I feel that my life is fulfilled and if death come, it's no big deal to me because I've already lived my life just being here with the family. Thank you, Dad.

JONES: Thank you.

CHILD: I'm prepared to die with this family if I have to for freedom. Thank you, Dad.

JERRY: I am also prepared to die after forty-four years of not being able to contribute anything to this life or find any point or reason for it at all, and not being well known at all there sure would be no glory in it, but for the children here, for the freedom, as long as there's one who remains on this earth that isn't free, none of us are free. And I am prepared to give my life if need be.

MAN: Could you take your daughter's life if it came to it?

JERRY: No, I'd give mine in the place of hers.

JONES: Hold it now. They brought up a sensitive question, and you may not understand the gravity of that question, but all of our children have faced this. We went through white nights so they'll not be hurt by it. We haven't had any child causing us any difficulty by facing this kind of thought.

MAN: Jerry, the question would be, If the fascists were coming up the road right now, and we were going to lay down our lives and fight for it, you say you would give your life for your child, but would you leave it for the fascists to have? What would you do in that case?

JERRY: If it came to that, I would have to take her life.

CROWD: Right. That's right.

JONES: Fine. Do you understand that? How old is your child?

JERRY: Eleven.

JONES: Oh, she's past the age. We fight at eleven. It's under that that we consider that. She would take up a cutlass and fight till she was dead, unless it came to an overwhelming invasion. Then we would gently put them to sleep which we have where they never know what hit them. We are already prepared for that. A people who are really loving and a father who's genuinely compassionate is prepared for all such emergencies. But you don't do that as long as there's alternatives in which you can make a mark. You don't do that unless there's alternatives. All alternatives are closed for you to make a mark against fascism.

WOMAN: Yes, I think we all should die tonight if it's our turn, and I'm willing, Father, to stand with you all the way just like I always have told you three years ago. 'Cause everything seems and will always be the same. I am not changing.

JONES: You don't need to say no more. I remember your face.

WOMAN: I know. I love you, Father.

JONES: I know you do.

✦ ✦ The tapes of the deaths at Jonestown were too horrifying to play on the air. The program ends with a description of what happened. "Father Cares: The Last of Jonestown" was broadcast in 1981, after Reston's book was published.

1979

♦ ♦ ♦ ♦ ♦ ♦ ♦ ♦ ♦

C okie Roberts went to Pennsylvania to cover the nuclear accident and the release of radiation at the Three Mile Island nuclear power plant, near Harrisburg. When she returned to Washington, she spoke with Noah Adams and played bits of tape she'd collected during a week of talking to the people who lived around the plant and were convinced that authorities were not being straight with them about this accident. Cokie began with part of an interview with a man who lived down the road from Three Mile Island.

All Things Considered, APRIL 8

MAN: I wish they would have told somebody. I mean, this worst release started Friday morning, about quarter of seven, and when it was over about ten o'clock, then they told us. And my wife and kids were here. I mean, that's not right! I wish they would have told me then so I could have got them away. But no. They — I don't know. It's just a credibility gap there.

ADAMS: The classic credibility gap. We heard a lot about that through the week and in the news reports that followed. Why was that? Didn't anyone know what was going on?

ROBERTS: Apparently not. And people felt that they were getting contradictory information. They were hearing one thing from the utility company, they were hearing another thing from the governor's office, they were hearing another thing from the Nuclear Regulatory Commission.

And they also worried that they weren't being told the whole truth, that people were holding things back, worrying about panicking them. On Friday, for instance, the people within ten miles of the plant were told to go inside and close their doors and windows, but they knew that glass wasn't going to keep the radiation out.

ADAMS: Why were they advised to go inside and shut everything down?

ROBERTS: Probably because the health officials worried about people inhaling the radioactive gases. On Saturday, we found out for the first time that people in the control room at Three Mile Island had been wearing gas masks, which means that the air must have been full of the radioactive stuff. And since then I've been talking to radiologists who say that inhaling radiation is far, far more damaging than absorbing it through your skin.

ADAMS: Well, were the people there ever warned about the dangers of inhaling radiation?

ROBERTS: No, they were just told to go inside, close their doors and windows.

ADAMS: Why didn't they all just leave, just get out of the vicinity immediately?

ROBERTS: Many of them did, of course. And the governor eventually recommended that pregnant women and preschool children leave. In fact, they're still out. But of course that was worrisome too. In a normal disaster, the disaster affects everybody the same way. When flood waters rise, they take away the house and everybody in it. But this was something different! This mysterious, invisible danger doesn't work that way. And I had many mothers of grade school children come up to me and ask, What's the difference between my four-year-old, my preschooler, and my first-grader? How is it going to affect them differently? Of course, many of those mothers did take their children and did leave. And the kids in the schoolyard in Hummelstown, which is just a few miles from the plant, did go back to school on Tuesday and they talked of nothing but the evacuation.

KID: An evacuation is, um, when you go away, when there's something really bad where you live.

SECOND KID: My friend went because they said on the radio and TV that pregnant women and preschool children might be scared of it.

THIRD KID: We didn't know what was happening, because all — the radio ones said we should evacuate and some said we shouldn't.

FOURTH KID: Evacuation is like something that — you leave your home until it's done. And then you come back and it's like — and you just like forget about it.

ADAMS: You know, when you listen to that tape, you can hear the natural confidence of youth, but you can also hear a little bit of fear too in that.

ROBERTS: Well, that's right. And the parents are frightened about the long-term effects on the children. They're worried about whether this incident will have any scarring psychological damage. After all, the government is talking about coming in and monitoring these people for years, the children maybe for the rest of their lives.

ADAMS: I was just wondering about that, if the people in that area, Three Mile Island, will feel for a long time that they're just a little bit on display, so to speak.

ROBERTS: Well, you know, they don't really know. There are an awful lot of bad jokes about it. When I got back here from Harrisburg, everybody made cracks about it. They could see through me or that they should put a lampshade on my head. Another reporter had a friend really refuse to shake his hand. And one woman in Hershey said that she had gone into a hospital outside of the area, just for some other reason, and that the nurse was afraid to touch her! Those kinds of things hardly inspire confidence!

But, of course, the people have much more serious questions than these immediate incidents after the event. These young parents are parents of an eighteen-month-old and they live right down the road from Three Mile Island.

MOTHER: I don't know whether I'll want to have any more children. I did want to up until this happened. Now I'm not sure. I would still like to have a child, but I don't know whether I would like to bear a child after being here.

FATHER: I don't know whether it's worth the risk. I'd rather have no other child than to have one that is, you know, a vegetable.

MOTHER: I hate being a guinea pig and that's what we are, because nothing like this has happened before. They don't know what the affects are. We are the guinea pigs. The statistics they use if there are any future accidents are going to be based on us. And it's a very scary feeling, because I, you know, we didn't volunteer for this experiment.

✦ ✦ ✦ ✦ ✦ ✦ ✦ ✦ ✦

We also had serious concerns about sending Cokie to cover a nuclear accident, and there was considerable debate around our egalitarian shop about whether NPR had the right to ask or to tell her to go. She went for the reason reporters generally go anywhere: it was a good story and an important one. Cokie told Noah that she had not worried much about potential danger while she was there, but, she added, she no longer wears the navy blue suit she wore to Three Mile Island.

A commission was formed to investigate the incident, and it was in the news the week that the Philadelphia Phillies beat the Chicago Cubs 23 to 22 in extra innings. Alex Chadwick called columnist Mike Royko at the *Chicago Sun-Times.*

All Things Considered, MAY 18

ROYKO: Had the Cubs won this game, it would have been a new record for coming from behind. Previously, the most runs any team ever came from behind was something like 11. At one point today the Cubs were 12 runs behind, 21 to 9. So, had they won it, they would have set a record for coming from behind.

CHADWICK: Were you sitting there in the newsroom listening to this game on the radio?

ROYKO: Absolutely. We had TV sets going all over.

CHADWICK: Did things kind of slow down in the office there as—

ROYKO: Yeah, everybody was running in and out of the sports department and running in and out of the managing editor's office and everywhere there was a television set.

CHADWICK: It must have been crazy.

ROYKO: Yeah, it was kind of fun, because early in the game, the reporters here who grew up in New York were snickering, chortling, because the Cubs were behind 21 to 9. And they mainly snickered and chortled at me because I'm the biggest Cubs fan here. And then I came back with reports, and their faces fell, the curs.

CHADWICK: Did you think the Cubs were going to pull it out?

ROYKO: No, I knew they'd lose.

CHADWICK: You couldn't have.

ROYKO: Yeah, it was —

CHADWICK: But they tied it up.

ROYKO: When they tied it up I was sure they were going to lose.

CHADWICK: The ninth inning, 22 to 22, they go into the tenth inning — why were you sure they were going to lose?

ROYKO: Because they're the Cubs. They lose games like that. They do something heroic right to the end, and then right at the last second they fail. That's what makes them so wonderful. Because that's basically the story of all of us. That's why the Cubs are so wonderful. They're losers and so are most people. I mean, the Yankees aren't real. Nobody goes around winning and triumphing over everything, being — 99 percent of most people don't triumph over anything, you know, they just get by.

CHADWICK: Is Chicago a good baseball town?

ROYKO: Oh, it's a marvelous baseball town. Fans are tolerant. They get mad, but they're basically philosophical and tolerant. They don't expect, they don't demand a pennant. If the Cubs play .500 ball, they'll draw a million people. Cub fans enjoy going out to the ballpark.

CHADWICK: I gather that Chicagoans don't have a great many expectations for the Cubs. It's not a team that you plan on making you feel good in August and September.

ROYKO: No. No. It's got the longest continuous record of failure, I think, of any team in professional sports. Last time they won the pennant, I think Hitler was alive. And then we had that terrible disaster in 1969 when we had the best team. It was even better than the wartime team that won the pennant. We had a helluva team in 1969. And the Mets, a bunch of real second-rate ball players with a good pitching staff, beat us out. It had to be New York. They needed another pennant. And they beat us out.

That was the last time Cubs fans really believed they were going to win a pennant because the Cubs had this enormous lead and really a fine team and a bunch of their — entire infield, I think, made the All-Star team that year. And they blew it. Since then, there hasn't been a year when any Cubs fan, any children, thought the Cubs were going to win a pennant. But we like them.

And, as I say, I think the reason Chicagoans generally are more sensible and levelheaded than people in many other parts of the country is that we've learned through experiences such as the Cubs not to expect the most and to be happy with small gifts.

Today we scored 22 runs. That's a remarkable thing. The other team scored 23, that's true. But we scored 22. So how many teams score 22 runs in one day? So we're happy. That's why we can survive great blizzards. We survive political corruption. We survive all the things, the gangsters that we're known for. We survive all that. We go on and we live and we're happy. And the Cubs help teach us that life is rough.

♦ ♦ ♦ ♦ ♦ ♦ ♦ ♦ ♦ ♦

In October, we went to the White House for a call-in program with the president. Susan Stamberg joined President Carter in the White House Library, the scene of FDR's Fireside Chats, to listen to the concerns of our listeners. This first call, with a child named Shanie Ridge from Colorado Springs, only slightly exaggerates the gently instructional tone of most of the president's answers. There were some questions on defense spending, but most of our listeners were concerned about energy costs and inflation.

All Things Considered, OCTOBER 13

STAMBERG: Go ahead, Shanie. The president's on the line with you.

RIDGE: Mr. Carter? Uh, do you like your job?

CARTER: Yes, I like it very much. I like the White House and the life there. So does Amy, by the way. And I like my job. It's the best job in the greatest country on earth.

RIDGE: That's what you think?

CARTER: That's what I think. Would you like to be president someday? You might have to run against Amy, I don't know.

RIDGE: My other question was, What can I do to help stop inflation?

CARTER: I don't know if you've been listening to the program or not, Shanie, but I think one of the things is that you could help to save energy. And around the house, you could observe ways to keep doors closed, to make your parents insulate the home better, to prevent heat from escaping. You can keep the thermostats set fairly high during the summer and low during the winter so you don't waste heat. You could cut off electric lights and other electrical appliances when they're not in use. And when you're driving along the road with your parents, you can certainly make sure they obey the speed limit. And I think that when your father or mother go to work, for instance, you could try to get them to join in a car pool so that one automobile could be filled before it rides up and down the highways with just one person in it.

We're doing all we can on this end, but there are a lot of things that a ten-year-old can do. Around the school, you ought to get together with other kids in your class, for instance, and try to share ideas with each other about what you can do in addition to those things that I've already described.

I wish you well. It's really good to see a ten-year-old interested in public affairs, and you can help me as much as anyone in this country can to cut down on energy waste and hold down inflation.

STAMBERG: Thank you, Shanie, for your question. Our next caller, Mr. President, is in Springville, Alabama. It's Lou Windham. Mr. Windham, go ahead, please.

WINDHAM: Mr. President?

CARTER: Good morning, Lou.

WINDHAM: We're in the petroleum business here in an area of the country that I'm sure you're familiar with. We own two LP gas companies and supply these rural people with propane for heating. At the same time, we're in the oil jobbing business. We find it tough to explain to our customers why every time they buy a petroleum product, it is higher. Now, we cannot see any evidence that the Department of Energy is doing anything. Now, I feel that the majority of the people in this country need a very good explanation as to what the Department of Energy is doing to put the lid on these producing companies.

CARTER: Well, that's not an easy question to answer, Lou, because there's very little the Department of Energy or a president can do to prevent foreign countries from raising their price of oil. And the basic thrust that we are pursuing is to cut down on that imported oil.

As you know, this past month the rate of increase of energy was more than one hundred percent per year on an annual basis. And as I said earlier, about four percent of our inflation rate is derived directly from energy costs. This is a very serious matter, and I think you've noticed if you've listened to this call-in show, how many people have raised this same question.

WINDHAM: Yes.

CARTER: I can't give you any easy answer. There's no reason for me to sit here in the Oval Office and try to mislead the American people. There are only three ways that we can deal with this question. One is to use as little energy as possible through conservation, savings. Second, to use more of the energy that we produce in our own country than we have been doing in the past. And, third, provide federal and other assistance for the low-income families to make sure that they do have enough fuel to heat their homes and to cook with and so forth, and also so they can have enough money to pay those bills.

But there's no way that I can mislead you. The prices are high now. They're going to get higher in the future than they are already. And unless our nation unites itself and deals with this very serious threat, we're going to be worse off in the future than we have in the past.

I inherited this problem. I'm not complaining about it. But it has been an extremely difficult thing to get the Congress to pass any legislation on this issue because it's so controversial. We have still not passed a single line of legislation in the Congress dealing with oil. This year we have a very good prospect of finally getting those laws on the books which will help you and help me and all your customers and people like them throughout the country. It's been slow in coming, but we're now making some progress.

WINDHAM: Mr. President, I would like to congratulate you and the Congress on the move that you have put forth to help these needy people in this crisis we're in, because I feel that that is one answer and you're to be congratulated on that move.

CARTER: Thank you. This will amount, by the way, I think between one hundred and two hundred dollars per family to help them with the fuel bills this winter. So if they combine that help, if they're a poor family, with saving as much energy as possible, I think we can get people through the winter.

WINDHAM: Thank you.

CARTER: Good luck, Lou, and thank you.

STAMBERG: Thank you, Mr. Windham. The next call is from Lancaster, Kentucky, Mr. Carter, Mr. President Carter, and it's from Robert Gordon. Go ahead, Mr. Gordon, you're on the line with President Carter.

GORDON: Yes, Mr. President.

CARTER: Yes.

GORDON: Well, first off I'd just like to say I love you very much, I'm praying for you, and my friends are praying for you.

CARTER: Thank you.

GORDON: You've got quite a responsibility. May I make a suggestion, Mr. President?

CARTER: Please.

GORDON: Well, what I would like to just suggest and encourage, sir, is that when politicking time comes, cut that time in half and spend it on your knees seeking the Lord Jesus Christ. Because, sir, Jesus is more important in this country. He will give you the answers, sir. He will give you the answers to lead as is his will. Excuse me, I'm a little nervous.

CARTER: It's all right.

GORDON: But the Lord Jesus puts the man in power, if you spend your time on your knees, seeking his will, and if it's his will that you stay in power another four years, then he'll put you in power. Mr. President,

again, I'm praying for you. I love you, and this is going to seem a little silly, but I was wondering if you could send me your autograph, sir.
CARTER: Yes, I'll be glad to. I'll do that.

✦ ✦ We followed the call-in program by checking back with some of the people who'd talked to the president to see what they'd thought of his answers. Most of them were impressed, respectful, and pleased to have had the opportunity. NPR's David Ensor and I called Lou Windham in Alabama.

WERTHEIMER: Mr. Windham, when you talked to the president, did it in any way change your own impression of him, of what he's like or how he approaches people?
WINDHAM: Well, it's nice to know that the guy that used to live next door is also up there talking to me on the other end of the phone. This is a very good program.

I think that I have a pretty dim view of the way Carter has done a lot of things in the sense that he hasn't really stepped in and taken the bull by the horns. Thank goodness it is an election year and the bull's standing there ready to be grabbed. Somebody's got to move it around.
WERTHEIMER: [*Laughs.*]
WINDHAM: And I think at this time it will give him some guts to stand up and say this is the way it is and this is what I've done, and quit apologizing for his mistakes and tell some people that he's doing the best he can and take some more forceful action. You can't always take your problems to the sitting room and hope that somebody's going to grant some, you know, answer upon your desk there in the Oval Office. It takes a little bit more forceful action, I think, in the White House.

✦ ✦ ✦ ✦ ✦ ✦ ✦ ✦ ✦

In November, we began *Morning Edition* and, once again, launched a program in the middle of the biggest story of the year. After the fall of the shah of Iran and the triumph of a conservative religious movement led by Ayatollah Ruhollah Khomeini, Iranian students took American citizens hostage in Tehran. The students wanted the shah returned to Iran to stand trial.

Morning Edition began with its own small share of turmoil. The first version we tried did not work. With one week to go before the planned debut, the executive producer, the producer, and the hosts left. The highest-ranking producer still standing was Jay Kernis, and it was our great good fortune that he had the same kind of vision that Bill Siemering had had years before for *All Things Considered*. Kernis begged and pleaded with Bob Edwards, who was hosting *All Things Considered* with Susan Stamberg, to at least help the program get under way. Bob liked his job and could see no reason to come to work at two in the morning, but for the good of the order, he did it. Kernis promised that after a few months, Bob could go back to his original post.

Morning Edition now has the largest audience in public radio and is the first place many Americans hear about things that happened overnight in Europe and the Middle East. Here is a sample of the first week's efforts to cover the hostage crisis. Jackie Judd joined Bob Edwards.

Morning Edition, NOVEMBER 5

JUDD: The State Department says it has gotten what it calls indications from the Iranian government that there will be help in negotiating the release of at least sixty Americans being held hostage at the U.S. Embassy in Tehran. The spokesman says that as far as the department knows, no one has been hurt in the takeover that began yesterday.

But what kind of help the Iranian government is considering is unclear. The Ayatollah Khomeini is reported to have called the embassy a center of spying and plotting. Khomeini's son arrived at the embassy a short while ago to talk to the five hundred student demonstrators occupying the building. The students are demanding that the U.S. release the former shah of Iran, now hospitalized in New York, and that Iran break its relations with the U.S. Yesterday, Iranian students living in New York occupied the Statue of Liberty, demanding the shah's extradition. NPR's Neal Conan reports.

CONAN: Several chained themselves inside the monument's crown, and a spokesman announced that they would stay there until the shah was returned to Iran to face punishment. Liberty Island was evacuated as a hundred-foot banner was unfurled from above the statue's right eye. SHAH MUST BE TRIED AND PUNISHED, it said.

Later it turned out that most of the protesters left along with the tourists. Only seven were there when national park police cut the chains. The seven have been held overnight to face charges of trespassing and disorderly conduct. They'll be arraigned in federal court this morning.

Neal Conan interviews First Lady Hillary Rodham Clinton on health care reform at the White House in 1993. *(White House)*

Ray Suarez, the host of NPR's *Talk of the Nation*, covering a demonstration in Durban, South Africa, in April 1994, before the election of Nelson Mandela. *(Marcus Rosenbaum)*

The current hosts of *All Things Considered:* Robert Siegel, Linda Wertheimer, and Noah Adams. *(Murray Bognovitz)*

EDWARDS: NPR's David Ensor has been following the administration's handling of the crisis. He's been talking this morning with members of the Iran Working Group at the State Department. David, since the information we get keeps changing, there are a lot of rumors around now. Why don't you start by running down what's happened overnight.

ENSOR: Well, Bob, the president has sent a special mission to Iran, headed by former Attorney General Ramsey Clark. Clark has met the Ayatollah Khomeini before and he's hoping to meet with him again when he gets there. I talked to the State Department a little earlier and asked them whether or not Clark was expected. And they said, obviously, he wouldn't have been sent if it wasn't known that he would be allowed to land and would be received. Who he'll be able to talk to, they don't know. They're hoping to go to the top, though. The other member of the delegation is William Miller, who is on the staff of the Senate Select Committee on Intelligence.

EDWARDS: What's the situation in Iran?

ENSOR: Well, overnight two more Americans were seized in their hotel and taken to the American Embassy compound, where about sixty Americans and thirty other hostages are being held.

Three U.S. citizens were stopped at the Tehran airport this morning and prevented from leaving the country. However, the State Department says that they are now scheduled to leave on a later flight and are going to be allowed to go.

The State Department has sent out an advisory to the fourteen oil companies that still have staff in Iran that they should start getting them out, saying that they can't guarantee consular protective services anymore.

And the Revolutionary Council that the ayatollah appointed to take over and to set up a new government officially accepted power and warned their followers that there should be no further attacks on foreigners.

EDWARDS: What has this Iran Working Group been doing overnight, and what's the mood over there?

ENSOR: Well, they've been answering telephones. The phones seem to ring every couple of seconds over there. They've been talking with everyone from Bruce Langen, the American chargé who is ensconced in the Iranian Foreign Ministry — in fact, has been sleeping over there, afraid to go outside. They've been talking to the press, to relatives of Americans in Iran who are wondering if they are all right. There's always about ten people over there and constant activity.

EDWARDS: So the administration is putting all its hopes in the Ramsey Clark mission?

ENSOR: Well, President Carter met twice yesterday with his National Security Council. And they sent out word that they have no thought of any kind of military reaction. And stressed that they expect the Iranian government to guarantee the safety of Americans and secure their release unharmed. However, they have been talking to third-country diplomats, including some from Muslim countries. Possibly they've been asking them to intercede as well.

Morning Edition, NOVEMBER 8

JUDD: The situation in Iran might now be described as a stalemate. American negotiators still haven't been allowed in the country. PLO negotiators say they want a specific invitation from the United States before they try to get help for the ninety hostages in the American Embassy. That could pose a problem for the U.S., since it has a policy of not dealing directly with the Palestine Liberation Organization. NPR's David Ensor has more on the state of negotiations.

ENSOR: State Department officials say the president's two-man mission is still in Istanbul, Turkey, waiting and hoping for permission to enter Iran and talk to authorities there. A spokesman said, "We've been able to keep in pretty good contact with the Iranian people in charge, we just don't have permission yet." He said, "The administration remains hopeful its special representatives, Ramsey Clark and William Miller, will be allowed to proceed."

The spokesman said that as for the people in the embassy, the American hostages, the State Department is still being told at the Iranian Foreign Ministry that they are well. However, there are now reports of physical and serious psychological abuse. A U.S. official said late yesterday that the hostages have apparently been pushed around, abused, intimidated, and mishandled.

✦ ✦ ✦ ✦ ✦ ✦ ✦ ✦ ✦

In the very early days of *Morning Edition*, Bob Edwards had a partner on the air. Barbara Hoctor left after a few months, but she helped us get under way with the new program. In this interview she talks to Dr. Fredrick Hacker, an expert on terrorism, about the difficult new problem of this kind of hostage taking.

Morning Edition, NOVEMBER 8

HACKER: The hostage taking that we have been concerned with recently was usually a band of people that were not particularly authorized, although they have been often in contact with sovereign countries. But here, a sovereign country, with the apparent approval of the highest authorities, commits an act of hostage taking that is almost an act of war, although this war has not been declared. The great difference is that here a whole country seems to totally approve of it, even officially.

HOCTOR: What is the motivating factor? Is it religious fervor?

HACKER: Well, apparently, it is this extreme fanaticism which has still not found enough attention because it really suspends all the civilized rules of dealing between not only people, but also between nations, and that creates an entirely new situation. I mean, even in times of war, it has been generally accepted that the representatives of a foreign country are safe and sacrosanct and are permitted to exit and whatnot. Now, here all that seems to be ignored and all the rules are suspended in the name of God.

HOCTOR: How can you deal with this situation?

HACKER: Well, you know, the fact that one side is in our opinion at least completely irrational and out of bounds does not say that the other side has to respond equally irrationally. We have to at least try to do some negotiating and then get a coalition of people that need not necessarily be law-abiding, but at least will agree to a minimal standard of conduct that makes international relations possible.

✦ ✦ ✦ ✦ ✦ ✦ ✦ ✦ ✦ ✦

One of the hostages being held at the American Embassy in Tehran was Michael Moeller, in charge of the marine guard at the embassy. Bob Covington, one of the producers on *Morning Edition*, called Moeller's wife, Anne, in Caruthersville, Missouri.

Morning Edition, NOVEMBER 8

MOELLER: It's now getting to the point that in a lot of ways I'm just — a lot of my emotions have just been cut off because I . . . I feel like I'm in limbo. I don't know what's going on really. It just gets to the point that you don't know where you are or what you're doing really and you just try to function in your day-to-day life as well as you can.

COVINGTON: Do you understand why this is happening?

MOELLER: Basically, yeah, I think so. It makes a little more sense, not much, but a little more sense if you understand the Muslims. Now, I'm no theological expert, not by any stretch, but I did live in Pakistan, which is another Muslim state, for two years. There's a great deal of national pride. They told us unequivocally they did not want us to accept the shah in this country. And when we took the shah in, even for medical reasons, it sent them off the deep end and it pushed them to very strong measures.

COVINGTON: Do you think President Carter and the administration have responded properly to this crisis?

MOELLER: That's hard to say because this whole situation has to go by a different set of rules. It's just not covered in the books.

✦ ✦ ✦ ✦ ✦ ✦ ✦ ✦ ✦ ✦

From time to time, Susan Stamberg would solve one of "life's little mysteries" with the aid of the mysterious Mr. Dumont. He spoke with a faintly Viennese accent, and in some ways reminded me of our London correspondent, Robert Siegel. I can say no more.

All Things Considered, NOVEMBER 16

STAMBERG: Hello, Mr. Dumont, can you tell us why there is no channel 1 on television sets?

DUMONT: Well, the frequency that would convey the video portion of a channel 1 is perilously close to the frequency of these synaptic impulses of the human brain. If television stations were permitted to use that frequency, human thought would be at the mercy of the television stations. Biophysical neurologists believe that freak variations in TV transmission account for many cases of mass delusion — for example, sightings of unidentified flying objects.

In order to prove that theory, you'd have to match up transmission lines of television stations with prevailing weather conditions and with all UFO sightings. It's a very, very arduous task and one that scientists are only beginning to undertake.

It has been proven though that a Detroit television station straying off frequency on April 15, 1964, is what caused residents in a two-block area in Windsor, Ontario, to file U.S. income tax forms instead of Canadian.

STAMBERG: Thank you, Mr. Dumont, That was Mr. Dumont, solving one of life's little mysteries.

✦ ✦ ✦ ✦ ✦ ✦ ✦ ✦ ✦

Our first science correspondent was Ira Flatow, who went on to a public television program called *Newton's Apple* and then back to us for a weekly science call-in program. Ira flew over the South Pole fifty years after Richard Byrd and then spent time at the international research facility at the South Pole weather station, built on a sheet of ice two miles thick, on the highest mountain range in Antarctica. There he spoke to glaciologist Dick Cameron, and took a walk with a geologist, Bruce Gaylord. The men are panting at that high altitude, crunching through the snow at forty-six degrees below zero.

All Things Considered, DECEMBER 19

FLATOW: This is absolutely amazing out here. You can't see anything as far as the eye can see around, except blue sky and white snow.
GAYLORD: Scott called it quite well when he finally got here back in 1911. He said, "My God, what an awful spot." And it is! But it's also pristine beauty. The whiteness is fantastic.
FLATOW: And the sun just hangs right overhead.
GAYLORD: It just circles around over the top of you. If you don't know what time of the day it is, you lose track of it, you become an insomniac.
FLATOW: It doesn't set in the west and it doesn't rise in the east.

GAYLORD: No, it just circles right overhead, gradually getting higher and higher until December 21, when she'll start her decline again.

FLATOW: And it's so clear out here, absolutely crystal clear.

GAYLORD: This is the best day we've had since we've been here two weeks.

FLATOW: Yeah. And the horizon is deceptive, I mean, since there's nothing to compare it to, no buildings on the horizon. How far away are we looking? The earth just goes. I can see how you think you're falling off the earth just looking straight out.

GAYLORD: OK, over here is the old Pole Station. You can see the antennas. That's about three-quarters of a mile away. You can make out the black markers at the end of the runway. That's a good mile, mile and a quarter. Other than that, you have no reference, no reference at all.

FLATOW: The gloves make it so hard to touch anything. You're just tempted to take — "Oh, I'll take my gloves off for a few minutes and fool around with the zipper or the parka or whatever." You can't do that because we've been out here maybe three minutes and already you can feel the cold coming right through the glove!

GAYLORD: If you don't have any moisture on your hands, you can get away with it, but you got any dampness there, you're going to stick to it. Bitter lessons people learn are: Don't put nails in your mouth if you're a carpenter. Don't drink a can of soda out here, it'll freeze to your lips. That happened to one of the guys last year.

FLATOW: And here's something new. I put my reporter's steno pad in my mouth, getting off the plane. Stuck to my lips!

GAYLORD: We're standing on eighty-five hundred feet of ice. Doesn't snow, just blows. This is one nice thing about the South Pole. The wind is always out of the north.

FLATOW: OK, better go in. Dick Cameron is the station's scientific leader, a glaciologist who studies the layers of ice that lock thousands of years of history at the pole.

CAMERON: During the National Geophysical Year, when we were trying to find out something about this vast continent, the United States established a series of seven stations around the continent, the South Pole station being one of the more important ones in that no one had ever wintered at the South Pole and we didn't know anything about how low the temperature is and we didn't know how thick the ice was and so forth. When we established the base in January of 1957, we felt that the research coming out of here was important enough to maintain a presence both for science and for the United States.

FLATOW: The U.S. has a research facility here, says Cameron, because the pole is the best place for special kinds of investigations, such as solar astronomy, taking pictures of the sun.

CAMERON: You can, during the summertime, watch the sun for a full twenty-four hours, and it's the darkest part of the continent during the winter. I mean, for six months the sun is below the horizon. So we can also do good auroral studies too.

And although the United States maintains the station, we usually have many cooperative programs with other countries. For instance, we've had Russian exchange scientists stay here. We've had Norwegians here and we've had Argentines and French and so forth. We always have many other nations that belong to the Antarctic treaty involved in research here at the pole.

FLATOW: Some researchers are studying the polar snowfall, a mere half inch a year, to determine the climatic history. Others are capturing polar air and sending it back to labs in the United States. The air is reputed to be cleanest in the world and scientists are using the pristine gas to detect pollution coming from the other side of the world.

Some of the research must go on in the dark of the polar winter, six months without sunlight. Researchers and support staff, seventeen of them, must stay here with the experiments, wintering in the dark and the cold, cut off from the rest of the world. The isolation of such an experience takes a toll on those involved.

CAMERON: You really don't know a person until you've spent some time with them on the ice. It's very different. Most of the people that come down nowadays are rather young people and they are rather keyed up and they're excited about the whole thing. But with time, during the winter, certain idiosyncracies of each person come out and that might bother you a little bit. So I think that wintering over is still quite a job.

FLATOW: What happens to them, what kind of traits are you talking about?

CAMERON: They get very irritable and become very aggressive, or other persons just will retreat and sleep a lot, and some people, of course, take up a little drinking too.

FLATOW: Has there ever been a case where you had to take somebody out because they just couldn't — it was going too far over the deep end here?

CAMERON: I think at the pole station, you see, we can't do that. After the first two weeks in February, this station is closed until the beginning of November, so if there is a problem at the South Pole station, that's it, you know. The temperature in the middle of the winter gets down minus one hundred degrees and we don't have any planes on the continent anymore after that, after the end of February. We probably could evacuate someone from here, you know, around the first of March, but after that, it would be too late.

FLATOW: So when you're here, you're here for good.

CAMERON: That's it. That's what the South Pole is all about.

FLATOW: [*Outdoors.*] Finally, the thing that people come to see most, of course, is really *the* South Pole. What does it look like? Does it look like the barbershop pole we think of? Does it look like something else? Everyone wants to go to the exact location of the pole. Well, where is that exact location? It's out here. It's a long walk from where the hut is, a few hundred yards. It's a good question because unless you know where to look, you could be misled.

You see, over here where I'm standing now is the familiar barber-pole with a silver round reflective bowl on top. It's like a globe on it. It's surrounded by all the flags of the treaty countries. It's used mostly for ceremonies and commemorative occasions.

But the real South Pole is a few hundred yards away, there are no fancy markings on it, no gimmicks, nothing to give it away as the South Pole. Just a twenty-foot-or-so wooden stick with green and red flags at the top. In fact, there are markings around the bottom of it. And you can walk 360 degrees, like this, walk around in a circle, and claim that just by circling the pole, you have walked totally around the world.

1980

✦ ✦ ✦ ✦ ✦ ✦ ✦ ✦ ✦

Jay Kernis, who led the team that created *Morning Edition*, occasionally conducted interviews for the show. Generally he spoke to people who could not manage Bob Edwards's schedule, but sometimes it
was Jay Kernis who scheduled those interviews. Jay spoke to Lauren
Bacall when she was promoting her first autobiography, *By Myself*,
illustrating the interview with music from the Broadway play *Applause*
and scenes from films with her late husband, Humphrey Bogart. Jay
asked Miss Bacall to light a cigarette because, he said, he wanted to hear
her do it. "You're contributing to my *demise*," she said, and laughed,
just like in the movies.

Morning Edition, FEBRUARY 18

KERNIS: I just saw *To Have and Have Not* and *The Big Sleep* again.
There's a lot of cigarette stuff going on in those movies.

BACALL: Well, Bogey, of course, he was not a chain smoker, but he was
an incessant smoker. You see, unhappily, now we're into this age of no
smoking, hopefully. But cigarettes definitely play a tremendous role in
male-female relationships, in moments, in scenes. When you light a
cigarette, you use it as a pause or a dramatic effect, when you're
thinking, when someone hands you a cigarette, when a man offers you a
cigarette, then when he leans over and lights it or you lean over. I mean,
there are so many things involved with smoking. A cigarette can become a very intimate thing.

KERNIS: What about Bogart?

BACALL: Bogey happened to fall in love with me. Now, Bogey, without
that, was a very generous actor. And he was, I mean, he did everything
to make it easy for me at the beginning. I mean, before he became
involved with me, to try to relax me he would crack jokes. But I didn't
write those scenes. Those scenes were written and directed and I
cannot honestly say that I — I mean, I played the scenes with Bogey, of

course, because a lot of our personal feeling, I suppose, finally did come into it.

KERNIS: Are we watching you fall in love with Humphrey Bogart when we watch *To Have and Have Not*?

BACALL: I would say probably. Certainly not at the beginning, but by the end of it.

KERNIS: Do you see it?

BACALL: Sometimes I, when I'm flipping the dial, I find that there's an old film on. Because I love to watch old movies. But I really don't like to watch myself. I don't enjoy it.

KERNIS: Why?

BACALL: Well, first of all, there are not that many films that I was in that I was crazy about. And second of all, it's painful to watch yourself! I mean, when you see all the things that you did wrong and that could be improved upon. And I don't look in the mirror a lot, so why? I don't want to look, you know. I know I don't look the way I looked then anyway, so that would be too depressing.

KERNIS: From watching Katharine Hepburn, were you able to discover just how she does it?

BACALL: No. No, I would say not. She's not a trickster, you know, Katie. She's a really good actress. She does it the way professionals should do it. It's the way Bogey did it, it's the way Spencer Tracy did it. It's the way really good, first-rate professional actors do it.

KERNIS: Why do you leave yourself out?

BACALL: Because I really don't think I'm in that category. I may get there, but I don't think I'm there. I'm a professional. I am a professional. But I just don't think I'm that good. But I will be! I'm not through yet! But they, they learn their lines and they know what the part is all about and they think about what they're doing and they do it. And there are no histrionics. There's no pounding of walls, and there's no getting in the mood, and do I feel this, and blah blah blah. There's none of that self-indulgence. They do it.

KERNIS: Do you know how you do it?

BACALL: No, I am lacking in technique. I have none. I cannot do it by the numbers. A lot of pros and a lot of brilliant actors do do it by the numbers. They really know exactly. They figure out what it's related to, what has to happen. I think about it in my head, but I don't really figure it out that carefully. I suppose maybe that's one reason I think I'm better on stage. Because there is the sense of continuity and a sense of growth in a character on stage. And then I grow with it.

I think life's a struggle. I think it's a struggle in work and finding out who you are and what you're all about in relationships. I just think it's tough. And I think that three-quarters of life is a fight for something. I mean, if you have any fight in you at all, and I have a great deal.

✦ ✦ ✦ ✦ ✦ ✦ ✦ ✦ ✦

I n March, Mount Saint Helens began to erupt after many years of dormancy. Eruptions continued in April. Then in May a terrific explosion blew off the top of the mountain and laid down the tall trees in the path of the blast, like strands of hair combed in the same direction. Howard Berkes, who covers the mountain west for NPR, talked to people who had lived near the mountain, in the town of Toutle, Washington. The eruption had blocked a creek and flooded the town, and the people of Toutle were evacuated several times because of smoke and gases and threatened eruptions. Thirty-four people were still missing on the mountain, but the people of Toutle wanted to stay.

Morning Edition, JULY 28

BERKES: Signs announcing ROAD CLOSED greet tourists that come here. They choke this dead end with their cars as they marvel at the mud-swollen river and scoop volcanic ash into paper bags and plastic cups.

Off to the side is a small log house. It, too, has a sign in front. NO PARKING, this one commands. It is a city sign, seeming out of place in front of this rustic country home. Norma Palmer built this house with her late husband more than thirty years ago. They took the logs that form its walls from a nearby stand of fir. Inside, it is a simple home. Pictures of children and grandchildren cover the mantel above the red-brick fireplace. More pictures of sons in uniform stand on a television in a far corner. The short, plump, gray-haired matron of this house would be alone here but for the company of her tiny white poodle and spotted Dalmatian and her memories of Mount Saint Helens.

PALMER: Like all the kids said, it looked like a great big ice cream cone sticking up there.

BERKES: Did you used to go up to Spirit Lake often?

PALMER: Yeah, we went up there, well, practically every summer. We'd go up there and pick huckleberries, black huckleberries.

BERKES: Is that even there anymore, do you know?

PALMER: I don't think so, because all of that's gone. That was the side, you know, where the Trumans' lodge was, where the road went up there and it just slid right down the mountain there and just took it all away. And here comes John.

BERKES: Johnny Palmer is thirty-two years old. He wears a rectangular hat identifying him as a veteran of a foreign war. He says dealing with the volcano is like dealing with war.

JOHNNY: I just go on off to sleep. I figure when it's my time to go, then I'll go. If I get buried, I get buried. I ain't afraid of dying. I spent two years in Vietnam and if I was afraid of dying, I wouldn't have went there. I volunteered both times. It's just part of nature. There's people that live in the other places, back in the South, that have hurricanes all the time and it's the same way. It blows things to pieces, but they still live there. There's people that live in countries have earthquakes all the time. It's something you get used to. We're getting used to it.

BERKES: What I hear just about everybody saying is there is a way to live with the mountain.

JOHNNY: Oh, yes, there's a way. You just take it as it is and pay attention. You can get out. As long as you don't defy it and try going right up on the mountain.

BERKES: Do you think the people around here are changing?

JOHNNY: Yeah. People are getting closer together, helping one another and people that lost their stuff and everything and need food, people help them with that, plant gardens, give each other vegetables.

BERKES: It is that willingness to share, to pull together, that gives Toutle its sense of community, and it is that sense of community that brought neighbor Ken Blackburn to Toutle a few months ago. Blackburn now operates a security patrol and is working with the county sheriff.

BLACKBURN: I don't know what we got here, probably some loggers working. The chain on a chain saw used to last, you know, half a day, three-quarters of a day. Now, they're completely wore out in about twenty minutes. And I mean, it's just shot, there's just nothing left of it.

BERKES: Why is that?

BLACKBURN: The ash. The ash just burned them up.

BERKES: I notice you've got a couple of surgical masks hanging from the rear-view mirror.

BLACKBURN: Yeah, you bet. There's oxygen in the trunk, last an hour, and we got it in all the cars that go up. Anybody goes up in the red zone has surgical masks and oxygen and chain saws and axes. And plenty of water in case you bust a radiator. You can run her till it blows. Any way getting out, you know. You can't get out, why, go far as you can, get that oxygen, and run, but that's about all you can do. We run flares, the type you shoot in the air, so if anybody gets caught up or timber blows down or something, why, they can shoot a flare and at least the choppers can find them then. So we're pretty well rigged out.

BERKES: Doing these patrols, doesn't that worry you? Heading into the area that everybody else is heading out of?

BLACKBURN: Yeah, it gives you a kind of a weird feeling. You know where that mountain is all the time. I don't care what direction you're going, when you're working there, you know where it is. The thing is, as long as there's still people up there we're going to go until we can't go any further to get them out. And then turn and run. I thought you might like to talk to these people here. This is Bobby Palmer.

BERKES: Howard Berkes. Nice to meet you. You're worried about flooding maybe after winter?

BOBBY: Yeah, Spirit Lake, you know, if something gave out up there, it would.

BERKES: Are you concerned about that?

BOBBY: No. Not really, we have plenty of forewarning, you know. If they give us fifteen minutes' warning, we could be out of the flood zone. We got all these high hills around us. We can get up and out. Far as taking my place, yeah. That concerns me, but far as our lives, I'm not worried about that. Because we can get out of the way.

BERKES: [*Addressing the children*] What do you think about the volcano?

BOY: I'm scared. I don't want to get out of this world.

BERKES: Is it exciting to have a volcano near your house?

BOY: No, it's stupid.

BERKES: You've had some bad dreams? Can you tell me about one of them?

SECOND BOY: I woke up last night and my dad was fighting somebody on the mountain and my dad fell in the mountain and I woke up screaming and hollering, Daddy, Daddy, Mommy, Mommy, all that.

WOMAN: I'll have dreams where I've left the kids up at my mom's house and they'll be playing out in the yard and the mountain will explode and the lava and everything will land on them and then my mother just says, "Well, I'm sorry, I couldn't get to them in time, there just wasn't any help for 'em." And then I'll go over and pick their bodies up and it's really terrible, it's terrifying.

SECOND WOMAN: You're afraid of it, but not to the point where it's going to push you out of your home. You just live with it.

FIRST WOMAN: I have a whole set of clothes by the bottom of the bed in case I have to jump into it and leave right away. And the same for the kids. We always have a small box of emergency supplies packed and on hand in case we have to get out fast.

✦ ✦ ✦ ✦ ✦ ✦ ✦ ✦ ✦

In 1980, interest in the Ku Klux Klan appeared to be growing, although the actual membership was around ten thousand people. The Klan held a rally in Connecticut that year, on a farm near the town of Scotland. They were met by a violent and hostile demonstration, injuring some members of the KKK. The police were out in force to protect the Klan. Neal Conan covered the events of that day.

All Things Considered, SEPTEMBER 14

DEMONSTRATOR: I'm not intimidated by the Klan. I've never feared the Klan, but I could understand, because the Klan, and particularly this group that's up here with the Grand Gizzard Wilkinson —
CHANTING DEMONSTRATORS: Jobs, yes. Racism, no. KKK has got to go!
SECOND DEMONSTRATOR: If we get our hands on them, we'll kill them. That's what we mean by "Death to the Klan."
CONAN: Counterdemonstrators gathered on Scotland's village green throughout the afternoon. A number of different groups were represented. Ad hoc committees from the University of Connecticut and nearby towns, more organized groups, too, including the Progressive Labor Party and the Committee Against Racism, militant communists who were determined to confront the Klan.

Late in the afternoon, many of the demonstrators set off from the village center to march the mile and a half or so to the dairy farm where the Klan was meeting. They walked along with people who were on their way to the rally. Without the banners it would have been impossible to tell one side from the other. Nearly all were young men with long hair and blue jeans, young women with set faces and heavy shoes. They both walked the same road to the rally and knew that anyone not with them was against them. There were taunts back and forth, nothing more serious until a man with a gun emerged from the side of the road.
THIRD DEMONSTRATOR: Well, I was coming down the road here, and I heard a shot go off, so I looked to my left and I saw somebody in

the yard with a rifle pointed toward the group. So I just took off and ran in the field.

FOURTH DEMONSTRATOR: Let me tell you something. The cops haven't done a thing to stop that guy. The guy in the yard is a Klan member. He took a rifle and fired like that. The Klan is using guns, and the cops aren't touching them.

CONAN: Then there were other incidents, one after the other, along the line of march. A van with Klan sympathizers inside had its windows smashed in. Fights broke out. Those on their way to the rally were heavily outnumbered. At one point the marchers set upon a group of bikers and many of them were beaten, a few seriously enough to need treatment at a hospital.

BIKER: They knocked a guy in the ditch. About five of them jumped on him. They had metal rods. Some had — one had a baseball bat. He started just beating the hell out of him. The guy got up, and one guy kicked him in the face. You know, I couldn't help the guy, it was only me.

CONAN: The incidents became serious enough that the police decided not to let the marchers get closer than shouting distance to the Klan rally. Some of the hundreds of cops moved down the road. The demonstrators moved in front of them, back down to the town.

At the entrance to Rood's Farm, the Klan was screening everyone who wanted to come in. The rally itself was in a pasture about a quarter mile off the road. State police were there, too, ringing the rough, hilly field. A crude speaker's platform was set up with a public address system at one end. At the other was the cross. And nearby hooded Klansmen dipped their torches in kerosene and waited for the dark.

The cross was twenty-five feet high, made of telephone poles wrapped in burlap bags that dripped kerosene on the grass below. Reporters and television crews made up about half the crowd at first, and people there were nervous in the daylight. Besides the press and Klan members, the crowd was largely young. There was a sizable contingent of men with chains and motorcycle boots and studded leather wristbands. A few had vacant expressions. A few were drunken old men. But most looked like college students and factory workers. Several said that they were to join the Knights of the Ku Klux Klan, many others said they came out of curiosity. One woman came from upstate New York.

WOMAN: I've seen them on TV, but I've never seen them close up. And I'd rather see them on TV.

CONAN: You look a little scared.

WOMAN: I'm definitely scared. Not a little, a whole lot.

CONAN: What was it, considering all of that, that brought you out to this field?

WOMAN: Curiosity. I'm not curious anymore. Now I'm just plain scared.

CONAN: As it grew darker, the rally got under way. The Grand Dragon of Pennsylvania made a short speech. A man was named Grand Dragon of Connecticut, and then he introduced Bill Wilkinson of Denhalm Springs, Louisiana, the Imperial Wizard of the Invisible Empire.

WILKINSON: The media will tell you the Klan doesn't have any members. The politicians say they're not strong, they're weak. They're nothing. The people in the state of Connecticut, you know, from all of your officials, they say nobody likes the Klan. Everybody hates the Klan's guts. So, why do they worry about us holding a rally out in the field if we have no power, if we have no backing, if no one likes us, if everyone hates our guts? Why do they fear us holding these rallies? You are the majority.

CONAN: Most of the speech was on familiar right-wing issues: ERA, forced busing, fair housing. "I'm being polite," Wilkinson conceded at one point. Toward the end, he concentrated more on racial issues, told the crowd that white people had to get themselves together.

WILKINSON: Now, if you don't believe there's a race war coming, you just look around you. You see, you remember Miami, rioting and burning, two hundred million dollars' worth of it. And it was only one business that was burned that didn't belong to a white man. What about Tampa, what about Orlando, what about Chattanooga, what about the blackouts in New York? Who is it that's always out there looting and burning and killing and raping? What happens when a cop in the line of duty shoots a nigger? Automatically, automatically the Negroes get on the bandwagon . . .

CONAN: Wilkinson went on to describe atrocities committed against white people in Miami. They had their ears cut off, he said, their tongues cut out. "These Negroes are just savages," he said. He appealed for applications for Klan membership before he led the audience over the field to the cross.

WILKINSON: Y'all move back, please. We got to get a little more distance here. That cross is going to be hot when it gets lit.

MAN: Yeah, really, I know it.

CONAN: Robed and hooded Klansmen stood in a circle. They marched three times around the cross, dipped and raised their torches in uni-

son. On Wilkinson's command, they saluted with their torches three times and then the Imperial Wizard led them to the base of the cross.
CONAN: What did you think of it?
MAN: Hey, it's great and it ought to happen again.
CONAN: Really think so?
MAN: Hey, I don't like niggers.
CONAN: OK, thank you.

As the flame on the cross subsided into a flicker, Bill Wilkinson returned to the speaker's platform to take questions from the audience. The small group of Klansmen, new converts, stood and cheered his remarks, the last of a long series of statements and declarations on this day.

Demonstrators had chanted their positions and left. The Klansmen set fire to their cross and were on their way home now. Everyone else kept their thoughts to themselves, let both extremes go unchallenged.

✦ ✦ ✦ ✦ ✦ ✦ ✦ ✦ ✦ ✦

In 1980, Cokie Roberts and I began a partnership in political coverage. I flew in the presidential campaign planes, listened to the speeches, and reported on what the candidates were trying to do. Cokie followed the campaign on the ground, asking people what they thought was happening. This pair of pieces does just that, our next-day coverage of a debate between President Carter and Governor Ronald Reagan in Cleveland. It was a critical moment for the campaign, the moment at which it became clear who would win. The day after the debate, I was traveling with Reagan in Texas.

All Things Considered, OCTOBER 29

WERTHEIMER: In Houston, with Roy Rogers and Dale Evans on hand for the occasion, the governor of Texas, William Clements, reflected the optimism of the Reagan campaign on this day after the debate.
CLEMENTS: What you are here for is to hear from the next president of the United States! We have a winner! We have a winner! We are winning this race! We will carry Texas for Governor Reagan and Ambassador Bush!
WERTHEIMER: In addition to polls related to the debate, the Reagan campaign is getting some indication that their appeal to blue-collar voters is working. But Governor Reagan is running a little bit ahead of

where winning Republicans have run in several states. Partly for that reason, several of the last days of the campaign will be spent in Pennsylvania and in the Great Lakes industrial states, including Michigan, for a series of rallies with former President Ford and Republican Governor William Milliken.

Governor Reagan's aides feel he did very well last night. The governor went into the debate intent on hitting President Carter on the economic issues. He did that, they say. But they acknowledge he spent quite a bit of time talking about the issues President Carter has tried to raise about Governor Reagan — questions of war and peace, of confidence in Governor Reagan's capacity to handle delicate issues of foreign affairs, of confidence in his judgment. Making a virtue of necessity, the governor said he was satisfied with the way the debate turned out.

REAGAN: Well, I feel very good today. And I welcomed the opportunity to at last, face to face, be able to refute some of the charges, accusations, and false statements that have been made about me in this campaign. And also, in company with the president, to be able to face him with what I think is the issue in this campaign, and that is the failure of his administration to deal with the economic and the foreign problems.

WERTHEIMER: About being on the defensive through much of the debate, Governor Reagan said President Carter would not be challenged on his own record. He denied that defensiveness hurt.

REAGAN: He refused to defend his record, and the statements I made about it were accurate, and he couldn't defend it so he just changed the subject.

WERTHEIMER: Despite his dancing to President Carter's tune for much of the debate, Governor Reagan's aides believe he clearly did the most important thing he had to do on Tuesday night — persuade the American people that he is a thoughtful man, capable of doing the job of president. And more, that he is a likable and sympathetic person, and not a harsh and doctrinaire radical.

✦ ✦ ✦ ✦ ✦ ✦ ✦ ✦ ✦ ✦

Cokie was in Pittsburgh the day after the debate, at a mall in a blue-collar neighborhood, to talk to the kind of voters Ronald Reagan needed to win the election. She remembers finding too many Reagan supporters, thinking she might be in the wrong mall. But what she was seeing was that crucial moment in October 1980 when the American people stopped worrying about Ronald Reagan and decided how they would vote.

WOMAN: I changed my mind, in fact. I decided to vote for Reagan. I just thought it was the thing to do, to vote for Carter, but I just can't do it.

ROBERTS: Why not?

WOMAN: I'm proud of the United States, you know? And I haven't been the last few years. I just figured I was going to vote for Carter, and then I read a little on Reagan and thought, Well, maybe. So I made my mind up last night.

ROBERTS: That woman is in the majority today in Pittsburgh's Allegheny Center, a shopping mall where families come to find bargains at Zayre's or Sears, and working mothers jam Woolworth's at noontime, frantically searching for last-minute Halloween costumes. Most of the dozens of people I talked to had seen at least part of last night's debate, and many of them turned off their TVs or radios as confused as when they turned them on.

This young mother normally votes Democratic. As she shepherded her children through Sears, she mulled over this year's choices.

SECOND WOMAN: It's still a shaky thing as far as I'm concerned because I still didn't get any firm answers to a lot of questions that are floating around.

ROBERTS: Was your mind made up before you watched it, about who you'll vote for?

SECOND WOMAN: No, not really. In fact, I'm not even sure I'll vote.

ROBERTS: Do you normally vote?

SECOND WOMAN: Oh, yeah. But this is a hard one. Especially because my husband's a mill worker, and I gotta figure where it's going to go. If he don't have a job, we don't live. So it's a hard decision.

ROBERTS: Many workers are confused this year. They say their unions are pressuring them to go for Carter, but they like Reagan's stand on issues like abortion and family values. Some said they were hoping the debate would help them choose, but they came out of it finding they liked the candidates even less than they did before.

MAN: I know cockfights are outlawed, but I guess it's OK to watch two turkeys battle it out.

SECOND MAN: I was very disappointed in the debate. I didn't think that either of the candidates addressed the questions well, and I didn't get that much out of it. It was the same rhetoric we've been hearing all along. I was very upset.

ROBERTS: Supporters of Jimmy Carter thought that he did well in the debate, that his answers were far more substantial than Ronald Reagan's, though several said they were nervous about how Carter might do, before the debate began.

THIRD WOMAN: I thought it was really good. It was interesting to see the differences between the two of them. There's really a lot of differences. The minimum wage thing got me, you know?

ROBERTS: So that made you feel better about Carter?

THIRD WOMAN: Yeah, than Reagan, yeah.

ROBERTS: Was your mind made up before you watched it?

THIRD WOMAN: Oh, yeah. I voted for Carter four years ago and I'll vote for him again this term.

ROBERTS: Several Carter supporters said the TV polls giving the debate victory to Reagan worried them. And a radio news station call-in poll here in Pittsburgh shows Reagan winning by two to one. And voter after voter in Allegheny Center agreed.

FOURTH WOMAN: Ronald Reagan was absolutely super. I was undecided at the time. But the way he stood up to President Carter and answered his questions and showed that he does have the intelligence and the ability to do it, he definitely sold me on the debate. You hear a lot of things, and you don't really know them, you read them in the paper. But when you see it on TV, it really changed my mind.

FIFTH WOMAN: Oh, I was undecided really until last night. I thought that he put on a better show, really. He had it more in command. I thought so, I don't know. It just seemed like Reagan did two-thirds of the talking.

ROBERTS: Were you frightened of him before last night?

FIFTH WOMAN: Yeah, I thought maybe he was a warmonger.

ROBERTS: And your fears were put to rest last night?

FIFTH WOMAN: Yeah, I don't think he is. I think it's just talk.

ROBERTS: So will you vote for him, as a result of the debate?

FIFTH WOMAN: I think so. Yes.

ROBERTS: Ronald Reagan just didn't seem scary to these people after an hour and a half on TV. And they figure that a man who can stand on the stage and take on a president can be president.

✦ ✦ ✦ ✦ ✦ ✦ ✦ ✦ ✦

H ere's a meditation on the limitations of politics from the sports-writer Frank Deford.

Morning Edition, OCTOBER 29

DEFORD: This is, of course, the high political season. This time has always had some association with sports. It is an old axiom, for example, that the country will pay no attention to the presidential election until after the conclusion of the World Series. Certainly that is true this year, if only technically so. This year, it seems, America will not pay any attention to the presidential election until after the presidential election is over.

Oh well. But certainly sports is in tune with the political times. It has gone unnoticed that the World Series was started and ended at Veterans Stadium in Philadelphia. And that the Phillies are now world champions, representing the district of a congressman who was just convicted of a felony. There's something real and warm about that. Only in America.

And politicians continue to intrude on sports. Predictably, the mayors of Kansas City and Philadelphia and two of the senators concerned, Heinz of Pennsylvania and Dole of Kansas, made those ridiculous wagers, betting indigenous local produce, in this case twenty-five pounds of beef versus twenty-five pounds of soft Philadelphia pretzels. God save us all. I would suggest that Senator Bill Bradley and Congressman Jack Kemp join together to produce a bipartisan bill banning all elected officials from offending us with this shopworn tomfoolery.

Surely you noticed that not a single politician was invited to throw out the first ball during the World Series. Of course there is no sense in belaboring here the oft-spoken fact that we don't trust our political leaders anymore. Not that we think they're dishonest, though that may be some of it, but we simply don't trust their ability to do anything. So far as I can see, the single thing that most Americans believe the president can still do is push a button and blow up the world. That's it. If I could cut off my fingers tomorrow and hence render myself non corpus buttonus, I could win the presidency in a landslide!

It is, I think, this sad disillusionment with higher governmental authority that has made coaches and managers so much more esteemed nowadays. The truism that Bear Bryant could become governor of Alabama is, for example, usually taken to mean that he is extremely popular there. But that is only the half of it. There is the feeling that Bear Bryant and coaches like him are the last bosses left who can actually control anything. The fascination with the feisty Earl Weaver is the most visible evidence of Harry S. Trumanism. Weaver is the heir to Truman that Carter tries to be. Reagan invokes Roosevelt, but who wears that mantle? Well, someone like Dallas Green does. He took a dispirited band of losers and turned them around, and never mind that a lot of people hated him for his excesses. And where in Washington is our Ike? Peace and prosperity, stability, a sense of order? Well, there is no one there. But you may find an Eisenhower in Pittsburgh in Chuck Noll of the Steelers.

Probably the more complicated the world becomes — and especially the more difficult it becomes for leaders to master it — or anyway, as that perception heightens, the more do the men who run things on the green fields grow in our stature. We impart to them the respect and admiration we once gave to our presidents. And more dangerous, perhaps, we compare our leaders to them, unfavorably. We do not seem to be looking for a president so much as we are for a head coach.

✦ ✦ ✦ ✦ ✦ ✦ ✦ ✦ ✦

John Lennon was murdered in December by a young man named Mark David Chapman. Chapman waited for Lennon and his wife, Yoko Ono, outside their apartment building just west of Central Park in New York City. When they came out, he asked for an autograph. When they returned, several hours later, Chapman shot John Lennon four times. Chapman then waited for the police. We did a series of reports, threaded with Beatles music, on the murder, the vigil outside the apartment building, and reactions around the country. Neal Conan wrote the script, which Sanford Ungar and I read. It includes an interview with the music writer Griel Marcus.

All Things Considered, DECEMBER 9

WERTHEIMER: I heard the news today, this morning, early on the radio. For some, there it was on the newspaper's front page. A few didn't read the paper or watch television, but noticed — noticed something — the way people looked on the way to work. A young girl at a coffee shop reading a paper over someone's shoulder said, "Oh, is that just New York?" What she really wanted to know: Did they mean to kill John Lennon?

We don't know where he'll be in history. Some have said that the classical music of future centuries will be today's rock and roll. But we do know the John Lennon of our times and the songs that are in our minds.

In the literature, he's listed as John Ono Lennon, formerly John Winston Lennon, born in Liverpool, England, in 1940. His first musical group, the Quarrymen, 1955. There were some other now forgotten groups, then the Beatles, 1960, and soon the Beatles changed the world.

MARCUS: I, you know, went down from my college dorm to the commons room, where there's a television to watch. I was mainly curious because I didn't even know they had rock and roll in England. And I figured when I got down there that there would be the usual argument with whoever was there over what to watch. And I walked into this room and there were four hundred people waiting to see the Beatles. And I didn't understand it. I didn't know where they'd all come from, why suddenly this crowd had formed.

And so they performed, and it was this bizarre religious experience. Everybody left the room chattering and excited, and I was chattering and excited, too, but I couldn't understand where all this had come from. It was like the world was starting over again. It was just amazing.

UNGAR: Writer Greil Marcus remembers that everyone had a favorite Beatle. The original litany went like this: Paul, the cute one; George, the quiet one; Ringo, the funny one; and John, the smart one. Smart and complex.

MARCUS: In a context of lightness, celebration, joyfulness, pleasure, which, John, you know, certainly communicated, John put an edge of struggle, of doubt, brooding, questioning, nervousness, all the sorts of qualities that one wasn't used to hearing in pop music, one wasn't used to hearing coming over the radio.

And it was really clear right from the beginning, and by the beginning I think I mean like two days after the *Ed Sullivan Show*, that there was someone in this group who was smart, who was self-conscious, who was nervy, who had an astonishingly mocking and sarcastic sense of humor, who was in one way just kidding and in another way not kidding at all.

People consciously and not consciously began to take the Beatles as a kind of metaphor for their own lives, not just their own personal lives, but the common lives they shared with other people, whether it was socially, politically, sexually, whatever.

And that became a very natural way to live one's life with this point of focus, which was the Beatles, and it was really a marvelously lucky thing to be able to do to play your life off against a symbol that was at the same time four real people who had a great sense of humor, who continually surprised you with their music. And surprise may be the crucial word, that for, I suppose, five or six years one lived in a culture of surprise, and that opened you up to any number of new possibilities that you might not have responded to otherwise.

WERTHEIMER: And around the country today, people remembered how they responded to the Beatles and John Lennon.

MAN: He first of all was an artist. He felt very strongly and very toughly about the condition of the world. But he always found a positive way to express what he had to say.

WOMAN: The fact that he had actively taken the role as a house husband, and proclaimed himself as such, kind of was an example to both men and women in this country.

SECOND WOMAN: I feel like a friend of mine has died.

SECOND MAN: He was everything that anybody was when I was a kid.

SECOND WOMAN: Just makes you think what kind of a world do we live in.

THIRD WOMAN: He was more than just, you know, a rock and roll star. To my knowledge, he's never told a lie and he always speaks the truth.

✦ ✦ ✦ ✦ ✦ ✦ ✦ ✦ ✦

A few days after his death, Lennon's widow, Yoko Ono, requested that his fans around the world observe ten minutes of silence in his memory. Vertamae Grosvenor was in New York City, but not because of John Lennon.

All Things Considered, DECEMBER 15

GROSVENOR: I believe in magic, and yesterday in an Upper West Side bistro, I saw it happen. Because my sixties was sit-ins, not love-ins, because it was not Monkees and Beatles, but Panthers and Young Lords, because my song was "We Shall Overcome," not "I Want to Hold Your Hand," I felt it would be a bit hypocritical for me to go to Central Park and light a candle for John Lennon. But because I believe that John Lennon was a righteous brother, I wanted to do something. So I met with several of my friends for brunch about one-thirty. Nobody announced two o'clock, but when it came, we knew.

A remarkable thing happened. The café became absolutely silent. The café became magic, and magic was the café for ten minutes. The magic transcended generations and color and culture and politics. Former flower children, ex–black militants, old longhaired Marxists, young shorthaired ad execs, shallow barflies, deep intellectuals, all came together in grief and fell silent. I swear I heard Aretha singing "Peace Be Still." Some folks actually prayed out loud. Most had their heads bowed. A few had tears. None was embarrassed. I had the feeling that people prayed for John Lennon's soul and their own. I know I did.

In these troubled times, when a pair of shoes cost as much as a month's rent, the cost of a Christmas tree equals a week's groceries, the Klan is on the rise, children are disappearing, men's hearts are being cut out, I prayed for John and me and you. I prayed for change. John is probably alive and well in rock-and-roll heaven, jamming with Otis Redding and Jimi Hendrix. Two P.M. yesterday was truly one of New York's finest hours.

The sixties are over. Let's not lament the loss of innocence and youth. If we can come together in peace and love for ten minutes, let's try to hold on to the feeling a little longer. My grandmama, Sula, used to say, "Prayer changes things." And for ten minutes yesterday, it did.

1981

The day the new president took the oath of office was the day the hostages were freed. Almost at the very minute that Ronald Reagan became president, Algerian planes carried the Americans out of Iran, headed for air bases in Germany. President Carter's negotiations with Iran, his agreement to release Iranian funds frozen in this country, came far too late for his reelection hopes but helped begin his opponent's term on a triumphant note. During the course of the fourteen months that Iran held the hostages, we spoke frequently with Dorothea Morefield, whose husband Richard was one of the hostages.

Months later, Susan Stamberg spoke with Richard Morefield. He is a foreign service officer, consul general at the embassy in Iran when the hostages were taken. Stamberg wanted to know about the Morefield family's stoicism, at their private and public diplomacy. Their conversation was broadcast in October, but we include it here.

All Things Considered, OCTOBER 6

STAMBERG: There has to be some residue of anger or rage. I mean, what struck me so much in talking to your wife over those 444 days was how reasonable she was always and how rational and how thoughtful in always saying that the government is right in not acting precipitously. We must wait it out, we must see what happens. You've said the same sorts of things since you're home. But where does the fury go? Where is that, the resentment?

MOREFIELD: I am a private person, and it's very difficult to show emotion publicly, if you will. And more than that, I think it's counterproductive.

STAMBERG: Why? What greater good is served by keeping it to yourself?

MOREFIELD: You have to realize that the bottom line in this was the U.S. national interest. Yes, it was very important to my family and to my wife, but the bottom interest was the U.S. government. Not the government, the American people. The U.S. society. And because we are an important country, that had implications for the rest of the world as well. We had to act responsibly as a people because only the small third-rate power has the right, the ability, to act irresponsibly.

STAMBERG: What have we gained from your experience of 444 days?

MOREFIELD: I think an understanding that we're far stronger morally and emotionally than people gave us credit for, that, in effect, we could go through this very difficult period and come out, I think, with not only the honor of the country, but the honor of the American people. It's a strange thing that the American people kept their cool.

STAMBERG: And they did. There's an enormous price to pay for that.

MOREFIELD: What? You mean that I was there? But I was there to represent the American government, the American people. I knew it was a dangerous assignment. I certainly didn't expect to go through what I did, but certainly, most of us, at one time or another, have had to worry about our personal safety abroad. We've lost five ambassadors in the last ten years, not because they were disliked personally but because they were there to represent a U.S. policy that unfortunately was unpopular in that particular area. And those are the sort of things that you balance.

✦ ✦ ✦ ✦ ✦ ✦ ✦ ✦ ✦

The inauguration of Ronald Reagan brought a change to the nation's capital. As Bob Edwards observed that day, there were more limousines and minks in evidence than had been the case four years earlier. Brenda Wilson covered an inaugural event, a reception honoring Mrs. Reagan.

Morning Edition, JANUARY 20

ANNOUNCER: Dear ladies, welcome Nancy Reagan.

WILSON: The soon-to-be First Lady Nancy Reagan was introduced to Washington yesterday at the Inaugural Committee's distinguished ladies reception at the Kennedy Center. Some six thousand were expected to attend, the wives of Republican congressmen and officials filled the center's theaters to capacity. Sprinkled here and there were a few men and a few blacks. The poor, if they attended, were in disguise. There was a noticeably tan delegation from the Sun Belt.

While Nancy Reagan and Barbara Bush made the rounds of the theaters, waiting audiences were entertained by mimes, comics, singers, and musicians. And if that wasn't enough, you went looking for celebrities, faces and names both familiar and unfamiliar to most Americans. Outside, it was bumper-to-bumper limousines. Inside . . .

BARRY: I'm Patricia Barry. I'm an actress. I was Ronnie's last leading lady in the *General Electric Theater*. And I'm working in New York now on a show called *All My Children* on ABC, and I came up for the inaugural. And they wrote me out so I could come and be here, and I'm just thrilled. And this is my mother-in-law, Mrs. Philip Barry.

WILSON: All right, so how do you both feel?

MRS. PHILIP BARRY: I think it's a lovely celebration. We're all having a wonderful time.

WILSON: So how do you think it will feel to have the Republicans in Washington? How do you think it's going to change the mood of the city?

MRS. PHILIP BARRY: I think it's already changed the mood of the city. You can tell by looking around.

PATRICIA: We had a very exciting lunch that Earl Blackwell and Eugenia Sheppard gave at the Jockey Club yesterday. And Senator Percy is a neighbor of Ellen's, and I was privileged to go with him over to the Warners', John and Elizabeth Taylor Warner, to a wonderful party.

All of these ladies, and one of them just turned to Ellen and said, "You're such a beautiful woman." [*Laughs.*] When you get these many ladies in a place and everybody's saying, "Gee, you're pretty," it's very nice.

UNIDENTIFIED WOMAN: There are more celebrities that are in town, and people seem to — there's more excitement, people are more excited. Before, everything was very blah.

SECOND WOMAN: I am glad to see some formality and some clothes and some dignity. With all the fur coats around, how do you know who's who? I mean, everybody's pulled them out of the closet and the mothballs. And I've never seen, I mean really, in a long time, I have never seen so many fur coats.

✦ ✦ ✦ ✦ ✦ ✦ ✦ ✦ ✦ ✦

P resident Reagan's inaugural, his stirring speech mixed with coverage of the hostage release, seemed to many to introduce a new era of American confidence and strength. The next morning, commentator Rod Macleish rearranged the symbols a bit.

Morning Edition, JANUARY 21

MACLEISH: Inaugurations of American presidents have taken place indoors, outdoors, in freezing rain, during wars, and once, under a cloud of scandalized suspicion that the vice president was drunk. But never has contrapuntal symbolism so attended the inauguration of a president as yesterday.

A half hour or so before Ronald Reagan assumed the prerogatives that stand for American power, a planeload of American hostages took off from Tehran, their torment and the confusion of American indignations over at last. Meaning sometimes works the crowd of history before events. If the whole hostage drama says something to us, aside from its human poignancy, that something has to do with the limits imposed on the use of power, especially military power.

Even as President Reagan was warning the shadowed side of the world, where enmity toward America burns, that we will never surrender to win peace, the hostages were rising into a Middle Eastern dusk, 444 days after they were grabbed. And 444 days later, in the long American attempt to use its power to get them free, in the end, bargaining did it.

Already, amid the jubilation of their return, angry clamors are heard here and there, saying that Jimmy Carter should not have bargained. By God, Ronald Reagan would never have done it. The comparison is preposterous. The uses of power have no more to do with the personalities and predilections of presidents than they do with tapioca. Undoubtedly, had the hostage crisis happened on Mr. Reagan's watch, to use Warren Christopher's phrase, the scenario would have been rearranged. The rhetoric might have been hotter in Washington, the rescue attempt perhaps tried earlier.

But Mr. Reagan would have been and will be imprisoned by the same realities as Mr. Carter. There was no way to nuke somebody and set the hostages free. The obdurate fanaticism of Iran's triumphant faction ruled out reasoning for their release. In the end, Mr. Reagan would have bargained too, giving back to Iran that which he had taken from it in return for that which it had taken from us.

The only question about new presidents is how long it will take them to learn what seasoned and somewhat disillusioned presidents know about the limitations on the use of power. In the shadow of that question, the Reagan years begin. And it's a mercy that the new president did not have to start his tutelage with the hostage crisis.

✦ ✦ ✦ ✦ ✦ ✦ ✦ ✦ ✦

R obert Krulwich covered business and the economy for us for a number of years, taking it on to see if he could imagine some new way to do it on the radio. With certain notable exceptions, like this book, radio can't be read. He couldn't use graphs or charts to help communicate complex ideas. What radio required, as Krulwich indelicately put it, was economics for the dummy. Squeaking mice replaced graphs, arias illustrated interest rates, and Krulwich suckered us in to subjects we'd probably skip on a newspaper page. Sadly for us, he's now moved on to the more lucrative, less flexible medium of television, but we like to think that in his time at NPR he made some of his best attempts to explain how money works. Here is a demonstration of good, old-fashioned American initiative, so celebrated in the eighties.

All Things Considered, MARCH 24

KRULWICH: Gladys Turnabin lives on Long Island. She is a very nice lady, except when it comes to grocers.

TURNABIN: I'm bad, I'm bad.

KRULWICH: To show you how bad she is, I should say first that she runs a coupon club. It has fifty members. They meet and compare notes and trade cents-off coupons for food and soap products. I'm sure you've seen these coupons.

TURNABIN: Here. This is a cash-off coupon. This says twenty-five cents off on turkey, on a Swift Premium turkey roast.

KRULWICH: Now normally, when you present such a coupon to a grocer, he will reduce the price of the turkey by twenty-five cents and take the coupon. But every so often, to bring in new customers and to please regular customers, a grocer will say that for a limited time only, I'm going to double the value of all coupons. That's called doubling.

TURNABIN: If the store is doubling, which we love, you get fifty cents. If it is tripling, which very rarely happens . . .

KRULWICH: But when it does — the idea of getting three times the value for your hundreds of coupons — wherever that grocer is, Gladys and her club will find him and pounce. Just the other month, there was this grocer in Queens, for example.

TURNABIN: His name was Bob Sugar, and the name of his store is Sea Town.

SUGAR: This is a small store, and I want to give this extra benefit to my regular customers.

KRULWICH: Mr. Sugar learned that a large grocery chain was about to build a store in his neighborhood, so he decided to triple for eight weekends as a gesture to his customers. The word, however, got to Gladys Turnabin and she was very happy.

TURNABIN: Eight Saturdays in a row. Unbelievable.

KRULWICH: Gladys told her fellow club member Gertie Katz, and Katz told her friends, and on that first Saturday, a small group was waiting outside the store just before it opened.

TURNABIN: Everybody from the club, everybody were there. Eight o'clock in the morning.

KATZ: About fifty people.

TURNABIN: Most of us came with our husbands to help us.

KATZ: And we have a lady from the Bronx that came down with an entourage.

KRULWICH: So this poor grocer, the door opens at eight o'clock, and there's the ladies from the Bronx and the ladies from —

TURNABIN: Long Island. We were a mob scene.

KRULWICH: You did this repeatedly? Saturday after —

KATZ: Every Saturday, yes. We set the alarm, we got up early, we went shopping.

SUGAR: That was a disaster for us. When ninety percent of your business is all triple coupons, that's a tremendous loss.

KRULWICH: But on the other hand, that's in your publicity budget or your marketing budget.

SUGAR: Yeah, but that's a little too extreme.

KRULWICH: According to Bob Sugar, by the final Saturday, every coupon club in greater New York had heard about his store and they all converged. It was the grocer's ultimate nightmare.

SUGAR: I got here about seven, but as my employees were coming in, they were saying that they couldn't park near the store because the whole street was blocked up with all these people waiting outside. And then when I really got worried was, as I said, one minute after I opened the doors, all of the wagons were gone.

KATZ: There was no other way.

TURNABIN: Some of us had two or three shopping carts because we were all loaded.

KATZ: You couldn't move.

TURNABIN: You couldn't move, really.

KATZ: We had the Bronx ladies.

TURNABIN: Oh, the Bronx ladies, the Bronx ladies were out of sight. They came with their children. And each child —

KATZ: Had a wagon.

TURNABIN: Each child watched a wagon, because you couldn't go through the aisles, so each child — she loaded up the wagons and each child stood on the sidelines.

KATZ: Because the women were taking groceries out from each other's wagon if you weren't watching because the shelves were empty already.

SUGAR: You should have seen the store that evening, after this was all over.

TURNABIN: The shelves were completely empty. When his regular customers came in, there was nothing to purchase.

KRULWICH: When grocers offer a promotion, coupons, sales, whatever, they are not allowed to favor regular customers. This is a general offer to the general public. Once made, it cannot be withdrawn. And Gladys Turnabin and her group were just always there first. As a result, Sugar's regular customers were regularly disappointed. Sugar found himself paying premiums to total strangers who cleaned him out of his very best brands.

TURNABIN: Green Giant vegetables, Campbell's soups, Ivory soap.

KRULWICH: And talk about being bad. Gladys Turnabin says there are now coupon clubs in the upstate New York area. When they hear about a triple, they can so terrify a grocer that, with a little bit of blackmail, they get their own private shopping tours.

TURNABIN: Let me tell you what the girls in Poughkeepsie did. The Poughkeepsie girls said that they wanted their club to come down, and they not only cleaned out the guy, but they helped the stores restock their shelves for allowing them to come. 'Cause don't forget, when we come with these big orders, we're holding up their Saturday, their regular people. So really they did him a favor.

KRULWICH: Wait a second, wait a second. The Poughkeepsie people called this man in — where was he?

TURNABIN: Not this man. The Poughkeepsie girls, the Poughkeepsie girls had tripling in their area, like in the Newburgh–Poughkeepsie area. And they called the store manager, and they said, "Look, if we come in there en masse tomorrow, you're going to have backup lines like you never saw." So she said, "Supposing we all come down Friday night and do our shopping and we will help you restock your shelves." Now, I offered —

KRULWICH: Did he say yes?

TURNABIN: He did. And the girls did it.

SUGAR: This store in Poughkeepsie allowed them to do that. I can't afford to do that. Maybe he can afford to do that.

TURNABIN: "Now, Mr. Sugar," I said to him, "would you like us to come down, let us all in . . ." He said, "Gladys," he says —

SUGAR: I am more interested in doing business with my regular customers, and I hope that we alienate the club and they don't come back to the store.

KRULWICH: You do?

SUGAR: Don't tell Gladys that, but — and this is going to be on the radio. Wonderful.

KRULWICH: Bob Sugar needn't worry about offending Gladys Turnabin. She can take it. When it comes to groceries, this woman is a fighter, and, as she says, she is bad.

TURNABIN: I told the man, I said, "You know, Bob," I said, "if you need anything, you can come down to my house and come visit your groceries."

[*Katz and Turnabin laugh.*]

✦ ✦ ✦ ✦ ✦ ✦ ✦ ✦ ✦

President Reagan was shot at the end of March, coming out of the Washington Hilton, where he'd made a speech. He was rushed to the hospital for surgery, greatly reassuring the nation when he joked gallantly to Nancy in the emergency room, "Honey, I forgot to duck." As part of our coverage, David Molpus reported that the young man who shot the president fit the pattern of a loner, obsessed with fantasies about famous people. In John Hinckley's case, it was the eighteen-year-old actress Jodie Foster, to whom he had written love letters.

MOLPUS: While no one will say so officially, it's now possible to theorize that the suspect's motives were not political in nature at all, but rather, the result of a seriously disturbed man overwrought by an unrequited love. It was not the first failure in John Hinckley's life. He had many, even though he was a child of privilege and wealth.

Hinckley is the son of a wealthy independent oil producer. Friends of the family describe his parents as "rock-ribbed Republicans" and "devoutly religious." A long-time acquaintance of John Hinckley, Sr., says, "If ever there was an ideal stable family, they were it." John Hinckley, Jr., grew up in an affluent suburb of Dallas, the kind of place where nearly everyone had maids, back yard swimming pools, and membership in a country club.

Writer Richard West is very familiar with the neighborhood. He grew up there too and graduated from the same high school that Hinckley went to, Highland Park High.

WEST: Well, Highland Park is a bedroom community of Dallas, it's an incorporated city, incorporated in 1913. It's in many ways the embodiment of the American dream. It's a beautiful place to live, very quiet, low crime, high-cost houses. For instance, the two vacant lots that are left in the city would sell for a total now, just the lots, of six hundred thousand dollars. It is a place of upward mobility. It is a place in which ninety-five percent of the kids graduating from Highland Park High School go to college. It's really not a question of will they go, but where. It's a town of intense competitiveness for kids and adults.

MOLPUS: A schoolmate recalls that Hinckley was not regarded as the top ten percent in brains or personality. He did go to college after high school, entering Texas Tech University in Lubbock in 1973, and kept taking courses off and on for the next seven years without ever getting a degree. Nor was he able to hold down a job. When he applied earlier this year for work with two Denver newspapers, he listed only two work references. He'd held neither job longer than four months.

While he had been apolitical in high school, a college professor recalls that Hinckley showed an unusual interest in the Nazi party and in Hitler's book, *Mein Kampf.* Apparently, it was not a mere academic interest. The new head of the American Nazi party, Michael Allen, claims John Hinckley joined the party in 1978, but Allen says Hinckley was kicked out of the organization in 1979 because of his, quote, "uncontrollable attitude."

ALLEN: He kept talking about going out and shooting people and blowing things up.

MOLPUS: What kind of people?

ALLEN: He didn't get specific.

MOLPUS: How did you interpret that?

ALLEN: Well, we have an old saying that's circulated amongst our party: it pays to be paranoid. And when someone comes to us and starts advocating shooting people and blowing things up, we, it's like just a natural reaction. We just make the assumption that the guy is either a nut or a federal agent trying to entrap us.

MOLPUS: The first indication that John Hinckley was prepared to commit armed violence on someone came last October. He was arrested at the Nashville, Tennessee, airport as he attempted to board a plane with three pistols in a briefcase. President Carter had arrived in Nashville two hours earlier that day and was to speak at a town meeting that night. Candidate Ronald Reagan had been scheduled to appear in Nashville two days earlier but canceled the trip. Hinckley was also in town when Reagan was to have appeared.

Hinckley paid a sixty-two-dollar bond but never returned for a court appearance on the gun charges. His guns having been confiscated, Hinckley apparently did not go on to New York as he had planned. Reagan and Carter were to appear in New York a few days later. Instead, Hinckley returned to Dallas, where records show he bought more pistols, twenty-two-caliber ones, the same kind used in the assassination attempt yesterday.

✦ ✦ ✦ ✦ ✦ ✦ ✦ ✦ ✦

Kim Williams was perhaps our most eccentric commentator, in a hot contest for that title. She was not odd, exactly, but she was unexpected. If you'd met her over the back fence in a New York neighborhood, wearing a shapeless sun hat and several other baggy garments, you'd have thought nothing of it, but we met Kim stalking the western range in Montana, hunting for huckleberries, plucking bitter greens, or making a breakfast of cattails. Kim died in 1986, but if you remind long-time listeners about her, they'll recite her name, rambling through the syllables as she did. This is Kim Willie-yums, of Mizoola, Mon-*tee-anna*.

All Things Considered, JUNE 30

WILLIAMS: If you drive by a cattail marsh and you see yellow pollen flying through the air, stop the car and climb out with a plastic sack in your hand. Take hold of the flower spike of the cattail plant and shake that spike carefully over your plastic sack. You will have, in your sack, a yellow powder that looks like talcum powder. That's cattail pollen, and that pollen is the special ingredient in my sunshine flapjacks. You can also call them cattail pollen pancakes.

Maybe you don't think pollen is edible. It is. In fact, you can buy pollen capsules in the drugstore. Pollen is supposed to be a very healthful food. I like the color it adds to the pancakes, both inside and outside, when they brown on the griddle. I like the taste, too. And who knows what magic undiscovered vitamins and minerals might be in that pollen.

Now, if you want to try my sunshine flapjacks, use your favorite pancake recipe and add three tablespoons pollen for each cup of flour. But first, remove three tablespoons of flour from each cup. I almost always use whole-wheat flour in cooking and baking, but for these pancakes, we use unbleached white flour. The delicate color and flavor of the pollen shows up better with the white flour. I know, it's a compromise. On the other hand, we didn't use syrup. We ate those sunshine flapjacks with just melted butter.

✦ ✦ ✦ ✦ ✦ ✦ ✦ ✦ ✦

In the fall of his first term, President Reagan issued a strong warning, a kind of signal of how seriously he regarded the conservative commitments he'd made during the campaign. Air traffic controllers were threatening a strike, arguing that their working conditions were so stressful that safety in the air was affected. Jacki Lyden talked to controllers Mike Finucane, Roger Perry, and Al Stone, who worked at Chicago's O'Hare Airport, about those conditions. The union had just voted down an offer, but talks were still going on.

All Things Considered, SEPTEMBER 2

LYDEN: The radar room at O'Hare International Airport is sunk underground, straight underneath the air traffic control tower, beneath the terminals, taxis, and other activities at this frenetic airport. Sequestered though it may feel, it is the nerve center of this operation, responsible for all passage of air traffic to and from the airport.

It is very dark in here. What faint light there is glows from a miniature galaxy of luminous control knobs, blinking red, white, yellow. And then there are the flat, circular screens of a dozen or so radarscopes, each two feet across, which cast a dull greenish light over the controllers who sit facing them, eyes locked on the rhythmic blips that remind you of a video space game. Do you ever think about the fact that there are three hundred people riding on that little blip?

FINUCANE: Not at all. If I thought about that, I wouldn't be doing this. I think it's like a three-dimensional chess game. I've got to get this blip here, this blip here, move this one over here. I've got altitude to keep 'em apart, I got air speeds to keep 'em apart, and I got distance between them.

LYDEN: Mike Finucane is a tall, athletic man who became an air traffic controller sixteen years ago in the military. Radar controllers guide all of the air traffic within a fifty-mile radius of O'Hare, stopping just short of the runways, which are monitored upstairs by the tower controllers. All of the controllers wear headphones, linked by radio to unseen pilots to whom they give directions in a rapid, staccato code of letters and numbers.

FINUCANE: One Nine Victor TWH at off your left, 727 going in for the parallel.

PILOT: OK.

FINUCANE: One nine Victor is cleared into TCA, 14 left's your runway. O'Hare Tower. So long now.

LYDEN: The traffic controllers at O'Hare like to compare their job to playing first string for the major leagues. They like to needle each other to keep each other loose and poke fun at the job.

FINUCANE: This is Chicago O'Hare Information, with the Top Fifty, the Middle Forty, and the Bottom Thirty, but we got 'em here at WORD Radio. What do you guys want to hear?

LYDEN: The sunlight and panoramic view from the tower make this small room atop a fifty-foot column appear larger than it really is. As Mike Finucane points out how things work on the runways laced beneath us, the men crowd over to good-naturedly razz him. And I comment to one of them, Roger Perry, on the competitive spirit among the controllers.

PERRY: It's very much a self-ego trip, you know. It's not a group ego, where you say, "My crew can do it better than your crew" It's "I can do it better than you, even if I'm on your crew." Now, a lot of these guys have worked together for quite a while, and it's not uncommon to see two guys working next to one another start yelling at one another, especially when they're working inbound ground and outbound ground, because they'll accuse one another of doing something wrong to affect his traffic. And so it turns out, well, you're-not-as-good-as-I-am and, I-could-work-both-positions-combined-if-you-want-to-take-a-break type of thing. And there's no one quite as good as you are.

LYDEN: A study released last week by the General Accounting Office shows that the O'Hare radar room is "significantly understaffed by thirty-two percent." The report also says it's imperative that the situation be corrected, but that, at present, it's not considered a safety risk. It does mean that the air traffic controllers here work a great deal more overtime than do their counterparts elsewhere. After six years, Roger Perry says he's leaving for a smaller place. Mike Finucane tried that once, but found that he actually missed the brain-boggling pace.

Today has been a relatively uneventful day for the controllers at O'Hare. Before going home, Mike Finucane and a fellow controller, Al Stone, stopped for a couple of beers.

FINUCANE: I don't have any close friends whatsoever outside of the job. Maintaining a relationship on any basis with somebody in civilian life is difficult because of the crazy hours and crazy days off you get.

LYDEN: Finucane is thirty-seven and single. Al Stone is thirty-three, married, with three children. And he's thinking of quitting the job he's loved for ten years and moving his family from their native Chicago because it's beginning to complicate family life.

STONE: It's gotten to the point now where my wife's just about ready to move anyhow. Because when I'm working certain shifts, I don't even see my children. They'll come home from school and I'm already at work and by the time I get home, they're already in bed. So it gets kind of hard. It's hard on her, it's hard on me. You can feel yourself when you get home, just totally mentally fatigued. You can sit down and stare at a newspaper, try and read it, and not realize even what you're looking at, just sit there and stare . . .

LYDEN: The fatigue and tension take their toll. Stress ailments are common among air traffic controllers and if they cannot pass an annual physical, they must resign.

FINUCANE: I'm thirty-seven years old, and I know I'm gettin' old for this job. I feel it, I feel it.

STONE: You start losing a little bit of your speed, you start losing, like with an athlete again, losing half a step. And the guys I've seen it happen to, they begin getting very overcautious, very touchy.

LYDEN: And that, says Stone, brings into question the possibility of the unthinkable moment, a collision.

STONE: When someone says, 'It's going to be a little close,' adrenaline really rises. And you feel your face gets hot and your hands get cold. Generally you get terrified.

LYDEN: To counter the fear, the men have a comic antidote known as the big sky theory of separation.

STONE: In other words, just let them go and leave it in the hands of fate as to whether they hit or not. It's all in a joking vein, though. You don't see that kind of thing actually going on.

LYDEN: Stone and Finucane each make about forty-five thousand a year. Because they feel the days in which they can earn the big money are numbered, they want more money now. They voted no on the current contract proposal, which they say not only doesn't give them enough money, but not enough time off. And although it would be illegal for them to do so, both men say they're willing to strike, even if it means being arrested.

✦ ✦ ✦ ✦ ✦ ✦ ✦ ✦ ✦

The air traffic controllers did strike, and found out exactly who they were dealing with. The strike was illegal, the president ultimately fired the entire union and filled their jobs. During that time, ridership on trains went up. One of our editors remembered my talking about traveling across the country by train, going to college, and sent me on a train ride.

Morning Edition, JANUARY 19

ANNOUNCEMENT: Now boarding, doorway letter D, Track 11. Thank you.

WERTHEIMER: The Broadway Limited is two trains, really. One starts in New York and the other in Washington. They're joined in Philadelphia by a dining car and proceed west as one.

The southern half of the Broadway rolled out of Union Station on this particular day and headed for Baltimore, rolling through the dusty, dark green high summer past houses where crape myrtles are in full bloom, riding a track trimmed with white, feathery Queen Anne's lace and droopy foxtail grasses.

My seat is in a slumber coach, a tiny, clever chamber, where a chair conceals a toilet and a dressing table is also a sink and the train seat disappears to make a bed.

ANNOUNCEMENT: Welcome aboard the Broadway Limited, service to Chicago and points in between. My name is Jerry Pritchard. I am your lounge car attendant . . .

WERTHEIMER: The train is just pulling into Baltimore. But Frances Bagley will stay on the train all the way to Chicago, and then take another train, to where?

BAGLEY: Spokane, Washington, is the last train travel that I will do on this trip. And the reason I leave the train in Spokane, Washington, is because that is the closest access to the place that I'm going up in the Cascade Mountains.

WERTHEIMER: What do you do there, way up in those mountains?

BAGLEY: The appeal is the mountains themselves. To climb, to hike, and, of course, this place is located, surrounded by, glaciers, and so naturally there are lots of lakes. And so a day's hike would take you to your choice of the lake that you would be interested in seeing that day. I haven't found it impossible up to this time. I wasn't there last year, so I was seventy-nine when I did my last hiking in the Cascades.

WERTHEIMER: Frances Bagley and I talked while the Broadway waited on a southbound New York train to clear the Baltimore Harbor Tunnel and then we were gone again. Out of Baltimore, we passed trains of hopper cars full of coal. We passed seedy trackside scenery masked by banks of black-eyed Susans. In Philadelphia, a switch engine tied the two parts of the Broadway together and we headed west, through cornfields, past Amish farms, past a girl in a lavender dress and a white lace bonnet, driving a horse-drawn surrey down a highway near Lancaster.

I made my way from the end of the train through six cars to the diner. The diner on the Broadway was changed this summer. Now it provides precooked food like airline food. I had dinner with two young people, Abby Huffman, who's an architecture student in Kansas City, and Bill Wood, who is a graduate student in business administration in New York. And he turns out to be a train buff.

WOOD: I remember once being on the Empire Builder, traveling towards Seattle, and I was eating dinner, or I was waiting for dinner with a couple of Midwestern farmers who were traveling to someplace in Montana. I don't have any idea where, but somewhere. And we'd been waiting for a while and we finally got a chance to sit down for dinner. And we had roast beef and potatoes. And the roast beef must have been about three — oh, half an inch thick or three-quarters of an inch thick, cooked over an open wood fire over what was then the kitchen in the diner prior to the refurbishment. It was just a tremendous meal. I was sitting around looking at, I guess it was the North Dakota countryside by then, and eating and talking with people of the sort that I've never encountered back east, where I'm from.

WERTHEIMER: I always remember breakfast as being the grandest meal on the train. And the Santa Fe served French toast. Do you remember that?

WOOD: I remember once on the Lake Shore Limited encountering the — I think the same thick French toast you're probably thinking of. It reminds you of bread that's been puffed up as if it had been deep-fried, the way you fry French fries or something, covered in maple syrup and butter and served with nice hot coffee on the side. Yes, I have memories of that as well.

WERTHEIMER: Dinner was no worse than what an average airline serves. The forks were plastic and the peas appeared to be. But it was served in a diner built long ago, with big windows which were looking at the broad and shallow summer version of the Susquehanna River as the Broadway climbed into the Alleghenies.

After dinner, the bar car was no place for soldiers and salesman to drink and play cards. It was strictly a family affair. The children of the Prestons, the Robertos, and the Lorings, two boys and four girls, ranging in age from seven to fifteen, found partners. They were playing cards, but it was crazy eights, and they had someone to help them explore the train. What have we got here? This is a Preston, and this is Tammy Roberto. What did you think a train would be like?

ROBERTO: Well, I thought it would be kind of cold and rough to ride. My aunts and cousins went on a train before and they didn't have microwave food, they had regular food, and I thought it would be like that, but we have microwave food. It doesn't taste that good.

WERTHEIMER: What do you do when you're here? What do you do for fun when you're on a train all day and part of the night?

ROBERTO: I would watch outside and read magazines and play cards. And eat.

WERTHEIMER: After a couple of hours, I went back to the tail end of the train, late at night, through coach cars rescued from the San Francisco Chief, with paintings of Indian symbols still decorating the walls, past cozy couples pillowed on each other, past all the vulnerable-looking sleeping people on the train, mouths opened, snoring, some minus the daytime disguise of teeth.

It's the middle of the night now, and I've just folded down my bed and turned out the light to watch Pittsburgh. The train passes by steel mills, looking just like they do in the movies, glowing and red and smoky. It stops at the station and then crosses the river and doubles back. From my window on the train, I can see all the bridges as we cross on a high railroad trestle. I can see the whole train curving out ahead on the opposite bank. Then I'm on the other side too, looking at the splendid city of Pittsburgh, sitting on its hills.

Now I'm going to try sleeping on this Broadway Limited, as we head for a fast, flat stretch through Ohio.

[*Sound of train going down the track. An alarm beeps.*]

WERTHEIMER: Nobody asks you when you want to be awakened on the trains nowadays, and nobody asks if you'd rather have coffee or tea. You have to work all that out for yourself. But you still get to open your eyes to a grain elevator leaning out of a foggy midwestern morning and sit up to see barns more beautiful than their houses, painted red and picked out with white. Fields of corn alternate with fields of beans and fields of stubble. Just as I looked out, another early riser, working in her garden, stood up to wave as we passed. From the platform at the back of the train, the track drops back now, straight as a plumb line, into the fog.

WAITER: Seven-Up in the morning, yes, ma'am.

SECOND WAITER: Out of one, here's fifty cents, thank you.

FIRST WAITER: Two coffees?

WERTHEIMER: Yep. Good morning again.

SECOND WAITER: Good morning again.

WERTHEIMER: We left Fort Wayne and we're headed for Gary, Indiana. It's raining and it's early in the morning and we're having a kind of breakfast, a microwave breakfast in the lounge car. We're just about to pull into Valparaiso. After that, we have only one more stop, and that's Gary, before we get to Chicago.

Brad Bowen, I've seen a lot of women traveling with their children, but you're traveling alone with your little daughter. How has it worked out that you're traveling that way?

BOWEN: My wife has a business in New Jersey, and she takes care of the store. And I work for a private computer consulting firm, so it's easier for me to leave than it is for her to leave. And my daughter hasn't seen her grandparents for a couple years. They live in Rochester, Minnesota. So we decided to take this trip. Too many times, her other grandmother has come out in an airplane and Heather has the opinion that her grandmother lives in the airport. And doesn't have a concept of how far Minnesota is from New Jersey. So I thought a train trip would instill in her mind how large the country is and how long it takes to really go to where her grandparents live.

WERTHEIMER: Train travel is almost a rite, a ceremony for some of the people I've met on this train. They like the idea of it, in some cases more the memory of it, as much as they like doing it. I haven't ridden a train to Chicago in nearly twenty years. I remember the dining cars with great regret, but apart from that I remember a lot of things I used to like and I find they're still part of the experience. I like looking into the backs of gardens as the train slows down for small towns. And I like riding at night with the horizon a dim line of dark blue, and farm-houses, little islands of light out on the plains. I remember the people who worked on the trains were very nice. I now find they're very young and they're still very nice.

We're rolling now past the Chicago Skyway toll bridge. We're almost there. I think I can say that there are things I miss in Amtrak's pared-down passenger trains, but for me this has been a grand trip.

1982

In the spring of 1982, we still did not understand fully the seriousness of the AIDS epidemic. We were not yet confident we could name the disease, and researchers were still speculating about its cause and nature. Ira Flatow, our science correspondent, began his interview with Larry Kramer of the Gay Men's Health Crisis. When Ira filed this piece, Susan Stamberg introduced it by talking about a "frightening medical mystery," a "serious homosexual health problem."

All Things Considered, APRIL 20

KRAMER: I have five, six friends now who have died, and I have four or five other friends who are in chemotherapy, and these are all guys who are in their twenties and thirties.

MAN: My best friend died of Kaposi's sarcoma. It was the second case of it in New York.

SECOND MAN: To think out of a community as big as New York there are 180 or 190 cases, or whatever it is. I know personally about 8 of them. It's incredible, when you think of it.

KRAMER: You can't not but be scared by all of that.

FLATOW: These members of New York's gay community have good reason to be concerned and scared. They've watched cancer, pneumonia, and other deadly infections kill homosexual men at an alarming rate. Drs. Alvin Friedman-Kien and Linda Laubenstein of New York University were the first to see evidence of an epidemic of a very fatal form of cancer, what is called gay cancer now.

LAUBENSTEIN: Every month we're seeing more and more patients.

FRIEDMAN-KIEN: There's no question that it's an epidemic.

FLATOW: In 1979 a young man entered NYU Medical Center with a case of Kaposi's sarcoma. Now, Kaposi's sarcoma normally causes a harmless skin tumor that attacks older European Jewish and Italian men. So when a man in his twenties appeared with the illness, Friedman-Kien and Laubenstein thought it to be no more than a medical curiosity.

LAUBENSTEIN: We see unusual cases not infrequently in a major medical center, but we had no idea how big a problem it was.

FRIEDMAN-KIEN: None of us at that time were aware of the fact that we were in the midst of an epidemic.

FLATOW: The extent of the epidemic of Kaposi's sarcoma in young homosexual men is now staggering. So far, 124 cases of Kaposi's have been reported in major American cities. The death rate is extremely high, at least thirty percent. And New York, with the nation's largest homosexual population, is seeing half the total number of cases.

FRIEDMAN-KIEN: We see here at NYU Medical Center at least one or two new cases now a week. Last week we saw three new cases.

FLATOW: But there's more, because as deadly as Kaposi's sarcoma is, gay men are dying in greater numbers from an illness that knocks out their immune systems, leaving victims vulnerable to an onslaught of deadly infections. In other words, these men are somehow acquiring an immunodeficiency so that germs that normally float harmlessly around us use this opportunity to attack, to turn into deadly pathogens in these people whose immune systems cannot fight them off.

FLATOW: Dr. Henry Masur, assistant chief of Critical Care at the National Institutes of Health in Bethesda is studying one of these opportunistic infections. He's especially interested in a pneumonia, *Pneumocystis carinii. Pneumocystis* usually infects organ transplant patients, people whose immune systems have been suppressed so that they will not reject a donor transplant. But now *Pneumocystis* has attacked gays around the country who are immunodeficient, attacked them with deadly results, and pneumonia is only the tip of the iceberg. Other germs, seizing the same opportunity, have joined the fray. So a whole slew of diseases that most people can harmlessly fight off have become killers.

MASUR: This is really an almost unprecedented kind of outbreak. And now we're seeing people with very severe viral diseases, very severe fungal diseases, very unusual bacteria. So that it would appear that once these people's immunity is suppressed, they are susceptible to all of these diseases, and the death rate is alarmingly high. Even with antibiotics, the patient has such a poor immune response that they don't recover. They get one infection after another and finally die due to that.

FLATOW: Well, is it just a coincidence that opportunistic infections and

Kaposi's sarcoma have appeared at the same time? Doctors do not think so.

FRIEDMAN-KIEN: In fact, it's thought that perhaps Kaposi's sarcoma, like the opportunistic infections that we are now seeing in these immunosuppressed individuals, is a tumor that is opportunistic, and that the tumor is developing only because these people are immunologically suppressed.

FLATOW: The Centers for Disease Control in Atlanta are now following the epidemic closely, and CDC now reports more than three hundred cases of Acquired Immunodeficiency disease nationwide, thirty-five new cases being reported monthly. The national trend reflects that of New York. Again, the overwhelming majority have been in young homosexual men, but about forty cases have been reported in heterosexual men and women. Homosexual women are not affected.

In searching for a precedent for this disease, researchers have uncovered similar cases of Kaposi's sarcoma in young males living in parts of Africa. Drs. Masur and Friedman-Kien say that in Africa a virus has been associated with the cancer: cytomegalovirus, the same virus that is seen in many homosexuals in America.

FRIEDMAN-KIEN: Cytomegalovirus, or CMV virus, which is closely associated with Kaposi's sarcoma, is now considered a disease which is extremely prevalent among gay men.

MASUR: So it would be interesting to speculate that maybe there is some viral disease which is suppressing immunity, making people susceptible to infection and also causing this tumor to occur.

FRIEDMAN-KIEN: But the question that one asks is why has this disease not been seen before. Why is it occurring now? And why among this particular group of individuals? The evidence seems to point to a multiplicity of factors.

FLATOW: One of the most obvious risk factors, say researchers, is the lifestyle of the disease victims. The CDC reports that the typical gay disease victim is thirty-five years old, lives in New York, Los Angeles, or San Francisco, and has had a total of eleven hundred different sex partners.

Larry Kramer, author, screenwriter, and cofounder of the Gay Men's Health Crisis, says the sexual liberation movement of the past decade evolved into a gay subculture that stressed sexual contacts and lots of partners.

KRAMER: Sex in the gay community I think has a slightly different connotation than in the straight community. There's so much of it, it's like eating meals. It's so easy that it becomes, I don't want to say devalued, but sex became like reading a book. We all fit in a nice portion.

FLATOW: Kramer says that gays developed their own meeting places, gay bars and baths, where men made repeated social and sexual contacts. And the more sexual exposures, say researchers, the greater the probability of exchanging viruses or developing new ones that might be involved in immunodeficiency disease.

In addition to sexual practices, Kramer says drug use is a large part of the gay subculture, and, in fact, Dr. Friedman-Kien says that many gays with Acquired Immunodeficiency disease use a variety of recreational drugs. Even more interesting, one apparent thing that heterosexual disease victims have in common is drug abuse. Of the forty heterosexual men and women with the disease, half have been intravenous drug users in the past.

Finally, the last risk factor might explain why some gays are susceptible to the disease while others can live the same lifestyle and be resistant.

FRIEDMAN-KIEN: An enormous number of our patients, namely sixty-three percent of all new patients with Kaposi's sarcoma, had genetic predisposition attached to their disease.

FLATOW: Dr. Friedman-Kien says that two-thirds of his cancer patients had a genetic marker that showed they were more susceptible to the disease than the rest of the population. So if you have a certain genetic makeup, it's possible that only then would you be susceptible to the virus, or whatever the unknown causes are.

MASUR: That, at least theoretically, might explain why if A transmits it to B, C, and D, B and C would not get the disease because they don't have the right genetic makeup, but D might.

FLATOW: As more cases of Acquired Immunodeficiency disease are reported each month, a clearer picture of the epidemic may emerge. But right now, being a promiscuous homosexual who lives in New York, Los Angeles, San Francisco, or other major cities puts you at the highest risk. After that, the picture is very fuzzy. For example, let's take the puzzling exceptions, the forty heterosexual cases, including a woman who has the deadly pneumonia but doesn't fit the profile at all. She's married. She has three children and can't be linked with anyone else with the disease. Finding the links between the heterosexual and the homosexual cases will be an important step in solving the mystery. In the meantime, doctors are coming up with a variety of possible new causes. Some wonder if immunity-suppressing agents found in semen are seeping into cracks in the skin or lining of the rectum, cracks open during anal intercourse, and then combining with viral infections to knock out immunity. Others suspect the wide use of steroids, like cortisone, used to soothe skin irritation of anal and genital areas. Steroids have the capability of suppressing the body's immune system. Some doctors are pointing to the parallel rise of over-the-counter steroids and the upswing in immunodeficiency cases. But right now these are just hypotheses. Some are being tested. But they are valuable leads for a disease that is so tough to track down.

✦ ✦ ✦ ✦ ✦ ✦ ✦ ✦ ✦

R ed Barber spent his last years in broadcasting with us. To be precise, he spent those years chatting with Bob Edwards. I've always wondered, if they'd been contemporaries, if they would have had the same warm feeling for each other, perhaps been a great baseball partnership? As it was, Bob cherished his Friday-morning conversations with Red. This one started with a listener letter asking about Red's phrase "I'll be a suck-egg mule" heard on the radio in 1947 when Cookie Lavagetto of the Dodgers broke up a Yankee no-hitter. The listener asked for Red's memories of that day. Bob read the letter, then turned to Red.

Morning Edition, APRIL 23

EDWARDS: Red, good morning.

BARBER: Good morning, Robert! And before we get into that, Bob, your voice dropped at six-thirty-five this morning. And that's the first time you made the announcement that the Braves' winning streak was over. I felt a great deal of sorrow for you.

EDWARDS: Why is that?

BARBER: Well, you seemed very sad about it, or maybe it's because you've got a head cold.

EDWARDS: That's probably it. You want to explain yourself?

BARBER: About the "suck-egg mule"?

EDWARDS: Yes, sir.

BARBER: Well, first off, that was the most exciting baseball game I was ever involved in. Bevens went eight and two-thirds innings, which was then the record in the World Series of a pitcher not giving up a hit. And suddenly the Dodgers had two men on, and with two men out, pinch hitter Lavagetto hit the second pitch for a double, and Ebbets Field exploded, and when all of the excitement was over for a little bit, I just sort of caught my breath and without thinking about it, Bob, I said, "Well, I'll be a suck-egg mule."

Ed Murrow was then in charge of news and special events for CBS, and he was my superior there. He had hired me to be director of sports, following Ted Husing. And he said to me later, he said, "You know, I think that's the perfect way to use rhetorical emphasis." And he had me come on his news program that night and explain it. And Bob, I don't know how to explain it, except when you're doing something, such as you and I are doing on live radio, without any preparation, no script, you just are concentrating on the event, you're concentrating on your work, and something just comes out.

In fact, later in that series, when DiMaggio hit what looked like a home run and Al Gionfriddo caught it at the left center field bullpen gate, I said, "Oh, doctor!" And people have remembered that. And I hadn't planned it. It just came out. That's what you do in ad lib broadcasting. And when you realize that things suddenly come out of your subconscious or your unconscious, when you're talking in front of an open microphone, it sometimes frightens you.

I know that's one of the reasons that many, many years ago, when I started broadcasting, I made a resolution that I would never say a word in private, a profane word or a foul word, that I could never say on a microphone, because I didn't want any speech habits to get to where sometime, in an unguarded moment, I might say something.

EDWARDS: That's what we're always afraid of, isn't it? Well, you've given us a lot in the language, "catbird seat," "rhubarb," "tearing up the pea patch," and "bases are FOB." You want to explain what FOB is?

BARBER: Well, FOB is one that I did sit down and create. I saw the word *FOB*, or the letters, and I thought to myself, Well, I'll see what I can make out of it. And it came to me: the bases are "full of Brooklyns," FOB. That was when I was with Ebbets Field.

EDWARDS: Thank you very much, Red. Talk to you next week.

BARBER: OK. Take care of your cold.

✦ ✦ ✦ ✦ ✦ ✦ ✦ ✦ ✦

A war was fought in the spring of 1982, over the Falkland Islands, tiny scraps of land off the coast of Argentina. The battle for the Falklands started as an almost comic-opera undertaking, with bands playing and British ships sailing for South America, easily recapturing their base on South Georgia Island. It turned very serious the first week in May, when ships were sunk and lives were lost on both sides. The war with Great Britain weakened the military government in Argentina and gave the opposition an opportunity to be heard all over the world about the activities of military death squads. In the confusion and bitterness that followed the fighting, people began to speak publicly about people who had "disappeared." NPR's Bill Buzenberg reported on the discovery that one of the Argentine prisoners captured by the British was wanted in other countries. Chris Hedges of the *New York Times* was then a free-lancer in Latin America. He talked to some of those who were speaking out in Buenos Aires.

All Things Considered, MAY 13

BUZENBERG: Navy Captain Alfredo Astiz is urgently wanted by the French and the Swedes in connection with three disappearances in Argentina in 1977. The Swedish government wants to ask him about the kidnapping and murder of eighteen-year-old Dagmar Hagelin, the daughter of a Swedish businessman living in Buenos Aires at the time. A spokesman at the Swedish embassy in Washington said today they believe Astiz was the leader of a death squad that picked up the girl and that he was the man who shot her in the head when she tried to escape. Her body was never found. The French want to question the Argentine navy officer about the disappearance of two French nuns who were working in Buenos Aires, forty-one-year-old Alice Domon, and seventy-one-year-old Leonie Duquet.

The French have testimony from released prisoners who had been held in Argentina. They say Astiz was the leader of a group responsible for killing the nuns. That was at the notorious Escuela Mecánica, the place where the Argentine government carried out its clandestine torture and murder operations in the late seventies, during its so-called "dirty war against subversion." In the five years since the three disappearances, both the French and the Swedish governments have compiled extensive evidence against Astiz, but they've never received satisfactory answers from the Argentine government. However, the British have not yet decided how they'll respond to appeals to interview him. Prime Minister Thatcher had this response today when asked about the case in Parliament.

THATCHER: For the moment, Captain Astiz has been held on Ascension Island. We shall of course comply with the Geneva Convention.

BUZENBERG: The International Red Cross in Geneva says the British can continue to hold Astiz as a prisoner of war until the end of hostilities. However, as a POW he has the right to give only his name, rank, and serial number. The Red Cross says that if the British turn him over to either the French or the Swedish governments, that would be a different matter. The law is not clear, and international war crimes issues could be raised.

In Argentina today, where the Astiz case has not yet been made public, reporter Chris Hedges found evidence that Captain Astiz also worked as an undercover agent to penetrate human rights groups.

HEDGES: Here in Buenos Aires, Astiz is suspected of infiltrating the group known as Las Madres, The Mothers, under the name of Gustavo. The Mothers, who have organized to ask the government for information about their relatives who disappeared here during the so-called dirty war, say he was a young man who claimed to have had a brother disappeared. But after the French nuns disappeared, one woman said this afternoon, he never came back. Mrs. María del Rosario was with Sister Alicia when the nun and thirteen other people, including small children, were abducted outside the Santa Cruz Catholic Church in Buenos Aires.

DEL ROSARIO: We went out from the Church gardens. A mother named Estelle Cariava was in front of me. She was a teacher. She was taken by a tall man with short sleeves. He grabbed her by the arms and the cord of her habit. I shouted, "What is happening? Why are you taking her?" But I couldn't see because there was another Mother beside me who they were taking as well. Alicia was young, dynamic, a good worker. She was only forty years old. The other nun was older. None of us knew her, but they took her as well.

HEDGES: She went on to read me a poem she wrote called "The Eighth of December, 1977."

DEL ROSARIO: "Where are those women? Cowards, mercenaries of death, you will have to answer to the justice of God. Those who ordered this will be judged, and the law will pay back the corrupt, the thieves, the bad seed, the assassins."

HEDGES: As the poem concluded, Mrs. María del Rosario grips my hand and begins to cry. "I'm sorry," she says. "This is an emotional day for us. Maybe it is our first day of justice."

BUZENBERG: No one can say with absolute certainty whatever happened to the Swedish girl or the French nuns, but an American businessman living in Buenos Aires at the time, who asked not to be identified, recalled an incident that occurred about a month after the disappearance of the two nuns.

BUSINESSMAN: I was at this party and I overheard a couple of Argentine officers laughingly talking about the flying nuns, referring to them as the flying nuns. And I asked one of my friends who was an American associated with them — I says, "What does that mean?" And he said, "Oh it just means they were taken out in a helicopter and thrown into the bay along with the rest of the prisoners."

✦ ✦ ✦ ✦ ✦ ✦ ✦ ✦ ✦

Ten years after Gloria Steinem began *Ms.* magazine, Susan Stamberg talked to her about that anniversary and about the death of the ERA, the Equal Rights Amendment to the Constitution. When *Ms.* was first published, Susan and I had thought it so significant for working women that we had insisted on reading selections from the magazine on the air. "Click," Susan said on that program, as a way of describing the recognition of common experiences that women attempting to balance marriage, family, and work had found in *Ms.*

All Things Considered, JULY 14

STAMBERG: Gloria Steinem, will you take a trip into the past with me, an oral trip, an oral journey?
STEINEM: Does it involve something I once said?
STAMBERG: Yeah, that, and some other things too.
STEINEM: All right, I'll try.
STAMBERG: Taking you back to a day at the end of January 1972, this is a moment from *All Things Considered* on that day, when there was this news that we wanted to bring our listeners. Mike Waters began with this announcement.

> WATERS: A new magazine is appearing on the newsstands this week. It is staffed by women, published by women, with illustrations and photographs taken by women. *Ms.* is edited by feminist writer Gloria Steinem. Two women from National Public Radio's staff, Susan Stamberg and Linda Wertheimer, look at the magazine.
> WERTHEIMER: Ms., capital *M*, small *s*, period. A salutation recommended by secretarial handbooks for use when a woman's

marital status is unknown. Editor Gloria Steinem spoke with me recently about what her magazine is trying to do.

STEINEM: I feel that even I am, and lots of other women are, very isolated from each other, so that we need a magazine that's a kind of consciousness-raising group in itself. A friend, you know, that comes into your house and is something that really tells the truth about your life and will help change life instead of just offering an escape.

STAMBERG: The standard-bearing article in this first issue is by Jane O'Reilly. "The Housewife's Moment of Truth" it's called. And it stands as a summation of many of the ideas . . .

STAMBERG: Listening to tape from the *All Things Considered* archives, ten-year-old tape. I'm talking with Gloria Steinem now about the tenth anniversary of the magazine *Ms*. There was so much that had to be explained in those days.

STEINEM: And I'm so glad you played that tape because I didn't hear it the first time around, and it explains to me why I've become your devoted listener.

STAMBERG: How sweet. What caught my ear in listening to that is what's true for us, for you, in listening to your voice, is in a way true for the people who read that magazine in these last ten years. We sure feel more confident these days. And we speak more confidently. It's not just simply a matter of age. It's that something has happened in these ten years that allows that, and you don't have to explain so much.

STEINEM: No, that's true, but I think the change you describe is exactly the right one because the ten years has brought an enormous change in consciousness and confidence and our knowledge of what the problems really are and the nation's knowledge of what the problems really are. We haven't really made very much institutional change, but we have made an overwhelming populist-consciousness change that must precede it.

STAMBERG: Yeah. It's interesting what you're saying about institutional changes and the lack of them because the women's movement has just gone through an incredible defeat and that is seeing the death, essentially, of the Equal Rights Amendment. Down but not out.

STEINEM: Yes, it will be introduced again. It's the temporary death. I think that also has to do with our lack of knowledge of history, at least in my case. I think if I had not been taught in my history books that women were given the vote — that was the entire treatment, that one sentence of 100 or 150 years of struggle to change the Constitution — I might have been less naive about how long it would take, having learned about the struggle for legal identity, how long it would take to gain legal equality.

We were naive in many ways. We thought that if we went to state legislators and demonstrated to them convincingly that the majority of their constituents supported the Equal Rights Amendment, they would vote for it. But we forgot the majority of those constituents don't vote them in. It's particular interests. And so in many cases they simply wouldn't listen.

STAMBERG: I must say, I was struck at the end of this last defeat when the ERA went down, at the kind of stiff upper lippedness that was so publicly demonstrated by the official speakers, by you and so many others. Why wasn't there room? Women are always talking about making room for feelings and making room for an honest expression of defeat and of grief. Why wasn't that kind of space made?

STEINEM: Well, maybe you're right. Maybe we're too worried about our stereotype of being emotional or too concerned that the country is going to blame the victim one more time instead of the legislators. But there was also a lot of anger. And the statement of mine that got the most response from women, now that you mention it, did have to do with talking about that anger. I was saying that, for me personally anyway, if the majority of the country had not supported the Equal Rights Amendment by now, I would have felt defeated, and that we had to go back to the drawing board, and depressed. But since the overwhelming majority does support ERA and it still didn't pass, I felt anger. And that seemed to be the single theme to which most women responded.

STAMBERG: There have been bad losses, though, of extremely good women, whose voices are no longer heard in public forums. Bella Abzug is one example. Yvonne Brathwaite Burke is another. Shirley Chisholm, who is leaving the House of Representatives now. That is a tremendous blow.

STEINEM: I think that cumulatively they are all casualties of the political structure and the pressures of the political structure as it exists. It's not a very humane world. I mean, women moving into the work world have this problem to a lesser degree, or maybe not to a lesser degree in lots of other areas.

We women, and I think many men too, are concerned about the inhumanity of the workplace, and if we are to be whole people, whether we're men or women, if we're to make time in our lives for children or for pursuits in addition to our jobs and not be workaholics, we are going to have to transform that structure.

✦ ✦ ✦ ✦ ✦ ✦ ✦ ✦ ✦

Another anniversary in 1982 commemorated the third year of a scientific experiment conducted right on the radio. Susan Stamberg and Ira Flatow repaired to a closet and chomped Wintogreen Life Savers, responding to a listener who wrote, asking why her teenagers were shutting themselves in the dark with rolls of candy. The tiny green flash in the closet, for some reason, made great radio. That summer, Susan and Ira relived their first tryst with Wintogreen and then the experiments that followed. This tape contains a reprise within a reprise, punctuated on the air with crunches and crashes and zipping noises, and the kind of music that accompanies romantic flashbacks in old movies.

All Things Considered, JULY 30

STAMBERG: Oh, that magic moment! And you explained — a year later, right, because we wouldn't quit, it was such a great idea — what was happening to make the sparks.
FLATOW: That's right. We learned that crushing the sugar crystals in our teeth caused an electric charge to be produced in the Life Saver. And the charge excited nitrogen in the sugar and in the air, and when the nitrogen relaxed after it was excited, it gave off this spark, an effect called triboluminescence.
STAMBERG: Triboluminescence. And the blue-green color?
FLATOW: That was due to the methylsalicylate in the Wintogreen Life Savers, known as the Wintogreen flavoring!
STAMBERG: Uh-huh. And that same year, Ira, we turned the lights out again. We tried another experiment.
FLATOW: We showed that plain old sugar cubes, when hit with a hammer or a mallet, would give off a glow also.
STAMBERG: That was a lot of fun. Now here it is.

FLATOW: See when I hit it hard. Oh, I saw blue, little blue, right under the hammer.
STAMBERG: I thought I did.

FLATOW: Right under the hammer. See if you can see it.

STAMBERG: Oh! I did! Now that was a fine green flash! And it reminded me a lot of the one in the closet with the Life Savers.

FLATOW: Let me try it one more time. That was a good one!

STAMBERG: That was even prettier, actually, because it lasted a little longer and it seemed to be more diffuse.

FLATOW: So you don't need to crunch your teeth on this, and probably ruin your teeth. You can try it with a hammer.

FLATOW: And now, Susan, in keeping with tradition on this third anniversary . . .

STAMBERG: You have another experiment, huh?

FLATOW: I'm afraid it's into the closet again. Shall we?

STAMBERG: Well, what is it this time, more Life Savers? Can't we get to chocolate?

FLATOW: No, I have a surprise this time. Adhesive tape!

STAMBERG: All right, into the closet with our science correspondent! OK, here's the closet. Close the door. OK, now wait, you said adhesive tape. That is, you're going to tape my mouth up with it, Ira?

FLATOW: No, I'm not!

STAMBERG: You're not?

FLATOW: No, no, that was the surprise. This time we're not going to use Life Savers to create that little spark.

STAMBERG: Oh, the very pulling of the tape is going to make that spark?

FLATOW: The very pulling of the tape, as the friction rubs against the back surface of the other tape that's still on the roll, will give off a little spark.

STAMBERG: OK, let's see. I can't see a thing.

FLATOW: We have to really get our eyes used to the dark here. That may take a few times. Let me see if this works.

STAMBERG: Nothing.

FLATOW: You didn't see that? I saw it that time.

STAMBERG: Oh. You did?

FLATOW: Yeah, let me try it again. Let me have your hand, so — I'm not getting fresh, I'm just going to show you where to look. You're going to look right up here at your hand, OK? There's your hand. Now I'm going to pull this very hard.

STAMBERG: I did see it! Oh, it was like a streak of green light across! Do it again!

FLATOW: One more time, OK. Look up at the tape.

STAMBERG: Fantastic! Ooh! It's better than fireworks! This might be the new Fourth of July thing to do! Ira, how wonderful of you to come. But listen, we have to end the program. Should we go back into the studio?

FLATOW: We'd better do that, yes.

STAMBERG: I think so. It's been lovely, Ira!

FLATOW: Well, we've got to stop meeting like this, I think.

✦ ✦ ✦ ✦ ✦ ✦ ✦ ✦ ✦

In July 1982, Israel invaded Lebanon, attempting to destroy the military capability of the Palestine Liberation Organization and force its withdrawal from Lebanon. Although the Israelis were ultimately successful in crushing the military power of the PLO, there was a considerable price. Israel's forces swept north through Lebanon and laid siege to Beirut, cutting off power and water to large sections of the city, relentlessly shelling and bombing. During this period, President Reagan repeatedly tried to persuade Israeli Prime Minister Menachem Begin to withdraw, but Israel repeatedly ignored cease fire agreements and continued to send in planes, long after the PLO had agreed to leave. The reporter William Drummond, the producer Deb Amos, and the engineer Marty Kurcias were in Beirut for the worst of the attacks. They sent back stories of Lebanese life in the middle of war. This report was filed shortly after a major Israeli bombardment.

All Things Considered, AUGUST 15

DRUMMOND: The protective gratings are being pulled up on shops around West Beirut as many people who fled are returning to find out what's left of their businesses and homes. Rema al-Kalil is lucky. Her pharmacy was virtually undamaged, but elsewhere in the city, whole neighborhoods were reduced to piles of rubble. Although West Beirut is devastated, to Rema al-Kalil, who is Lebanese, the city is still her home.

KALIL: No damage. Everything is all right, but because of the aircrafts which Israel is coming to Lebanon, when the airplane comes it makes *wooooooo* and everything comes down. It's not because of damage. Look, everything is in its place.

DRUMMOND: First of all, tell me why you decided to come back into West Beirut today.

KALIL: Because I can't leave it, it's my country. Wherever I go, it's like the heart of Lebanon. Nothing goes in Lebanon or runs except in this part of Lebanon.

DRUMMOND: Rema al-Kalil and many other Lebanese and Palestinians are angry about the Israeli shelling and air raids. The neighbors on the street outside her shop are angry with the United States as well, for not stepping in sooner to stop the bombing.

MAN: The west area of Beirut, we can't say completely have been destroyed, but let's say it's sixty percent destroyed. That means this is a catastrophe. It's a humanity catastrophe.

ANOTHER MAN: We are living here without no water, no electricity, nothing to eat. You know, I am coming from six kilometers to bring bread for my children, for my family. All the world can see in television what is happening here, can see people smashed into pieces. We are human beings here!

DRUMMOND: For days, the Israelis shelled and bombed Palestinian refugee camps in the south of the city, claiming that the civilians had abandoned that area and only the PLO strongpoints remained. Actually, thousands of civilians remained in the camps, either because they chose to, or because they could not leave.

The patients of the Islamic asylum for the aged and mentally handicapped stayed throughout the bombing. Over the weekend, Nobel laureate Mother Teresa, working with the International Red Cross, evacuated some of the younger patients from the hospital, where one of the few things still working is the chime clock in the reception lobby.

I'm walking down one of the wards of the mental asylum here in Sabra. There are still around five hundred patients left here, even though around thirty or so children were evacuated this morning. The conditions here are very bad because the staff is much reduced. People have just not been able to come here to work. This hospital has been heavily shelled.

Jean-Jacques Coeurs of the International Red Cross:

COEURS: Mother Teresa wanted to come in West Beirut on her own, without any advertisement or publicity around it. She asked to see the most dramatic places in West Beirut, one of them being clearly this asylum for aged and mentally handicapped people. During the shelling and bombing, this asylum has been hit several times, so it was the worst of hell right in the middle of another hell. And since the beginning of June, there were eleven dead and twenty-three wounded among the patients in this asylum.

DRUMMOND: Is it possible to say how people who are mentally disturbed react to war situations? Does it cause them any special kind of fear or grief?

COEURS: I came here in the morning after shelling, the night shelling. And the only thing I can tell you is that normally people can react against their own fear. They can try to master this fear. But these poor people just can't. They are totally victims of their own fear, of their own nightmares. And for normal people the fear or terror lasts for a couple of hours, but to them it can last for days and even months.

DRUMMOND: Let me ask you one final question, Mr. Coeurs. Why would anyone want to shell a mental hospital? What purpose would there be in shelling a mental asylum?

COEURS: That's exactly the question I am asking myself, and I still haven't found any answer.

✦ ✦ ✦ ✦ ✦ ✦ ✦ ✦ ✦

The peace movement in Israel gained strength because of growing opposition to the furious attack on Lebanon, and the international attitude toward the fierce nation of "never again" changed as well. But more shocks were in store when the Israeli army either permitted Lebanese Christian militiamen to murder refugees in the Palestinian camps of Sabra and Shatilla or ignored what was happening. Robert Siegel was in Israel that fall, when the Lebanese army was conducting a brutal mop-up of the Palestinians left behind in Beirut, and Israelis were establishing a buffer of settlements in captured territory. It was three weeks after Sabra and Shatilla when Robert spoke with some of those settlers, members of Gush Emunim, the Bloc of Believers.

All Things Considered, OCTOBER 6

SIEGEL: At a time when many Israelis are divided and uncertain about their country's future and its present policies, the believers of the Gush Emunim enjoy a political advantage far beyond their relatively small numbers: their certain belief in the need to make and keep the West Bank part of Israel. A majority of Israelis probably agree with the Gush Emunim's aim but for other reasons, for Israeli security, for water from the Jordan River, or in the belief that neither Jordan nor the PLO will ever accept Israel with Jerusalem. So why leave the adjacent West Bank in limbo, in anticipation of a peace that will never happen? The Gush

Emunim settlers approach the issue with greater conviction. One of the movement's founders, Rabbi Moshe Levinger, says that without the biblical lands of Judea and Samaria, the Jewish people are incomplete, mutilated, abnormal. Would he trade land for peace? Rabbi Levinger calls the question impossible.

LEVINGER: It is an abnormal life, an abnormal idea, to cut your body and then to say I can continue to live, I can continue to do my duty. With a piece of life, with a piece of body, you cannot receive peace.

SIEGEL: But you use the image, this is a figure of speech, to describe the land of Israel. In Lebanon, it wasn't a figure of speech. Israeli young men did lose arms, legs, or their lives. Can one really compare this figure of speech about the land with a real loss of life?

LEVINGER: I cannot understand that we can continue to live with only a part. If we are ready to give a part, then they will say perhaps give another part, give also Netanya, and give also Ashkelon. Is this enough for you? Also Tel Aviv? And we can also divide every place in Eretz Yisrael, in the Jewish state. If we are ready to divide our body, then we must be ready to divide and divide time after time, until we will come back to the Diaspora.

SIEGEL: The loss of lives in Lebanon seems to have had a greater effect on some of the younger West Bank settlers. At Tekoa, south of Bethlehem, fifty families, a third of them from the United States, live in small homes, sharing a single communal telephone, being paged and hearing public messages by loudspeaker. Bobby Brown, raised in New York City, is the settlement's manager.

BROWN: I think that every night when the casualties came out — there were eight one day and five the next and seven the next — every Israeli made a mental calculation as to the morality involved in losing our soldiers. And here it's very strongly felt every time one Israeli soldier dies. So I think that as much as any other war, that had a tremendous effect here. I don't believe that any time during the war, even when we lost one of our members here in Lebanon, when he was killed fighting on the Syrian front, did we ever feel that the war wasn't justified, or wasn't a war that had to be fought.

SIEGEL: Bobby Brown told me that he and most of the settlers at Tekoa wanted a commission of inquiry into the Beirut massacre. But no one protested publicly since that might have threatened Menachem Begin's government. A new government could mean a new settlements policy, perhaps the freeze that President Reagan wants, perhaps the eventual dismantling of existing settlements as part of a territorial compromise.

The believers of Gush Emunim may have a serious political fight on their hands soon, if the National Religious Party, which they've become closest to, drops out of Menachem Begin's government with other smaller parties to form a new coalition with the Labor Party. The fight will be for the allegiance of young religious Jews who might be convinced to settle on the West Bank, who in Lebanon suffered casualties disproportionate to their numbers in the army, and some of whom staged rare antigovernment protests after the Beirut massacre.

The Gush Emunim's best weapon in that fight will not be the merits of their scriptural case for the West Bank, but their certainty in it at a time when many Israelis opposed to Begin's government have their doubts about whether any Israeli compromise would bring lasting peace to their country.

1983

✦ ✦ ✦ ✦ ✦ ✦ ✦ ✦ ✦

Vertamae Grosvenor grew up in North Carolina and knew people who lived on the Sea Islands, off the coast of South Carolina. Since the Civil War, descendants of slaves had lived on the islands, free people, farming and fishing, isolated from the mainland, preserving some of the language and traditions of Africa. In 1983, nearby Hilton Head Island had already been rebuilt into a resort, and Daufuskie Island was on the brink of development. The islanders were philosophical about progress, although they were skeptical about its benefits. The developers were promising to preserve the grace of Daufuskie's past, but as everyone but the developers seemed to understand, they intended to preserve a past which had never existed.

All Things Considered, JANUARY 17

GROSVENOR: Long before "day clean," as Gullah calls the dawn, our ferry chugs across Calibogue Sound. The water is wide, and it's been too long. Four years since I've been on 'Fuskie. From what I hear, this may be the last time I see 'Fuskie as I know it. A money man from upcountry has bought one-third of the island. They say he plans to build houses and condos for the rich. Daufuskie will change. And I know everything must change, but like the islanders, I wonder what it will mean.

As we get near the shore, I can see them. There they are, Ellie Mae, Jake, the newlyweds, Bertha and Tom and Willy. There's Willy. Willy knows every shortcut through the woods.

All the high school students are waiting at the dock, too. They're carrying their schoolbags and suitcases. These four kids are bused and boated. The ferry will take them to Hilton Head Island. They'll take a bus from there to school on the mainland in Bluffton. They'll spend the week on Hilton Head with friends or relatives. Friday, the ferry brings them back to Daufuskie.

First- through eighth-graders go to school on the island in a two-room schoolhouse. There are ten of them. Six preschoolers go to class in a trailer next door. They can greet you in Gullah, English, or Swahili.

Daufuskie lies somewhere between the future and the past, like the Gullah expression, "It's seen worser days and better times." Old-timers like to talk about better times, of the days when they sailed boats full of produce to market in Savannah, days when the winery and oyster factories were open, when there were hundreds of people on the island, when life was fine, as fine as the Scuppernong or Muscadine wine they made.

Today they live on pensions, welfare, their wits, and whatever else they can do. For money, they'll take you around the island or taxi you across the sound. And they sell deviled crabs. Daufuskie deviled crabs are a gourmet's delight, world famous. The recipe is a century-old secret. They hold onto that secret like they hold onto their language.

I grew up in the Carolina lowlands, so I understand Bertha Robinson Stafford's Gullah speech. Gullah's a patois, a dialect, a way of speaking English with an African rhythm. Sea Island people are warm, witty, generous, loyal. But they're very independent, and it takes awhile to get to know them and awhile for them to let you know them. They divide people into two groups, "forbeenyers" and "forcomyers," natives, newcomers. After some years and many visits, I've made some friends on 'Fuskie, like Mr. Johnny Hamilton. He's my friend, but even so, I have to coax a song out of him.

You know, "Sweet By-and-by," "Further Along"?

HAMILTON: "Further Along"?

GROSVENOR: There used to be a lot more to sing about on Daufuskie, back before pollution destroyed the oyster industry and the boll weevil destroyed the prize Sea Island cotton. The oysters were choice, served on tables in New York and Boston, and favored by the czar of Russia. I don't know that, but that's what they say.

Work was hard, but like trouble, it wasn't all the time. There was big fun. What Tom Stafford liked best in those days were the leg parties, a kind of mass blind date.

STAFFORD: Leg parties, ain't nothing to it. It's a common dance, but what I'm talking about, you can't see the women, you know. And they got a big, old, long curtain, you know, come all the way down. You can see the shoes, but if you come in with a blue sock, I can't see that no more, because they set you all the way back. But anyone you grab, if it's ninety years old, that's what you got to treat.

GROSVENOR: You have to treat 'em?

STAFFORD: Yeah, that's right. Anyone you grab that night would be your mama. You're going to treat 'em.

GROSVENOR: That was big fun, huh?

STAFFORD: Oh, man, that was joyful time I do in them days.

GROSVENOR: It wasn't unusual for people to stay up all night singing and telling stories. Sea Islanders love a good story and they love to talk in parables and proverbs. "God don't love ugly." "Most kill bird don't make soup." "Every grin teeth ain't a laugh." "Every shut eye ain't sleep." "Every good-bye ain't gone." There was a message in everything.

Back in those days there was no telephone service on the island. Now there are thirty-six listings in the Daufuskie directory. That's including the repair service number. Bertha's unlisted.

Before the phone, if you wanted to get a message to somebody, Fast Man could do it for you. His real name is Daniel Mitchell. They say he walked so fast, on the mainland he could be arrested for speeding. Fast Man works in Savannah because there are no jobs in Daufuskie for him. He'd rather be on the island, where he found a rich life.

MITCHELL: You could get your conch free, your oyster free, crab, shrimp, fish. There are so many things you can get. Rabbit, deer, or anything you want. That's a good living. You could go, man, and have fun here, have fun there, and it was nice at that time in the younger days. But the biggest thing is, there are no jobs. But if you'd have a job there, a man could live a millionaire life there.

GROSVENOR: Times could be good again on Daufuskie. The man who bought the real estate has said so. He says folks will be able to come back and find jobs on the island. There'll be golf courses, tennis courts, and newcomers. Some islanders think that's too high a price to pay. Geraldine Wellahan drives the mosquito spray truck and the community ambulance. She wants to keep things the way they are.

WELLAHAN: You know, when you can get up in the morning and walk around on the outside in your pajamas, sit on the front porch and drink your coffee in your pajamas. Where else can you do that? I mean, that's living, to me. We know everybody. We know everybody's babies, and people trust me. And I mean, now, when you get all these people, you're not going to have that trust. Because what's going to be is they're going to bring strangers to the island.

GROSVENOR: Daufuskians have a good idea of what progress is all about. All they have to do to see progress is to look across Calibogue Sound at Hilton Head Island.

RECEPTIONIST: Good afternoon. Hilton Head Inn. These are your inn charge cards. And you can use these to put your food and beverage charges directly to your room, OK. They also serve as identification cards. And this is your car pass. You'll need to keep this on the dashboard of your car. This will allow you to get through the security gate.

GROSVENOR: Hilton Head's gotten real crowded and built up in the past twenty-five years. It's so crowded, animals are leaving. Rattlesnakes have been found three miles offshore, and deer have been seen swimming across to Daufuskie. Not long ago, these two islands were very much alike. Blacks were the majority. Then in 1957 they built a bridge from the mainland to Hilton Head. That sure changed things.

Tourists arrived, unpacked their bags, and stayed. Today blacks are the minority on Hilton Head. Emory Campbell was born on Hilton Head Island. For him, development has been a mixed blessing. He earned money for college working at the new golf course, but he lost his freedom.

CAMPBELL: I could go anywhere on Hilton Head, put down a boat anywhere, hunt anywhere, ride my horses all over the island, get firewood all over the island. And all of a sudden, I can't do that. The first time I ever faced anything on Hilton Head that would make me believe that I didn't belong was I was coming from the golf course one day after caddying, and the sheriff stopped us because the car was overloaded.

And he said, "What in the hell are you all doing down here, anyhow?" And, boy, did that put some things in my mind. I said, "What am I doing here, anyhow?" What does he mean by that? I've been here all my life, and nobody ever questioned me being on Hilton Head.

GROSVENOR: When Emory travels around Hilton Head these days, he has to go through security gates to enter the subdivisions. His family used to own land at Braddock's Point. Now Braddock's Point is called Harbor Town, an elegant, private community of shops and apartments and a golf course.

CAMPBELL: That's the eighteenth hole of the Heritage Golf Classic, right over there to your right, right opposite my grandparents' cemetery. This is the graveyard as it is now, but there was much more than this before development came in. Some of the graves weren't marked, and when they started developing, nobody came and staked out the graveyard. That house right there, definitely on graves, and maybe a part of that golf course, as well. Many of the headstones have been taken away by tourists for souvenirs. And what it's referred to as is the "slave graveyard." My great-grandmother over here was born in 1861.

GROSVENOR: Susan Williams.

CAMPBELL: Mmm-hmm. That's my great-grandmother. Now, when we come to bury people here, what happens is the security guard will meet us at the gate and bring the processional down here, and after the casket is out of the hearse, then they ask everybody to leave.

GROSVENOR: Why?

CAMPBELL: They just think that it's too much congestion here and they're blocking traffic. Just can't stay any longer.

GROSVENOR: There's less and less room for the real past on Hilton Head. It's replaced by a fictional past, modern-day renderings of the Old South, romantic magnolia mint-julep time. It's implied and conjured up in the names, Sea Pines Plantation, Palmetto Dunes Plantation, Hilton Head Plantation. A plantation is a plantation is a plantation, depending on who you are. Ask Charles Cauthen, the man who bought one-third of Daufuskie.

CAUTHEN: The plantations of yesteryear were exciting places, exciting for both the landowners and laborers.

CAMPBELL: To us, it brings fire in us. We hate that word, *plantation*. It's a slave word to us. It's a slave term. It's a term that means that you have a big house and you have slaves working for you.

GROSVENOR: Emory sees it one way. Charles sees it another way. Charles is forty-four, bearded, with an intense gaze and a casual attitude. When he moved here from the Carolina uplands, he fell under the spell of the lowlands. His plans for Daufuskie include a big house. He calls it the Great House Inn. To create a hushed antebellum charm, he wants to keep the roads unpaved. Travel will be by horse and surrey only. Even though no work has started, Charles likes to give tours.

CAUTHEN: We're right now riding down a live oak lane shrouded with Spanish moss. We're in the twilight of this afternoon, and you can almost hear Miss Scarlett calling from the Great House saying, "I hear Mr. Rhett coming up the lane now."

GROSVENOR: Well, I don't know about that. It's hard to picture Sea Islanders at Tara. Legend has it, they made terrible slaves, too clever, too independent-minded. Ironically, this independence has attracted people, even tourists.

WOMAN: We have visited the Hilton Head Island several times, and for years we've enjoyed looking across to Daufuskie and now we're having the opportunity to see what Daufuskie's all about.

GROSVENOR: You're interested in the island or you're interested in the coming development?

WOMAN: Well, just the island. We didn't know much about the coming development until this trip, but now it certainly sounds fantastic.

GROSVENOR: Well, the islanders aren't sure it's fantastic. They'll wait and see what it is. Charles claims it won't be a crowded development. He expects six thousand residents. His plans are wonderfully thought out: the Great House Inn for overnight visitors, a restaurant featuring Daufuskie deviled crab, a graceful marina for yachts and small boats, and plenty of jobs, a chance to recapture the prosperity the island lost.

CAUTHEN: I like to look at it as a re-creation rather than changing it. So those people who want to stay home and want to come home can do so.

GROSVENOR: Charles tells people all about the jobs his development will create. He wants to help the islanders. Tom Barnwell's heard this kind of talk before. He owns land on Daufuskie and lives on Hilton Head Island. He saw his neighbors become chambermaids and busboys. He says all this job talk is too vague.

BARNWELL: No one is being specific. And you have to be specific, because there will not be an abundance of jobs, you know, certainly beyond domestic and the service area. And what I'm talking about, we've done that. We've proved ourselves in life that we can do that. And you know, those of us who are native blacks, there are those of us who would like to and want to and intend to and will do more than that in our lifetime.

GROSVENOR: Some Daufuskians are looking ahead, hoping their kids can learn management skills before the boom comes. They want Charles and his company, the Daufuskie Island Land Trust, to provide training. Emory Campbell says that Hilton Head blacks were left out in the cold. He worries the same thing will happen on Daufuskie. Real estate taxes will rise and people's paychecks won't keep pace. Islanders worked hard since emancipation to get land and keep it. Emory knows they'll need help to hold on.

CAMPBELL: I think the developer has a moral obligation to the people on the island to make sure that those people are developed as he develops the island. And I think he has a moral obligation to make sure that those people are able to remain on their land and be able to provide for their family.

GROSVENOR: Charles says he'll live up to his obligation. He's gotten to know these islanders by name. He brings them medicine and supplies from the mainland. He prays in their church on Sunday. He says he understands the people. From the start, he's felt their fate was in his hands. He'll never forget the day, a few years ago, when he came to the monthly town meeting to tell the people of Daufuskie about his development plans for the first time.

CAUTHEN: That was in June and it was hot. And everybody sat down. And pretty soon there was a little toe tapping, and Frances Young had begun to start a little beat with her wooden crutch. And she broke out, and she said, "Precious Jesus, don't pass me by. Precious Jesus, don't pass me." At that point, the hair stood up on the back of my head, and I said to myself, Charles, get up, go home, and leave this island and these people alone. Forget it. And by the time she got through with the hymn and everybody joined in and sang along with her, I changed my mind, and I'm still here. And the reason I changed my mind was that I knew that their island was going to change, and I felt I can do it the best and change their island as little as possible.

GROSVENOR: Well, I don't know what to make of all this. I suppose the people of Daufuskie are just as confused as I am. Progress may save and sacrifice Daufuskie at the same time. But maybe, just maybe, these people are tougher than that, strong enough to hold onto the past, as their little island is packaged into somebody else's dream.

Since every good-bye ain't gone, I'll wait and see. Some of my friends, like Louise Wilson, are weary of all this crazy talk.

WILSON: Yeah, my daughter, we used to have some swell time on Daufuskie, but it gone, gone, gone, gone, gone. The man bought the land, and it's his place to do whatever he want to do. It hurts because, you know, all the older ones is dead, and even some of the younger one, and half of them is off the island and gone. So there's nobody but a few over here. So I guess, the white man say, Well, ain't but a few people. We can just take over, do what we want to do. And that's all I see. But we had some real nice times on Daufuskie. It was real nice. Yeah, well, that's what all I know, darlin'. That's all I know what to tell you. I don't know any more.

✦ ✦ ✦ ✦ ✦ ✦ ✦ ✦ ✦

A ndrei Codrescu's first essay for National Public Radio was a fairy tale about bears.

All Things Considered, APRIL 27

CODRESCU: I told my son, Tristan, this story. In a forest far away a bear ate a certain mushroom, and lo and behold, he was transformed into a schoolchild.

Finding himself in a regular school unable to convince anyone that he's really a bear, not a child, he takes to the road and wanders, forlorn.

When he meets another child on the road he tells him, "I'm a bear." To his great surprise, the fellow traveler answers, "*I'm* a bear."

It turns out that something similar had befallen this bear-child, too. The two of them team up and soon they meet another child. "I'm a bear," "I'm a bear," "I'm a bear," they confess, and the third bear-child joins them.

To make a long story short, they are joined by seven more bear-children, wandering the roads in search of their lost bearhood, and then they meet another child.

They joyfully greet him with, "I'm a bear," "I'm a bear," "I'm a bear," to which the newcomer says, "I'm a bird."

I won't tell you all the rest of what happened. If you want to know, you have to ask Tristan. But this much suffices for what I have been thinking about all these many days and more, namely that bears are the few successful survivors of the rich bestiary that once populated our fables and yarns. Maybe it is because bears have been humanized to the point where very little bear survives in them. There isn't much mouse in Mickey, so maybe bears only bear a faint resemblance to the animal bearing that name. But I refuse to believe that. I like to think that in spite of everything, a little bear survives in our fabulous bears.

On the cover of *The Three Bears* in the little Golden Book edition, I behold a mischievous nymphet being looked over with varying degrees of solicitude by a greedy little bear dressed in lederhosen, a mother bear who looks like Edith in *All in the Family,* and a giant daddy bear with his hands behind his back and a carpenter's apron around his formidable waist.

And in looking at them, the meaning of my little story comes suddenly to me. If there are no more bears left in the forest, surely there must be some among us disguised as humans. Where could all that bearness go: If not in us, who so delight in it? It is possible that at any given time in any given gathering, a number of us are bears and birds and mice. I am bird-bear.

✦ ✦ ✦ ✦ ✦ ✦ ✦ ✦ ✦

Tom Shales of the *Washington Post* has reviewed movies for *Morning Edition* for more than ten years. Many of his reviews are memorable, but we like him best when he really hates a movie, in this case, a very popular one.

Morning Edition, MAY 6

SHALES: Surely it can't be only a coincidence that the release of the movie *Flashdance* coincided with the publication of a report by the Commission on Educational Excellence, which said, in effect, America's kids are getting dumber every day.

Ninety minutes' exposure to *Flashdance* makes you think you're getting dumber, even as you watch it. You can feel the synapses shorting out inside your head. It's not just the numbing experience of the usual bad movie. This is something a little more insidious. Watching *Flashdance* is like drowning in Ping-Pong balls. And when you come out of it, your mind may be so parched that it's shriveled. You want to dash off to one of your college textbooks or just go over your tax return again, anything that would give food for thought.

Richard Corliss in *Time* magazine has called *Flashdance* a perfect movie for 1984, one year early. It does seem to have been designed for an audience of zombies, young people so hypnotized by use of television and rock music that they can only respond to something subprimally banal and free of all content.

Nominally, *Flashdance* is the story of an eighteen-year-old girl who lives in Pittsburgh, is a welder by day and dances to Giorgio Moroder music in a twilight zone bar called Maudie's at night. The camera concentrates on her pulsating fanny. Director Adrian Lyne cuts her up into body parts, as if there were a commercial, say, for Jovan's Night Musk. And indeed, Lyne cut his teeth, until they were sharp as fangs, on pop chic TV spots.

In the very first of the preposterous flashdance performances, the girl sits on a chair in the middle of the stage, pulls a cord, and, *sploosh!*, is doused with a couple of buckets of water. The movie becomes another entry in a genre we might call "saga of the soggy teenager." Wet teenagers sell orange soda and beer and suntan cream on television. Here the pitch is a shrink-wrapped eroticism that seems as dehumanizing as hard-core pornography.

The ditsy heroine is played by actress Jennifer Beals, her boyfriend boss by former soap opera heartthrob Michael Nouri. Beals puts in one of those perky-jerky performances that brings to mind Didi Conn in *You Light Up My Life*. She bubbles and burbles and interrupts the cute act only to spill out a few abrasive obscenities every now and then. The questions one asks oneself are, What makes this girl tick, and how can this ticking be stopped? The film has writers listed in the credits, but it's really a screenplayless movie. There's just some small talk wedged between the cornpone porn. The business of the movie is business. It's welded together like a commercial war machine, an Avon lady coming to your door in a tank.

The heroine's goal is, to quote, "make it happen," unquote. She has a dream, the old dead dream of movies like *Fame*, and that is to dance seriously with a ballet company. Another dancer's body had to be dubbed in for Beals when this consummation finally wishes itself true. Along the way, the girl and the boy smooch and spat, and the soundtrack coos with modern dip-think lyrics like "Frightened by a dream? You're not the only one. Running like the wind, thoughts can come undone."

Indeed! *Flashdance* has been compared to MTV, the Warner cable channel that plays rock videos twenty-four hours a day, Vuzak for home consumption. But the film's really more like a ninety-minute commercial for lip gloss or nail gloss or just gloss gloss. It's android foreplay, Bubble Yum for the brain dead, filmed in voyeuristic glitzorama and living lobotovision. As a movie, the film has no significance, a flashdance in the pan. But as a symptom — whoa boy! It's the stuff term papers are made of.

Corliss reports in *Time* that the film is doing big business and that happy, happy Paramount Pictures thinks of it as maybe the *Saturday Night Fever* of 1983. Imagine, a movie that makes *Saturday Night Fever* look like Eisenstein. Emptiness on this magnitude is stupefying, but *Flashdance* is more and less than that. One may feel like a fuddy-duddy, or like, totally groady for thinking it, but as you watch the movie commit aerobicide right in front of you, you wonder, perhaps in terror, what's to become of a generation that is capable of being entertained by the likes of this.

✦ ✦ ✦ ✦ ✦ ✦ ✦ ✦ ✦ ✦

Perhaps also anticipating 1984, ABC produced a movie about nuclear war, called *The Day After*, which was previewed in the Kansas town where it had been filmed. There was considerable debate about the project, which made an obvious argument against those nuclear strategies that so concerned our leaders. In the film, Kansas City is destroyed, but the action takes place in nearby Lawrence, where people survived for a time. Lawrence, Kansas, saw the made-for-TV version of nuclear war about a month before the rest of us, and Susan Stamberg talked to people in the town and people involved with the movie. The first people we heard were Kansans reviewing the preview.

All Things Considered, OCTOBER 13

MAN: The movie scared me very badly. It was nothing I hadn't known before, but seeing it in front of me, seeing other people going through that, scared me deeply.

SECOND MAN: We knew it was fake, we knew it was all pretend. But you couldn't help getting caught up in it. I definitely agree that most people are ignorant of the fact that it could happen.

FIRST MAN: I'm hoping this gets past the censors. I'm hoping ABC has the guts to put it on.

SECOND MAN: It was not a very uplifting film at all.

FIRST MAN: If anything it was underdramatized. It could have been much worse.

SECOND MAN: I was always pronuclear and thought that to prevent war we had to make sure we were as strong as the other person. I'm not so sure anymore.

STAMBERG: Also in the audience in Lawrence yesterday was Nicholas Meyer. He's the director of *The Day After.*

MEYER: The idea of going back to Lawrence was a deliberate choice on the part of the filmmakers, myself and ABC, because without the people of Lawrence, Kansas, we literally could not have made the film. When you see the film you'll see that Lawrence and the citizens of Lawrence are the stars of the movie.

STAMBERG: You said that you would like for it to be shown to the Russians. Why?

MEYER: Well, I think that the movie — it is a cautionary fable, I suppose. I likened it at one point to a giant public service announcement. It does not take a political stand. It does not deal with generals or politics or global strategies. It does not suggest we arm or disarm. What it does is attempt to show nuclear war from a point of view of regular Americans. And in that sense, the film is not ultimately about Lawrence. It's about everybody. And "everybody," I think, also includes the Soviet Union.

It's supposed to be sobering. And it is also supposed to supply vivid imagery to those words we read and throw around so that we have become completely inured to their meaning; "fallout" and "shelters" and "megaton" and so forth. Our movie tries to update things so we can all get a handle on what all those words mean.

STAMBERG: And, as you said, you're updating it in the middle of a wonderfully ordinary part of the country, Lawrence, Kansas. Is that the reason you think there's been so much hullabaloo in advance about this film?

MEYER: It's a bit confounding, to tell you the truth. I find it a rather sinister aspect of the social scene or the media scene that this film is being judged by people who haven't seen it.

STAMBERG: Isn't that inevitable, though? Are you being a little naive to have thought that might not happen, that prodisarmament groups would want to use the film for their purposes, just as antidisarmament groups would?

MEYER: I think we expected it to some degree. I don't think we were naive in thinking that it wouldn't occur at all. I think what was stunning to me was the level of the acrimony, the level of the attempt to sort of co-opt the movie into one political or ideological camp or another. Very shrill.

STAMBERG: I can't remember a similar reaction, can you, to other films which dealt with the same subject, and there've been a number of them. There was *Dr. Strangelove*, there was *On the Beach*, there was that NBC television program *Special Bulletin*, which showed the simulated destruction of Charleston, South Carolina.

MEYER: I'll tell you why, I think, and that is that most films that are made on the subject of nuclear war have always chosen to distill that event through a particular filter. *Dr. Strangelove* distilled it through humor. *On the Beach* distilled it through distance. *Special Bulletin* distilled it through television journalism. *The Day After* is a very literal-minded film. It just takes a kind of plodding look at the before, during, and after with a camera that never blinks.

STAMBERG: Whose fault is this destruction? Who fires the first missile?

MEYER: Uh, you never know. And by the way, that was never decided out of political expediency or wanting to get off the hook. But if you are in Kansas or in most places in the world when a nuclear war begins, you'll never know who started it.

✦ ✦ ✦ ✦ ✦ ✦ ✦ ✦ ✦

O ne hundred million people are believed to have watched the film when it was broadcast in November, just before Thanksgiving. There were seminars, conferences, city council resolutions, and peace demonstrations around the country.

Just a few days after the preview in Lawrence, Kansas, a truck blew up in front of U.S. Marine headquarters in Beirut, killing more than two hundred marines. And at the same time, the president decided to send troops to the Caribbean island of Grenada, to rescue U.S. students endangered by an attempt to take over the government. NPR's Ted Clark said that the invasion of Grenada might serve as a distraction from questions being asked about the deaths of the marines in Lebanon and from a discussion of their not very well defined mission there. Two weeks after the invasion, Scott Simon was in Grenada, as the U.S. military continued to pursue Cuban troops that had helped topple the government of Maurice Bishop.

All Things Considered, NOVEMBER 8

SIMON: The phrase isn't used here, but during these days when Grenadians speak so ecstatically of regaining their liberty, the dictionary definition of "martial law" exists on this island. American soldiers patrol the streets. American warplanes scour the skies. American soldiers inspect each automobile, grocery sack, and children's schoolbag. An eight o'clock curfew is enforced at night, but by seven the streets — already dark in the absence of electric power — are empty and silent. And yet by day, there seems a kind of happy contagion among Grenadians. North, away from Saint George's, driving onto the red dust roads riding up through jungle mountains, we met a cocoa farmer named Boise Childs who told us he just delivered a load of fruit and fresh water to American soldiers nearby.

CHILDS: And they are very friendly, and they are very courtesy, and they are very nice, and very generosity. Very, very nice. And I cannot find sufficient words to shower praise on these people for the tremendous assistance we have gotten from them here. They come at a time of need.

SIMON: You don't often hear Grenadians speak of an American invasion of their island. "Rescue" is more likely the word they choose, and they tend to set aside misgivings that Americans might voice over the invasion — or the rescue — by citing the terror and dread they recall in the days just before the invasion occurred. For most Grenadians, that story begins on October 19, when thousands of them marched to force the release of Prime Minister Maurice Bishop — Grenada's Sweet Man, as he was often called — from the prison where he and five more members of his cabinet were being held by the People's Revolutionary Army. Moishda and John Bruce are Baha'i missionaries who live in an apartment above the harbor in Saint George's. Mrs. Bruce works at the hospital adjoining the army complex at Fort Rupert, and she remembers that day with exhilaration, as being nearly like a second Grenadian revolution.

MOISHDA: Everybody was so rejoicing, hugging each other, and there was such a feeling of joy, and such a feeling of victory, the people felt so united, that they felt such a pride that they saved their leader. We were standing and waiting and then suddenly there was a big gunshot, and everybody started running.

JOHN: We saw the armored cars coming down the road and we had some Grenadians with us, and they mentioned that, Oh, the military is for Bishop, and we thought nothing of that . . .

SIMON: From their balcony above the harbor, John Bruce saw that crowd of thousands encircling the stone walls of the prison, chanting, cheering, linking up arms and hands in a kind of human wreath.

JOHN: We thought that was fine and we saw them disappear here out of view and then we saw them come back in view as they were entering up the fort, and I heard one large explosion, and we saw it in the sky above the fort, and that was one of the guns from the armored cars. And then after that, machine-gun fire opened up and people were jumping from rafters and off of forty-foot walls and there was dust everywhere, and cannons were going off, and cars were exploding, and it was really a bloody, dirty mess.

SIMON: The drivers who taxi reporters around the island these days will often point down from the hill here towards a mass grave in the lot that's below the Richmond Hill Prison. It's not certifiably known how many people may be buried here. One number is 100. So is 50, so is

150. Those are Grenadians who may have died on a single afternoon in a small island nation of a hundred thousand people or less. It's an event that is absolutely without echo or precedent here. Grenada is a nation which gained its independence from Great Britain peacefully, almost reluctantly, back in 1974. The revolution which brought Maurice Bishop into power just five years later was also without violence. But now there was a government in place which not only ruled by force, but maneuvered in secret, imposing a twenty-four-hour curfew in the country. Through the split sides of a rusted shed in which he works in a northern jungle village called Paradise, Grenada, a coconut farmer named Raddix Robertson found himself afraid to sprint across the street into his bedroom.

ROBERTSON: There was mad dogs with armored cars just roaming up and down the street and just driving everybody crazy and we was wondering, What next, what next. You know, some people said what the English is doing, what the Queen is doing, and eventually in the morning we saw the American up here, and everybody heart was just glad.

SIMON: To many Grenadians, this is the symbol they seem most to evoke of the American mission — something heaven-sent, something swirling in from the shores and the skies, rumbling with power and fire. Now, it must be noted that although the People's Revolutionary Army had threatened to shoot down anyone seen on the streets after their curfew, there is so far little real evidence that this actually happened. The PRA imprisoned maybe eighty more people on political charges, but did not torture or execute them, which was not always the case for a number of prisoners held during the time of Maurice Bishop. Still, the conviction was holding among Grenadians that they were in the sudden grip of a regime that was violent and demented, a government which had murdered Grenada's own Sweet Man and hundreds of those who loved him.

ROBERTSON: And up to now we have to say thank God to the Americans. If they didn't come to our rescue, maybe all of us would have died by now.

SIMON: American reporters, anxious to discover if there is any difference of opinion among Grenadians over the invasion of their island, can sometimes feel hard and foolish as they search for it. It's often pointed out in the United States that there is something ironic in the American government now so loudly lamenting the loss of Maurice Bishop. They had seemed to distrust him so when he was alive. And it was Mr. Bishop who brought in Russian advisers, Cuban construction workers, and Soviet weapons to this island. But there is also something ironic and sometimes comic about the way in which Maurice Bishop's supporters have moved from asking the Americans not to be involved in the affairs of Grenada, to now setting a permanent place for them here. Lincoln Lessie, for example, owns the Freedom Disco in the northern city of Grenville. He was personally close to Maurice Bishop and a district member of the People's Revolutionary government.

LESSIE: I would bloody well suggest to who is ever in the interim government to allow America to have a base in Grenada, like they did in Trinidad, for saving not only us, but the entire Caribbean. This is our wish.

SIMON: And in his tin shed in the small town of Paradise, coconut farmer Raddix Robertson has taped up two newspaper portraits. One is of Great Britain's Prince Philip, the other of Princess Margaret.

ROBERTSON: I'd like to have a picture of President Reagan to hang up in my house.

SIMON: Oh, in addition to Philip and Margaret?

ROBERTSON: Yeah, and Philip and Margaret. And I would like to get more than one picture of President Reagan.

✦ ✦ ✦ ✦ ✦ ✦ ✦ ✦ ✦

The year 1983 also introduced the Cabbage Patch doll. The dolls were first made by hand for special-order customers and adopted by little girls, whose parents paid a fairly stiff fee for the privilege. When Coleco began mass-producing the dolls, they were an instant hit and there were reports that customers were fighting over the cuddly, pudding-faced creatures. Susan Stamberg consulted Carole Klein, who had written a book called *The Myth of the Happy Child*, and cohost Noah Adams added some of his own thoughts about the Cabbage Patch Kids.

All Things Considered, NOVEMBER 30

KLEIN: The doll is not an attractive doll, and you can identify with that doll better than you can, let's say, with a Barbie doll. I mean, one of my objections to the Barbie doll has always been that it's so bizarre in terms of what a child can really identify with. These children are growing up in a time of broken homes, and single-parent homes, and it may be a way of acting out that anxiety.

STAMBERG: You mean the idea that the doll comes complete with these adoption papers.

KLEIN: Yeah, and that the child is not really the secure baby in the home. I think that may be part of it.

STAMBERG: And, Carole, don't children very often have that fantasy that they themselves were adopted?

KLEIN: Yes, that is absolutely a very real anxiety that almost any child has, whether they articulate it or not — am I really an adopted child? And I think this is probably for that reason a very positive toy to have. Children have a great many fears and feelings that they don't have the words to express, and dolls and play have always been traditional ways of grounding these anxieties, acting them out. So it's a way of communication.

STAMBERG: You know, there's a shortage now. That's part of the reason for the stampede in the stores. There aren't enough of these dolls. And there are hospitals — the ones I know about are in Arkansas and Iowa — which are offering now to send birth certificates for any doll, even if it's not a Cabbage Patch doll.

KLEIN: Yeah, that's really fascinating.

STAMBERG: But, you know, what's interesting about this is it's not the kids that are stampeding the stores, it's the grownups!

KLEIN: Yeah, well, they're meeting a child's needs. You know, this is a generous act, to adopt a child. I mean, this may be far-fetched, but I think if I had a small child that age, I would not consider it a bad thing to develop this idea of generosity and love. I mean, here you are going to take this homeless child and give it a home. It's a nice idea that your little girl wants to adopt a homeless little baby.

STAMBERG: Uh-huh. And parents have their own anxieties?

KLEIN: Yeah, I think so. I also think mothers are very heroic figures to children. There's a very real kind of identification that can be made with a mother by being this heroic to another baby. I mean, when you play house, you try to identify and copy what your mother does. But I think the awesomeness of a mother figure — the child may feel more identified with that by being this heroic figure to a baby doll.

ADAMS: Susan, something very sinister I'm afraid has occurred to me about these Cabbage Patch dolls. It has to do with the television commercial. You've seen that?

STAMBERG: No.

ADAMS: It's an animated thing. A cabbage plant opens up, and inside there's a little creature, a little doll. But suppose for a moment — bear with me now — that an alien force is trying to take over the earth. People from another planet, like the *Invasion of the Body Snatchers*. Now, they figured out the way to do it is to send down a lot of these little, cute Cabbage Patch dolls. Now, people say cute, but they also say ugly. They in fact can't figure out why everybody likes them so much. That's the power of these dolls. Anyway, right after Thanksgiving, this frenzied urge develops around the country. People have to have the dolls. A few million or so, then millions more to come very quickly. And then, late in February, in the dark of night, they start to multiply in your house. And they start walking around. You look around, and they're someplace else, and maybe there's two of them or three of them. And then suddenly they start biting at your ankles.

STAMBERG: Oh, come on. Wait a minute.

ADAMS: You trip over things, and you have a lot of trouble. And then one morning you wake up in bed and you can't move. You're tied down. About twenty of these beastly little creatures are right there in your bedroom and they're grinning at you. And then they send out the beam to the mother ship. The mother ship comes down, and all the little Cabbage Patch dolls go marching off to the field right outside of town there. And the door of the ship opens, and the big Cabbage Patch people come down the ramp and they are smiling. And the little Cabbage Patch people start getting on board, but they don't look the same. They've changed, and they have the faces of the people they've been living with. And, back of the house, the people are still tied up in bed, and they've changed too. They now have the faces of the Cabbage Patch dolls. The spaceship goes up and out of sight, and below, the earth starts to turn green all over. The planet Earth, you see, is turning into a giant cabbage.

✦ ✦ ✦ ✦ ✦ ✦ ✦ ✦ ✦ ✦

On the last day of the year, Lee Thornton interviewed the new president of NPR, Douglas J. Bennet, who came to work for us at a time of debt, deficit, and fiscal crisis. Bennet talked about the crisis with typical Yankee understatement. "Things got out of hand," he said. "They lost track of their financial accounts, lost track of management, made some bad assumptions about revenues. I think that in a broader sense, this is a very new institution, relatively speaking, and that it was due for some adjustment. Some of that adjustment was taking place in a sort of dramatic way in the course of the year." Dramatic indeed. The fact is that in 1983, we nearly lost the network. In the course of trying to get back on an even keel, NPR laid off employees and canceled programs. Member stations and foundations came to our aid, and the Corporation for Public Broadcasting was persuaded to lend emergency funding to keep us on the air. Mr. Bennet was asked that New Year's Eve if we should now put it all behind us. "I don't think we can put it behind us because I think we've got some lessons that are very important. In terms of my own management mission, part of it is to ensure that nothing like that ever happens again. But I think the more important lesson really is the support we found, that National Public Radio found, from people across the country. No normal organization could possibly have survived this crisis without that kind of constituency support." Doug Bennet nursed us back to fiscal health, and on to considerable growth and prosperity. One of his last acts at NPR was to organize the purchase of a new building. He stayed ten years before leaving us to go back to the State Department to serve in the Clinton administration.

1984

Susan Stamberg and Noah Adams had a short list of resolutions to open the year, followed by a Larry Massett production. The creator of the program *Soundprint*, Larry Massett is one of the best sound producers I know. Smoothing his work out on a page often does not do it justice, but this particular piece is an apt beginning for this particular year. First, though, the resolutions.

All Things Considered, JANUARY 2

ADAMS: In 1984, we resolve never to allow the name *George Orwell* to again cross our lips.

STAMBERG: In 1984, we resolve never to do stories on Cabbage Patch dolls or Pia Zadora.

ADAMS: We never did stories on Pia Zadora.

STAMBERG: But you never know when her name might pop up.

ADAMS: Or Joan Collins.

STAMBERG: Definitely.

ADAMS: But I would like to talk with Judy Collins. Or Tom Selleck.

STAMBERG: I think it was Tom Selleck, you will remember, who said, "In the scheme of things, I'm not as important as Dr. Jonas Salk."

ADAMS: In 1984, we resolve to avoid stories about pasta and whether jogging is bad for your knees. And men getting in touch with their feelings. And no reports on the quality of education in the United States.

STAMBERG: In 1984, we shall not discuss the amount of pine tar allowed on a baseball bat.

ADAMS: Coping over forty and National Public Radio's financial difficulties.

STAMBERG: Especially NPR's financial problems.

ADAMS: Especially coping over forty. However, there have been a number of stories we've always meant to do on *All Things Considered*, and this year we resolve to do them!

STAMBERG: To wit, in 1984, we will present interviews with all of Brooke Shields's professors at Princeton.

ADAMS: A complete annotated list of all the wives of Norman Mailer.

STAMBERG: And in 1984, we resolve to do a story about people who have spontaneously combusted.

ADAMS: Susan, wait a minute.

STAMBERG: What's wrong? That's a very legitimate story.

ADAMS: We actually have this story right now, coming up.

STAMBERG: You're kidding.

ADAMS: A story about people who have spontaneously combusted, from Larry Massett.

MASSETT: This is the time of year when people worry a little bit about catching on fire. Mostly about the Christmas tree catching on fire. But Joan Retallack, a writer teaching at the University of Maryland, collects stories about people who catch on fire, people who spontaneously combust.

RETALLACK: Miss Phyllis Newcombe. Miss Newcombe, a twenty-two-year-old British girl, combusts before a room full of people while waltzing in a dance hall, August 7, 1938. I'm sure Miss Newcombe was a virgin and destined to be a spinster, fulfilling the destiny of that label imposed by society, and somehow her cells conspired to give her a kind of racy and graceful way out of all of that. So in her last moments, she was a spectacular exhibitionist and chaste.

MASSETT: I suppose everyone stopped, and said, "Look at Phyllis!" Or "What's Miss Newcombe doing?"

RETALLACK: Well, actually, I think of her as a sort of anonymous figure, except for this. I imagine the reaction was, Who was that?

MASSETT: Joan Retallack finds these stories in old books, newspaper accounts. She collects them the way other people collect old beer cans or antique furniture.

RETALLACK: Then there's Mrs. Patrick Rooney. Mrs. Rooney combusts spontaneously on Christmas Eve 1885. Mr. Rooney dies of asphyxiation from smoke inhalation. I love it because it's the ultimate passive-aggressive act. She needn't have said a word to Mr. Rooney in all of those years.

None of these things strike me as odd. After all, we're volatile creatures. We live in a volatile world. Why not?

MASSETT: But it doesn't seem to happen very often. About how often does it seem to happen?

RETALLACK: I think that's in dispute. I've read figures like three hundred cases in four hundred years. That isn't very much.

MASSETT: Joan Retallack calculates that it would take about three thousand degrees Fahrenheit to produce the spectacle of spontaneous combustion. That's very hot, and apparently it's very fast.

RETALLACK: The suddenness is illustrated in the case of Aura Troyer in 1942 in Bloomington, Illinois. Aura Troyer, fifty-nine, was found in the basement of the bank where he worked as a janitor, almost all his clothing burned off. "It happened all of a sudden" was all he said before he died.

MASSETT: Many of these stories, she says, are badly documented, suggesting the work of amateur minds. There have been few really scientific studies.

RETALLACK: Probably the most scientific thing that I've read about was a case that occurred in Florida. The case concerns a Mrs. Mary Reeser, who combusted and was totally incinerated. And the incident was investigated by the police and by a physician and by a physical anthropologist, Dr. Wilton Krogman. He is said to have conducted a full-scale scientific study of the case and declared it baffling. This happened, like most accidents, at home.

MASSETT: The fire can be put out simply by beating on it or stamping it, but Joan Retallack finds no overall pattern that would suggest any way of preventing it before it happens.

RETALLACK: I think probably the one thing these accounts do have in common is suddenness and lack of control. I don't think it's something that you feel coming on, you know, saying, "I'm feeling a bit under the weather. Actually, I'm feeling like I might, in a few hours, combust." I think it comes on totally unawares, and that's part of the beauty of it.

✦ ✦ ✦ ✦ ✦ ✦ ✦ ✦ ✦

The political reporting partnership of Roberts and Wertheimer was going strong in 1984. We were both in San Francisco for the Democratic Convention when former Vice President Walter Mondale announced that his running mate would be Geraldine Ferraro, a member of Congress from New York. It was an extraordinary moment, personally and professionally, for us both. We talked about it with Bob Edwards on *Morning Edition*.

EDWARDS: What's the reaction at the convention?

ROBERTS: Well, the reaction yesterday afternoon and through the evening, as people began to hear this news, was one of tremendous excitement, especially as you might expect, among the women here. The women political professionals, many of whom have been pushing the notion of a woman vice president and pushing the notion of Geraldine Ferraro for a good while — they were just tremendously excited, but just a little bit disbelieving, saying, "I'd like to see it signed in parchment with Walter Mondale's fingerprint on it."

But I think it basically changed the whole atmosphere of the convention instantly, from one of going through the motions, hoping that Jesse Jackson would not cause any great trouble, to one of real excitement.

WERTHEIMER: Also, though, that excitement was kind of followed by a gulp and a kind of hesitation. The women we talked to last night said, "We have to make it work." Walter Mondale can't fail to be elected *because* he took the step of putting a woman on the ticket. This is scary stuff, this is a new adventure, uncharted territory. Nobody really knows whether it will work.

EDWARDS: Well, you two have covered the campaign for months. What do you think?

WERTHEIMER: Well, I think that if I were Walter Mondale, I could very clearly see why it would make some sense to do a thing like this. He's nineteen points behind in the polls. Everybody talks about him as the vanilla candidate. He's not exciting. So here he is, taking an incredible chance. At the very least, he should be able to shake off the notion that he's an ultracautious candidate.

ROBERTS: It's confusing because it's one of those situations where all of the traditional measures don't help you much. The polling data is not very good. Different polls tell you different things. Some people lie in polls that ask questions that they think they should answer one way, when in fact they feel a different way. But there is some indication and a good deal of what we call anecdotal information, which is just wandering around talking to voters, that women are attracted to a ticket with a woman on it.

EDWARDS: But aren't some to say that Mondale was bullied into the decision, that he's caved into another special interest?

ROBERTS: It's possible. Women have made demands on Walter Mondale, and the women's groups, especially in the very recent National

Organization for Women convention, were there making threatening noises about walkouts or nominating a woman from the floor. Geraldine Ferraro, by the way, handled that very well because she was the woman they were threatening to nominate from the floor and she made it very clear that she would not allow her name to be placed into a situation like that if Walter Mondale had already picked his running mate.

WERTHEIMER: I think that people will certainly say that Walter Mondale has caved in, but I think it's more likely that he was boxed in by his very own process, raising very high expectations that he was going to do something unusual: pick a minority, perhaps a Hispanic, Mayor Henry Cisneros, or a black, Mayor Tom Bradley of Los Angeles. I think that he left himself with very few choices. And I think he had a strong feeling that people didn't like the way he'd handled this vice presidential choice. They decided to cut their losses, get it over with, do something dynamic, do it now and get it done. And I think when he made the decision that he did not want to pick the obvious choice, which I think we'd have to say was Gary Hart, then Geraldine Ferraro, out of the group that he had left himself with, made the most sense to him.

EDWARDS: Why not Hart?

ROBERTS: Well, you have to remember it was a long and bitter campaign. I remember sitting at Texas A&M when Gary Hart talked about the "days of shame" under the Carter-Mondale administration with the blindfolded Iranian hostages. Those kinds of things went on through the entire campaign. You have to remember Walter Mondale served as a vice president, knows what that relationship was like, and I think he was just not ready to make that step toward someone that made him so uncomfortable.

EDWARDS: So why Ferraro, then?

WERTHEIMER: Well, if she is the one, she has some traditional vice presidential aspects to her. She's an ethnic Catholic from a very big state. Vice presidential candidates have been picked on that basis alone. Besides that, she's a solid, establishment politician. She gets along with the big boys in the Congress. Speaker Tip O'Neill says that she's his favorite candidate.

ROBERTS: She's been the unlikely candidate of an awful lot of Queens, New York, Democrats, Archie Bunker's own district, it's said. She was a prosecutor, which makes her very amenable to the law-and-order types. She's a mother and she's a good Italian Catholic and she's a good campaigner who tends to end her speeches by saying, "Look, I've been here awhile, I've been happy to listen to you, but it's time for me to go home to my children now. They're expecting me to make a little manicotti, a little ravioli, and my mother is expecting me to call."

✦ ✦ ✦ ✦ ✦ ✦ ✦ ✦ ✦ ✦

In political years, I generally spent most of my time on the road, traveling with the candidates of the party out of power, lugging boxes of tapes representing critical moments in the campaigns of Walter Mondale, Gary Hart, Jesse Jackson. Periodically, I would do a review, drawing on my traveling library. I called these pieces "greatest hits from the campaign trail." Bob Edwards and I summed up the Democratic campaign just before the San Francisco convention.

Morning Edition, JULY 13

EDWARDS: Let's go back to the beginning, back to Iowa.

WERTHEIMER: When I think of Iowa, what I remember was that it was cold. There was snow blowing around on the cornfields. But I think my dominant memories are of the Hart campaign, traveling in a camper, Hart getting out and speaking to people, just wearing a suit in nine-degrees-below-zero weather. The little towns, Spencer, Emmetsburg, Algona, Clear Lake, and Hart was saying this kind of thing:

HART: I intend to surprise the pundits and the pollsters, demonstrate that someone who was not well known but does try to represent the future of this country can do well in a state like this and go ahead and get the nomination, with the help of people like yourselves, and become the next president of the United States. Thank you all very much.

EDWARDS: Iowa belonged to Mondale, as predicted, but Hart came in second in a crowded field. Mondale was the man in those days, leading up to the Iowa caucuses.

WERTHEIMER: His campaign slogan was that he was ready to be president. He said he had the experience to be president, and he went around collecting endorsements with every hope of success, from the AFL-CIO and the National Education Association, from the teachers.

MONDALE: By the end of this decade, I want to walk into any classroom with the brightest youngsters in that class and have many of them tell me, "I want to be a teacher."

EDWARDS: Those endorsements had a backlash too. He became

known as the special-interest candidate and they're still charging him with that.

But back to the winter. At about that time, we began to hear a new voice out of the Reverend Jesse Jackson.

WERTHEIMER: The incredible preaching, the rolling rhetoric that black people have heard for years, but white people had never really heard in a presidential campaign. He made history, came into the race saying that if all the unregistered blacks eligible to vote in this country had registered and had voted, then the last election would have come out differently. Remember, he called them rocks, just laying around.

JACKSON: Rocks! Laying around! Hold your head high! Dry your tear-stained eyes! Pull out your slingshot! Pick up your rock! Say, Goliath, it's 1984 now! Hands that once picked cotton now gonna pick presidents!

EDWARDS: Jackson got out the black vote all right and carried about seven of America's biggest cities, but he stumbled over charges of anti-Semitism.

WERTHEIMER: At the very beginning of the campaign, it was reported that in private conversation he referred to Jews as "Hymies," New York as "Hymietown." He came to New Hampshire to apologize for that.

JACKSON: It was not in a spirit of meanness. An off-color remark has a new bearing on religion or politics. However innocent or unintended, it was insensitive and wrong.

WERTHEIMER: That apology was a long time in coming, and it happened again when Louis Farrakhan, who is an associate of Jackson's, made very strong anti-Semitic remarks, and Jackson was a long time in denying him. Had that not happened, I think that Jackson would have done even better than he did, that he would have made a remarkable mark on this election.

EDWARDS: The New Hampshire primary. Everything changed there. Gary Hart won it.

WERTHEIMER: Everything certainly did change. Maine confirmed that it was not a fluke. Independents came in to vote for Hart, and Hart was on his way. Mondale was stumbling. Mondale was trying to find his voice. Finally, at Emory University in the South, where the campaign headed next, he basically said, Here I am, this is me.

MONDALE: I am seasoned, and that experience will make me a wiser president. I have deep values, and my commitment, those commitments, will make me a stronger president. I am who I am. What you see is what you get.

EDWARDS: It was down in Georgia that Mondale got things going again for his campaign. He asked the only question that counts, as I recall, "Where's the beef?"

WERTHEIMER: That was in the Atlanta debate. Gary Hart was talking about how Democrats should support small business.

HART: . . . own and operate businesses that create jobs.

MODERATOR: Mr. Glenn?

MONDALE: May I respond to that?

MODERATOR: Well, we'll come back to you. Let some of the others —

MONDALE: What's new about coming out for entrepreneurs?

HART: There are some specific ways to do that.

MONDALE: When I hear your new ideas, I'm reminded of that ad, "Where's the beef?"

EDWARDS: Was, in fact, a campaign turned around by a fast-food commercial?

WERTHEIMER: I think it was, because at that point, Mondale survived in the South. He won two states, and then he went back to the area where he should be strong, in the labor states. He went to Illinois, where he beat Hart, who made some mistakes. Hart had trouble filling the shoes he'd stepped into. His campaign really wasn't up to being the front-runner. Mondale beat him in Illinois and then beat up on him in New York. This was the New York debate, where Mondale made a really strong attack on Hart, and it worked very well for him:

MONDALE: Why do you run those ads that suggest that I'm out trying to kill kids when you know better? I'm a person who believes in peace. All my life I've been opposed to any kind of use of American force that isn't totally justified and sensible under the circumstances. And to run ads as you run them suggests there's something to my policies that will lead to the death of American boys. I think you oughtta pull those ads down tonight.

EDWARDS: In Illinois and New York and other states, Mondale used an ad to plant and nurture seeds of distrust of Hart.

WERTHEIMER: That's the famous red-phone ad.

TELEVISION COMMERCIAL: The most awesome, powerful responsibility in the world lies in the hand that picks up this phone. The idea of an unsure, unsteady, untested hand is something to really think about. This is the issue of our times.

WERTHEIMER: Mondale somehow wanted to make people believe that Hart was not really ready to be president, as Mondale kept saying *he* was. And that worked very well for him. And he used it in Illinois and New York and in later states.

EDWARDS: But even when Mondale won Texas, beating Hart down there, it wasn't over because Hart won in Ohio.

WERTHEIMER: That's right. Walter Mondale just somehow could not bring this campaign to a close. So it went on to California and on to New Jersey, and in California, Hart did something silly. Once again, something silly changed the course of the campaign. A joke about Hart campaigning with his wife.

HART: The deal is that we campaign separately. That's the bad news. The good news for me is that I campaign in California, and she campaigns in New Jersey.

WERTHEIMER: A good news–bad news joke about New Jersey told on a poolside patio in a Beverly Hills house, and Gary Hart's last chance dwindled away. It was in the paper for days and days and days in New Jersey.

EDWARDS: What, for you, was the big moment of this campaign?

WERTHEIMER: I think I would have to say it was Jesse Jackson, who was by far the most exciting campaigner in this whole race. I remember Jesse Jackson at Jackson State, a black college in Jackson, Mississippi. He led a march to the courthouse to register these kids. Jesse Jackson fired up, tired, roaring, preaching to youngsters who were just hanging on his every word. It was one of the most electric moments of the campaign for me. And this was one of the most electric moments of his speech:

JACKSON: [*Shouting.*] Change! Feed the hungry! Change! Clothe the naked! Change! Liberate the captives! Change! Make democracy real for everybody! Our time has come! Thank you very much.

WERTHEIMER: I think when you add up this campaign, you have to say that Jesse Jackson and moments like that and the fact that he did change history is what we will remember.

✦ ✦ ✦ ✦ ✦ ✦ ✦ ✦ ✦

While I climbed on and off airplanes during the campaign year, Cokie Roberts tended to stay on the ground, closer to the voters. This is another way we summarized campaigns, listening to voters, hearing where the country was headed. The campaign was almost over when Cokie stopped at Bogue's Cafe in Birmingham, in Alabama, to talk to the owner, Andy Straynar, and his customers and employees.

ROBERTS: Bogue's Cafe in Birmingham isn't what you'd call a fancy place by any stretch of the imagination, but it attracts a loyal clientele of over-the-coffee-cup philosophers.

STRAYNAR: You could get yourself an earful just by sitting over there. That's where the gang hangs out.

ROBERTS: Bogue's owner of seventeen years, Andy Straynar, is happy to let a reporter join his table of regulars, but first, Straynar wants to register his own opinions.

STRAYNAR: God save the United States if a woman gets in there, and my wife feels the same way. She said a woman's place is not in there. She says it's not because they're not smart, it's because they just don't think like a man. And I agree with her that women don't think like men.

ROBERTS: The one woman at the table, registered nurse Kathy Caldwell, couldn't disagree more.

CALDWELL: I like that there's a woman vice presidential candidate.

ROBERTS: And is that likely to sway your vote?

CALDWELL: It has, yeah, I think so. There are a lot of women who'll never speak up for things that they believe in, and when she's up there they feel stronger and are able to come out with what they believe.

ROBERTS: It's giving you the nerve to open your mouth?

CALDWELL: Maybe, yeah. That's a good way to put it. 'Cause I wouldn't be talking to you now. You know?

ROBERTS: With these guys here.

CALDWELL: Good point, yeah. This is the guy's table.

ROBERTS: The guys at the table are almost unanimous in their support of President Reagan. Though most of these southerners were raised as Democrats, this year they'll be voting Republican. Robert Gwin is in the lighting supply business.

GWIN: I personally don't like Mondale. From a personal standpoint — now, I guess that goes back to the association with Jimmy Carter. Of course, this is the Knights of the Round Table. Anything you want to know in Birmingham, I mean, you came to the right place. I mean, it seems like all the knowledge is right here. You know, we talk about Jesse Jackson and things. I made a comment: I'd vote for Jesse Jackson before I'd vote for Fritz Mondale. But I mean, I don't know, I just don't like his views. In particular, taxation.

ROBERTS: Bob Gwin sits sipping coffee at the Formica-topped table that serves as the magnet in the middle of a room lined with plastic-covered booths. Most of the men around the table know each other. They come in every day to read the paper, have some coffee or perhaps a full breakfast of ham and eggs, grits, and biscuits. At this one table, in this one town, they personify the numbers so starkly displayed in the polls. Ron Gaiser is a real estate developer.

GAISER: I don't like the Democratic ticket. I haven't liked the Democratic ticket in many years. I don't. I think it would be nice if they could get a John Glenn or somebody that was more responsive to Middle America and to goals and objectives that people have in Middle America.

The Democratic ticket is basically built around labor unions and around minority groups. There's nothing wrong with minority groups, but when you build a ticket around special-purpose legislation and around special-purpose groups, I believe you're building a ticket that doesn't reflect working people and doesn't reflect their values. Their values are basically family, recreation, children, schools, good schools, low taxes, lack of government interference in their business affairs and their family affairs, independence, a self-confident role in life, and the right to do your thing.

ROBERTS: Lawyer Gene Caldwell likes the Reagan program.

CALDWELL: It's beneficial, generally, for most of the people. I think maybe it's slanted a little bit to the upper class, but, you know, upper-class people are high achievers. They seem to do better when they have the rein to do it, you know.

The people on these welfare programs, they've been on them for years. Generations have gone, passed down. That's their livelihood, that's what they do and that's what they've always done. And he's just giving them some involuntary incentive to go out and do something. I don't think, on the other hand, he's cut everybody off and threw them in the street either.

ROBERTS: Among the men sitting around the table at Bogue's in Birmingham, only Bill Lowe, a woodworker, supports Walter Mondale.

LOWE: Foreign policy? Reagan has no foreign policy whatsoever. His foreign policy in Lebanon has frightened us out. Domestically, in this town, two years ago, there were people — I mean, I was working on a job in North Birmingham, and every piece of scrap wood that hit the ground, somebody picked it up to burn to keep warm.

ROBERTS: Then Ron Gaiser summed up for the men.

GAISER: Mondale, though, is basically a joke. I mean, he is an absolute joke.

ROBERTS: When he said, "Mondale's a joke in the South," and you said, "*She's* not," tell me why.

KAREN HABERSTROH: I just think the people that are the Reagan people are more outspoken, louder, and are basically more men in the South. I think the women, who don't get heard as much, are more for the Mondale-Ferraro ticket. I'm not necessarily that crazy about him, but I think she's excellent.

ROBERTS: Bogue's cashier, Karen Haberstroh, had circled the table, listening to the men. She finally could keep her peace no longer. Neither could the woman who waits on these men every day, Dale Smith, who says she's had her troubles in the last four years.

SMITH: This is my table. I hear it day in and day out, and I just try not to get involved in it. Because, you know, I think that Mondale and Ferraro are a great pair. As a waitress, they tax us eight percent, that new tax. Sometimes I draw a month with seven dollars in my paycheck. And if I have fifteen customers sit down and they don't leave a tip, they still say that I owe them eight percent of whatever was not even left on that table.

ROBERTS: You mean these guys who are all talking about the economy being good for them don't tip you?

SMITH: That's right. Some of them don't. Most of them do. Most of them are my friends, really. We have great discussions here, we have a great table here. I love 'em, every one, but we really give it to each other sometimes.

ROBERTS: The crowd around the table at Bogue's in Birmingham drifts out. The men go off to work. Dale Smith mops the table with a cloth, Karen Haberstroh returns to her cash register, and all promise to bring their views to the voting booths a week from today.

✦ ✦ ✦ ✦ ✦ ✦ ✦ ✦ ✦

The table at Bogue's had it right. President Reagan was reelected. Cokie Roberts and I have both been back to Bogue's since then, for grits and opinions.

Right around election day, Noah Adams interviewed a man who advocated harvesting organs from executed criminals. Dr. Jack Kevorkian was not yet famous, but he clearly had star quality.

KEVORKIAN: The ancient Alexandrians in 200 and 300 B.C., the kings, the Ptolemys, decreed that all condemned criminals would be subject to experimentation in the process of execution, and I thought that was a good idea and I thought I'd propose it today, with one addition — that they all be under deep anesthesia during the process.

ADAMS: California pathologist Dr. Jack Kevorkian proposes that condemned criminals could provide many needed transplant organs if they were removed immediately after or even just before the executions. In the October issue of *MD* magazine, Dr. Kevorkian writes that many death-row inmates are eager to suffer more meaningful death this way. The option would, he says, enable the condemned truly to repay society for their crimes.

KEVORKIAN: The man would be given a choice, or the woman, of execution the way the law says in each state now or instead to be put under with an injection in the arm at the exact instant the time was set for execution. And while they're under, we'd experiment on their body, but they would never awaken. And not necessarily with lethal experimentation. They may survive the experiment. In that case, a layman would come in and just push in an overdose of anesthetic.

ADAMS: So you're, in a way, updating this proposal to suggest that people who are going to be executed have the option of donating their organs to other people.

KEVORKIAN: Or submitting to experiments. If a condemned person is too old or too ill to donate organs, he should have the choice of submitting to experiments to atone.

ADAMS: You point out that to pay for one's sins involves an actual transfer of value, and this is about the only way it could be done.

KEVORKIAN: Absolutely. It's the only time. It's the first time in history, in human history. It's the only way you can have a positive aspect to the death penalty, at the same time giving the man the most humane mode of execution.

ADAMS: You maintain that twelve hundred people now on death row have been surveyed and are willing to do this.

KEVORKIAN: No, but I myself have talked to six condemned men in this country in three states, and I have now got a written petition, entirely spontaneous, from thirty-three condemned men in San Quentin in California, endorsing this idea. I can't go around this country and interview thirteen hundred people. First of all, they don't let me in because they're all against the idea, the prison authorities, politicians, and the medical authorities.

ADAMS: Well, you point out that the people making this decision, or making the decision by not making the decision, are not on death row and would not benefit themselves from the organs.

KEVORKIAN: Well, that's — I'm just guessing that's part of it. They're all selfish. They're not there. They don't care. It exposes the hypocrisy of those for and against the death penalty who are against this idea. Those for it are a little bit uneasy because it makes death a little too easy. They want revenge. Those against it, it makes capital punishment too valuable. They don't want anything that would retard their campaign, which is based strictly on the macabre aspects of capital punishment. And this would eliminate the macabre aspects.

✦ ✦ ✦ ✦ ✦ ✦ ✦ ✦ ✦

In 1984 San Francisco had the largest share of people with AIDS in the country, almost all of them gay men. Caring for hundreds of seriously ill people created a health crisis at a time when no city was set up to handle AIDS cases. A San Francisco organization called the Shanti Project, which had worked for ten years to provide counseling for people facing terminal illness, shifted its focus to AIDS, to train counselors to deal with this new disease. Margot Adler talked with some of the people learning to live and die with AIDS.

All Things Considered, NOVEMBER 23

ADLER: Volunteer counselors are picked very carefully. They undergo an intense training that includes role playing, patient advocacy, learning how to wend your way through the state and federal bureaucracies, and learning to help someone with AIDS not to see himself as a victim. All trainees go through an hour-and-a-half exercise in which they imagine their own diagnosis with AIDS, their own sickness, and their own death.

There's a small building on Fillmore Street near the Shanti office. It's one of the four residences for people with AIDS. I went with Lynn Eubanks, a counselor, to see her client, Patrick, who had taken ill six months before with *Pneumocystis* pneumonia, one of the two most common illnesses associated with AIDS. Now at home, speaking by holding a cloth over a still-open incision in his throat, Patrick is recovering, hoping against hope that he will not have a relapse. We sat at his bedside and listened to his story.

PATRICK: It had a lot of effects on me, frightening effects. Obviously, I was very upset and it was very helpful to me to have Lynn come in every day at the hospital. She's wonderful. She came in every single day while I was at the hospital and even stayed two separate nights when I was in agony and in pain, by my bedside. And there were two occasions when I nearly passed away and on both occasions she was always there.

EUBANKS: When I met Patrick, he was in intensive care and on a ventilator with lots of tubes and on a morphine drip. And I remember, he couldn't talk at all, so he would write. And his first sentence to me was, "I can't believe the horrible, horrendous pain I'm in, the total suffering, and it's been nothing but suffering since I've been here."

And then his next sentence was that he planned to recover, that he was going to spend his energy recovering. And then he looked at me and he wrote, "Am I in your care now?" And I said yes. And he said, "OK, can I go to sleep now?" [*Laughter.*]

PATRICK: I remember that distinctly. Your visits certainly had a lot to do with my recovery.

ADLER: Despite the prevalence of death, Project Director Jim Geary says the focus of Shanti is on life, is on the now.

GEARY: Probably over ninety percent of the people with AIDS after diagnosis view themselves in the process of recovery, rather than as in the process of dying. Despite the statistics and despite the vast number of people that have died of AIDS, we really attempt to hold onto a belief in miracles and the possibility that someone is going to beat this illness. Either in terms of being cured or living a lot longer than expected.

We don't see ourselves as there really to teach anything. We see ourselves as available to offer support, to be a sounding board, to not shy away from the painful issues that the people with AIDS deal with, the rejection, the issues of sexuality, coming out maybe to family members, both as a person with AIDS and possibly as a gay person at the same time. It's that willingness, the volunteer's willingness to not run away from very painful emotions, that enables the clients to explore their own pain regarding certain emotions.

PATRICK: I haven't told my family yet because I felt it would take too much psychologically out of them, because I don't want them to have any worries.

ADLER: Mary Redick is a Shanti counselor.

REDICK: There are plenty of mothers that have flown into San Francisco that are wringing their hands, not understanding why their twenty-seven-year-old son died of pneumonia. And the doctors say it was a very fierce form of pneumonia, we're sorry we couldn't save your son. AIDS and being gay has never been mentioned. Why? A person with AIDS had a right to privacy and if their parents are not to know, they're not to know.

Then there's the whole process of saying, Hey, I'm going to deal with the whole thing. And beautiful, incredible scenes of parents flying in and finding out within a forty-eight-hour period that not only is their son gay, but also that he has AIDS and he's going to die within a week or so. And mothers and fathers holding their sons and loving them and asking how they can help their lovers make decisions. And the kind of working together is incredible, you know?

And then there are horrible scenes like, I remember one: a mother came in and started screaming like, get the fags away from my son, and he's already repented, and all of this horrible stuff. And, I mean, she really basically needed to be put in a straitjacket. I mean, it was not like — it was not Christianity or something, it was like being bananas. And her son was in a stage of, what I would say, it's as though he was treading water. He had definitely seen the other side, there was no doubt about it whatever. And he had not died.

Mother phones, the same crazed mother phoned from wherever it was in the Midwest and asked the church nurse if she could talk to her son, and the church nurse said no, figuring that she would just rant and rave again and that it would be awful and a disaster. And Mother finally prevailed. So the church nurse took the phone, and put the phone up to the person with AIDS's ear, and then the nurse listened. And this very mother, who six weeks before had been causing such incredible chaos with her homophobia at the General Hospital, now phoned to beg her son's forgiveness for her behavior.

Somehow, in the middle of all that, she came to her senses. And her heart connection with her son was made. And this particular man could not respond at that point, so the nurse said, "Blink if you know your mother loves you. Blink if you understand that she forgives you and she wants your forgiveness. Blink if you know that she loves you exactly the way you are and always has." And he — at each point he blinked. He could hear still.

Mother hung up. He went into a huge spasm of coughing. It took almost ten minutes to suction him. He went into a deep and very gentle sleep. He went into the act of dying twelve hours later. I was present and at the moment that he died — a man who was thirty — I could show you a picture of him. He was thirty and looked like he was a hundred and five. At the very moment of his death, he looked like a twelve-year-old. And that moment of death — there was that incredible sense of release.

ADLER: Although Shanti counselors seem to experience a relentless flow of crisis and loss, all told me the experience was a gift, an opportunity to face the issues every human being ultimately faces. All the counselors I spoke to told me their lives had changed utterly. "I won't eat something I don't like because it might be my last meal," Mary Redick said. "I live every day in the present."

REDICK: Everything's accelerated. The level of authenticity has gotta be there. There's no time to play games. If I looked at you and said, "OK, you're gonna be dead in six months," how different our interaction would be at this point.

ADLER: It would be more intense.

REDICK: Absolutely. And at the same time, it would be much more relaxed. A whole series of issues are solved. Are you worried about dishes? Hell, no. You know. You're not worried about dishes. Are you worried about your mother's second cousin's fourteenth birthday? No, you're not worried about that. Much more relaxed. Much more relaxed. There's a beautiful day. Hey, there's serious cloud watching to do. It's a starry night? You gotta put four hours in on the Big Dipper. These men have given me an incredible gift. Yeah, I've put in my hours. But the stuff they've taught me is just extraordinary.

1985

When Pine Bluff, Arkansas, edged Flint, Michigan, out of last place in the *American Demographics* magazine rating on quality of life, Michael Moore spoke up for Flint. He was then editor of the *Michigan Voice*, not yet the producer of the documentary film about General Motors, *Roger and Me*.

All Things Considered, JULY 1

MOORE: Greetings from the second worst place to live in America. You have no idea how it feels not to be number one anymore. For the better part of this decade, Flint, Michigan, has ranked at the top of all the worst lists in the country: worst unemployment, worst crime rate, worst number of cars repossessed, worst everything, it seemed. But not anymore.

You're probably wondering, How did Flint put itself back on its feet to become only the second worst city in which to live? The turning point, I know for me, was back in 1983, when the unemployment rate here hit twenty-seven percent. And the mayor of Flint, in search of a miracle, sought the help of TV evangelist Robert Schuller. The city of Flint paid Reverend Schuller ten thousand dollars to come to Flint and hold a citywide revival to lift the spirits of the poor and downtrodden and lead them from the unemployment line to the promised land of lowered expectations and minimum-wage jobs.

His sermon, to the thousands assembled in the sports arena, was simple. Tough times don't last, tough people do. The message was clear: Wimps hit the road. Recessions build men. Pump gas or get out of town. According to a recent survey, twenty thousand people apparently took his advice and left Flint in search of work elsewhere. With twenty thousand fewer jobless people to count, the unemployment rate here looks a lot nicer.

Flint is also number two now in violent crime. The FBI's uniform crime report has declared that only Miami is worse than Flint. Wouldn't that make you feel safer, knowing that you barely beat out Miami in per capita number of murders, rapes, and assaults?

I guess the point of this is that it doesn't feel all that good to be number two. In some ways it's even worse. At least if you're the worst city in which to live, you get a lot of attention from the national media and supply-side evangelists. But who wants to save the second worst city? People don't like a loser, and now Flint has even lost at losing.

But there still may be hope. Eighteen thousand families still collect food stamps here every month. The poor still line up every morning at the Flint Plasma Center to sell their blood for some extra cash. And General Motors is still talking about closing two more factories, throwing another five thousand people out of work. So what more does it take to regain our rightful place as the worst of the worst? Being number two, we'll try harder.

✦ ✦ ✦ ✦ ✦ ✦ ✦ ✦ ✦ ✦

In the middle of June, the Reagan administration suddenly had its own hostage crisis. Lebanese Shiite Muslims, the extremist Hezbollah, hijacked a TWA jet flying out of Athens. For days the plane shuttled between Beirut and Algiers, as attempts were made to negotiate release. On one stop in Beirut, the hijackers murdered a young American marine, Robert Stethem, and dumped his body on the tarmac. By the end of the month, most of the passengers had been released, except for a group of American men who had been taken over by the more moderate Amal militia, which demanded that Israel release Lebanese prisoners in exchange for the American hostages. In the end, that is what happened, although statements were made that there was no link between the two releases.

Scott Simon talked to some of the hostages about a week after their return home. Scott first worked for us in our Chicago bureau. We sent him all over the world and finally brought him to the mother ship to anchor *Weekend Edition* on Saturday. Scott is almost as vivid and beguiling on the radio as he is in person. Listeners know more about Scott than they do about the rest of us. He makes no secret of his strongly held views on war and violence and is famous for this kind of sympathetic interview with the TWA hostages Robert Peel, Thomas Cullins, and Jeffrey Ingalls. Some had formed a relationship with their captors.

PEEL: Well, you have to look for funny things in this, and one of the gentlemen in our group — after eight days we were allowed to get our luggage and it was very dark and it was very late at night and everybody was sleeping — went down and he grabbed his wrong luggage. He grabbed his wife's luggage. So he spent the next eight days wearing her blouses, which made for a little bit of humor. Another time, we had become friends with this guard. He came into our room and was very panicky. He had lost his gun and wanted to know if any of us had seen it.

SIMON: That's former hostage Robert Peel, Jr., on his arrival back home in Hutchinson, Kansas. What seems to stay in the minds of the former hostages as vividly as the terror of the taking of that aircraft and the overheard murder of Robert Stethem is the experience they had as captives in another country. Those who did not share their anger, their fear, their confusion, and the small acts of kindness that became so critical cannot begin to understand what's happened to them.

Thomas Cullins, for example, an architect in Burlington, Vermont, remembers he actually issued orders of a kind to the men in the Amal militia who held him prisoner.

CULLINS: Such as, "We're out of water. Bring water now," and saying it very sternly. Or "Food is late, please bring food now." Or that kind of thing. So that was one category of communication.

SIMON: You felt free to behave that way with men who were carrying guns?

CULLINS: Absolutely. This may sound really ridiculous to you, but I believe that the — we were told over and over again, and the central focus of their movement is based on their religion, and we were told over and over again, which I believed to a certain degree, that the Koran and their beliefs to some degree allowed the killing of people who were guilty either of spying, et cetera, et cetera, but that we were innocent people and they believed that. And we would absolutely not be touched even to the point of having a pinprick.

SIMON: Much of the time, he says, they watched television, American programs, in fact. Mr. Cullins recalls this conversation with one of his captors.

CULLINS: I asked him what he did for a job, besides being an Amal militiaman. He said he was a barber, and I asked him to cut my hair. And I sat in the chair, and he put his AK-47 against the wall, and he cut my hair.

SIMON: But you felt safe. Not safe maybe . . .

CULLINS: I felt safe in a general sense. I was, I had a constant fear level, a constant anxiety level, but I felt confident that, aside from getting killed by mistake or having to be shot by being backed up politically to save face, we would not be shot.

SIMON: Navy seaman Jeffrey Ingalls was told by the Hezbollah he was being held to ensure the release of Lebanese prisoners in Israel, men they described as being their brothers, though that term was probably metaphorical.

INGALLS: You know, anyone that we saw or talked to, they said they were very sorry.

SIMON: If everybody was very sorry, and everybody said that no harm would come to you, and everybody that you had any contact with seemed to be — at least after you were taken off the plane — seemed to be provisional of your interest, did the Hezbollah ever tell you why you were being held, or why they didn't let you go home?

INGALLS: Well, they told us we were being held because they themselves had been pushed into a corner.

SIMON: How do you feel about that?

INGALLS: Well, I can see their point.

SIMON: You know, when some of you fellows expressed those kinds of sentiments in the press conferences we saw in Beirut and then Damascus, a lot of that was explained away in this country by the fact that you people were judged to be suffering from a psychological affliction, something called Stockholm syndrome, that you couldn't really be sincere, you had to be psychologically ravaged. How do you react to that?

INGALLS: Well, I'm no psychiatrist, you know. Maybe it is true. I don't know. This is the first time it's ever happened to me. But I think I'm mentally sane myself, and I have clear thoughts about it. And, you know, as I said before, we saw a different side of the world, and, you know, when we were moved throughout the streets of Beirut, I've never seen so much destruction in my life. We could've been treated a lot worse.

SIMON: Could've been not hijacked at all, of course.

INGALLS: Right.

SIMON: Mr. Ingalls recalls that the man guarding him, like most soldiers and civilians in Beirut, wore a pistol.

INGALLS: But most of the time he tried to take it off and leave it outside the room. We asked him why he did that, and he said that he didn't want us to be afraid of him. And he didn't like guns anyway.

They just gave it to him while he was going to be with us and told him to wear it. But most of the time, he always tried to take it off and not wear it around us. The man had actually even, you know, fallen asleep in there one time, wearing a gun, and, you know, he realized we weren't gonna hurt him and we realized he wasn't gonna hurt us.

SIMON: Mr. Ingalls, I've got to ask you. You're a member of the United States Navy, right? You're being held hostage, your captor falls asleep with his gun. Why didn't you filch the gun, hold it at his head, and say — you've seen all those movies!

INGALLS: That's just it. You said it right there. They're movies, and in a real-life situation there's a whole lot more to it than that. I probably would've made it two steps out that door, and that would've been it. And then the other three individuals who would've been in that room — they would've been, they wouldn't have lasted too long either. There would've been a couple more trips up to Arlington.

♦ ♦ ♦ ♦ ♦ ♦ ♦ ♦ ♦ ♦

During the eighties, the world began to be aware of desperate conditions in Africa. A combination of drought and revolution moved enormous numbers of people away from their agricultural land. International efforts began to feed people in Ethiopia and Chad. And 1985 was also International Women's Year for the United Nations, and the occasion of a massive conference held in Africa. NPR sent a crew to Kenya for the Nairobi Conference, including Ellen Weiss, now the executive producer of *All Things Considered*. This piece was about a fact of life for women all over the world, something one of the delegates described as women's "double burden." Women bear and raise the children, and in Africa they are the traders and the farmers as well. Ellen talked about women's work in Kenya.

All Things Considered, JULY 16

WEISS: The life of a rural Kenyan woman, a woman like Grace Njeri in Murang'a, is incredibly difficult.

NJERI: I wake up at about five that day in the morning. I go and milk. And I take my milk to the dairy and then I go about the business of the home, feeding my family and preparing them for school. And after that, I go to the farm.

WEISS: She brings food and fuel home from the farm, walking as much as ten miles a day, carrying a pot of water which may weigh thirty pounds.

NJERI: If I am wading or planting or harvesting, whatever it is I do, until the evening, when I have to milk again and prepare the supper for my family.

WEISS: In the rural areas of Kenya, only women work in the fields. In fact, only women work because almost all of the men have moved away. In the capital Nairobi and the coastal city Mombasa, the population has swelled with men working as security guards, in hotels, factories, any job that pays. The women are left behind to produce all of the food and care for the family.

When British colonizers at the turn of the century started planting coffee, tea, and other cash crops, changes began to take place in the division of labor between Kenyan men and women. Men worked for money, while the women's traditional tasks kept them at home. As the men moved farther and farther away for paying jobs, the women assumed all of the responsibilities of providing food for the family.

NJERI: Actually speaking, about ninety percent of the actual farmers, the ones who do the work, are women. The men — most of the men are in formal employment, so they leave the women behind.

WEISS: Little if any of the husbands' salary reaches their wives in the country. And the occasional visits home usually result in another child for the woman to care for. The women work small plots of poor-quality land almost entirely by hand. Women rarely hold the title to the land, so they are ineligible for credit.

Alone, poor, with children to feed and all of the farming to do, women in Kenya have learned to survive by working together. In fact, there are more than fifteen thousand women's groups scattered throughout the country, each with anywhere from twenty to forty women members. Through these groups, women are producing food for their families, getting their goods to the market, drinking cleaner water, and improving their health. There's a quiet revolution taking place among the women in rural Kenya.

The Lamani women's group raises goats in western Kenya. This area is known as the breadbasket of the country. Many of the large farms are run by black and white absentee landlords living hundreds of miles away in Nairobi. Kenyans call them telephone farmers.

Almost all of the food produced in this area is transported to other parts of the country. And in the last few years, dairy products have become more and more scarce. The Lamani women are trying to change that. Wilkesta Maketa chairs the group.

MAKETA: We started our group in 1979 to help each other. We saw some women who are not able to raise the food for their children. So I decided to call them and study together to decide what we can to do so that we can help each other.

WEISS: The group began raising goats through a donation by the affiliate of CARE in Kenya. Each woman contributes nine dollars to join and her time to keep the project going. All the women gather for big activities such as dipping the goats, coaxing the animals into a bath of special insect repellent solution. The women work shifts feeding and cleaning the animals, two days a week per member. When they sell some of the goats, the group keeps the profit, and from the rest of the animals, the women get all the milk they need for their families.

Ironically, while the women across Africa produce most of the food grown on the continent, it's the men who have received the greatest part of the aid and training from governments, private donors, and international agencies. Since the start of the women's decade in 1975, Kenya has received money specifically for integrating women into development activities. It is through the country's thousands of grass-roots organizations that some change is taking place, but it's a slow process.

The members of the women's group in Mbita earn their living by fishing in Lake Victoria, the world's second-largest lake, located on the Kenya-Uganda border. They are one of six thousand groups belonging to Maendeleo Ya Wanawake, which means Progress of Women. It's the largest women's organization in Kenya and was started over thirty years ago. The fishing is plentiful, but the work is long and hard, and right now the women must depend on men to transport their fish to city markets. Esther Okenye is the leader of the group.

OKENYE: Here we are, when we have got the fish from the lake, they go and weigh it, and for one kilo they give us two shillings. But when they go to Mombasa, or to Nairobi, one kilo is thirty shillings. And so we have realized that we are working for them. And therefore we have thought out what to do next. And we have thought of maybe we could all unite to form a big group, one big body which will trade in fish.

WEISS: The women want to buy their own truck, eliminate the middle-man, and, they hope, get more profits for their labor. So far, no money from the government or outside the country has reached the women. One member, Penina Oketo, says that fact doesn't detract from the gains the women have made.

OKETO: This lady here with the baby, ten years ago, it would have been very difficult to get her here, convince to leave her lands and come here. I think she's more aware of what her baby needs.

WEISS: Rosemary Massumba is a reporter with the *Voice of Kenya*. She says that for all the well-organized, numerous women's groups working on the local level in Kenya, few advances have been made by women nationally.

MASSUMBA: In our Kenyan constitution, there is no discrimination against a woman, but the women have never seized that opportunity. We don't speak as one voice. We're not united. If we were, you know, we are the majority in this country and we could get anything. But we'd rather give out this chance to the men just because we are not united. And you see the men will capitalize on that.

WEISS: Both Kenyan men and women are reluctant to incorporate changes into their traditional roles. There are more women lawyers in Kenya today, but many stay home after marriage and don't practice. Although more than half of the registered voters in Kenya are women, only 3 parliamentary seats out of 172 are held by women. Theresa Shitaka, director of Maendeleo Ya Wanawake, says her organization is trying to educate women to become more active in the national political process.

SHITAKA: Women now who are ready to stand for politics are very few. They still think that the men are the only ones who can be members of Parliament.

WEISS: Phoebe Asiyo is the only woman elected to Parliament. The other two female MPs were appointed by the president. She represents Nyanzu District in western Kenya, where three-quarters of her constituents are women and children.

Phoebe unseated a powerful male incumbent in 1980 and survived his challenge in 1983. She won by mobilizing the women's groups in her district. They raised money and votes for her campaign. In return, Phoebe has successfully channeled development money into her district, money to start income-earning pottery and weaving projects and money to train midwives and set up health clinics. But Phoebe Asiyo is just one member of Parliament. She and the few other women in positions of power know that the vehicles for improving the social, economic, and political position of Kenyan women are the grassroots organizations. Progress has been made in the last ten years, but Phoebe says that change must be carefully balanced with tradition and with the life of the already overburdened Kenyan woman.

ASIYO: Women have usually worked for sixteen or more hours a day.

There are children to take care of. There are also husbands that must be taken care of because we really cherish our family life. We then have the leadership responsibilities, so that, really, the woman is tired. You know, she is worked out.

And somebody has to devise a method of sharing, sharing so that we know that we are not alone in this work — in our role as new leaders of our societies — and so that we get the spiritual strength and the mental strength to want to carry on.

✦ ✦ ✦ ✦ ✦ ✦ ✦ ✦ ✦

Alex Chadwick took a walk among the trees with Norman Maclean, the author of *A River Runs through It*. (The movie came out in 1992.) Alex is one of our best writers, and Maclean, who died in 1990, is one of his favorites. The story begins with the sound of the two men walking on a woodland path by Seeley Lake in Montana.

Weekend All Things Considered, NOVEMBER 9

CHADWICK: Maclean guides a visitor off a logging road and down a trail a few miles north of a Seeley Lake cabin. We are going to a place he and his brother once fished. The woods are enormous. Before we duck into them and out of the light, Maclean stops and looks up above us.

MACLEAN: Such beautiful mountains, you'd have thought they had diamonds in them. I would have. I've gone looking for diamonds. Such a beautiful mountain.

CHADWICK: The story that Norman Maclean wrote is about his brother, who was reckless and daring and a great fisherman. Either there are a lot of families with reckless, daring, great fishermen, or there is something else in this book that leads those who have read it to press it onto others. It continues to sell fifteen to twenty thousand copies a year, all of them by word of mouth. The publisher hasn't spent a dime on advertising in a long time, and it's been nine years since the book came out and the critics called it a new American masterpiece. Maclean was seventy-three then, and he hadn't written a book before.

A River Runs through It begins, "In our family there was no clear line between religion and fly fishing." And right in that first sentence, Maclean has managed to tell you what his story is concerned with, family and fishing and some sense of godliness.

When we reach the end of the trail, Maclean points out a spot on Clearwater Lake, where he and his brother once spent an afternoon fishing from an inflated boat that leaked. They didn't catch anything. By the time he's told the story, it's evening.

MACLEAN: Let's go and eat. Or drink, anyway.

CHADWICK: All right. (We go back to the cabin to talk about the book.) When people ask me what it's about, I often feel I can't really tell them what it's about.

MACLEAN: Neither can I. Don't ask me.

CHADWICK: I was going to ask you. How do you describe it?

MACLEAN: It's about a family with serious problems, but a family that loves itself infinitely, and the love spreads over everything. We stood by each other, we tried to support each other, we tried to excuse each other. And outside we thought it was a real rough, rugged world, full of bastards. We weren't under any illusion about that. But we tried to set up this world of love as a world against that world. And, ultimately, it's a tragic story, of course. Ultimately we couldn't understand each other.

CHADWICK: You wrote *A River Runs through It* after you retired from a long and very successful career of teaching.

MACLEAN: At least a long one.

CHADWICK: What got you started writing then?

MACLEAN: Well, in a way, having taught so many years, I discovered that the problem of identity is, of course, very strong among younger people. And even stronger among those who write about it. They act as if the problem of who we are is only the problem of the young. And the older I got, the more I realized that you go on wondering forever who the hell you are and what you can do and what's best for you. So I was determined when I got to retirement age to find out a little bit more about myself, for one thing. So I committed myself to that, with the knowledge that to find out whether I could write would mean that I would probably have to sacrifice many of the things that normally people associate with happiness in old age.

I figured I would not have time for much company, I figured I would have not much time to run around with women, I figured I'd have to give up my plans to travel and go to Scotland and so on. It was a very monastic decision I'd made because I had not written and I did not have the habits built up. I had to do it by what I knew and by my great powers that I hoped I had of self-discipline, that I could do without things.

CHADWICK: It took you about two years, I understand, to finish the book, the three stories.

MACLEAN: I suppose it did, yeah.

CHADWICK: In the process of that, what are the new things that you did learn about yourself?

MACLEAN: Well, I learned that I could write well. What else have I got for it? I've withdrawn from so many people, even, it's not really — I didn't form new friends, but I even had to withdraw, in part, from old friends, not spend the kind of time I used to spend with them. And it's, in a way, it's a sorrowful journey.

CHADWICK: How do you know you're a good writer? When you read what you've written, how do you know it's good?

MACLEAN: I think I just know. I spent a life trying to point out what I like in literature and, in so doing, enriched my own power to write.

CHADWICK: You taught Shakespeare and Wordsworth.

MACLEAN: I taught both of those quite frequently. Shakespeare, I taught every year. I thought it was important, to me. I don't think I was a Shakespearean scholar and I never meant to be, but I thought it was important for me to teach Shakespeare once a year just to keep my literary values straight so I wouldn't be around, as I thought as many academic people do, exalting some second- or third- or fourth-rater. You know, if you like some second- or third- or fourth-rater, that's fine. But you ought to know he's a second- or third- or fourth-rater. And just to keep sure you know, you better teach Shakespeare once in a while.

CHADWICK: Norman Maclean will be eighty-three next month, although he doesn't look that old. His eyes are clear, he's solid in the middle. His knees no longer work easily. He walks stiff-legged, carrying his weight in front of him, as though he's leaning into whatever's coming at him. If he's irritated, he can still look physically dangerous. This is a retired English professor from the University of Chicago.

A little while before he stopped teaching, his wife died. She, too, had come from Montana. His children got him to try writing down his stories. He sent *A River Runs through It* around to publishers, who sent it back, one of them noting with apparent distaste that these were stories with trees in them. A colleague suggested the University of Chicago Press, but because the press prides itself on a scholastic reputation, publishing such a fanciful memoir was completely out of the ordinary. A faculty committee finally decided the writing itself fulfilled the requirements for publication, being true and original and a contribution to learning. Toward the end of the story, Maclean and his brother, Paul, and his father are together on the last fishing trip they will share.

MACLEAN: [*Reading.*] "We sat on the bank and the river went by. As always, it was making sounds to itself, and now it made sounds to us. It would be hard to find three men sitting side by side who knew better what a river was saying.

"On the Big Blackfoot River above the mouth of Belmont Creek the banks are fringed by large Ponderosa pines. In the slanting sun of late afternoon the shadows of great branches reached from across the river, and the trees took the river in their arms. The shadows continued up the bank, until they included us."

CHADWICK: Maclean, who eventually got a doctorate in English, started without going to school at all. His father, a Scotch Presbyterian minister, kept him home and instructed him each morning. He had the boy write an essay and rewrite it and rewrite it again. Seventy-five years have gone, and the father's lessons still guide the son. Maclean writes in longhand, on tablets, sitting at an uncomfortable desk. He rewrites paragraphs again and again, until they're ready to confess.

He's been writing a second book for eight years. A number of his friends simply think he'll never be able to finish. He's infinitely patient in waiting for satisfaction with words, so that if you ask him if there's a sentence in his story that he was never able to get exactly the way he wanted it, he says no, there isn't. Nonetheless, Maclean remains uncertain about what the story means.

MACLEAN: When I was young and — very young — and turned loose in the afternoons in the woods, and when my father used to read to us every day from the Bible or from a religious poet, especially Wordsworth, I began to feel that I would have some wonderful moment that was so designed that it seemed like a story that had been designed by an author. And the older I got, the more my life seemed that way, a series of moments so exquisite, really, and beautiful and true and moving, that they seem as if they'd been planned or plotted by an author. This is still a great problem with me. I have no trouble seeing the designs of many lives, including my own, but I don't know whether that's something I make up or whether it's in the thing itself or in between.

CHADWICK: Someone listening to this might say, This man's talking about God.

MACLEAN: Well, I wouldn't blame them. I don't have any conventional religion left. What I told you really is my religion. But I got it also from my father.

CHADWICK: Here goes a man who was seventy-three and had never written a book before, ending his story, reading the last paragraphs of "A River Runs through It."

MACLEAN: "Of course, now I am too old to be much of a fisherman, and now of course I usually fish the big waters alone, although some friends think I shouldn't. Like many fly fishermen in western Montana where the summer days are almost Arctic in length, I often do not start fishing until the cool of the evening. Then in the Arctic half-light of the canyon, all existence fades to a being with my soul and memories and the sounds of the Big Blackfoot River and the four count rhythm and the hope that a fish will rise.

"Eventually, all things merge into one, and a river runs through it. The river was cut by the world's great flood and runs over rocks from the basement of time. On some of the rocks are timeless raindrops. Under the rocks are words, and some of the words are theirs.

"I am haunted by waters."

✦ ✦ ✦ ✦ ✦ ✦ ✦ ✦ ✦

As soon as we could manage it, we expanded our coverage of South Africa, a commitment we have maintained over the years. In 1985 violence in the black townships was increasing, there were terrible riots in Durban, and the government had declared a state of emergency. A worldwide movement to stop investing in South Africa began that year, and the U.S. House approved sanctions. But as this report reflects, many white South Africans were still claiming that their country lived happily under apartheid, seemingly oblivious to coming change. Susan Stamberg felt it important to say that the unlikely names mentioned here are real. Mike Hanna reports.

All Things Considered, NOVEMBER 12

HANNA: The suburb of Oakdene is twelve kilometers away from Johannesburg city center. Here, on Johan Meyer Street is Kosta Plenty, the home of Jeff and Carol Kokaine, both in their late thirties and, like others in the neighborhood, relatively affluent. They're comfortable speaking English, as well as Afrikaans. Inside the modern split-level home, I sit and talk to Jeff and Carol in their living room as they watch state-controlled television, their main source of information.
BABY: Daddy?
JEFF: That's right, it's the news, darling.
HANNA: Both work in the computer industry, and Carol breeds pedigreed cats in her spare time. Around them, symbols of the good life, like a remote-controlled video machine. And outside the sliding glass

doors, their seven-year-old, Ryan, plays next to a kidney-shaped swimming pool. For them, the troubles in the black townships could be on another continent.

Jeff, does the situation, the reports you hear of the violence, unrest, does it worry you at all?

JEFF: It doesn't really worry me because I think it's very much under control by our security forces. Basically, it's not inspired by, you know, within this country. We firmly believe it comes from without. And, you know, this is what's causing the unrest.

You know, I speak to black people at the office, and they're quite happy with the situation and they mention that it's the outside influences that are causing this. They don't want trouble. And yet they have to just live with it.

HANNA: Do you feel that you are kept informed of what is happening in the townships by SA television, by the newspapers, Jeff?

JEFF: Look, I think we're informed reasonably well, you know. Obviously, they don't want to make mountains out of molehills. But we are aware there is trouble in the townships, but as I said to you just now, that the trouble is caused by themselves. It's not a white situation that's causing it, it's a black situation that's causing it.

I think the average black person in this country is quite happy with his deal and his lot, and as long as he's got a job and a roof over his head and food for his family he's quite happy to carry on. And when you look at the rest of the world, all the rest of Africa, really, the way they're starving, our blacks are far better off than they'll be elsewhere in Africa.

HANNA: Everybody accepts that the society is changing. To what degree would you be prepared for it to happen? Would you, for example, object to having neighbors who are black?

CAROL: Well, that's a bit of a difficult question to answer. They're totally different to the way we do. You generally find, I think, whites are quieter. Blacks can be terribly noisy. From that point of view, I might object to the noise side of it.

JEFF: No, I wouldn't object if they could sort of come up to the sort of same socio-economic standards that we're at. And, you know, they can only achieve that by proper education and that sort of thing. And it's quite obvious to us that they don't want education. They burn their schools down and, you know, we have to pay higher taxes so they can build the schools back up again, you know. So sure, I wouldn't mind them living next door as long as they could be, you know, on the same standard of living as I am, as an equal.

The typical black in this country, as I said, is quite happy just to have a roof over his head and a full belly. And that's all he needs. You know, he doesn't want to live in these areas. You know, if you spoke to the actual black people, they don't want to live with us. They want to live in their own areas.

And if you want to take it, it's — you know, I was over in America in April, and it's exactly the same there. The blacks don't live with the whites. They live in their own areas. They don't frequent the same bars or nightclubs that the whites do, so what difference would it make here? I think it would end up being the same thing. Like will stick to like.

✦ ✦ ✦ ✦ ✦ ✦ ✦ ✦ ✦ ✦

M ikhail Gorbachev came to power in the Soviet Union in March, and in November the Soviet premier and the American president met in Geneva. Although no agreements were signed at that meeting, this was the beginning of the end of the old relationship between the two powers. Scott Simon discussed it with our news analyst Daniel Schorr. Dan has had several careers, notably at CBS for many years. He takes pride in having been thrown out of the Soviet Union and landing on President Nixon's enemies list. Dan reviews the news each week with Scott Simon on *Weekend Edition, Saturday*. This conversation began with Scott suggesting that despite smiling photo opportunities the meeting between Reagan and Gorbachev was not always cordial.

Weekend Edition, Saturday, NOVEMBER 23

SIMON: Dan, you spent the entire week in Geneva. I shouldn't — I don't like people who laugh at things the audience can't see, but you have just unbuttoned your shirt to reveal a Reagan-Gorbachev meeting T-shirt, Geneva, Switzerland, November 19 to 21, 1985.

Do you know of any other private moments that can be related now which you found out about through your sources in the sessions between the two? Is the State Department convinced that Mr. Gorbachev represents a new regime and a new chance to deal with the Soviet Union?

SCHORR: Yes, and so does President Reagan. President Reagan was actually rather taken by Gorbachev. Now, it was interesting, that in the days before the summit started, there was an awful lot that was the so-called war of briefings, in which the Soviets really unloaded a lot of very strong language against the United States, which suddenly stopped when the principals arrived, when Gorbachev arrived.

But President Reagan was especially irritated by one remark that had been made by Georgy Arbatov, the Kremlin's big America-watcher, when he had said at one point, made a reference to President Reagan as a grade-B actor. And when they took the famous walk down to the poolside villa, the president said, "I'm really not a grade-B actor. Did you ever see *King's Row*?" And that was surprising enough, but what was even more surprising was that Gorbachev said, "Was that the one about the man with his legs cut off? Yes, I did see it, and I thought it was a very interesting picture," which showed that Gorbachev had done his homework too.

Well, after that, Gorbachev could really do no wrong. He did pound the table, he did point his finger at the president, all of that. I think that both of them agreed that while it was vigorous, sharp at times, it was all in a spirit of give-and-take, and the phrase "table thumping" gives a rather false idea of the way things went. The fact of the matter is that Reagan came out and said something that I think is rather remarkable, considering the way he talked of Soviet lying and cheating all these years, but he talked about Gorbachev as being, "Well, he's a communist all right, but I've decided he's very sincere." And I think that really marks the beginning of some kind of relationship.

SIMON: The charm that has been reported about Mr. Gorbachev in private sessions and semipublic sessions in particular seems to have affected Mr. Reagan. I'm wondering if you have any reading as to how our own president's charm seemed to ingratiate itself with the Soviet leader.

SCHORR: To be frank, that's harder to tell because you don't get the kind of briefings from the Soviet side that the American delegation will give you. I attended a press conference of Gorbachev, and the only indications I got there were that at one point Gorbachev made a reference to the president as having talked banalities. And that had to do with the fact that the president said that Moscow has to stop making trouble for us in our back yard, in Nicaragua, Africa, and so on. And what Gorbachev said was that the president does not seem to understand that there are social revolutions in progress — that if Brazil and Mexico cannot pay their debts and there's a big social revolution, are we still going to say this was all done by Moscow?

So I have the impression, but less clearly than you can get Reagan's impression, that Gorbachev came out feeling kind of like he's a nice man but not a heavyweight.

SIMON: I'm still impressed by the fact that Mr. Gorbachev held all these press conferences, that he met with Jesse Jackson in a forty-five-minute session and actually broached the question of his treatment of Soviet Jews. I'm assuming that none of that was for television back in the Soviet Union.

SCHORR: Oh yes, twenty minutes of the forty-five-minute meeting with Jesse Jackson was on Soviet television. Because no matter what else happens, they would like to tell the people back there that there's not only Reagan in this country, but there is a peace opposition in this country. That remains very important from the point of view of their ideology.

But speaking of television! Let me tell you the one worst moment that Reagan really had, which almost held up the signing of a cultural agreement. The cultural exchange agreement was really ready several months ago, and they continued negotiating it up until a week ago Friday. There was only one line in it that held up its being signed. President Reagan had instructed them to get in something about the exchange of television appearances. He wants to be on Soviet television. And the Russians wouldn't give in, and in the end all they got was that in principle they'd agreed there might be an exchange of Soviet television appearances. With the result that the only and first time that President Reagan has been live on Soviet television was in the concluding ceremony on Thursday when he appeared with Gorbachev. That was the one time he's been live in the Soviet Union. But a quarter of a billion audience, not bad.

SIMON: Better than 20 Mule Team Borax, I guess.

SCHORR: Better than 20 Mule Team Borax, right.

SIMON: Here's the question I've been preparing all week. Does our world become a safer place now that the two men have met and managed to get on with each other?

SCHORR: Marginally, yes, because what we have not said was that there was not a single agreement on anything of any substance. They did not get anywhere on so-called Star Wars or anything else. It becomes marginally better because Reagan comes back and no longer talks about lying and cheating, but thinks he understands that there is a man back there who heads a country with a different point of view, and they have somehow got to find ways to come to terms. They are doomed, as you might say, to coexist.

1986

On January 28, 1986, the space shuttle *Challenger* exploded about four miles above the coast of Florida, with the New Hampshire schoolteacher Christa McAuliffe aboard. Susan Stamberg was pressed into service to anchor our live coverage. "The space shuttle blew up. Those words flashing across America today," Susan said, "heard on the streets, in offices, people calling home. The shuttle missions have become almost ordinary events: the weather delays, the experiments, the satellite deployments. This morning's launch was of somewhat more interest because there was a schoolteacher among the crew of the space shuttle *Challenger*. But the nation wasn't watching on television until later when the videotape provided a shared experience." The pictures showed the shuttle climbing into the sky, rising on its white column. Then a puff of smoke and orange flame appeared, and the white column divided in two and turned downward. I spoke later that day with Jo Miglino, our reporter covering the *Challenger*.

Special Coverage, JANUARY 28

MIGLINO: Linda, it's a very strange situation. Outwardly, here at the Kennedy Space Center, there are very few signs of today's disaster. There's a flag flying half-mast outside on the green, which is opposite the launch pad about five miles away. And it's right next to the clock that usually counts down to the launch of the shuttle. That's one sign. But here inside the press area, things are going on almost as if the mission were in progress and things were very routine. Reporters are busy at their work, staring at their computer terminals. NASA information specialists are answering phone calls. Even the countdown clock that usually marks the mission elaspe time, hours, minutes, and seconds, is still counting from this morning's liftoff.

Eighteen miles away from here, though, you should know that planes, helicopters, and ships have been searching frantically all day long, searching the waters, for any sign of debris or any sign of life. We just heard Jesse Moore, director of the Johnson Space Center, not come right out and say the astronauts were dead, but it was a pretty hopeless message that he gave reporters here. We understand that family and relatives of the crew are still in seclusion here at the space center. Reporters have not been able to talk with them.

WERTHEIMER: Jo, you've seen these launches before. Where were they, the family members who were watching the launch? Sitting in bleachers, special VIP viewing area? Where is that?

MIGLINO: They were sitting in bleachers in a VIP area a short way from the press area here, altogether about five miles away from the launch pad. I can't tell you what a glorious sight these launches are, and I'm sure they were feeling just jubilation at the moment of launch, and then to have the rush of feeling that something horrible, tragic, went wrong. There's just no way that we can really know what they were feeling at that moment. Such a joyous occasion normally. I've seen ten of them, and every time I've been filled with this sense of wonder at the experience. I just can't imagine what was going on through their minds at that time when people froze and just realized that something that we had never seen before had just happened.

WERTHEIMER: Jo, you've been there briefly. Have you had any chance to talk to any of the people there? I assume they must be speculating, as we are speculating from the pictures, about what happened — even though NASA has no official word.

MIGLINO: The people here are holding to the NASA line, which you just heard Jesse Moore say: "We are not going to speculate based on the film footage so far." The NASA people are very tightlipped, so there is very little speculation of any kind going on here about what caused this. Up until seventy-two seconds after the launch, it was another picture-perfect liftoff, the way we always describe when one of these things happens. So I just don't think they'll say anything until they are certain about what the cause was.

✦ ✦ ✦ ✦ ✦ ✦ ✦ ✦ ✦

Until the *Challenger* fell, we believed our space program was the dramatic exception to our national dim view of government projects. A presidential commission charged with identifying the source of that failure began to concentrate on the solid-fuel booster rockets, which carried the shuttles into orbit. The boosters were built by the Morton-Thiokol Corporation in Brigham City, Utah. NPR's Howard Berkes reported the story in Utah, and, acting on a tip from Howard that the engineers who built the rockets had tried to stop the launch, Daniel Zwerdling raced to Huntsville, Alabama, to find someone who would talk about it. He found men tortured by guilt who felt they had not done enough to prevent the launch that unusually chilly January morning.

Danny first talked to the wife of one of the men involved, who felt strongly that her husband should speak to someone. She told Danny how to find her husband, and NPR broke the story of why the *Challenger* fell.

Morning Edition, FEBRUARY 20

ZWERDLING: A Morton-Thiokol engineer sits before me, his eyes getting red with tears. "I fought like hell to stop that launch," he says. "I'm so torn up inside, I can hardly talk about it, even now." But here's the story, according to this and other company engineers I talked to, of what happened the day before the launch. Top NASA and Thiokol officials refuse to talk about it.

It's about noon at company space-shuttle headquarters in Brigham City, Utah. Several key engineers learned that temperatures around the shuttle launch pad in Cape Canaveral are unusually low, colder than they've ever been just before a launch. They meet hurriedly, urgently, in company hallways and they all agree that they've got to warn top management fast that the shuttle could be in serious trouble. A handful of worried employees crowd around the desk of vice president Robert Lund, and they lay out the evidence.

If the temperatures in Florida don't get a lot warmer, they say, then the crucial seals which hold the first- and second-stage booster rockets together might fail during takeoff. Says one engineer, "We all knew what the implication was without actually coming out and saying it. We all knew if the seals failed, the shuttle would blow up."

Six P.M., a bigger and more formal meeting in one of the company's main conference rooms. About a dozen engineers are there, along with four top managers, poring over charts and photographs of rocket seals and joints. They all agree that it's too risky for the shuttle to take off.

Eight P.M. They call NASA officials over a special telephone conference network and, one by one, four key Thiokol engineers lay out the troubling evidence.

Point number one: Both NASA and company engineers have

known for several years that when the shuttle starts to take off, tremendous forces work the joints where sections of the solid rockets fit together. Some of those crucial seals don't work right.

Point number two: The colder the weather, the worse the seals work. In fact, they emphasize, when the shuttle took off in January 1985 in fifty-three-degree temperatures, the coldest it's ever been till now, half the seals in both solid rockets were damaged.

Point number three: Thiokol's own laboratory studies show that as temperatures drop below fifty degrees, the seals dramatically lose their ability to hold the rockets together. And tomorrow at Cape Canaveral, the engineers warn, it's going to be only around thirty degrees.

Thiokol executive Bob Lund wraps up the presentation to NASA with the company's official recommendation: Do not launch the shuttle tomorrow.

The NASA officials listening on the telephone lines are shocked. "I am appalled," says George Hardy, of NASA's Marshall Space Flight Center in Huntsville, Alabama. "I am appalled by your recommendation." Another top official, Larry Malloy, argues with the Thiokol engineers. He challenges their figures. He says the company doesn't have firm enough proof that the seals will fail in cold weather.

But Thiokol engineers vehemently disagree. At some points almost shouting with anger they insist that NASA should postpone the launch until the weather climbs into the fifties. And at that point, according to one engineer, NASA's Malloy exclaims, "My God, Thiokol, when do you want me to launch, next April?"

It's eight-thirty P.M. now. Thiokol managers put NASA on hold on the telephone network and they ask their staff engineers one more time, "You're sure about all this?" "Absolutely," the engineers say, and virtually no one in the conference room disagrees.

But now Thiokol's general manager, Jerry Mason, speaks up. "Look," he says, "this has got to be a management decision." So while a dozen engineers look on, fuming with anger, Mason asks the three other managers what they want to do. They each nod, OK, let's go ahead with the launch. "Who knows why our managers overruled us," one engineer tells me now. "As you know, our company's competing with several other corporations to get future shuttle contracts. I can only guess," the engineer says, "at the enormous pressures they were feeling."

Eight-forty-five P.M. Thiokol general manager Mason takes NASA officials off hold, and he tells them, "OK, we'll approve the launch after all." NASA's Malloy tells them, "Then sign the document right away and send it to us by telefax." One top Thiokol manager, Alan MacDonald, who's been taking part in the conference call from the cape, refuses to sign the paper.

The meeting breaks up. The engineers go home feeling downtrodden and defeated and terribly worried. "I kept having fantasies that night," says one engineer, "that at the moment of ignition the shuttle would blow up instantly. See, we thought that if the seals failed, the shuttle would never get off the pad. There would just be a big fireball and everything would vanish. I was so scared I didn't even want to watch the launch."

But the next morning the engineer joins fifty other colleagues back at company headquarters in the same conference room where they'd argued the night before. They were all watching the countdown together on a large-projection TV.

"When the shuttle lifted off the pad," he says, "I thought, Gee, it's going all right. It's a piece of cake. And when we were one minute into the launch, a friend turned to me, and he said, "Oh, God, we made it. We made it." Then a few seconds later, the engineer says, "The shuttle blew up, and we all knew exactly what happened."

✦ ✦ ✦ ✦ ✦ ✦ ✦ ✦ ✦

In February, the American people watched the elections in the Philippines with almost as much interest as we watch elections here. The long-time president of the Philippines, Ferdinand Marcos, was historically pictured as a friend of the United States, a barrier in the Pacific against communism. But the woman who wanted to replace him, Corazon Aquino, immediately captured our imagination. She is the widow of Benigno Aquino, who had fought the corruption of the Marcos regime. He was assassinated when he returned to Manila in 1983, after years of political exile in the United States.

Cory Aquino was persuaded to take up her husband's fight. Although the Aquinos were a leading family of the Philippines, Cory was a housewife, not a crusader. Still, she led a crusade against the aging Marcos and his acquisitive wife. Wearing bright yellow dresses, the colors of her cause, Aquino fought two campaigns, one for the presidency and a second campaign to be sure the vote count would be fair. Bill Buzenberg filed this piece on the campaign the week of the election.

BUZENBERG: A neighborhood rally for the president is an elaborately staged affair. Some have compared it to a Las Vegas show. A specially built platform is wrapped in red, white, and blue, the colors of the president's KBL party, and festooned with balloons. Across the top are giant letters with the names of the two candidates, MARCOS-TOLENTINO.

Marcos rallies attract relatively small crowds that tend to leave early. Campaign aides have attracted this audience with free hats, free T-shirts, free sack lunches, and perhaps fifty pesos, or two dollars and fifty cents. There are also big buses and small jitneys bringing in the party faithful from other neighborhoods. This rally will last about four hours. Three hours of it will be entertainment. There are comedians, musicians, including one who gives an impression of Elvis Presley, and movie stars, some of whom hint that if they don't attend these rallies they won't get work in the Marcos-supported movie industry.

Perhaps the biggest star to come out is Imelda Marcos, Ferdinand's wife. She makes a dramatic entrance to her own fanfare, moving with the regal bearing of a former beauty queen. She reaches down into the crowd nearest the stage, much to their delight, not to shake hands but to let people touch hers. At one point, she removes her wristwatch, almost disdainfully dangles it over the edge of the stage for a moment, and lets it drop.

In a short speech, Imelda Marcos tells the crowd that if they want change, her husband will give them change. She also says if they reelect the president, they'll get her as a bonus. The speech is less well received than what follows, the First Lady singing a popular Tagalog love song. What this crowd really seems to be waiting for, however, is for President Marcos to join his wife.

Generally, the crowd closest to the stage is made up of these party loyalists. They cheer on cue when urged to do so by arm-waving prompters on the stage. The rest of the crowd appears less interested, even listless, as President Marcos begins to speak.

MARCOS: I have come to see you not just as a candidate, I have come to see you as president of the Republic of the Philippines and, more than that, as a small, young soldier who is bent on the protection of our country.

BUZENBERG: Ferdinand Marcos has not faced a real election since 1969. He's kept himself in power by rewriting the constitution. He appears slightly feeble at this rally. He has a hard time raising his hands above his head, and he has a coughing spell whenever he does. Yet he will speak for almost an hour. His standard stump speech is much the same as when he first ran for president in 1965. He dwells on the role he claims to have had as a guerrilla fighter in World War II, and he dismisses all evidence to the contrary as politically inspired. He tells the crowd he has shrapnel wounds which cause him to limp and because of that limp, he says, the political opposition makes fun of him.

MARCOS: They laugh because Marcos limps from his old wounds of the war. I laugh back at them, and say, "It is an honor from little Ferdinand Marcos, the little soldier, to have been wounded five times in the fight for freedom."

BUZENBERG: The toughest part of his speech, another old theme, is an attack on communists and his opponents, which to him are one and the same. He says it's his duty to be the eyes, ears, and tongue of the nation.

MARCOS: I come to you therefore, as president of the Republic of the Philippines. And I'm crying out to you, Danger! We face danger once again. We fought the enemy that tried to occupy our land. Now the enemy is inside. He is already within us, already campaigning for the highest position of the land.

BUZENBERG: President Marcos accuses Benigno Aquino, his former political rival who was murdered three years ago, of founding the Communist party and its guerrilla army. He says the opposition plans to put communists in the Cabinet and bring communist generals into the armed forces. The opposition denies this, but Marcos insists and says it will cause a civil war.

MARCOS: We must not allow this! No! While we can still prevent it. No! While we still have the power of the ballot to stop all of this. No! We want you to use the weapons that are at your command. Here are the loyal protectors of democracy who will fight communism to the death and who will not allow the communists to take over our country. Those are your weapons, and who are they? Marcos, Tolentino, the fighters against communism.

BUZENBERG: An Aquino rally is a bit different. "Enough, too much, and let's change" is the slogan of the Aquino campaign. If a Marcos rally is like a Las Vegas stage show, then an Aquino rally can be likened to a cross between a revival meeting and a huge block party.

Here the crowd swells out in all directions from a simple makeshift platform. Many people have waited for hours for the rally to begin. Confetti floats down from office buildings, where workers line the windows and ledges. Everyone in the crowd has something yellow, but they weren't given these props. Hawkers wade through the crowd, selling them. Hats, T-shirts, ribbons, flags. The Aquino campaign has its stars too, but they're folk singers, not rock or movie stars. Freddie Aguilar sings what has become something of a theme song for the Aquino campaign. It's an old patriotic song called "Bayan Ko," my country. As he sings, people in the crowd raise their arms in the air and with fingers make L signs for Aquino's Laban party.

This song is one that the Marcos-controlled radio stations have officially banned from the airwaves. Signs in the crowd poke fun at the Philippine First Family. One reads, ALL THIS TIME A FAKE HERO. Another shows the grave of Benigno Aquino and makes reference to the many building projects of the First Lady. The caption above the tomb reads, ANOTHER PROJECT OF IMELDA MARCOS.

All this is a kind of joyful catharsis. The crowd revels in the use of satire, puns, and digs at the Marcos family. One speaker at the Aquino rally entertains the crowd with tales of the First Family's alleged hidden wealth, calling it the number-one issue in the campaign. What's the difference between a Cory Aquino rally and a Marcos rally?

WOMAN AT RALLY: Oh, this is spontaneous. At a Marcos rally, they've got to bring them in from the provinces. Plus, they pay them. They haven't paid any of us.

SECOND WOMAN: All the people here, campaigning for Cory, are smiling. They do it out of their hearts. But Marcos, you see their face falling apart just like him.

BUZENBERG: Are you supporting Cory Aquino?

THIRD WOMAN: Yes, very much so. I think she's the hope of the country. If we still do not change Marcos now, I think we'll have an almost impossible task of removing him. Because already, there is so-called second-generation cronies, and not only his family, his children, his grandchildren, his great-grandchildren. It will just be too much. They will be like snakes, multiplying so fast that, even though we want to get rid of them, we cannot anymore get rid of them if we don't do something now.

BUZENBERG: Mrs. Aquino is not a politician, not a great orator. Sometimes she just stands on the stage in her yellow dress and smiles. What matters most, according to her supporters, is her simplicity and sincerity, which they contrast with what they see as the duplicity of President Marcos.

Mrs. Aquino says that for most of her life she was a housewife, and she also acted on her own for eight years while her husband was in prison. And she has been politically active since his death. At this rally, she speaks in Tagalog. At other rallies, she uses English.

AQUINO: My friends, tomorrow Mr. Marcos will say again that I have stolen his social ideas. He has already accused me of stealing his economic program. This is just like Mr. Marcos, who can think of nothing but stealing.

BUZENBERG: Her usually short campaign speeches include references to her husband, Benigno. She links the suffering of the Filipinos under Marcos to her own suffering.

AQUINO: I cannot expect justice while Marcos is head of our government. And I have said from the very beginning that Mr. Marcos is my number-one suspect in the assassination of Benigno.

BUZENBERG: She says that Benigno gave his life for democracy, and she is willing to give hers. The crowd boos when she speaks of a government poster at one rally that warned it would only take one bullet to stop her. They cheer when she says it will only take one ballot to stop Marcos.

✦ ✦ ✦ ✦ ✦ ✦ ✦ ✦ ✦

On Fourth of July weekend, corporate America returned a restored Lady Liberty to her people. The statue had been showing signs of stress from millions of tourists trooping up inside it, and its island home needed a reworking as well. President Reagan handed the job to Chrysler president Lee Iacocca, who franchised Liberty like a basketball star. For months, the statue was shrouded in scaffolding and plastic, preparing for Liberty Weekend, part of that year's Independence Day celebration. Ian Shoales, our fast-talking kid from San Francisco, talked about Liberty on *Morning Edition*. As Bob Edwards says, "There are many waves in the currents of culture. Catch them with Ian Shoales. It's all rock and roll to him."

All Things Considered, JUNE 25

SHOALES: Art museums are filled with the broken statues of the distant past, and in a nation which has no distant past, I suppose I should feel the faint stirrings of nationalistic pride with the coming of Liberty Weekend, during which the most famous statue in the country will once more lift her lighted lamp of freedom. Products will be sold, gala extravaganzas will occur, magazine prose styles will become grave and stately, and America will go back to work on Monday sunburned, heartwarmed, and proud.

Me, I'll sit at home with the official soft drink of Liberty Weekend and be mildly overwhelmed, not so much by the spectacle of the weekend as by the commercial machinations that made it possible. It seems like the Statue of Liberty is just a big pawn in the cola wars. In the endless media parade of extreme close-ups of Ms. Liberty's face, I've noted more than a passing resemblance to Elvis Presley, but beyond that, I haven't seen anything I haven't seen before.

I like the Statue of Liberty as much as anybody, but how many images can we see? It's not like she does anything. She lifts her lamp beside the golden door. That's about it. One picture framed against the sunset is nice, but one thousand pictures are worth only one word, "Enough."

Now, when I saw the Temple of Dendera at the Metropolitan Museum of Art, I was struck by how this temple, separated from its natural environment in history in a new context of Manhattan skyscrapers and commerce, seemed just tiny. The Statue of Liberty hasn't been moved, but she also keeps getting tinier and tinier, just not as big as the corporate hype surrounding her.

Now frankly if you're going to offer me a symbol of freedom or freedom, I'd take the freedom, but Ms. Liberty isn't even a symbol anymore. She's a logo. That's OK. I may be a cranky futz, but I don't want to spoil America's fun. I appreciate that tax dollars were saved by corporate sponsorship of the statue's renovation, but that doesn't mean that the land of liberty should be turned into Libertyland.

Sometimes I think we have no history, no broken statues. What we have instead of tradition are tricentennial laser light shows. Well, folks, there's more to time and life than Time-Life Books, as my mother used to say. And on my mantel, if I had a mantel, I've always wanted one of those little Statues of Liberty under glass. You know what I'm talking about. When you turn it upside down two things happen: snow falls, and the words MADE IN HONG KONG appear. I will really be impressed if on Liberty Weekend they encase the statue in a glass dome, turn it upside down with helicopters, and make it snow. And if David Wolper, the producer of the event, can put the words MADE IN HONG KONG under the base in letters twelve feet tall, I'll be even more impressed. But that's not going to happen. Instead, we'll have Lionel Richie again, and the melting-pot parade of smiling dancers and babushkas and cats roller-skating to a dance mix of "God Bless America." Wake me up when it's over, OK? I'll be over on the teeming shore, taking a nap with the wretched refuse. I gotta go.

✦ ✦ ✦ ✦ ✦ ✦ ✦ ✦ ✦

Americal attitudes toward AIDS changed some in 1986 after the actor Rock Hudson died of the disease. In the United States, it was still considered a homosexual illness, concentrated in areas where there were substantial populations of gay men. But in Africa, the disease took a different course. Laurie Garrett and John McChesney went to Tanzania that summer to report one of the first stories on the AIDS epidemic in central Africa. They found doctors who described how they had realized they were dealing with a new kind of venereal disease.

Morning Edition, AUGUST 14

GARRETT: The waves of Lake Victoria wash up on the shores of Bukoba. Egrets and cranes stand at attention watching children swim. Green marshlands meet the white sand beach. The town of Bukoba is small. About ten thousand people live in the general area. It's quiet here. Not many people have gasoline for their cars or motorbikes, or batteries for their radios. At times the only sounds in downtown Bukoba are the busy chatter of the marketplace and the evening call to Muslim prayers.

But two years ago, the peace of Bukoba was disturbed by a deadly invisible enemy. Something started killing the young people of the surrounding villages. The sick came to a government hospital in Bukoba. They seemed to have some strange kind of venereal disease, and the hospital director, Dr. Jayo Kidenya struggled in vain to help them.

KIDENYA: These patients, they were all dying. The so-called venereal diseases were presented by very dreadful genital abscess, very frightening, very big, very deep. They never responded to more treatment. And the characteristic feature, which was present to all these patients — we had the severe wasting, weight loss, very severe.

GARRETT: Some patients lost up to thirty percent of their body weight within three months' time. Dr. Jayo Kidenya had never seen anything like it.

KIDENYA: At the same period there were rumors from the villages that there was a new disease which was believed to be probably of witchcraft origin, and it was believed that it was coming from the nearby bordering countries, such as Uganda.

GARRETT: The people of Bukoba are wary of Ugandans. Just eight years ago Ugandan dictator Idi Amin crossed the nearby border and occupied this area, called the Kagera region. When the first young people died of this mysterious disease, the people noticed all the dead came from villages along the border, villages that frequently traded goods with Ugandan travelers. The first woman to die of this strange disease had met with a Ugandan trader. He had beautiful cloth with the name Juliana printed on it. He wanted to make love to her. Bukoba Dr. Juste Tkimlenka says she in turn demanded the Juliana cloth.

TKIMLENKA: So the man accepted. He gave that piece of cloth to that woman and then they went together. They had sexual intercourse. And from that point, that woman contracted the disease and she died. So the people started saying she has died because of Juliana.

GARRETT: So the people gave the new disease a name. They called it Juliana disease. Dr. Jayo Kidenya, his assistant, Dr. Tkimlenka, and Bukoba surgeon Dr. Clint Nyamrerekunge were stumped. They knew Juliana disease wasn't the result of witchcraft, as the people believed. So what was it?

There was a link, they believed, with Uganda and perhaps other neighboring countries, Rwanda, Burundi, Kenya, and Zaire. Rumors had reached the doctors of a mysterious disease the Ugandans called "slim" disease, a disease that produced the same symptoms they saw in the Bukoba patients, acute diarrhea and massive weight loss. And Kidenya noticed something else. All his patients were strangely vulnerable to other diseases, especially to tuberculosis. It was as if their bodies were no longer able to fight off infections.

KIDENYA: So that is when we started asking ourselves, what is happening to this society?

GARRETT: Dr. Nyamrerekunge noticed twenty patients had something in common. Each of them had had sex with a particular barmaid or they were the wives of men who slept with the barmaid. Nyamrerekunge collected blood samples from the patients and set off for Tanzania's capital, Dar es Salaam. He traveled all night by steamer across Lake Victoria, then waited days for a plane to take him south.

Once in Dar es Salaam, Nyamrerekunge sought out help at Mwambile Hospital. But doctors there could find nothing in his blood samples. One doctor suggested Nyamrerekunge look up some research papers in the medical library, papers on a new disease found in America and central Africa.

NYAMREREKUNGE: So that is the day when I came to know that in the world is a new disease called AIDS.

GARRETT: In March of 1985 the three Bukoba doctors presented a paper to a meeting of their medical colleagues that said that the AIDS epidemic had come to Tanzania. But their colleagues were not pleased with their diligence.

NYAMREREKUNGE: Doctors were refusing. They said, "How do you know? You don't have a good laboratory. How can you be sure that it is AIDS? You are just raising a false alarm."

GARRETT: The Bukoba doctors couldn't prove that they had an AIDS epidemic. They didn't have the AIDS blood test. So the Tanzanian government stepped in and asked the U.S. Centers for Disease Control to go to Bukoba and find out if Juliana disease and AIDS were the same thing. Last June at the International AIDS Conference in Paris the CDC's Dr. Joe McCormick presented the results.

MCCORMICK: This study confirms the existence of AIDS in the Kagera region of Tanzania. AIDS in Tanzania affects men and women in approximately equal numbers. Our study suggests that heterosexual contact with multiple partners is an important route of AIDS transmission in Tanzania.

◆ ◆ ◆ ◆ ◆ ◆ ◆ ◆ ◆

Toward the end of 1986, on November 2, Islamic Fundamentalists released a hostage, David Jacobsen. He said that he'd been a prisoner for 524 days. Alex Chadwick talked about that slow passage of time in captivity with two other hostages, held for months and years by the Islamic Jihad, which wanted to use them to negotiate with the West. The Reverend Benjamin Weir is a Presbyterian minister. Father Lawrence Jenco is a Catholic priest.

Weekend All Things Considered, NOVEMBER 9

CHADWICK: Father Jenco, do you remember the moment of your capture?

JENCO: I do. It was on January 8, around seven-forty-five in the morning. I was on my way to work at Catholic Relief Services that morning. I had just gotten into the car. I turned the corner and within two minutes the hostage takers were running down the street from a car, two cars in front of us, and they're running from behind from two cars in the back. And I saw it and I told my driver, I'm going to be kidnapped.

CHADWICK: By this time Father Jenco knew it was dangerous for any

Westerner to remain in Beirut, especially dangerous for an American. Indeed, although the two men had never met, Father Jenco knew about his fellow clergyman Ben Weir, that he had been abducted earlier from the streets of Beirut.

WEIR: A bag was put over my head. I was taken out of the car into a room, and there I was taped with adhesive plastic tape from my ankles to the top of my head, with just enough space to breathe through my nose. Once the guard had gone out of the room I raised my blindfold to look around. I found that I was in a very bare room. I supposed it was something like maybe ten by fourteen feet. I was seated on a mattress. Otherwise the room was completely bare, with the exception of a radiator, to which I was chained.

CHADWICK: That incident took place in May of 1984, eight months before Father Jenco was kidnapped. During all that time, Reverend Weir's conditions of captivity remained constant. He was held alone in a room, and that was what Father Jenco began to settle into as well: isolation.

JENCO: I would get up very early because you sleep in the course of a day. So I am up early with sunrise, and I would offer Mass. I tried to recall to mind the Scriptures and do a thematic approach to that. I knew the Eucharistic prayers by heart, so daily I would celebrate Mass, and that was an extremely nourishing thing for me. And in the course of the day they'd bring in breakfast, which is basically, you know, cheese and bread and tea. And then the rest of the day I would read if there was a book available to read and then wait for lunch, and lunch would come in. It would sometimes be rice and beans or whatever they themselves were eating because they didn't eat any differently than what I ate.

WEIR: I did what I could to structure the time, so I thought I would try to have some kind of a calendar for keeping track of time and decided I would try to make a mental calendar. I noticed on the wall in front of me holes in the plaster where someone had previously driven in nails, probably to hang pictures. So I decided to use the pockmarks in the plaster as something on which to hang my mental calendar and put Tuesday, May 8, on the first hole and then filled out the rest of the month and then I reviewed that regularly. That helped to give a sense of structure. Later on I found I could hear off in the distance the Muslim call to prayer five times a day, so that also helped to give some structure of time to the day.

CHADWICK: Neither man was physically abused, but the torment of isolation proved terrible. Both men were still held in solitary confinement, moved occasionally from hideout to hideout, but always left alone. Benjamin Weir recalls the delight he found in even the most trivial interruption of the dreadful monotony.

WEIR: I had a wrapper that had been with vitamin C. It was in both Arabic and French, so I would read that over and over. I learned some new terms, not very useful, but I learned something new. Later on one day I got a sandwich with a piece of an Arabic newspaper wrapped around it so I saved that piece and I would read that over and over again. And where there was a half of a column I tried to figure out the words that filled out the rest of the column.

JENCO: In the course of the day there was extreme isolation, extreme loneliness of not knowing what the next hour or the next day was going to hold. But basically it was just trying to survive the course of the hours and get through each hour. And when night came, I was glad night came. You know, at least sleep took me away from it and I could dream.

WEIR: There certainly were times of great fear. On several different occasions I would be awakened in the middle of the night, the chain taken off. I would be led out by a guard, having no idea of where I was going or what would happen. And it time and again ran through my mind, Now maybe the time has come for my execution. That never, of course, happened, but I found that to be a very fearful experience.

One day I was told by a man who came newly to me that he would tell me a message in Arabic and I was to write it in English. So I proceeded to do so and, as he was telling me, I learned for the first time that I was being held as a hostage because of seventeen men held in Kuwait. That came as really quite a shock, and I realized it was a very desperate situation and the likelihood of being released from that condition was very narrow.

JENCO: There was one time that I was extremely alone and hadn't been even talked to for about a month and a half. And I think that was the worst period of my life. Even a violent touch would be a touch that I accepted as . . . you know? I don't know even how to explain that. But it was that I had some sense of worth as a person. But in that closed, lonely place, I think that was the worst for me. And I celebrated Mass, and I would keep a piece of the Eucharistic bread. Whenever I really got depressed and couldn't cope with it, I would hold the Lord in my hands, and one day the guard asked what was in my hand, and I opened up my hand and there was a piece of bread. And he couldn't understand it was Jesus for me, but he said, "Oh, just bread." And he thought I was hungry, and it wasn't a question of being hungry. It was a question of being hungry for freedom.

CHADWICK: By the early summer of 1985 there were thirteen Western hostages in Beirut, held by different groups with different demands. Father Jenco and Reverend Weir did not know this, though. They got almost no information from the outside.

Finally, in July of 1985, an end to the terrible isolation. Reverend Weir was moved. But this time he was left in the room with another prisoner, who turned out to be Father Jenco. Reverend Weir begins the story.

WEIR: When I arrived in that room I was chained and told to go to sleep. After the guard had locked the door, I lifted my blindfold and looked around and saw that I was in the room with another person.

JENCO: And I just looked at him, because I asked — I said to the guard, "May we talk to one another?" That was the first night. And he says no. So I just stared at him, and he stared at me because this was the first time that we were allowed to take our blindfolds off.

WEIR: Then we began to whisper after a while, and at least I found out who he was.

JENCO: That was a glorious experience to be able to talk, even in one's own tongue and then to share, you know, one's own grief, one's own joy and sorrow.

WEIR: It's an experience I will never forget of having a relationship with another human being. It was almost like being born, I guess.

CHADWICK: When he came to freedom in July, Father Jenco carried with him a videotape from David Jacobsen with a plea for renewed efforts on Jacobsen's behalf. And at last, a week ago, after 524 days as a hostage, David Jacobsen was released.

✦ ✦ Alex noted that Terry Anderson and Thomas Sutherland, two other hostages who had been Weir and Jenco's companions, were still being held. Since Weir's release, three others were taken. Father Jenco said in that interview that he hoped the intervention of the envoy of the Archbishop of Canterbury would help. Terry Waite did intervene, and he too was taken hostage.

JENCO: I know that, even in captivity, I realized, it was a question of time. And the difficulty is, you know, being able to cope with that, cope with that time. When, Lord, am I going to go home? And that's the frustration.

And just a tremendous waste of one's life, I believe, two years now for Terry Anderson and Tom. You know, two brilliant men who have so much to offer to that part of the world, and sitting behind closed doors surely doesn't help.

1987

S ome of the most important work we have done covering the AIDS
crisis has been done by Patricia Neighmond. Patty proposed that
we personalize AIDS by following the course of the disease with one
person. She chose Archie Harrison. Archie was personable and candid,
never refusing to answer questions, determined to help us understand
his situation. When we first met Archie, he had known for about a year
that he had AIDS and had been selected for experimental treatment
with AZT. At that time only about three thousand people were taking
the drug.

All Things Considered, JANUARY 16

HARRISON: I feel like now I want to make a difference in what I do. I
don't want to sound morbid about this because I don't feel morbid
about it, but when you get a diagnosis of a disease where they don't
have a cure, and you're told something like, "Oh, your life expectancy
will probably be eight months to a year, maybe longer," you can go one
of two ways. You can take that as a death sentence and lie down and
wait for it to come, and then I really think that if that's the route you
choose you will fulfill their prophecy and you will be dead in eight
months to a year. Or you can start making every moment count.
NEIGHMOND: Archie Harrison lives here, in the theater district on the
far West Side of Manhattan. Even though he has AIDS, he's determined to pay attention to his fitness, and so every day he tries to get
outside to walk. The walking, he says, strengthens his muscles.
HARRISON: And so I make myself get out, and it's usually in the
morning. I will go out when there's not a lot of traffic and just walk. Go
somewhere if I have to go somewhere or, if not, I'll just walk around. I
try and read every day. I have important things that I like to read. I like
to read the *New York Times*. I like to just keep up on what's going on in

the world, and then I have novels, you know, things that are fun that I also want to read. I also have been working on my acting class.

NEIGHMOND: Nine years ago Archie came to New York to work as an actor. He had worked in the theater in high school and in college. He was twenty-three years old and tall and slender, sandy-haired and good-looking. He did what most actors here do. He worked odd jobs in an office, a restaurant, handing out flyers on the street, while he looked for acting work. And there were some successes, parts in Off Broadway plays and roles in television. But when he went into the hospital last February with *Pneumocystis* pneumonia, everything changed.

HARRISON: While I was in the hospital there was a man there who was a member of the AIDS unit at Bellevue at the time, where I was, and he came in to see me, to sort of make me aware of what it meant to have a diagnosis of AIDS, what it meant to have *Pneumocystis* and, you know, my life expectancy and all of that, and had I made a will?

He said all these things to me about my life and about, you know, choices and, well, all of that, and then left me alone for the weekend. It was Friday and his time off. I liked this man right away. He had a wonderful sort of attitude about everything, and he was very straightforward with me. It was no-nonsense, which I appreciate a lot, but I was devastated when he left the room. I cried for about half an hour, thinking about my own demise. And then I had the time to really think about, well, you know, anybody who lives in a city like this should have made a will the minute they got off the boat. You never know what's going to happen to you here, and if you don't do a will, you're just fooling yourself. That was when I really started to think, yeah, you know, it's not the end of my life. It's a challenge, and I started to really reflect on it over that weekend as a challenge that I could meet head-on and come out of feeling good about. And when he came back in on Monday, I was so thankful that he had done this, that he had really forced me to take a look at my life in terms of my death is really what he did.

NEIGHMOND: After that, Archie did see life differently. He became honest with himself and with those close to him in a way he had never been before.

HARRISON: I informed my parents in the hospital that I was — that I had AIDS, and we also discussed my sexuality for the first time over the phone, long-distance, at the same time, something that had never been discussed, but it was part of that change. It was part of, well, you know, they have a son that they don't really know or hadn't really known for most of my life. And if the only thing I could do for them with what remains of my life is let them know who their son really is, that's wonderful, and that's what I want to do.

Now I am as honest with them as I can possibly make myself every time I talk with them. And they're more interested, as a consequence, because I think they detect that what they're getting is really me. It's not a washed-over story that's supposed to make them feel good.

NEIGHMOND: Archie decided that it was time to do the things he'd been putting off, the hard things, like making a will, and the fun things, like a trip to Ireland with two close friends. He started writing again, went back to acting class, and he says when he works in the theater again it will be for different reasons. A few weeks ago Archie read an ad in a trade paper. Casting was to begin for a play about people who work with AIDS patients. It isn't the type of acting job he's used to, but Archie says it's something he really wants to do. The play is called *Report from Team 14*. It's the story of a support group for AIDS–crisis intervention workers.

HARRISON: And I feel honored to be a part of this. I was so excited when I was called and told that they wanted me to be a part of the cast because I felt as though I would do anything to be a part of this. I think it will certainly open a lot of people's eyes. I think it will help. It will do what I feel like I want to do, by doing this with you, to make this a human, down-to-earth thing. It's not a mysterious, horrible, ugly disease. It's real people hurting and real people helping real people that are hurting. And the more that I feel that I can be public, the better for people who suffer from the fear of this disease, the fear of being around people with AIDS.

NEIGHMOND: Next week there will be a public reading of the play, to find financial backers, and for the past week Archie's been in rehearsals three to four hours at a time. He says he feels stronger these days. For the past eight weeks he's been taking AZT.

HARRISON: I was really happy and I was also cautious. I watched myself very carefully. It's really easy to get caught up in, Oh, is this a cure? Is this a cure? and start looking at, well, this drug specifically as a cure. It's not.

Sure, I could be perfectly healthy, and that would be wonderful. I want that, but if it has to be where it is right now, that's where it is, and that's OK. That's really OK.

MEDICAL TECHNICIAN: OK, 112 over 78. Very good. That's normal.

NEIGHMOND: Every Friday Archie goes to the Spellman AIDS Clinic in Saint Clare's Hospital, where he gets weighed and has his temperature and blood pressure taken.

HARRISON: Hi, I'm Arthur Harrison. I have a prescription to pick up.

PHARMACIST: All right, sir, it's just like last week. Just take two capsules every four hours, around the clock. If you miss a dose, you know, the same thing. If you miss a dose, don't double up. We'll see you next week.

HARRISON: OK, thanks a lot. Look at this. This is what it looks like now. This is a hundred capsules, my weekly dose. I take two of these every four hours, day and night. So I take them at seven in the morning, eleven in the morning, three in the afternoon, seven at night, eleven at night, and three o'clock in the morning. So if I'm lucky, I get about three and a half hours sleep in between that, but usually it's a little less. I just kind of catnap all day long if I can.

I didn't have a real good appetite before, and for the most part I feel like my appetite is a little better. I haven't put on any more weight as a consequence, but I feel like I'm getting more nutrition during the day. I haven't really noticed anything else. I hear about a lot of side effects, like itching, kind of like dry-skin itching. Nausea, which I experienced once, just yesterday. I hadn't experienced that before, and it's kind of just gone away. Headaches. You can have problems with your bone marrow and your red blood cell count, but my diagnosis today is really good. In fact it's better than it was last week, which is a really good thing. The main thing it means is they don't have to cut my dose of AZT or take me off. This is a life-and-death struggle. And I want the life part of it. I want the length and the quality.

✦ ✦ ✦ ✦ ✦ ✦ ✦ ✦ ✦ ✦

Archie Harrison died in the summer of 1988. Through a series of conversations over many months, our listeners had grown fond of Archie. We received calls and letters of condolence, as if we were members of his family. People who met Archie over the radio made a panel for him in the AIDS quilt. Patricia Neighmond talked with Archie a few days before his death, after he'd made the decision to stop taking drugs and to have feeding tubes removed.

All Things Considered, AUGUST 9, 1988

NEIGHMOND: Another visit with Archie. Wednesday, last week. Archie sits on his bed, a new water mattress. He's so thin now that the regular mattress is uncomfortable. When he leans back, he props his knees up with a pillow, his back against two cushions. His face is chalk-white. The hollows of his eyes are large and reddened, but they are dramatically different from the eyes I saw one month ago, eyes that were angry and frightened, eyes that seemed to ask a thousand questions. Now Archie's eyes seem to sparkle again. They seem to give a thousand answers, not to be sad or uncomfortable, to know that this is the right decision for Archie, that this is how he wants to die.

Archie's friend Sarah is here. Sarah came to New York ten years ago with Archie. She wants to be a costume designer. Sarah holds on-to Archie's hand tightly. She does not let go for the entire evening. And Archie's companion, Drew, sits close too, listening to every word. He holds Archie's shoulder, strokes his arm, laughs now and then as Archie talks about the night he made the decision to stop taking the medication and the feeding.

HARRISON: That night I went to bed and I slept so well, for the first time in weeks, talked a lot in my sleep. I think I talked to a lot of people because I've been getting a lot of phone calls from people who I haven't talked to in a long time, good friends, loving people who I just haven't seen, and I think we made psychic touch somehow, and they've called and are coming by to see me now.

NEIGHMOND: In fact the days have been filled with people coming to say good-bye. It's beautiful, says Drew, to watch. I asked Archie if he has spoken with his parents. He has. His parents listened to what he had decided to do. His mother, he says, was too upset to talk about it. His father finally agreed to support him in whatever decision he made. The next day Archie awoke feeling better, he says, than he had felt in months. Drew says Archie woke up early, saying he wanted to go to the museum. Archie listened as Drew describes their day.

DREW: I got to push him in the wheelchair and we went to the modern wing of the Metropolitan, and it was like seeing paintings but like seeing every square inch of the paint and really relishing, just relishing, that day. God, that was such a great day. Now that he's feeling this way, it's like I don't want him to go. It's as if, you know, it's like he was never sick. It's like now that he's living again, I don't want him to go.

But the whole lesson for me is the letting go, and realizing that this is what I and several of his friends around him had wanted all this time, for him to reach this level of peace, regardless of whether he stayed in his body or not. We just wanted him to be at peace, and he is, and so I can't tell you the relief that is, knowing that he will pass at a place like this, and how blessed he is, how blessed we are, that this happened. It is a miracle. It's a real miracle that he reached this point.

HARRISON: I still get a little afraid sometimes, but I know this is the right thing. It's time to let my body have a rest now. It just, it worked real hard, and so did I, and my spirit is going to soar. And I, I feel so much love now. I just really do. That's all I want to say. That's it. I can't say any more about it.

NEIGHMOND: That was eight days ago. Yesterday at 11:52 in the morning, after two days of semiconsciousness, Archie died. As he wanted to. At home, with Drew and two close friends by his side, holding him.

✦ ✦ ✦ ✦ ✦ ✦ ✦ ✦ ✦

I think Nina Totenberg is the best reporter now covering the Supreme Court. In addition to her grasp of the issues the Court considers, she is right at the top of the very short list of reporters who have broken stories about the Court. As you will see, Anita Hill was Nina's story, as was the marijuana use of an unsuccessful Supreme Court nominee. In 1987, we broadcast a lengthy conversation with Nina and Justice William Brennan. He was eighty at the time. Nina said he had a springy step and a mischievous grin that reminded her of Jimmy Cagney. But behind that grin, Nina said, was a "mind of enormous force and determination, a mind that has by most accounts been at the forefront of molding American jurisprudence over the last thirty years." Here are some excerpts from that conversation, broadcast over two days in January 1987.

All Things Considered, JANUARY 29 AND 30

TOTENBERG: Over the last three decades, Justice William Brennan has written dozens of opinions about the religion clauses of the Constitution, the clauses that guarantee freedom of religion and at the same time bar the government from in any way establishing religion. Brennan has written some of the landmark opinions striking down aid to parochial schools. He's concurred in the Court's abortion rulings, and in 1963 when the Court struck down prayer in public schools Brennan wrote perhaps his longest opinion ever, seventy-five pages, setting out his views on almost every aspect of the religion question.

Justice Brennan, are you a religious person? Do you go to Mass?

BRENNAN: Every Saturday, five-fifteen Mass.

TOTENBERG: How do you reconcile your personal views, your religious views, for example, when they are at war with what you think the law requires?

BRENNAN: Well, you were too young. I guess you weren't born when I had my confirmation hearings.

TOTENBERG: I was old enough, but not old enough to be covering them.

BRENNAN: In any event, there was an organization, I've forgotten the name, that asked the Judiciary Committee to submit to me a question, which, in effect, was, When you come into a conflict between a principle of Roman Catholic faith and the Constitution, which prevails?

TOTENBERG: Now, this was the 1950s, before John F. Kennedy was elected president, and a question like this was considered an insult by many Catholics since similar questions were not asked of Protestants and Jews. The Senate Judiciary Committee determined that the question was improper but asked it anyway. And Brennan answered.

BRENNAN: Obviously, where there was a constitutional principle that was in conflict with any principle of my faith, my responsibility as a justice of the Court was, of course, to apply the Constitution as I saw that it should be applied. And that's the way I have acted, and I don't see any inconsistency whatever between that responsibility, as I defined it, and my going to church and receiving the Sacraments, as I do every week.

TOTENBERG: And what is the principle, for example in the abortion cases, that you think is embodied in the Constitution?

BRENNAN: Well, it's the right of privacy, of course, and the right of choice. It's a constitutional right that every individual has, male and female, and it happens, in the case of the female, to include the right, within the limitations set out in *Roe v. Wade*, to have an abortion.

TOTENBERG: Because you've written so many opinions in this area about school prayer, you've written a number of decisions striking down provisions that give parochial-school aid, and because you have concurred in the abortion decisions, I think sometimes your views are misapprehended as a hostility to religion. Could you explain?

BRENNAN: Oh, my, they could not be more wrong. They could not be more wrong. Of course, I'm not hostile to religion, good heavens. I'm a devout Roman Catholic. It's as simple as I tried to suggest earlier. The

Constitution has the religion clauses. They are not self-defining when any conflict has to be resolved. That's the responsibility of this Court to do.

As Justice Jackson always said, this Court's not final because its members are infallible. It's infallible only because it is final. Meaning only by that that what we pronounce as the Constitution becomes the law of the land and will remain such unless we change it or there's a constitutional amendment. And when I work on the religion clauses, that's all I focus on.

TOTENBERG: When you're focusing on the religion clauses, what is it you're trying to figure out?

BRENNAN: What I have said was that under our Constitution government has to stay away from trying to regulate religion, and religion has to stay away from butting in on matters that are for government. The whole notion of separation of church and state, and the notion that this means the Constitution sponsors hostility to religion is just so very, very wrong. We have learned through bloody experience, indeed the sort of thing that's going on in some places in the world today, that religious conflicts can be the bloodiest, most cruel kinds of conflicts that seem to turn people into fanatics. And that's the kind of history that prompted the framers to write the prohibitions of the religious clauses in the Constitution.

TOTENBERG: Perhaps no subject has impassioned Brennan more than capital punishment. He has consistently pushed the Court with all his might towards his belief that the death penalty is a violation of the Constitution's ban on cruel and unusual punishment. In 1972 a majority of the justices agreed that the death penalty as then administered was unconstitutional, but four years later, after states had readopted the death penalty with fairer procedures for sentencing, the Court declared in a case called *Gregg versus Georgia* that capital punishment was then and is now permissible punishment under the Constitution. Since then, Brennan has repeatedly dissented from every decision by the Court allowing a person to be executed.

I want to ask you about the death penalty cases which have been so important to you and about which you've written so much. Why do you continue to dissent in these cases?

BRENNAN: Well, you have to remember, these are not the only cases in which I continue to dissent. You have to remember this, this goes back to what I said earlier to you that, as Justice Jackson said, we're not final because we're infallible or infallible because we are final. We can't always be right. And one dissents and has to dissent, is expected to dissent, when he disagrees with the constitutional interpretation of the majority. Because the day may well come when what he says in dissent, when greater wisdom prevails, may become the law of the land as it did with *Plessy versus Ferguson,* separate but equal. *Brown versus the Board of Education* said there's no such thing as separate but equal.

Particularly in the death penalty, all over the world, nations have been ambivalent about whether there should or should not be a death penalty. And indeed, in the United States, even today, eighteen, twenty, or something states don't have the death penalty. And the reasoning that leads me to that conclusion, that it violates the cruel and unusual punishment prohibition of the Eighth Amendment, I hope will someday persuade. If not that reasoning, some other reasoning that the death penalty is indeed unconstitutional as cruel and unusual punishment.

We've had that happen with a great many other punishments which were in force at the time we adopted the Eighth Amendment: for example, cutting off arms and hands and all that sort of thing. Those things still went on in places supposedly civilized. And no one today would ever suggest that they were not cruel and unusual and in violation of the Eighth Amendment. The day, I think, may well come when that will also be the considered conclusion about the death penalty.

TOTENBERG: Have you always thought, since you've been on the Court, that the death penalty is unconstitutional?

BRENNAN: I thought so before I came on the Court.

TOTENBERG: In view of the fact that the death penalty existed at the time of the adoption of the Constitution, it existed all during your boyhood and your early manhood and even your middle age too.

BRENNAN: Way back, I've forgotten, 1890s, 1880s, this Court decided *Weems versus the United States* and said as to the death penalty that its validity — oh, how the dickens was it put? — depends on the maturing standards of decency of a civilized society, or words to that effect. In other words, as I have said, there are some penalties that were in effect when the Eighth Amendment was adopted that nevertheless had been said to be violative.

TOTENBERG: Your opponents have said in written opinions, No matter what the maturing standard is, the body politic says it wants this punishment — so whose standard is it other than yours that doesn't want it?

BRENNAN: Well, the answer is that we'll have to wait and see. This is my idea of where I think my colleagues of the majority have fallen into error. And just as those who felt that the Court that wrote *Plessy and Ferguson* had fallen into error, it took *Brown versus the United States* to agree that, indeed, they had. And I hope the day will come when there will be an opinion here that will agree that *Gregg versus Georgia* also is a case in which my colleagues have fallen into error.

TOTENBERG: Following that logic, you would, of course, urge your colleagues who have dissented in the abortion cases to continue to dissent?

BRENNAN: Of course, if they want to, that's exactly what they should do. Absolutely. Of course they should.

TOTENBERG: In the hopes that one day they'll win.

BRENNAN: Oh, certainly. It is no different in my case than from theirs.

TOTENBERG: If everybody keeps hoping that it will change, then why would they obey it now?

BRENNAN: While it's the law of the land, it's the law of the land.

◆ ◆ ◆ ◆ ◆ ◆ ◆ ◆ ◆

We are always noting the passage of seasons at NPR, possibly trying still another way to send those mental pictures through the radio, to add the smells and sounds of shared experiences. I once wrote an essay on Crayolas and how they evoke the fall and the school year. Our reporter Brenda Wilson wrote about the spring. Her essay begins with the sounds of church bells.

Morning Edition, APRIL 19

WILSON: Some Sundays, these bells have awakened me. No matter how rankling it is to have those last few precious hours of pagan sleep disturbed, I stop in a kind of wonderment. I pause. That sound, as if the day is being broken open, is followed by a flurry of commotion, the sound of scuffling feet, voices. The corner where Canaan Baptist, St. Stephen's of the Incarnation, and the AME Zion Church conjoin comes to life. It is one of the few places in Washington with gridlock on a Sunday morning. Sometimes I sit and watch as families climb from cars. Men with church robes tossed over the arm, women with large hats and matching dresses, wearing heels that seem as high as church steeples, move in unison toward the churches.

More so than any calendar date or any series of warm, sunny days, there is that one Sunday that chimes with some internal clock, which signals the return of spring. It is the festival of spring, Easter. As if in an old sentimental movie, I hear the voices of small children singing, "He arose, he arose, he arose from the grave." A certain literalness from a Fundamentalist childhood takes over. There is the face on the Sunday school card of a young man with dolorous looks surrounded by a jeering mob and one or two isolated figures standing to the side. A drop or two of blood stains his forehead. Sometimes he is stripped to the waist, at others, draped in a loose-fitting gown. The vague teachings of suffering are recalled, the pain of the thorns as they pierce the brow, the weight of the cross. Perhaps the pains of youth, no matter how real, are too vague. It took years to make sense of the lessons of suffering. Then it was almost comical seeing a wooden cross of two-by-fours being carried down the church aisle by solemn adults.

Spring was christened by a new outfit, top to bottom and sometimes underneath. And forever and always, it seems, new black patent leather shoes, with everyone looking to see how everyone else turned out. Still in mind from the day before was the pungent smell of vinegar, and the steaming water being poured over the pellets of dye, and the impatience of letting the eggs set until the dye had taken and the eggs were a darkened hue of primary colors. By Saturday night, there was the simple happiness of a bowl of eggs in the center of the kitchen table, which miraculously the next morning had multiplied, giving birth to chocolate rabbits and marshmallow ducks and a basket stuffed with new green paper grass.

What did the newly born know of rebirth, much less suffering? So as Brother Gilbert labored with his real or imagined suffering under the old homemade cross, the children were already wandering among high grass in search of brightly colored eggs. If, centuries ago, these dramas were initiated, as the scholars say, to make as vivid as possible for the uneducated laity the deep significance of the events that were being celebrated, I suspect that the laity had long since imbued them with a significance all their own. Faith, then, as I recall, was not so hard a thing to find.

✦ ✦ ✦ ✦ ✦ ✦ ✦ ✦ ✦ ✦

NPR covered the entire Iran-contra committee hearings live, from May 15 to August 3, more than eleven weeks of extraordinary testimony. Lieutenant Colonel Oliver North was the most important witness, but one of the most revealing days of testimony came earlier.

The committee heard a panel of witnesses, wealthy people who had agreed to give the government money to carry on projects that Congress had not agreed to fund. To my mind, they told a far clearer story than many of the administration witnesses did. I particularly remember Ellen Garwood. She seemed quiet and shy, an unlikely person to be financing arms purchases. I remember picking up several of the old-fashioned hairpins she scattered as she testified. I also remember Ellen Garwood as a passionate patriot. What follows is from our nightly summary of each day's testimony, prepared on this occasion by Cokie Roberts.

Special Coverage, MAY 21

ROBERTS: The day began with three civilians, nonmilitary, nongovernment, but not altogether ordinary Americans. Texas cotton heiress Ellen Garwood gave two and a half million dollars to the contra cause last year. Most of the money was solicited by Carl Channell, who set up a series of meetings between Ellen Garwood and Oliver North. At one meeting last spring, North gave Mrs. Garwood a list of rebel needs. House Counsel Thomas Fryman asks Mrs. Garwood about the list.

GARWOOD: The list had different categories of weapons, had hand grenades, I remember, and bullets, cartridge belts, possibly surface-to-air missiles. And there were quantities opposite each category and after that there was a sum of money that was needed to provide those weapons, what those weapons would cost.

FRYMAN: What was the approximate total amount?

GARWOOD: The approximate total amount was over a million dollars. And I'm not sure just exactly what it was. It was over probably a million and a half, something like that.

ROBERTS: Mrs. Garwood says that Oliver North did not ask her to come up with the money, but Carl Channell did. Mrs. Garwood first had to consult her banker.

FRYMAN: What did you do with the list?

GARWOOD: Well, I returned on Sunday afternoon, and on Monday morning I took the list to Mrs. Ann Glance, who is the manager of my trust account at the Interfirst Bank in Austin, and asked her if — and showed her the list — and asked her if it were possible for me to supply the funds needed for that.

FRYMAN: And what was her response?

GARWOOD: She said, "I think you can, but I think we will have to sell some stock. We certainly don't have the cash."

ROBERTS: Ellen Garwood did make the stock transfers to Carl Channell's group, the National Endowment for the Preservation of Liberty. A few weeks ago, Channell pled guilty to conspiring to defraud the U.S. government because he claimed his organization was tax-exempt. Mrs. Garwood said that Channell had assured her that she could take a deduction, even though she thought she had been purchasing weapons. But her concerns about the matter led her to turn it over to her lawyer, Mr. Osborne.

OSBORNE: I had made efforts to get more detailed information from Mr. Channell and from his attorneys without success. And we further, on April 13, contacted the Internal Revenue Service in Washington, D.C., a Mr. Larry Batdorff, who confirmed that the National Endowment for the Preservation of Liberty had been tax-exempt throughout all of 1986 and was still tax-exempt. Based on that information, we filed a return and claimed the deduction. About two weeks later, around April 30, Mr. Channell pled guilty, which made the conversation that he had with Mrs. Garwood highly suspect. And on the basis of that new information, we amended the return and did not take the deduction.

ROBERTS: Ellen Garwood testified that she would give whatever she could to stop communism in this hemisphere, that tax deductions meant nothing to her. As the contributors described the solicitations, the whole story took on the air of a sting operation. A classic set-up-the-mark (done by Oliver North), then collect (Carl Channell's job).

New Hampshire Republican Warren Rudman insisted that it was nothing but a legal fiction to claim that under these circumstances Colonel North was not actually doing the soliciting. Rudman asked Ellen Garwood about a meeting with Carl Channell and Oliver North in Dallas.

RUDMAN: Mr. North met with you at the airport that day. And told you, according to your deposition, that there was a need for all sorts of things down in Nicaragua, particularly, I believe, possibly trucks and other supplies.

GARWOOD: Yes, he told me the terrible news that supplies had arrived, but there was no way to transport them. Much like the way supplies arrived to feed the starving people of Ethiopia, and they were left on the docks and rotted.

RUDMAN: And they didn't have trucks to move them with.

GARWOOD: That's right.

RUDMAN: And then Colonel North left. And then Mr. Channell took you back to your hotel in a cab. Is that correct?

GARWOOD: Yes, sir.

RUDMAN: And then, essentially, within a short time frame after Colonel North told you, Mrs. Garwood, that trucks were needed, Mr. Channell said to you, "Mrs. Garwood, you can help."

GARWOOD: Yes, sir.

RUDMAN: And in fact, you did.

GARWOOD: Yes, I did.

RUDMAN: Then and there, you issued a check, or shortly thereafter, for thirty-two thousand dollars.

GARWOOD: Yes.

RUDMAN: Now, that's, where I come from, we call that the old one-two punch.

ROBERTS: Mrs. Garwood took offense at that characterization. Despite the general air of levity at the morning session of the hearings, the committee members did voice some underlying concerns, chiefly the ongoing question of just how much President Reagan participated in soliciting funds for the contras. The witnesses testified that no one in the government had ever asked them directly for money, but they knew they were doing what the president wanted. Mrs. Garwood attended a meeting where President Reagan expressed his gratitude.

Democrat Peter Rodino asked her where she thought the actual request for aid to the contras was coming from.

RODINO: Colonel North didn't ask you, White House officials didn't ask you. But nonetheless, it was Mr. Channell who asked you for the contributions, but you recognized that this was a request coming from the principals at the White House.

GARWOOD: Oh yes, that it was the executive department at the White House.

✦ ✦ ✦ ✦ ✦ ✦ ✦ ✦ ✦ ✦

President Reagan took the extraordinary step, in the Iran-contra hearings, of ordering his staff to talk, to tell exactly what they had done. Despite his orders to be candid, there were lingering doubts that White House officials could have treated the president as they said they had, proceeding without his permission, to perform missions outside the law. Whatever the real story, the Iran-contra affair had the effect of making the president a less significant figure in his last years in office. One of our conservative commentators, the columnist Cal Thomas, offered these observations on the survival of presidents.

THOMAS: Now that the Iran-contra hearings have mercifully ended, it's time to ask whether we can go on like this. There seems to be a perverse enjoyment of these events, like the man in New Jersey who was recently convicted of an inhumane act for shooting his dog just for the thrill of watching him die. We have treated our presidents in recent years as if they were vegetables to be sliced or diced by journalistic and political Veg-O-Matics. Then we wonder when we're through with them why they can no longer function.

Political analyst Kevin Phillips has been among those prophesying the doom of the current president. He wrote recently that President Reagan now "verges on irrelevance and that, at age seventy-six, he is no longer on top." Well, even if that is true, which is debatable, is it all the president's fault? Did he jump or was he pushed?

And we have become equal opportunity destroyers. In recent years it hasn't mattered whether the president has been a Republican or a Democrat, a liberal or a conservative. *Newsweek*'s Eleanor Clift summed it up for me when she said, "We go after whoever is on top, regardless of their ideology." Opinion polls, our current substitute for truth, helped the process along, but polls are really nothing more than seismic readings which measure whether the critical bombardment by the media and the president's adversaries have shaken the faith of the masses in their leader.

It is not just the criticism of Ronald Reagan that is bothersome. Some of that criticism is valid, some is not. What should concern us is that we no longer seem pleased with any president, regardless of party or persuasion. We appear not to know what we want or how to be happy even if we get it.

Much of the press's natural skepticism long ago mutated into an unhealthy cynicism that seriously impedes our national goals. Even British Prime Minister Margaret Thatcher made note of it on her recent visit, when she lectured us on what we are doing to ourselves with this Iranian-style self-flagellation. The press ought not to be a cheerleader, but neither should it be a boo leader.

I wonder how effective this or any other president might be if those who have been calling for his head and treating him as washed-up would begin to build him up instead. Whoever is president, with so much at stake, can we really afford for him to fail?

✦ ✦ ✦ ✦ ✦ ✦ ✦ ✦ ✦ ✦

S usan Stamberg was the host of *Weekend Edition, Sunday*, when it began in 1987, closing the circle and making *Morning Edition* available every day. Scott Simon created a very personal version of the Saturday show, and Susan's show was also very personal, with live music and an emphasis on cultural turning points. She also introduced America to Tom and Ray Magliozzi of the Good News Garage, in Cambridge (Our Fair City), MA. They are NPR stars with their own show these days, and even people who wouldn't think of looking under the hood love them. On this occasion, Tom and Ray thought it was hilarious that Ms. Judith Fishback of Flagstaff, Arizona, was driving a 1964 Plymouth Valiant. Valiants are not as funny to the car guys as, say, Ford Escorts, but it still took awhile to get around to advice about stalling in damp weather.

Weekend Edition, Sunday, AUGUST 30

RAY: You may have a condition whereby the carburetor is putting in an excessively rich mixture, which would not be a problem when the weather was nice, but would be a problem when the weather was inclement.

So if the ignition system, and all the pieces that we mentioned, the cap, the wires, the points, the condenser, the coil and its tower, if those things all check out OK, the next thing is to see if the carburetor is running too rich. And they can do that with an emissions test. When the engine finally warms up, after like fifteen minutes of driving, is it then OK?

FISHBACK: It's not really, he's not really himself. He's still complaining about the wet. That's why I moved to Arizona.

RAY: You have to move to El Paso. There's a lot more sunshine in El Paso, and it almost never snows there.

FISHBACK: OK, I'll do it.

RAY: Nice town, you'll like it.

TOM: See, here's another woman who loves her car. She's willing to go literally to the ends of the earth for her car.

STAMBERG: What if she got a tiny little umbrella, put it in under the hood, right over her spark plug?

FISHBACK: That's it.

RAY: Let the mechanic check the simple things first, and of course the wires and the coil are the simpler things, and then if he doesn't turn anything up there he can go ahead and check the carburation.

STAMBERG: Ms. Fishback? Sounds like you've gotten good advice.

FISHBACK: I did, I love it. Will you guys marry me?

RAY: Both of us?

TOM: I'll marry your sixty-four Plymouth. My brother can marry you.

STAMBERG: Thanks, Ms. Fishback. Tom and Ray, before we say good-bye I want to remind folks how we usually say good-bye to you because we've gotten a lot of mail about it. Hold on.

That sound, that wonderful sound, our so-long sound effect to the car guys gets plenty of mail. Listeners want to know what kind of a car that is. Do you, either one of you, have a clue?

RAY: Sure, that's a Triumph.

STAMBERG: What?

RAY: That would be my guess. That sounds like a British sports car of old.

TOM: Well, my guess is that it's not a car at all.

STAMBERG: It's a former producer.

TOM: Lawn mower?

RAY: I think it's a Briggs and Stratton, a 1984 Briggs and Stratton.

STAMBERG: No, you are on the money. It's from a sound-effects record, and the label says a Triumph TR3. I'm so impressed. What hearing you've got.

TOM: I'm telling you, this guy is brilliant. Brilliant!

STAMBERG: Congratulations, you both are brilliant, Tom and Ray Magliozzi, up at member station WBUR in Boston. So long.

RAY: Bye-bye, Susan.

TOM: That was good.

RAY: Oh, it just had that familiar ring to it.

STAMBERG: Let's hear that sound again.

[*Car engine starting.*]

TOM: Yep, that's what it is all right. I should've known. I used to have one. Except mine never ran. I only heard the first half of the noise. *Rrrrrr.*

1988

✦ ✦ ✦ ✦ ✦ ✦ ✦ ✦ ✦

S ex was part of the election campaign in 1988. Former Senator Gary
Hart, who had made a respectable showing in the 1984 fight for the
Democratic nomination, came after it again. This time, he was undone
by a short cruise on a boat called *Monkey Business*. A photograph of the
candidate with a beautiful blonde on his lap was published everywhere.
Hart tried to assert that his private life and his marriage vows were no
one else's business, but that didn't work. Frank Browning wrote this
piece on politics and private lives. It began with a recording of "Happy
Birthday," sung at a party for the president in 1961.

All Things Considered, JANUARY 29

BROWNING: The singer was Marilyn Monroe, fourteen months before
her apparent suicide, when she was reportedly obsessed and distraught
over her long-standing affairs with both President Kennedy and his
younger brother Attorney General Robert Kennedy. In that time, the
president's sexual appetite was a poorly kept secret in the elite circles of
the Washington press corps. Indeed, Kennedy's succession of brief
affairs was, according to biographer Garry Wills, a matter of presidential pride, a badge of his manliness, as it also had been for his father,
Joseph Kennedy. But in the 1960s, rampant womanizing, so long as it
was performed with discretion, was not a story in the responsible press.
In those days, discreet sexual adventures were simply accepted as part of
the privilege of power. To see how that transformation has come about,
we need to look at the era of political sex scandals played out during the
1970s.

Paula Parkinson used to be a Washington lobbyist. Tom Evans used
to be a Republican congressman from Delaware, until he and another
congressman, Tom Railsback of Illinois, were discovered to be sharing
a Florida weekend house with Parkinson. Evans acknowledged the
relationship, asked forgiveness, and lost his seat in Congress. Railsback,

who denied any improprieties, held onto his seat. Paula Parkinson, who was also featured in a *Playboy* magazine photo spread, now lives in Texas. She says that when she was in Washington male congressmen simply assumed that attractive young women would be ready to sleep with them.

PARKINSON: I was sitting with a group of people and — some of them being congressmen — and they introduced me to a freshman congressman from California. Then he sat down next to me and leaned over, and said to me, "I want to spend the rest of my term trying to make love to you."

One of the first members I met was Tom Railsback, and I had been trying to get through to him to see if he would speak at a seminar. Couldn't get through, couldn't get through, couldn't get through. The Polo Club had a grand opening, and I ran into him and I said, "My God, I've been trying to get ahold of you," and he said, "Well, you know, you just give me a call tomorrow, and they'll put it right through." Bam! The next day I did, I was put straight through. So then, he said, yes I'll do it. But then he said, you must have dinner with me and you must have a drink with me. But then, OK, I said, when I started to do lobbying, I wanted to talk to some other ones. And all he'd do is he'd call on the phone and say, I'm sending so-and-so over, and she doesn't want to talk to any staffers. You know, she wants to talk to you. I mean, it was immediate entry.

BROWNING: Stories like Parkinson's were part of the turning point in the etiquette of the Washington sexposé. Throughout the 1970s, congressman after congressman fell from power as a new generation of journalists began to write about the hitherto taboo territory of politics and sex. Long-time *New York Daily News* reporter Joe Voles was part of a pack of reporters who specialized in congressional girlfriends.

VOLES: And we were going around interviewing young women who might be having affairs, making house calls, so to speak. Actually going out at night, interviewing these gals at home, running around town. We were this small group of zealot journalists. And one night you had a congressman from Louisiana arrested for trying to solicit a prostitute downtown in the red-light district. Of course, you did have the *Washington Post* story where Congressman Bob Leggett of California actually had two families, two wives, supporting both of them.

I think we were suddenly discovering that not only are people interested in the personal lives of these politicians, but we could get it in the paper for some reason. The stories that had been booted about in private, told from one reporter to another, from one politician to another, now are considered — since the Elizabeth Ray thing and since Watergate — fair game.

BROWNING: The Elizabeth Ray whom Voles mentions was a blond secretary to Ohio Congressman Wayne Hays, one of the most senior and most powerful members of the House of Representatives. Miss Ray gained some notoriety when she declared that the secretarial skills for which she was paid did not include the ability to type.

The first and perhaps the biggest of that era's sex scandals involved Arkansas's Wilbur Mills, chairman of the House Ways and Means Committee, who found himself in an embarrassing situation down at Washington's Tidal Basin with a striptease dancer named Fanne Fox.

Congressional philandering, of course, was not new to the 1970s. Lyndon Johnson, never far from a bawdy anecdote, used to boast about his sexual prowess. And even Dwight Eisenhower and Franklin Roosevelt had mistresses. And so the deeper question may not be why the press began to report these stories, but why in earlier times the press did not. Eileen Shanahan has been a top Washington reporter for more than thirty years, many of those with the *New York Times*. Shanahan argues that the stories weren't written, in part, because most of the writers were men.

SHANAHAN: When it was an old-boys' club, lots, not all, but lots of the old boys had extramarital affairs whether they are journalists or politicians. And therefore, there was, I think, some sense of, well, we won't tell, because that was in fact the male locker room bonding.

BROWNING: Locker room bonding almost certainly played an important role in controlling reporting on Kennedy's and Johnson's womanizing. But University of Michigan historian and former reporter Terrence McDonald says there was a deeper collusion between the press and America's political leaders.

MCDONALD: The premier media organs, in particular the print organs, had, and to some extent still have, a sort of overburdened sense of their responsibility for the stability of the political system. So I think this notion of the media, in particular in the fifties and sixties, the print media, as responsible political institutions which have a stake in the stability of the political system, led them in many ways to a form of self-censorship. Not just because of locker room solidarity, but I think there was a broader image too, which was that these kinds of things tended to cast doubt on the American system as a whole.

BROWNING: McDonald argues that before Watergate, before the Vietnam War, before the muckraking exposés that marked those times, the press was much more like a fourth branch of government. National politics in that earlier era was the purview of a few hundred party leaders. And the nation's top editors and commentators, often as not, behaved as advisers to those leaders. But by the 1970s the old collusion between press and state had begun to break down, on everything from CIA law breaking to the clubby security that had always protected the country's political bosses. As public presidential primaries came to replace brokered party deals in the selection of candidates, and as candidates began campaigning against the party system itself, the press's role changed too.

SHANAHAN: If presidential candidates are going to be nominated by the public at large, rather than people who really know them, then maybe the press has a different kind of obligation than existed before. To really spread on the public record things that may be wrong with, or perceived by many voters to be wrong with some of the candidates.

BROWNING: If the press felt it had new responsibilities in a new political era, it also was facing big changes of its own. Namely that by the mid-1970s the boys on the press bus weren't all boys anymore. And the women who were there didn't snigger and roll their eyes about the womanizing pols as their male colleagues always had. The battle cry of the feminist movement, that the personal is political, began to raise new and often uncomfortable kinds of political issues, which a changing press corps had to acknowledge.

SHANAHAN: The fact of the matter is that the people who were running the parties didn't care if someone was a womanizer, it was not viewed as the kind of character flaw that it is viewed as now, in many quarters. That there is a certain shallowness in the man who compulsively must try to bed any woman who seems attractive to him. That such a man is generally incapable of forming deep relations, such a man who views women as something to be used and perhaps discarded rather quickly. And all of those things, I think, are now viewed more than they used to be as character flaws. In major part because women are speaking up about it and have been for fifteen or twenty years now, and are saying, hey, we're human beings, we're full human beings, we're not objects, we're not toys to be played with. We are total human beings, just as you are, Mr. Man.

BROWNING: Still, if press attitudes toward privacy and sexual politics were changing, the changes did not come easy. In 1979, years after Wilbur Mills and Wayne Hays had passed from the Washington scene, *New Yorker* writer Suzannah Lessard took on the prince of Washington liberalism, Senator Edward Kennedy. In an article for the highly respected but iconoclastic *Washington Monthly*, Lessard charged Kennedy with compulsive philandering. She said that his aides would even go out looking for young attractive women to ask them if they would like to have a date with Kennedy. Kennedy denied the charges, and Lessard drew a chorus of denunciations from the predominantly male Washington journalistic community. The magazine's editor, Charlie Peters, said he personally took many complaints from close Kennedy associates, but that none of them disputed the facts of Lessard's article. The problem was that such material was still considered scandalmongering. Indeed, Lessard says that many prominent Washington women were afraid to be named simply because they were afraid of being ridiculed in the male-dominated world of Washington politics and journalism.

LESSARD: I interviewed a lot of women, and nobody wanted to be quoted, or very, very few people, women, wanted to be quoted, women who had some standing in the political world, because they would sound like jerks. They didn't want to sound like jerks, you know. And they said so. They were very frank about that. They just didn't feel free to express it, and they didn't have the right terminology to express it. And it still remains very, very difficult to express this correctly without sort of slopping over into strident moralism or appearing to be very puritanical and those things. It's hard to talk about. It's a very subtle thing.

BROWNING: Gradually, the sex issue was maturing into a feminist womanizing issue. But in the process, all the old distinctions between public and private were torn apart. And, says Yale social historian David Plotke, there was opened up a whole set of unresolved social problems, well beyond sex.

PLOTKE: The sex-scandal aspect of it is just one part of a set of ways in which people see their own family and personal experiences as intertwined with public decisions, the quality of public life. People are anxious about their kids, how to take care of old people, how to take care of disabled people, how to handle the kind of incredibly difficult issues that arise in divorce and child custody today. All these are matters for important public policy debate, but they often get recoded or recast as dramatic tales of individuals' success or failure to cope with them.

BROWNING: Or, in short, character. Beneath that one word, which has so occupied this year's political discussion, lies a multitude of social conflicts that were never acknowledged as critical issues. For liberal feminists concerned with womanizing, character has to do with basic issues of social justice and equality. For New Right conservatives, womanizing also has to do with character, character failure to maintain traditional codes of family morality. Both use the same term. Both care about morality. But, says Plotke, each argues for very different social agendas.

PLOTKE: Well, it's a real problem, because the old moral code, if one went back to the forties or fifties, is still firmly in place as a kind of high-level official morality about how people are supposed to conduct themselves. The proper candidate is supposed to be heterosexual, to have been married, to have a couple of children, to behave respectfully toward their family and spouse, and to go to church. And to have a kind of single path through their life, organized around those experiences. But what's happened in the last two decades is people's actual practices have changed enormously.

BROWNING: Now about half the country's marriages end in divorce. More than half of all Americans born since World War II have lived with other partners prior to marriage. Most middle-class wives now work outside the home. And church attendance is erratic at best. The social contract upon which the traditional moral code rested is as faded as a scratchy rerun of *Ozzie and Harriet*. Yet the new lifestyles that have emerged in the postwar generation are themselves so diverse that no new social contract has yet emerged. And consequently, historian Plotke says, there is no coherent moral code to justify the lives that so many Americans, perhaps even a majority, are now living.

PLOTKE: So you have huge numbers of people, millions of people, especially people of say, between the ages of thirty-five and fifty, who have lived lives that for some substantial period were at variance with the official moral code of this society. And they don't have a clear language within which to articulate why it was OK to do what they did. And that, that makes for big trouble when these people's lives come up for inspection.

BROWNING: As a result of such inspections, the character crisis for political candidates is only likely to expand. In the old days, when politics was reserved for a fairly small group of conventional white middle-class men, such issues seldom arose. Both journalistic codes and the codes of political etiquette protected politicians from too much inspection. And in those old days, most voters were loyal to party rules. Now, less than a third of America's voters follow their party. "Conventional lifestyle" is a meaningless phrase which applies to fewer and fewer people in either private or public life.

And the moral code has itself become the subtext for political debate, an eventuality little dreamt of in 1961, when the love goddess of American male fantasy sang to the prince of Camelot.

MONROE: [*Singing.*] "Mr. President, for all the things you've done, the battles that you've won, the way you deal with U.S. Steel, and our problems by the ton, we thank you so much. Everybody, happy birthday!"

✦ ✦ ✦ ✦ ✦ ✦ ✦ ✦ ✦

The cartoonist and commentator Lynda Barry joined Renee Montagne for this conversation broadcast just before Valentine's Day. Barry was introduced as a great, unrecognized expert on love, prepared to answer questions.

All Things Considered, FEBRUARY 12

BARRY: Why does love pester us so? Who started it anyway? Was it just some dirty trick that kind of caught on? If it is your time, love will track you like a cruise missile. It starts looking for you the second you say, "No, not right now." And that's when you'll get it for sure. But the minute you want it, really want it, you will find yourself alone on a grease pole to hell.

WOMAN: I want to know why the first date is always so horrible. They're awful. They're awful. If you go out to dinner, you can't order a salad. It's awful.

MONTAGNE: Lettuce gets stuck in your teeth, right?

WOMAN: Things fly off the plate.

BARRY: Well, I think the most promising kind of date would be the one that parallels the situation in that one movie where Sidney Poitier is handcuffed to this white bigot and they're prisoners and they escape from this prison and they have to go handcuffed together through the swamps of Louisiana. I mean, I think going through some kind of grueling, wet, muddy event that's inescapable and you're handcuffed together would let you know right away if the relationship is going to work. And you wouldn't have to make small talk. And I think they should create facilities like this, like health clubs, that you go to on your first date and you spend two days fighting off nature together and then you can know by the end whether this is the person you want to stay with or not.

MONTAGNE: A word — whenever people talk about romance and love — a word that always comes up is "chemistry."

MAN IN BAR: What is chemistry? Is it some sort of sexual fantasy? I mean, I've seen a lot of relationships where it's all neurosis.

BARRY: I think chemistry is the astounding and deft human ability to gaze across a crowded room and instantly find the one person there who is the most like your mother. Even though it takes from seven to ten years to actually find that that's true. It's sort of an ability to locate the person who can bring you the greatest possible amount of misery.

MONTAGNE: And how does lust fit into that? One of our people wanted to know if chemistry really was lust. It doesn't sound like that's what you think it is.

BARRY: Well, no. I think lust is definitely the wiggling worm on the hook of love. I mean, I think lust is there, but what attracts us to someone sexually has more to do with neuroses. And I think that there is a real nice ecosystem involved in it where you pick somebody who is going to fulfill your worst fears about them and yourself, thus allowing you to work out the problem and kind of move on, kind of like those video games that have increasing degrees of difficulty even though it's the same game and that if you can actually get to the bottom of it without getting a brain tumor, then you can have a good relationship and enjoy your last two years on earth happily. I think it takes about sixty years to be able to achieve this.

MAN IN BAR: Maybe Lynda can deal with some of the phoniness. I think a lot of that has to do with first dates or especially people meeting in bars because they're trying to impress people.

MONTAGNE: Now, let me just tell you this is a bartender.

BARRY: Well, I think the question every person wants to know with someone on the first date is who is getting the better deal. And people are phony or they lie in an attempt to raise the stakes. I think you're phony or you lie in direct proportion to how much of a gap you perceive between your miserable worthless self and the other person's extreme desirability. And so the stakes keep getting higher and then there's a crash, like on Wall Street.

MONTAGNE: Well, we have a question that comes right out of this conversation.

WOMAN IN BAR: You know, in relationships, women are very honest and emotional. We're honest. A man, even if you catch him red-handed, he will always deny it to the nth degree. He'll lie, and I would like to know why.

BARRY: Well, like you learned in school, that the two instinctual responses to fear are fight or flight. But with men, there's a sort of third option, a built-in option. And the third option is: or lie. It's either fight, flight, or lie. And men lie because they are afraid of women yelling at them. I think the real question is, Why do they keep doing things that they have to lie about? And I think the answer to that is that men are pack animals. They move in packs and they have to do what the pack leader exemplifies for them, and a lot of times a man's pack leader is Rod Stewart or David Lee Roth.

MONTAGNE: OK, we have one last one for you here.

SECOND MAN IN BAR: Why is it that you never fall in love when you want to fall in love, and you always fall in love when you don't want to fall in love, like when you're ready to go off to school or when you're moving to a city? You always fall in love then. It's always the worst time.

BARRY: I think that the reason is that cupid is a monster from hell. You know, they call this little creature that we draw and see a lot around Valentine's Day with the arrow, this little flying baby, flying red baby or pink baby, who is shooting you with arrows, they call it cupid and surround it with hearts so we think this is actually a nice spirit. But if a red baby flew into the room and aimed an arrow at you, you would know instantly that there is some kind of malicious intent, and I think the fact that we fall in love right when we're ready to leave for some-place or split up or right when we fall in love with somebody else is an indication that these kind of funky imps are active.

MONTAGNE: Lynda, happy Valentine's Day.

BARRY: Happy Valentine's Day to you too, and watch out for them flyin' babies.

✦ ✦ ✦ ✦ ✦ ✦ ✦ ✦ ✦

In 1988, Lady Bird Johnson, the widow of President Lyndon John-son, was seventy-five, and in two days of celebrations in Washing-ton, she received a medal from President Reagan and recognition from the Congress. In all her years in Washington, Lady Bird must have heard that official bellow from the doorkeeper of the House hundreds of times, but this time the double doors at the back of the chamber opened, and he hollered, "Mistah Speakuh, Mrs. Lady Bird Johnson!" Cokie Roberts heard it too.

Morning Edition, APRIL 29

ROBERTS: These are the trappings of official Washington, the an-nouncement by the Speaker of the House, the appointment of an honor guard to escort the dignitary to the chamber, the presentation of the colors by the guard of the joint armed forces, the singing of the national anthem by the Men's Glee Club of the Naval Academy. These symbols of nationhood and tradition provide a sort of stability in the capital city, a place of pomp and purpose, where the citizenry seems secondary to monuments and documents, the people merely passers through, transients who call someplace else home.

But this was a celebration of a more personal and permanent Washington, a place of remarkable beauty, where every year the tulips rise out of the brown winter earth to reflect their profound purples and blood reds against the shimmering stone of the nation's shrines. Some 145,000 tulips, to be exact, along with 95,000 daffodils, 17,000 trees, 50,000 shrubs, the profusion put forward in the parks and pools, fountains and flower beds, of the capital, planted at the insistence of Lady Bird Johnson, who organized the Committee for a More Beautiful Capital.

Texas Democrat Jack Brooks addressed Lady Bird.

BROOKS: Your dedication and energy and hard work to beautify our country deserves the gratitude of every American. And every year, with the first warm breath of spring, our lives are renewed when we gaze upon the brilliant colors of the flowers and the budding trees that have been planted in our nation's capital as a result of your commitment to beauty and the poetry of nature.

ROBERTS: Brooks looked out over a House chamber where the Johnson children and grandchildren occupied the front row, Lynda and Luci's oldest daughters now the ages their mothers will forever be in our national memories. Mixed in and among members and former members of the House sat stalwarts of the Washington establishment: Clark Clifford, adviser first to President Truman. Joseph Califano, brought to government by President Johnson. This is family in official Washington, where Lady Bird Johnson touched individuals as well as institutions. And it was her everyday gutsiness as a wife that her old Texas friend Congressman J. J. Pickle first remembered.

PICKLE: LBJ was a volatile one. Lady Bird was the one who would come in and soothe tempers. She would apply the balm necessary to make everything all right. One morning Lady Bird was belatedly asked to attend one of the president's functions. And she hastily attempted to get dressed for the occasion. Restless as usual, the president stood outside the door, and began to shout, "Bird, Bird, come on. Hurry up! Let's go! We've got to go!" He made the mistake of speaking a little bit too loudly and a little bit too harshly, whereupon Lady Bird came to the door, and said, "Lyndon!" One word, that was all. And the president of the United States, the most powerful man in the Western world, came back to his coterie of workers and sat down and wisely observed, "Mrs. Johnson's not quite ready to go yet."

ROBERTS: And then that special grace few wives are called on to confer.

PICKLE: One endearing memory of her was when the president's body lay in state in the Capitol Rotunda. People kept filing by the casket until two-thirty in the morning, and Mrs. Johnson stood there almost all the time, greeting people. Old friends and strangers alike, comforting them. A young bearded man was in line, and said to her, "Mrs. Johnson, I'm sorry we were so ugly to him." And Mrs. Johnson patted him gently, and says, "Don't worry. He wanted to change things, too."

ROBERTS: If the memories of that night under the Capitol dome must be hard ones for Lady Bird Johnson, they've not wiped away her happier recollections of this place. The former First Lady rose to the lectern on the dais of the House of Representatives, where Lyndon Johnson stood five days after the assassination of John F. Kennedy, beginning the painful process of bringing the nation together. Now it was his widow, receiving the only gift the House of Representatives knows to confer, a resolution.

LADY BIRD JOHNSON: To be back in this place, Mr. Speaker, strikes a very deep chord. Lyndon used to say, the Hill is my home, and we were a life centered around this room for twelve years. Before that, he'd begun, I think, as a doorkeeper, so this was for long his habitat and then mine. And these walls have echoes, but to be back here under these circumstances was the farthest thing from any thought I ever had. I just want you to know that all of those seventy-five years have been rich and good, even some of the painful ones, because I learned from them.

ROBERTS: And as Lady Bird Johnson prepared to make the trip down Pennsylvania Avenue to the White House again, past the pink and white dogwood, the fuchsia and salmon azaleas, of her legacy, the Naval Academy Glee Club sang "America, the Beautiful," a farewell made more meaningful as a result of her making the capital her home.

✦ ✦ ✦ ✦ ✦ ✦ ✦ ✦ ✦

Anne Garrels was the ABC bureau chief in Moscow in the early eighties and one of the few correspondents working in the Soviet Union who spoke Russian. She went back, for NPR, to cover the discussions between Mikhail Gorbachev and President Ronald Reagan. At that time, there were many reports about liberalization in the Soviet

Union, about former dissidents pushing out previous limits. Anne wrote about psychiatric practices, particularly the practice of committing dissidents to mental hospitals. The same people, she wrote, who were guilty of the most serious abuses were still in charge.

All Things Considered, MAY 31

GARRELS: Over the past twenty years, human rights organizations have documented over five hundred cases where mentally healthy political and religious dissidents have been committed to mental hospitals as a form of punishment. Many were suddenly released over the past year with no explanation. It is estimated that between sixty and seventy dissidents are still hospitalized, but there have been no new commitments in the past eighteen months.

The Soviet press has not yet addressed the government-approved policy of committing dissidents. But it has come startlingly close. Several articles have accused local bureaucrats of committing mentally healthy ordinary citizens for nothing more than being a nuisance. Until these articles appeared, public discussion of psychiatric abuse in any form simply did not occur. Upon publication, the floodgates opened. The editor in chief of _Komsomolskaya Pravda_ has received hundreds of letters, one of them from a man who will only be known as Volodya. While working as a policeman in the Tambov region, about three hundred miles from Moscow, he complained about bad management and official corruption. He says he was fired and subsequently ordered to spend forty-five days in the Kaschenko psychiatric hospital in Moscow.

VOLODYA: When I asked for an explanation, I was told I was incapable of adapting to the collective, or adapting to circumstances. I could not agree with this.

GARRELS: Situated on the outskirts of Moscow, Kaschenko is surrounded by wooded grounds. A hundred-year-old compound holding two thousand patients, it's Moscow's foremost psychiatric clinic. The director, Dr. Vladimir Kosalyov, was impatient with the questions posed. Like other senior Soviet psychiatrists, he flatly denied that Soviet authorities have used psychiatry to punish dissent. As for the Soviet newspaper reports, he said, they're wrong.

KOSALYOV: Insofar as the concrete cases that were highlighted in the papers, there is nothing so terrible about them. Perhaps the treatment used was very rough, but in fact the cases discussed were cases of truly ill people.

GARRELS: So you are saying you do not believe there are such cases?

KOSALYOV: I don't know of any. I haven't encountered any. Maybe some people have behaved improperly, but that is not a problem specific to psychiatry. There are bad people everywhere. We can't take responsibility for that.

GARRELS: The Soviet press won't let up and is planning more stories. Though it's begun to discuss abuse by officials, its main focus continues to be the original criticism raised, that psychiatry here is just bad. Peter Reddaway is the leading expert on Soviet psychiatry in the West. He is encouraged by the prospects for change in the Soviet psychiatric system. But he believes any changes are first and foremost for economic reasons.

REDDAWAY: Gorbachev regards improving the state of the Soviet economy as the basis for all his other reforms. And clearly it's important to try to get a healthy work force. It's important not to waste a whole lot of money on a highly inefficient psychiatric system which is simply badly organized, corrupt, inefficient.

GARRELS: But as Reddaway notes, those who stand to lose from another of Gorbachev's reforms, those who supported the old system, are fighting back.

REDDAWAY: It's a very, very fierce fight in which the reformers have documented at great length the dreadful state of Soviet psychiatry. It is supported from above by Mr. Yakovlev, Gorbachev's strongest supporter in the leadership and the political leader who has a bigger control of the media. But the conservatives are resisting every step of the way. They are launching their own counteroffensive and it is an enormous battle and it could end up going either way. The conservatives could stem the reformist tide, turn it back, and essentially very little of substance would be changed.

GARRELS: So far the results of this battle have been mixed. Many senior psychiatrists have been investigated for corruption.

REDDAWAY: The typical pattern is that a criminal who has committed serious crimes knows that if he is sentenced in the ordinary way, he will get ten, twelve, fifteen years in a labor camp for his crimes or even conceivably execution. And if he can only get a psychiatrist to diagnose him and claim that he's schizophrenic, then he will be sent to a psychiatric hospital instead, and one bribe is necessary for that. And the going rate apparently is between six thousand and eight thousand rubles, something like eleven or twelve thousand U.S. dollars at the official exchange rate. And you then need a second bribe to get out of the psychiatric hospital after a couple of years, when you get the psychiatrist to say that you've now been cured.

GARRELS: To the dismay of reformers, charges against most of these psychiatrists have been dropped. Reformers have succeeded in getting a law passed. The special psychiatric hospitals where many dissidents have been kept will no longer come under control of the police. And patients are now guaranteed the right to appeal their cases. Also doctors who commit a patently healthy patient will now be prosecuted. However, a Soviet lawyer who helped draft the legislation has said it's inadequate. Patients must first appeal to the very doctors who committed them. It's still unclear if and how patients will get access to courts. As it is, there are no independent court-appointed psychiatrists here.

Galena Vasiliovna's son had suicidal tendencies. After four years in a hospital, she believes he's now well enough to be released. However, she's not been able to have his case reviewed, despite the new law. She's seen no change in the system since the law came into effect three months ago.

VASILIOVNA: I think if it were really enforced it might work. But too much still depends on the individuals at the hospital. And as for lawyers, they can't help because no one knows what's going on.

GARRELS: The head of Kaschenko insists the new law simply codifies existing practice. But he notes his doctors are now more cautious about committing patients, perhaps too cautious, he adds. Dr. Kosalyov worries the Soviet Union now will have mentally incompetent people living on the streets.

U.S. officials and human rights activists are waiting to see how this new law will apply to dissidents, if indeed the political abuse is ending. While bad psychiatry is certainly part of the problem, they say bad politics must be tackled head-on too. Widespread publicity in the West about the commitment of religious and political dissidents led to protest by the World Psychiatric Association in the late 1970s. Rather than risk likely expulsion, the Soviet Union withdrew from the association. It would like to be readmitted now.

As a first step towards restoring their standing, Soviet psychiatrists have agreed, in principle, to meet with U.S. psychiatrists in the fall. Details still have to be worked out, but a senior State Department official has said, "There seems to be a genuine interest in bringing the problem of abuse to an end." But before the Soviet Union is taken back into the fold, it's widely believed Soviet officials and Soviet psychiatrists must publicly acknowledge and condemn the political abuse.

REDDAWAY: If the authorities, the psychiatric authorities in particular, get away with their present tactics, which is to try to reestablish the good name of Soviet psychiatry in the world without admitting that any political abuses have ever taken place, then it's of course entirely possible that if there is a switch back to a more conservative leadership in the Soviet Union in the future, the abuses will simply become much more frequent again.

✦ ✦ ✦ ✦ ✦ ✦ ✦ ✦ ✦

Peter Breslow is a quiet adventurer. Most of the time he's a gardener, a quick and decisive producer, and a killer on the basketball court. But when we went to Kenya he took a few extra days and climbed Mount Kenya, and in 1988 he asked for time off to join a Wyoming expedition that called itself Cowboys on Everest. Pete called in from time to time. Here he speaks with Renee Montagne.

All Things Considered, SEPTEMBER 2

MONTAGNE: Peter, what have you got there, tents and a phone booth?
BRESLOW: No, it's a little more elaborate than that. We have a whole communications hut. We inherited a fair amount of the equipment from a British expedition. We took over the same base camp that they had, and they have this device. This telephone that we're talking on now is basically a satellite uplink. A TCS 9000, it's called. And you can just pick up the phone, and if it's not busy you can call me.
MONTAGNE: It must be startling after, what, traveling on roads that weren't even roads?
BRESLOW: Yeah, well, it's definitely the most technology we've seen in a while. Just to update you a little bit on what happened, if you heard my last story, we were stuck in a cruddy little town called Chegar, and we were waiting for our gear to arrive, which was traveling overland across China, from Beijing into Tibet. That was about forty thousand pounds of gear. It finally did arrive, and we were all excited. We were finally going to get under way, and we drove out of Chegar and got to the bridge and, lo and behold, there had been an earthquake and a landslide and the bridge was washed out. Some of the trucks tried to run the river, and it was a pretty rapidly rising river and some trucks made it across, one way, and then another truck tried to come back across the river. As that truck was driving across, it got swamped.

Inside the truck with the driver were another man and a seven-year-old kid. We were standing on the shores watching this traumatic scene of people trying to rescue this little seven-year-old child from this raging river. The river began to flow into the cab of the truck. It passed through the windows and started to edge up very near the top of the truck, and that's where everyone was sitting. The child did make it ashore. He wasn't even crying. It was really amazing.

We finally got to base camp at about two-thirty in the morning and just kind of flopped into a tent, and the next day I woke up and there's Mount Everest right in front of me. It's almost surreal. It almost looks like you could just throw on a daypack and go and hike up there, but —

MONTAGNE: But you can't. How far is it, exactly?

BRESLOW: I think it's about twelve miles. About twelve miles and twelve thousand feet. We're at seventeen thousand feet here. And today, I sort of got my first dose of high-altitude hiking. We're starting to establish our upper camps, and I carried a load up to just over eighteen thousand feet, which left me pretty much huffing and puffing. The weather finally appears to be breaking, and so we would get some pretty good views of mountains all day long, and it's really beautiful because the light changes. And even at night you get the alpine glow on the mountain, and it turns orange. The first couple of nights here we had a full moon, so that was really spectacular.

MONTAGNE: Now, you're not going to be heading up the mountain until the end of September, right?

BRESLOW: Well, no, teams have begun heading up right now. We're behind schedule, and it's a real tightrope that you walk between when the monsoon ends and when winter begins. Because once winter officially begins, you get incredible winds, which would just blow you off the mountain. So we have to work fast now to make up the time we lost. It took us a whole month to get here. We were hoping, you know, maybe ten days to get here. The one advantage for the long time arriving is that we've acclimatized quite well. So anyway, a bunch of folks are up on the mountain starting to establish higher camps, and we just need to ferry supplies, food, oxygen, tents, sleeping bags.

It is almost like a military assault, very well organized. Teams, certain teams are responsible for certain camps, and establishing those camps and supplying those camps so the next team can come in, use the facilities, and establish the upper camps. And then finally, the summit climbers. We've each got six designated summit climbers. We try to save them a bit. They don't have to carry quite as many loads as other people. Hopefully, they'll be a bit fresher, they'll be able to establish themselves at the upper camps, and then, if all goes well and the weather's good, make a summit attempt sometime. Now we're talking end of September, first week or two of October.

MONTAGNE: You know, after all that dragging to get there and all that waiting for this and that, sounds like morale is pretty good. You sound like you're having a good time.

BRESLOW: Oh yeah, it's really, it's really great. It was nice to get out today and go for a hike, you know, and carry a load up the mountain. And every so often, I just sort of have to pinch myself to actually realize that I am, in fact, looking at the highest point on the earth.

◆ ◆ ◆ ◆ ◆ ◆ ◆ ◆ ◆ ◆

Vice President George Bush and former Massachusetts Governor Michael Dukakis debated in Winston-Salem, North Carolina, at the end of September. The tone of the debate in this summary that I wrote for *Morning Edition* is bristling. In this campaign Dukakis talked about budgets and plans to finance college educations, and Bush talked about the Pledge of Allegiance and the pollution in Boston Harbor. By this time, the very tough hot-button campaign designed by Lee Atwater, campaign manager for the vice president, was looking like a winner.

Morning Edition, SEPTEMBER 26

WERTHEIMER: The debate was as scrappy as the campaign has been, with the two candidates waiting for opportunities to land punches. The tone was set with the answers to the first question on drugs. Why do so many Americans use drugs and what can be done about it. George Bush went first, saying American values are not being upheld. We condone, he said, where we should condemn.

BUSH: We have to change this whole culture. You know, I saw a movie, *Crocodile Dundee*. And I saw the cocaine scene treated with humor, as if this were a humorous little incident. And it's bad. Everybody ought to be in this thing. Entertainment, industry, people involved in the schools, education. And it isn't a Republican or Democrat or a liberal problem. But we have got to instill values in these young people.

WERTHEIMER: Michael Dukakis set off a string of tough exchanges between the two candidates with this answer.

DUKAKIS: I agree with Mr. Bush that values are important. But it's important that our leaders demonstrate those values from the top. That means those of us elected to positions of political leadership have to reflect those values ourselves. Here we are with a government that's been dealing with a drug-running Panamanian dictator. We've been dealing with him, he's been dealing drugs to our kids, and governors like me and others have been trying to deal with the consequences.

WERTHEIMER: Vice President Bush responded to that, saying he'd had a CIA briefing, which he could now reveal, where he learned that seven American administrations had dealings with Panamanian strongman Manuel Noriega, but there was no evidence of his complicity with drug deals until recently. And Bush said Michael Dukakis had the same CIA briefing.

This was the first face-to-face exchange of the fall campaign, and it gave both candidates an important opportunity to answer major charges their opponent has made in campaign speeches. George Bush was asked why he refers to Michael Dukakis as a "card-carrying member of the American Civil Liberties Union" and what that is supposed to mean to voters.

BUSH: He has every right to do it. But I believe that's not what the American people want. And when he said, when he said at the convention, ideology doesn't matter, just competence, he was moving away from his own record, from what his passion has been over the years. And that's all I am trying to do, is put it in focus, and I hope people don't think I'm questioning his patriotism when I use his words to describe his participation in that organization.

DUKAKIS: Well, I hope this is the first and last time I have to say this. Of course the vice president is questioning my patriotism. I don't think there's any question about that. And I resent it. I resent it. My parents came to this country as immigrants. They taught me that this is the greatest country in the world. I'm in public service because I love this country. I believe in it, and nobody's going to question my patriotism as the vice president has now, repeatedly.

The fact of the matter is that if the Pledge of Allegiance was the acid test of one's patriotism, the vice president has been the presiding officer in the United States Senate for the past seven and a half years. To the best of my knowledge, he's never once suggested that a session of the Senate begin with the Pledge of Allegiance.

I don't, Mr. Bush, I don't question your patriotism when you were attacked for your military record. I immediately said it was inappropriate, it had no place in this campaign. And I rejected it. And I would hope that from this point on, we get to the issues that affect the vast majority of Americans: jobs, schools, health care, housing, the environment. Those are the concerns of the people watching us tonight, not labels that we attach to each other and questions about each other's patriotism and loyalty.

WERTHEIMER: Dukakis repeated on a couple of occasions one of his stronger campaign statements about George Bush's record concerning his involvement in the Iran-contra scandal. Dukakis was asked which he would place higher, the lives of American hostages or the commitment not to negotiate with terrorists. This country must never negotiate with terrorists, Dukakis said.

DUKAKIS: As a matter of fact, Mr. Bush was the chairman of a task force on international terrorism which issued a report shortly before that decision was made, and said, rightly so, that we never, ever can make concessions to terrorists and hostage takers. And yet, after sitting through meeting after meeting, he endorsed that decision, endorsed the sale of arms to the ayatollah in exchange for hostages, one of the most tragic, one of the most mistaken foreign policy decisions we've ever made in this country, and, I dare say, encouraged others to take hostages as we now know.

WERTHEIMER: Vice President George Bush responded, saying the Reagan administration has made improvements in its anti-terrorism. He cited the American attack on Libya.

BUSH: I have long ago said I supported the president on this other matter, and I've said mistakes were made. Clearly nobody's going to think the president started out thinking he was going to trade arms for hostages. That is a very serious charge against the president, and that has been thoroughly looked into. But the point is, sometimes the action has to be taken by the federal government. And when we took action, it had a favorable response.

WERTHEIMER: One of the last questions raised was about Bush's choice of a vice president, the forty-one-year-old senator from Indiana, Dan Quayle. Quayle is a source of growing concern among voters, including Republican voters, according to polls. Reminded of criticism of Quayle's qualifications, Bush was asked, What do you see in him that others do not?

BUSH: I see a young man who is knowledgeable in defense, and there are people on our ticket that are knowledgeable, in the whole, in the race, knowledgeable in defense, and Dan Quayle is one of them. And I am one of them. And I believe he will be outstanding. And he took a tremendous pounding, and everyone now knows that he took a very unfair pounding. And I'd like each person to say, Did I jump to conclusions, running down rumors that were so outrageous and so brutal? And he's kept his head up, and he will do very, very well, and he has my full confidence. And he'll have the confidence of people that are in their thirties and forties and more.

So judge the man on his record, not on a lot of rumors and innuendo and trying to fool around with his name. My opponent says "J. Danforth Quayle." Do you know who J. Danforth was? He was a man that gave his life in World War II, so ridiculing a person's name is a little beneath this process [*applause*] and he'll do very well when we get into the debates.

MODERATOR: Governor?

DUKAKIS: Well, when it comes to ridicule, George, you win a gold medal. I think we can agree with that. [*Applause.*] In the course of this campaign, did I sense a desire that Lloyd Bentsen ought to be your running mate, when you said the three people on your ticket?

BUSH: No, I think the debate —

DUKAKIS: I think the American people have a right to judge us on this question, on how we picked our running mate, a person who is a heartbeat away from the presidency. I picked Lloyd Bentsen, distinguished, strong, mature, a leader in the Senate, somebody whose qualifications nobody has questioned. Mr. Bush picked Dan Quayle. I doubt very much that Dan Quayle was the best qualified person for that job. As a matter of fact, I think for most people the notion of President Quayle is a very, very troubling notion.

1989

✦ ✦ ✦ ✦ ✦ ✦ ✦ ✦ ✦ ✦

A IDS education began to slow the spread of the disease among the gay community, but other risk groups emerged. The incidence of sexually transmitted diseases began to rise among young people, especially among young blacks. Vertamae Grosvenor went to an AIDS education night at a halfway house in Washington, D.C., for this story.

All Things Considered, APRIL 13

GROSVENOR: Between Hollywood and the tabloids, you could believe that only rich, famous, and beautiful do it. But in fact everybody does it, the young and the old, the middle-aged and the adolescent. The physically disabled and the hearing impaired do it.

You don't have to be rich and thin to do it. Sexuality, passion, romance all over the world, is expressed and appreciated in many forms. A short, squat man will give some people fever. Some go wild over tall and bald. Some are turned on by hair in the armpits. For others, skinny legs are exciting, and there are contests where big-boned, big-hipped women win. We are turned on by as many ways as there are languages: by zee French "ooh la la" to the Puerto Rican "m-m-m-mamita" to the black man's "please, baby, please, baby, baby, baby, please."

Dr. Reed Tuckson is the health commissioner for Washington, D.C.

TUCKSON: For black men, we know that the way that we express our sexuality, by the frequency of it, the number of quote, "conquests," unquote, is in many ways the only opportunity that black men have to exert their will on the world, to show their control of the world.

What that means in prevention of AIDS, then, is that if in fact people, especially young men, are going to continue to define themselves only by the variety or the frequency of their sexual conquests, then it's going to be very difficult for public health commissioners to say to them, "By the way, because of the disease called AIDS, we want you to stop being sexually promiscuous, and if you do, at an absolute minimum, you need to wear a condom in every one of those experiences." That becomes a difficult message to give out.

GROSVENOR: I saw firsthand what he was talking about when I saw him speak to a dozen boys in a large parlor room of a downtown row house, a halfway house for teenage boys. The boys, dressed mostly in sweats and Reeboks, sat slumped down on couches, feet wide apart. They wore their "I'm bad" attitudes like armor. They kept a distant silence when Dr. Tuckson talked about homosexuality, warmed up a little when he talked about IV drug use, and then he talked to them about doing it. When asked how many were sexually active, all raised their hands. It was hard to tell whether it was true or it was worth lying about.

TUCKSON: How many of you all have been in a locker room? How many of you all have ever talked about who you been with in a locker room? What did you say? C'mon, it's all right, we're friends.

TEENAGE BOY: Said I was with so-and-so last night.

TUCKSON: How did you feel when you said that?

TEENAGE BOY: I felt like a big boy.

TUCKSON: You felt like a big boy.

TEENAGE BOY: Yeah.

TUCKSON: Powerful. Is there any other moments when you get to feel powerful?

TEENAGE BOY: At school. That's all.

TUCKSON: When at school?

TEENAGE BOY: When I'm doin' my work.

TUCKSON: You're lucky.

TEENAGE BOY: Like we got little conduct sheets, and whenever I get all A's and B's and they applaud me, I be feeling powerful.

TUCKSON: Most times, people say that they never get to feel powerful unless they have controlled somebody. And the way they tell me they control people is through violence or through sex.

GROSVENOR: Of course, it's not hard to find the reasons for these feelings among the boys in this room. Unemployment is higher among black youth, more black men go to jail than to college, and homicide is the leading cause of death for black men, age fifteen to forty. All of these things and machismo will have to be addressed to convince this group that to take control of the sexual kind, to be educated about the disease called AIDS to protect themselves and others, is a form of empowerment.

TUCKSON: And what it teaches me, in my observations then, is that the fight for AIDS, the fight against AIDS, is the same fight that we have been engaging in since our experiences as people of color in this country. It is going to mean that we have to give people other ways of feeling good about themselves or feeling powerful, of feeling a part of this world, and also other ways of feeling loved and appreciated.

Now focus on something beyond yourself for just a minute. Do you all have families?

TEENAGE BOYS: Yes. Yes.

TUCKSON: You care about them?

TEENAGE BOYS: Yes.

TUCKSON: You love your mama?

TEENAGE BOYS: Yeah.

TUCKSON: Seventy percent of all the women in America with AIDS are black or brown. Eighty percent of all the children in American with AIDS are black or brown. Is it fair for you to be part of bringing into this world a baby who's going to die of AIDS? Is that fair? Is it fair?

TEENAGE BOYS: Nope.

GROSVENOR: It was easy to agree on the traditional values of loving mom and family. But when it came to the personal responsibility and practical act of wearing a condom, putting on a rubber, the tension in the room rose to a suffocating level. The baaad young men were teenagers again.

TUCKSON: If you're gonna do it because you feel so important, then at a minimum you have to wear a condom. [*Laughter.*] Oh, now that's funny. OK, tell me why that's funny.

SECOND TEENAGE BOY: 'Cause it don't feel right to me, it don't feel right.

TUCKSON: It doesn't feel right to you. Would you risk infecting another person? Do you have that right? I'm curious.

SECOND TEENAGE BOY: No, I ain't got that right.

TUCKSON: But you're gonna take it. You would risk giving somebody a disease that they could not recover from?

SECOND TEENAGE BOY: No, I wouldn't do that though. I wouldn't, seriously, I wouldn't do it.

TUCKSON: So you'd wear a condom every time.

SECOND TEENAGE BOY: Not all the time.

TUCKSON: Please. Let me ask you, Do you care about black people? Are black people important to you?

SECOND TEENAGE BOY: Yeah, all types.

TUCKSON: Do you know whether or not you've been infected with this virus?

SECOND TEENAGE BOY: I know I ain't got it. I go see the doctor, go see the doctor next week.

TUCKSON: Has the doctor given you a test specifically for this disease?

SECOND TEENAGE BOY: No.

TUCKSON: Then you don't know whether you have it or not. You don't know whether you have it or not. And I ask you again, Do you have the right to infect another human being?

SECOND TEENAGE BOY: No, I ain't got the right, I told you that.

TUCKSON: I ask you again then, If you have sex with somebody, and you do not know whether you are infected or not — and *you* do not know — do you have the right not to wear a condom?

SECOND TEENAGE BOY: No comment.

GROSVENOR: The boy seems so unreadable, unreachable. The oldest was eighteen, but they were all older than I, whatever past they had had brought them to the halfway house, their future uncertain. They only had the present, which caused me as a parent, as a black person, to feel very sad and very frustrated. I kept thinking, what could be done to reach them and whatever that something was had better be done quickly. It's unrealistic to think that what took decades to do can be undone in less time.

TUCKSON: These young men have had multiple experiences, year after year, that have convinced them that they are not worthy, that they are not loved, that they are not appreciated, that the future for them is bleak and rather immediate. I think that at least having one person come on one day to give them facts and information and to share with them the fact that one person cares very deeply about whether they survive and the quality of that survival is important. But in and of itself, no, it is not enough. Somebody tomorrow has got to come and hug that child and somebody the next day has to be prepared to put this young person into a job-training program and give them the opportunity to succeed at something instead of being always told that they are going to fail.

GROSVENOR: The threat of failure, by us or by them, means something different to these kids here in Washington, D.C., now called the murder capital of the country. Their choices are simple, violent death on the streets, slow death from poverty and untimely death from AIDS. And it is here, at the intersection between all the other threats they face and this new one, AIDS, that Tuckson ties together his various roles as the man who tries to stop the dying and who cleans up after his and our failures.

TUCKSON: [*Addressing the teenagers.*] One of the things that I get, which is the worst part of my job, is that I'm in charge of the morgue. So I go to the place where all these shooting victims wind up, and I look at them. Let me tell you something interesting about them: they look just like you. Every one of them. You're the same age, built the same way, and you got on the same clothes. Those, those black Reebok — those are Reeboks? — black high-top Reebok tennis shoes, usually a sweat-shirt like that one. They look like young fresh-face kids like this one. They look like somebody's kid, except for a few little strange things about them. They got a little hole, about the size of an eraser, it's like you put an eraser there. And you put one here, always one here, and one here and one here, and then two or three here, one, two here, one here, and maybe one, two in the legs.

THIRD TEENAGE BOY: What is that, where you stick the needles at?

TUCKSON: No, it's where you stick the bullets. The bullets. The semi-automatic bullets.

FOURTH TEENAGE BOY: Why is there always more right here?

TUCKSON: Because we hate each other so much. We always shoot each other in the head because we hate each other so much. We always shoot each other in the head. We hate ourselves so much, we always shoot each other in the head, that's why. And that's about choices and that's about decisions. And what I'm supposed to talk to you about and end up with is about your sexual behavior, that you got choices to make and the choices you make have consequences.

GROSVENOR: In times of trouble and crises, my grandmother used to say the devil is at work. Well, he's on overtime in Washington, D.C. Like Dr. Tuckson, I'm not an optimist, but I am hopeful that we can put the devil out of work, so that these young people can have chances that will change the quality of their lives. One thing is for sure: Mother Nature will have her way, and the boys will do it, and the consequences of their choices will affect us all.

✦ ✦ ✦ ✦ ✦ ✦ ✦ ✦ ✦

Student demonstrators began to gather in Tiananmen Square in Beijing in mid-May, calling for reform, for the old men to give up the government. As that demonstration was beginning, Lynn Neary talked to Chinese American Amy Tan about her book, *The Joy Luck Club*, a novel about Chinese mothers and their American daughters. Just three weeks later, the Chinese government moved with force against the students in Tiananmen Square. Here are two of Lynn's interviews from that spring, first with Tan, and then with Kate Adie of the BBC, who was in Tiananmen Square when the shooting started.

Weekend All Things Considered, MAY 14

TAN: When I started to write, it was about the time my mother turned seventy. And she had said to me, one day, "I am getting old now. If I die, what would you remember?" And I, at the time, said, "Well, I'd remember all kinds of things, but you're not going to die, but I would remember many things because you're my mother." And she just looked at me, and said, "I think you know little percent of me." And I remembered that, later on, when she had been hospitalized and in intensive care with an apparent heart attack, and I thought at that time, Here I am going to lose my mother, and I'm going to lose all the things she wanted me to know about her. Well, it turned out that she didn't have a heart attack, she was fine. But I thought, if my mother lives, I will take her to China, I will get to know her, I will meet my sisters for the first time. And she turned out to be fine, so I fulfilled that promise. And I took her to China, met my sisters, and I decided I wanted to see what I did know about my mother. And that's what I wrote in my book.

NEARY: So you, like one of the characters in the book, have Chinese sisters, sisters in China that you had never known.

TAN: Yes. I had actually three sisters that I had never met before. They're not twins, as they are in the book, but they were sisters, however, that my mother was forced to abandon in 1949. And lost contact with for over thirty years. She did not leave them on a road in Kwelin, as described in the book, but she did, she was cut off from them.

NEARY: Did you feel, once you set out to really know your mother, did you begin to feel that you did know her more than a little percent?

TAN: I was surprised at how much I remembered because when I was growing up and she'd tell me things, little stories or advice, I didn't want to listen to her. But I must have been listening with at least one ear because it stayed in my memory, and as I was writing all these memories started to come back. And I remembered things she said about her mother or about herself growing up in China. And I remembered the advice she gave me when I was growing up. And how I had heard it one way, and now, remembering it, I heard it another way. And after I wrote the book, a lot of my friends said to me, "You must have done a lot of research to write this book," and I said, "My research was my mother." And it made me feel that there was a lot in me that had been planted there that was Chinese, and I had just been denying it for so many years.

NEARY: Well, part of what's fascinating about the book and just the pure joy of reading it is the Chinese mythology and symbolism and the folktales that seem to be there. Did you grow up with them?

TAN: I grew up with a mother who naturally talked in a narrative, storytelling manner. She didn't sit down and tell me whole stories, but she would say very provocative lines, like, "Once when my grandmother was dying, my mother took a knife and cut a piece of meat from her arm and boiled this meat in a soup and fed it to her mother, to try to save her one last time, but it didn't work. She died that day." And she would just say these little gems that would fill my imagination with a whole scene in China. And I would take these little nuggets and expand a story from them.

NEARY: And, of course, you use that exact story in the book, and it gives you one of the central images of the book, I think. And I wonder if you could read a passage about it on page forty-eight, it comes just after what you described happened in the book, where a woman takes a piece of her flesh and puts it into a soup to try and save her mother. The passage begins, "Even though I was young."

TAN: OK. "Even though I was young, I could see the pain of the flesh and the worth of the pain.

"This is how a daughter honors her mother. It is *shou* so deep it is in your bones. The pain of the flesh is nothing. The pain you must forget. Because sometimes that is the only way to remember what is in your bones. You must peel off your skin, and that of your mother, and her mother before her. Until there is nothing. No scar, no skin, no flesh."

NEARY: What does that mean to you, that idea that your mother is in your bones?

TAN: There is so much that we don't see that has been given to us and it's in our character, but it's almost a sense that no matter how much we try to run away from that, it is within us, and cannot be taken away. The other part is that once you recognize that, you must go deep within yourself, so deep that it removes all the pains of years of misunderstanding, of both the psychic pain and a physical pain, and that you would go to that length to show that respect and that love that you have for a mother. The bond and the connection is something almost inexpressible, but it is there within your bones.

NEARY: Kate, were you out there? Were you surrounded by this violence? What did you see?

ADIE: Last night, I was out for four hours. There were several thousand people running around, jeering, standing and yelling at the troops, screaming abuse at them, shouting at them. There were so many people around, to a certain extent you felt they surely can't fire into the middle of the people. Without warning, there was an enormous and lengthy volley of shots. It seemed to go on and on. I had turned away to take a cassette of our video coverage back to our hotel, and I was about a hundred yards from the frontline, the frontline of students. And I was running with everyone else, and I saw people going down in the road, shot, and I felt something graze my elbow, and a man two feet in front of me threw his arms in the air and dropped dead. And I fell, stumbled, crashed, straight over him. And I was on the ground, and I saw a bullet strike the ground four feet from me. There were another two people dead, another six feet from me, and two more injured. It was appalling, people were being shot wildly, randomly, and there were so many people going down.

NEARY: Did you just stay down then, or did you keep running? What did you do then?

ADIE: I didn't know what to do. I have to say that I genuinely, for about three seconds, did not know whether I was going to be killed if I lay there or killed if I got up and ran. I decided to run, and I made it about fifteen yards to the trees at the edge of the road. I have been extremely lucky. So many others have not been.

NEARY: When you first realized that the soldiers were firing bullets at these people, these unarmed people, what went through your mind?

ADIE: I think, probably, the same as a lot of people here, virtual disbelief that soldiers were opening fire on unarmed civilians. I was in the side streets leading down to the road along which trucks, lorries, tanks, armored personnel vehicles, were thundering into town. And as we went down the side streets towards the main road, the soldiers were opening fire from the lorries as they passed the ends of the streets. Passersby, people sitting outside their houses, people inside their houses, were shot.

NEARY: Did you also see something that we have heard described, students sort of coming in waves against the soldiers and just being mowed down?

ADIE: Well, this morning, on the main boulevard near the square at about 10:23, there were several hundred students, and they're not exclusively students, all sorts of people are out on the streets, but it was mainly the young people this morning, both young men and women. And they were forming in a line across the road, facing huge rows of soldiers with tanks behind them. They must have been two hundred and fifty, three hundred yards apart. And some of them ride bicycles, some of them running around, some of them jeering at the soldiers. With no warning, there was a huge volley of shots. And some people ran and some were left behind. And they took away as many as they could, by bicycle, rickshaw, they dragged people away who were injured. And half an hour later, with again the students, the young people back there, there was another volley of shots. And the estimated total is between thirty and forty people killed in those two incidents.

NEARY: We have also heard that now, as people have gone out trying to collect victims, trying to find their relatives, that they are being shot.

ADIE: Two ambulance drivers I know of were shot. Ambulance drivers were prevented from getting into the square when the troops were trying to take it over. And in the square itself at five in the morning, when the students were leaving, they were pushed in something of a panic, down from the steps of the monument, and people were crushed. The Red Cross, very brave Red Cross people who'd stayed in, tried to get to them, and they were not only beaten back, but beaten to the ground by the soldiers and left there.

NEARY: You visited one of the hospitals recently, is that right?

ADIE: I've been to two hospitals. I went to one last night and one this morning.

NEARY: What did you see at the hospitals?

ADIE: The first hospital I went to, which is actually a children's hospital, was in a state of near mayhem when I'd got in there. We'd actually brought in our car a woman who'd been shot in the head. We picked her up and somehow got her into the car with a couple of relatives and the film crew and our driver and an interpreter, and we hurtled off to the nearest hospital, the children's hospital. We got in there. As we raced down the corridors with her, carrying her to the operating theater, there were people stampeding in behind us, one after another, with people being carried on park benches, on chairs, on planks. They were brought by rickshaw, they were brought on the back of bicycles, they all had bullet wounds.

I had a brief glimpse of the operating theater. There must have been eighteen people lying in there, with staff frantic, blood splattered everywhere, shouting and yelling, absolutely desperate. As we came back out into the corridor, every few seconds people were coming along, bringing injured people. There were over a hundred people into that hospital within an hour.

A second hospital I visited this morning was still taking casualties in. I went to the morgue. There were thirteen people there. Half an hour later, there were forty people there. There were people lying in the corridor, being operated on in the corridor. The operating theater couldn't take any more. The medical staff were in tears, so many of them, particularly the young nurses. They were so distraught at what had happened, they were so enraged. They were shouting at me, they were saying, "Tell people, tell the world what has happened, tell them what they're doing, they're butchering people."

I've got to say, I just heard quite a loud noise in the distance. I can't tell what it is, like a — either very heavy fire — I can't say.

NEARY: I'm sure it's impossible to predict, but at this point as we are talking to you, it is after midnight, the streets are deserted, do you think people will come back on the streets tomorrow? Will this continue?

ADIE: Who can tell? A few hours ago, tanks roared down the main boulevard about two blocks away from us. There was gunfire, small-arms fire, and the tanks roared back again. There's retribution being meted out. There's been gunfire all day. I mean, twenty-four hours since it started. There have been lulls, but then again, it has started up.

I think people are frightened, but on the other hand they are enraged by what has happened. This is the People's Liberation Army of China, it is the people's army. Last night when I was on the streets, people were shouting, "You are the people's army, but we are the people. Why are you killing us, the people?"

NEARY: Would you dare go out again at this point?

ADIE: We have to be very careful. Several Western journalists have been beaten up today. One or two are missing still since last night. We are not willingly going to provoke anything either, because there is a danger in us talking to Chinese. This is forbidden by martial law, that we, as it were, consort with people who may be involved in any, what may be construed as illegal acts under martial law. There are very, very tight regulations. So the authorities have every excuse to drag us in and perhaps drag in Chinese who might be with us, helping us, or interpreting for us, or just near us. So we cannot risk their lives. We are having to be very circumspect.

✦ ✦ ✦ ✦ ✦ ✦ ✦ ✦ ✦ ✦

S usan Stamberg invited a number of reporters to give up temporarily the distance they all must try to preserve between themselves
and their stories. She asked them to go back to their hometown and see
it again, for her program, *Weekend Edition, Sunday*. Richard Gonzales
offered this personal portrait of Richmond, California, an industrial
town on the San Francisco Bay. By 1989 Richmond's smokestack in-
dustries were closing and developers were looking at its miles of shore-
line.

Weekend Edition, Sunday, SEPTEMBER 17

GONZALES: As the dense fog rolls in off the San Francisco Bay, a
chorus of powerful horns blow, guiding commercial ships and small
sailing crafts to their ports. I'm standing near a marina in my hometown of Richmond. Several hundred boats are docked near brand-new
waterfront condominiums. The condos are surrounded by expansive,
vibrant green lawns. This is a new Richmond, I've been told, developing to change the rough-and-tumble image of the city's south side,
where we lived on a dead-end street.

My family still lives there. They first came in 1923, and when I
return on occasion I look for changes among the rows of single-family
houses and apartments. Some things haven't changed. When we were
growing up, there weren't more than a half dozen Mexican families
living in the south-side ghetto neighborhood. In those days, the Black
Panthers were strong and popular. Just a few days before my return,
Huey Newton was killed in nearby Oakland. To many people in South
Richmond, Huey was a hero because he stood for black self-defense,
and the fact that he succumbed to the trap of crack addiction only
enhanced their identification with him as a human being.

For me, growing up in Richmond was like growing up in two
worlds. In public school, all my classmates were black. After school, we
joined the mix of Mexicans, blacks, whites, all from working-class
families attending catechism at St. Mark's Parish. Today, St. Mark's
Parish is still a cultural melting pot but with some new elements: Thais,
Cambodians, Bolivians, Peruvians, Salvadorans, Nicaraguans, most of
them refugees from violence-torn areas of the world.

It's early, Sunday morning Mass, seven-fifteen. The fog outside
creates a dampness among the wooden pews inside St. Mark's. About
sixty members of the Laotian refugee community begin Mass with a

Buddhist-like chant. Men sit on one side of the aisle, women on the other. These people are Kamu, from the highland of Laos, and by a strange fate find themselves unwelcome strangers in the poor, drug-infested neighborhoods of Richmond.

After the Lao Mass, there are two services held in Spanish, both standing room only. The congregation prays for the farmers and farm workers, for the alcoholics, and the drug addicts. This Sunday, the Mass is devoted to Señor García, who was born before the Mexican revolution and is celebrating his birthday as mariachis stroll up the aisle to serenade him.

About a year ago, the archdiocese recommended closing down St. Marks because it needed structural renovations, but the parishioners are raising money to save their church. Brother Jude Solario works for St. Mark's youth groups and he's also the main AIDS educator in the neighborhood.

SOLARIO: If St. Mark's had gone, I think we would have seen a higher incidence of the crack cocaine problem in Richmond also. When you hear gunshots down the street, you know what's going on or that we have crack houses here where kids are being used for sexual purposes. So, in one way, if St. Mark's were to disappear, it would become a crazy madhouse around here.

GONZALES: Some say it's already a madhouse. St. Mark's is located near what's left of downtown Richmond. These are mean streets, much like any poverty-stricken city. And it's been that way for a long time.

World War II brought thousands of workers to Richmond to help build ships in the yards of industrialist Henry Kaiser. By the end of the war, thanks to prefabricated parts, Richmond workers were building Kaiser Liberty ships at the rate of one per day. After the war, most of the newcomers decided to stay and went to work for Chevron or Ford. During the fifties and early sixties, the town was reasonably prosperous. I recall, as a child, my folks taking me downtown, where there were active department and grocery stores. Later, as a teenager, downtown McDonald Avenue was a popular cruising strip for kids, just like in the scenes from George Lucas's movie *American Graffiti*. It is a memory I shared one morning with a friend, Ron Tennady.

When you think about how McDonald Avenue used to be this happening place, and you see it now, what's your reaction in your gut?

TENNADY: It's like watching your home go down. It's like somebody came in and dropped the bomb.

GONZALES: The bomb was the racial strife that hit Richmond during the mid-sixties. Portions of downtown were set ablaze one night. It was the beginning of the end of downtown Richmond as retail businesses relocated to a mall in the northern part of town. Almost ten years later, as a college senior back east, I met a woman from nearby Marin County. I was trying to find some commonality in cold Cambridge, so I told her I came from Richmond. She raised her eyebrow, and replied, "Richmond, huh. Is it still burning?"

In a way, I'm afraid it is still burning. The fire is now called crack. But I saw signs of hope: immigrant parents bring their children to register for school and are served in their native languages. Perhaps the most astonishing thing was that I kept hearing about unusual coalitions of corporate leaders and social-service types who have joined together to find some solutions to the problems that led to the explosion of crack in Richmond.

Developers have plans to bring in software, research and development, and perhaps biotech firms into Richmond, firms that have no room for expansion in nearby Marin County or the Silicon Valley. That would help update the city's industrial image. It may also begin to displace some of Richmond's old neighborhoods. I began to wonder, if the developers are successful will I recognize my hometown five years from now? I came home and I found two Richmonds. As I stood on a freeway overpass, on my right, my old neighborhood, South Richmond, is like an old boxer, battered but still standing. To my left is the waterfront development on the San Francisco Bay. The contrast is unavoidable. I wonder, can the city propel itself into the twenty-first century while being dragged down by a legacy of poverty and hard luck? And I worry that there may be two futures for Richmond, one for the rich and one for the poor.

✦ ✦ ✦ ✦ ✦ ✦ ✦ ✦ ✦

Half a dozen mostly peaceful revolutions were in progress in Europe that winter as the Iron Curtain fell away. Each day brought more extraordinary news about attempts to dislodge communist regimes put in place at the end of the war, preserved by the arms and authority of the Soviet Union. The Berlin Wall, the strongest symbol of Soviet domination for most Americans, fell in November. Alex Chadwick covered Czechoslovakia's Velvet Revolution in December, and he filed this piece after he came home. Alex felt that although he'd seen a revolution happen, filed stories, and attempted to explain grand

and historic events, he'd not yet told the important story of his time in Prague. This is it.

CHADWICK: I left Berlin by train on Friday, two weeks ago. It was a six-hour journey across the border, time to read a little, prepare for a place I'd never been. The anticommunist revolution that transformed Poland and Hungary, and then East Germany, was present now in Czechoslovakia.

A week earlier in Prague, the government had blundered in its brutal reaction to a peaceful demonstration near Charles University. There were demands that the Communist party leader, Milos Jakeš, give up his power. But no one even knew if it made sense to make such demands, no one knew what would happen. Jakeš was among those who'd run Czechoslovakia for more than twenty years, ever since the Soviet army had gone in to stop the reforms of Alexander Dubček back in 1968.

A journalist friend who'd been in Prague back then offered some advice about people to see, some of the old reformers who would still know things. But I would need a translator, he said, and so I decided to go to the university to find a student, and that is how I met Natasha Dudinska. I just found her, in the entryway to the school of philosophy and languages at Charles University, the first person there who spoke English and said she could work right away. It was already dark, but we walked toward a taxi stand to get a cab to take us into the hills, and Natasha began to talk about the student strike.

DUDINSKA: So democracy is something very fragile because we were not brought up, my generation was not brought up in democracy. And we don't know to express ourselves because we were not allowed. I am twenty-two, and all my childhood, all my young days, we were just pushed down. And we also don't know how to listen to each other. We want dialogue, we want discussion, but discussion means at least two people are speaking. Both of them are speaking and listening to each other.

CHADWICK: I didn't realize then that the translator I had hired was one of the organizers for the Student Strike Committee, although I could tell she had unusual insight. The cab drove several miles to a political institute owned by the Communist party, where we'd been told an emergency meeting was under way. We asked the driver to wait, and we got out. Some Czechoslovak students started yelling at us.

DUDINSKA: They cry, "Go home. Please, go home."

CHADWICK: We went to ask the police guards to let us in to talk with someone, but they told us to go away. So we left without learning what the communist leaders inside had decided, but it didn't matter. When we got back to the cab, a news bulletin was on the radio.

DUDINSKA: Yes, that's true! Jakeš. That's fantastic. Central Committee exact words are "Gave their places or their seats to the disposal of somebody to take them."

CABDRIVER: Yes, that's incredible.

DUDINSKA: Maybe it's history, but maybe we shouldn't be so much excited because who will change, who will come . . . ? The driver, he is crying. He wants to cry, he's really excited about it. It's fantastic. We should go to the Wenceslaus Square after.

CHADWICK: The cabdriver wept with joy and took us to Wenceslaus Square, the site of huge demonstrations last week, where hundreds of thousands of Czechoslovaks demanded change.

Now thousands gathered in the square again. Jakeš, hated Jakeš, had quit. Other top communists quit with him. They were gone and, as important, everyone in Wenceslaus Square was beginning to see that the communists might not know what was possible any longer either. My student activist translator said it was too soon to celebrate, there was too much left to do, and then she jumped in the air with pleasure.

DUDINSKA: Champagne! You see champagne already.

CHADWICK: Two days later, in Prague, I was working with Natasha again. We were at a theater, where the opposition group Civic Forum was giving a press conference to report on a discussion that morning with the prime minister. It was in English, so Natasha simply stood and listened with me. After the spokesman finished his statement, a reporter asked again the question that always got asked, How had this occurred so quickly? After all, this same Civic Forum man who was speaking had fled across a rooftop eight days earlier to escape the police. Now his group negotiated with the government. What had happened? It was a student demonstration, he replied.

CIVIC FORUM LEADER: You see, this is the first demonstration when the riot police deliberately surrounded several thousands of people. They didn't give them a chance to escape. You can see it on those videos that the students are sitting there.

CHADWICK: The most famous and powerful pictures in Czechoslovakia today are seen on television screens that show what happened in Prague just three weeks ago, when a group from the university held a march for democracy. On the videotape, the students sit in the narrow cobbled street. Many of them are under a stone and plaster archway that runs along one sidewalk. It's nighttime. In the police lights, everything has an orange glow. Then they come, the police, in white helmets, some in red berets. They carry shields and long thin clubs or batons and, without any provocation that you can see, they begin to beat the students and it gets extremely violent and bloody. The students don't fight back.

Natasha Dudinska told me that that very night a group of students decided to strike. There was already an informal network of activists. They called each other and arranged to meet. For two days they moved from restaurants to clubs to cafés, talking for a while, agreeing on a new site, and going there in small groups, afraid that the police would discover them. They agreed to strike, to seize the university buildings, and to call for a two-hour general national strike for a week from that Monday. They thought they would need that much time to organize support. Though if you consider that they had no access to the news media, no money, no real contacts with outside groups, no experience in what they were seeking to do, none whatsoever, the notion of organizing a national strike in eight or nine days was laughable. They didn't know what they were doing, but on the other hand they didn't know they couldn't do it either. The Strike Committee decided to send teams of students into the countryside to explain what had happened in Prague. They carried with them copies of a videotape of the beatings.

DUDINSKA: So we needed workers and agricultural workers and people all over Czechoslovakia to communicate with them, to be listened to, to have the chance to speak.

CHADWICK: Why did you think that sending the videocassettes was going to get them on your side?

DUDINSKA: Because common people in villages, you can talk to them, but when they see this violence, they somehow couldn't stay ignorant. And also, yes, this is very important. Who was beating students? State police. And also, who represents these police? Communist party. The police is the tool of Communist party, and if a party or a government beats their own people, that means it is out of any ideals, of any ideas. That's why they use force or violence.

CHADWICK: They don't have any ideas left, they don't have any ideals left.

DUDINSKA: So that's why they use violence or force. I can't think properly about this because two weeks ago nobody of us had the courage to think like this. We simply didn't imagine that it will come so quickly. So we are still a bit excited, a bit perplexed, a bit we don't know what to do. Much helpless and becoming hopeful.

CHADWICK: They were hopeful, but they were almost worn out too. They were always meeting about something. Anyone could get up and talk and then everyone got a vote. But the leaders began to see that this was a very difficult way to make decisions. The philosophy school was in a big drafty building, and they were in it all the time. They slept there and talked all night, and they ate there too. Different groups met in different classrooms. The desktops held scattered bottles of cough syrup and pills and throat tablets and, for balance, cheap cigarettes. Almost everyone smoked.

The committee was still sending teams of students out from Prague to build support elsewhere, but sometimes the students were arrested. Other government opponents had organized themselves into Civic Forum, which joined the call for the national strike. Amazingly, Czechoslovak national TV began covering the daily demonstrations in Prague and reported news about the growing strike movement. And although the foreign reporters who came to town now went to Civic Forum to learn the news, the students knew how the movement began.

At noon on Strike Monday, I opened my hotel window as wide as it would go and held a microphone outside. People carrying banners and flags marched across a bridge below, and the cars that passed waved other flags, and Prague made noise. On TV, there were pictures from other cities, showing pretty much the same. In nine days, a group of beat-up university students enlisted the help and support of what had been a psychically battered political opposition and somehow shamed and inspired what had been a cowardly controlled press and called five million of their countrymen into the streets. The next day, the government agreed to resign and to change the constitution in ways that should allow for political freedom.

Natasha Dudinska's grandfather was named Alexander Langfelder. In the 1920s, he became a Communist. After he joined the party, his father never spoke to him again. But Langfelder was good at politics. He became the first editor of the party's first newspaper in Slovakia. Later he went to Spain to join the war against Franco. He was shot and lost a lung. And he went to London when the Second World War broke out and joined the Czechoslovak government in exile. His father and the rest of the family couldn't get out. They all died in concentration camps.

When the war ended, Langfelder returned to his homeland and

worked for the election of the Communist government in 1948. But Langfelder was a Jew, and when the Communist party purges against the Jews began in the early fifties, he was sent to jail. Years later when he got out, he insisted it was only a mistake. And then his granddaughter was born in 1967. He took her into his house and wanted her to have some chances in her life, and the way things went that next year, he thought she would have them.

And then the Soviet invasion and the treachery of the new leadership in the Czechoslovak Communist party. And the old man thought, For this I gave up my father and my family. And so in the years that followed, he told the girl what had happened.

I last saw Natasha Dudinska on Sunday. There was a rally in support of Chinese students. She'd come out between meetings on how to completely revise the curriculum and another meeting on how to vote the then dean of the school of philosophy out of office, which effort she appeared to be leading. She told me the strike leaders wanted to suspend the strike at that point, but they thought they could not get the students to vote to go along. They couldn't inspire them to get the work done though either, and they were absolutely exhausted and again didn't know what to do. I said that I had asked another student about the strike leaders and that this student had said many people considered Natasha different, enormously intelligent, a fine speaker, but so busy she had no real time for anyone else.

I saw the most beautiful moment of this revolution, or burst, or whatever it is. Ten days ago, in the big hall in the philosophy building, where the huge group meetings took place, they were going to vote again on whether to continue the strike. It was late in the afternoon, the light was already shrinking from the windows and the patterned glass in the ceiling. A violinist and a pianist from the National Philharmonic had come to play. We will do Dvořák, they said, his one hundredth sonata, which he wrote for his children. There were several hundred students there. They filled the long stepped rows of bench seats and writing places. And they stood in the aisles where there was room and crowded the balcony in back, and they looked down to where the musicians stood near the low platform and the lectern at the front. Each face grew still.

Natasha Dudinska was at one end of a long desk where the Strike Committee sat on the platform. She was wearing the same thick-knit red cotton sweater and green flannel shirt and black pants that she'd had on for three days. Her dark tangled hair was tied back with a piece of black lace she'd gotten somewhere. She looked pale and colorless, except for a yellowing bruise the size of a dime on her forehead. At last she folded her arms on the desktop and lowered her head. Her eyes closed for a moment, then struggled back open and closed again. For the only time in the ten days I saw her, she looked at peace. I thought she might actually be sleeping, but then her small head began to move with the rhythms of Dvořák.

✦ ✦ ✦ ✦ ✦ ✦ ✦ ✦ ✦ ✦

Just before Christmas, the revolution in Romania ended the terrible rule of Nicolae Ceausescu. The Romanian poet Andrei Codrescu had been on *All Things Considered* for seven years by that time. On this day, Noah Adams introduced him with the phrase that begins Romanian fairy tales, "Once upon a time, when there was no time."

All Things Considered, DECEMBER 22

CODRESCU: I've been dancing since six A.M. this morning when the phone first started ringing. Ceausescu's bloody regime is gone. I still can't believe it. I just heard the news that Ceausescu was arrested in Tirgovişte. That's the town Dracula is from, an appropriate bloody symbol.

The old proverb is true. Dawn comes even after the longest night. Last night, December 21, was the longest night of the year, and it looked for a while that on the blood-spattered streets of Romania, dawn was never going to come again. But it did come this morning, and the Romanian people have given themselves the greatest present in a quarter of a century of unhappy history.

For me, personally, it's even more than a Christmas gift because yesterday was my birthday, and nobody ever gave me a gift this good. I was born in 1946, the year communism came to Romania on the turrets of Russian tanks. My mother named me Andrei so the Russians wouldn't harm us. The Russians didn't, but the misery of life under two consecutive hard-line Stalinist regimes did, and in 1966 we were forced to leave our homeland.

There is an untranslatable Romanian word that expresses with great precision the kind of unbearable longing and nostalgia that grips one's heart when thinking of home. The word is "dor," d-o-r, nostalgia for the beautiful medieval town of Sibiu in Transylvania where I grew up, longing for certain golden autumn afternoons at an outdoor café, drinking new wine with friends, all of us young, intoxicated with poetry and song. I miss the smells of flowering linden trees, the blue reflections of deep mountain snow in the evenings, the old peasant villages that Ceausescu's insanity almost wiped off the face of the earth.

I heard someone say today on Romanian television that the word "comrade" was dead in Romania. It's about time. Like all the other Orwellian speech of the soon-to-be-dust tyrants of the world, comrade has meant exactly the opposite for twenty-five years. Few things are certain in this life, but good things are even less certain than the few that are. The next months will be critical for the Romanian people. They need the goodwill and support of the world. Personally, I have my bag packed for a look. I've had it packed for twenty years.

1990

✦ ✦ ✦ ✦ ✦ ✦ ✦ ✦ ✦ ✦

M any things were set in motion in 1990. President Bush mobilized thousands of American troops in Saudi Arabia to go to war against Iraq. And South Africa began to move toward majority rule. In April, we heard this conversation between John Matisonn and Major Craig Williamson, both white South Africans. Williamson was an officer in the security forces and, posing as a white liberal, had infiltrated groups sympathetic to the African National Congress. John Matisonn was one of the people Williamson spied on. John is back in South Africa now, building a public broadcasting system for his country, but when Williamson was keeping an eye on him, John was a crusading newspaperman. He was banned in South Africa and spent several years working for us. This interview with a man he knew, but did not always know as a spy, is an illustration of the situation in which many South Africans found themselves as their country changed direction. Bob Edwards said on *Morning Edition* that when President F. W. de Klerk made the decision to legalize the African National Congress, "it meant that Williamson's twenty years of work fighting the ANC had been reversed by a single speech."

Morning Edition, APRIL 26

MATISONN: When President de Klerk made his speech, it had been five years since Williamson resigned as head of Police Intelligence. Williamson was now a president's counsellor, a senior member of the ruling party, and an adviser to Cabinet colleagues on security matters. Even though he's become a voice in favor of accommodation with the ANC, his years of betraying those who befriended him in the ANC have made him many enemies. His biggest fear is still that he might encounter an ANC guerrilla with an assault rifle.

WILLIAMSON: One of the most wonderful feelings over the weekend, after the president spoke, was a feeling of, that's almost over. That one can stop at one's gate, get out, and open it without worrying about the guy with the AK behind the tree.

MATISONN: Williamson knows that the old order must pass. But like many of his colleagues in the National party leadership, in this period of transition he seems to lack a moral compass. In conversation, he veers from admissions about government violence to pride in having helped keep the white man in a position of power.

WILLIAMSON: We're admitting openly that we dominated as a minority, we dominated the majority. And now what we're saying is, Please, let's work out a system whereby the dominated majority of the past can achieve their rightful place in the political circumstances of South Africa, but in which they'll never have access to the type of power that we, as a minority, have had for the last forty years. Because if any other government in South Africa ever gets its hands on the type of power which we have at this time, we fear for our future.

We know exactly what we did with that power. We maintained South Africa, yes. We maintained the integrity of the party and the white man and we built the country economically. But at the same time, we did some pretty serious oppression as well. And if we're just going to change seats, move a black man or a black party into our white-party seats, then there's going to be problems. So we have to build a totally new South Africa, one in which there will be universal franchise, but one in which individuals will be protected from excesses and abuses of power of the state.

MATISONN: As soon as de Klerk made his speech, Williamson realized that the ANC leaders were coming home and that their status will change. They will be negotiating with President de Klerk because that's the only way to end the war. I asked him if he accepted that the ANC would be an important part of the government.

WILLIAMSON: Yes. The role of the ANC in the future government of South Africa is certainly going to be a dominant one.

MATISONN: How does that make you feel?

WILLIAMSON: Apprehensive. But also excited. And I suppose I'm one of these lunatics that has gotten used to living on adrenaline rushes, so maybe I'm one of the few people that'll enjoy the exciting days to come. But, of course, apprehension.

MATISONN: Williamson wrote to the man he betrayed in the ANC who became his counterpart as head of ANC military intelligence, Ronnie Kasrills. It was a personal letter. He said that his message was part plea, but also part warning.

WILLIAMSON: At the end of the day, my message to Ronnie and the others was that they must take seriously the step we've taken, because the step we've taken was not taken lightly. And I know it will be difficult. They're going to have to be compassionate and they're going to have to be magnanimous. And they're going to have to be big enough, not only individual men, but the whole ANC and the whole Communist party, big enough to let the past be the past and the future be the future. Because if they can't do that, then they also must be big enough to understand that the constituency represented by the National party and other conservative parties, et cetera, in South Africa is not going to roll over and lie down and play dead. They'll fight and that's got to be stopped.

MATISONN: What Williamson and de Klerk are now fighting for is a place in the future government. They want to persuade the ANC to agree to a governing coalition that includes both the presently ruling National party and the ANC. But I reminded Williamson that he's written similar letters to exiles in the past, inviting them to come home, promising that all will be well, when in fact those letters were simply a trap he was setting for his enemies. And I asked him why they should believe he's telling the truth now.

WILLIAMSON: We played all sorts of games. I wrote and distributed all sorts of documents, yes. It was part of the war. It was disinformation, it was psychological warfare, it was what we call communication operations or strategic communications. But that's exactly what it's about. We have to stop. Somewhere or other we, the guys who have been fighting, have to say, Enough! We're now stopping. And until we do that, this country is going to continue heading down the abyss.

MATISONN: After talking with him for six hours, he seems to be speaking frankly, but it still leaves the impression that there's another agenda. I said I wondered whether a spy ever stopped being a spy. And he said nothing.

Williamson reminded me of Boris Pasternak's *Doctor Zhivago.* The character Williamson made me think of was Victor Komarovsky, shady and successful under Czar Nicholas, then again shady and equally successful under Lenin. There were signs of it already, in the way he talked to me of Nelson Mandela, the leader of the organization that Williamson spent twenty years trying to smash. Williamson said he would be happy to work in a government headed by Mandela.

WILLIAMSON: If you read what Nelson Mandela said in the early fifties about negotiating, it's precisely what is being implemented today, exactly forty years later. And those are forty lost years. In fact, the entire, my entire life circle. Nelson Mandela was talking the type of negotiations he's talking today with the National party, of which I am now a senior member, in the same year as I was born. And in a sense, that means a lifetime has been lost politically. And I hope that we're young enough to now turn it around and spend the next forty years doing something constructive instead of destructive.

MATISONN: Maybe Major Williamson is tired of the futile battle. And maybe there is a chance to an end to all that waste. For Nelson Mandela, twenty-seven years in prison and a lifetime of confrontation. For Williamson himself, if he can ever unlearn the terrible skills he's acquired. For me as a journalist, the years of conflict and tension while Williamson's intelligence network was trying to curtail news reporting. And most important of all, for ordinary South Africans in the millions, who have to try to pick up their lives midstream and to learn what it means to live a life that's normal.

✦ ✦ ✦ ✦ ✦ ✦ ✦ ✦ ✦

Ted Clark generally covers the State Department, explaining U.S. interests, patiently unraveling the complexities and the confusion of foreign policy. He is the son of a foreign service officer and spent much of his childhood outside this country. He lived in southern Africa, and he returned there to report on the long civil war fought in Mozambique. Renamo were the rebels on the right, and Frelimo, the government on the left, one of the many "sponsored" conflicts of the cold war period. In 1990 the rebel forces were waging the kind of conflict we are seeing in many countries now. More than a million people were driven from their homes, agriculture was disrupted, and families separated by war and confusion, in an effort to create economic chaos and force the government to fall. As is always the case, children were especially victimized by this kind of warfare.

Ted reported on a project sponsored by the international organization Save the Children, attempting to reunite children with their relatives. He described an airfield in Mozambique, near the Zambezi River, where social workers waited for a seven-passenger plane to ferry two dozen children to a relocation center. The children, he said, were passive and silent. Only the smallest ones showed any emotion, a trace of fear. Ted talked to ten-year-olds Felice and Manicu, who described the deaths of his parents. Then they waited together for the plane.

CLARK: We finish our interviews and have nothing to do but wait. We watch a tractor cutting grass on the far side of the airstrip. The sun is now directly overhead. It must be a hundred degrees here. People from the town drift by, hoping we'll take them with us in the plane when it returns.

Renamo's tactics, to destroy the country's economic lifelines, have taken their toll here. An old man approaches, sits at the end of the bench, tells us that he has not eaten in three days. He lifts his shirt to show us how thin he is. He asks us to take him to Beira, Mozambique's second largest city, where we are in fact going. He says his son works on the docks there. We cannot take him, but we give him something to eat.

Other people drift by, like characters in a play. A young man, obviously drunk, rants at us about the deprivations of his life. And then an ancient woman, an apparition almost, with white hair and frightfully thin, naked from the waist up, asks to be taken to Beira. We have to refuse. She walks away without a word. War has turned the citizens of this town into prisoners.

When the plane returns, I feel relieved. He's flying very low to avoid detection by Renamo. He circles once and lands. People rush to the plane. Suddenly there's activity again and the mood seems to brighten. The airfield's only employee hurries onto the landing strip and stands at attention with a fire extinguisher.

I'm on this flight and am pleased that Manicu and Felice will be among the children on board. There's excitement in their eyes. It's obvious they've never flown before. Their concepts of distance and time become confused. As soon as we're airborne, they think we've arrived in Beira. The children are smiling and animated. For the first time since I met Felice and Manicu, they seem like normal little boys. When we reach our cruising altitude, Felice looks at the ground far below and says, "We're not moving." To prove that we are, Terry puts the plane into a shallow dive and the boys laugh. Up here, the air is cool and fresh. We land in Beira after an hour. Here, the children will get into a van and go to the city's orphanage to spend the night. In the morning, if all goes well, they will finally be reunited with their relatives.

We arrive at the orphanage early the next morning. The building is austere, made of cement blocks on a dry, sandy lot. There's the frame to a swing set here, but no swings. Just across the street is the Indian Ocean. We ask Manicu and Felice how it was last night, in this unfamiliar, impersonal place. They say it was fine, they ate well, they slept well. The children in this country never seem to complain. But when the orphanage staff begins to round up the kids and shoo them inside for breakfast, Manicu's stoicism fails him. With the prospect of family so close at hand, he cannot bring himself to go back in that orphanage, even for a few more minutes. It's the first time I've seen him cry, or fail to obey.

Manuel, our interpreter, asks what's wrong.

MANUEL: He says he want to see his uncle.

CLARK: The women who work at the orphanage coax Manicu inside one last time. I'm told the Mozambiquan government intends to close orphanages like these. And it's a realistic goal. The extended family is still a strong feature of Mozambiquan life. Grandparents, aunts, uncles, older siblings, traditionally share the task of raising children. If a child's parents should die, other relatives are always willing to step in. For this reason, it's often said there are no true orphans in Mozambique.

It's time to go. Felice and Manicu must say good-bye to each other. The relatives they're going to live with are in different towns. Manicu and a few other children will get in the van with us and drive to Chiringoma, twenty miles away. Felice learns that he will have to stay in the orphanage one more night. I can see disappointment creeping into his eyes as a social worker explains all this to him.

Chiringoma is a *deslocado* village, a village for people displaced by war. It's named after the district of Chiringoma, sixty miles north of here where there's been a lot of fighting. The people fled, built this new town, named it after their old home, and are now trying to reconstruct their lives and their families. In the village center, there's a Mozambiquan flag on a crooked pole. A few trees offer shade. A piece of scrap iron hanging from a branch serves as the town bell. In a small, open-sided mud hut, the village clerk is recording births and deaths.

The children we have brought all have relatives here. They've been located through a remarkable tracing program. Whenever social workers find children alone, they take Polaroid photos of each one and write down whatever they can learn from the children about their families. The photos and the information are then turned into posters which are hung in public places around the country. When relatives identify children, the Mozambiquan government and Save the Children arrange the reunification. That's what's happening here in Chiringoma. Within minutes of our arrival, an expectant crowd has gathered.

The reunification process begins immediately. It is totally without ceremony. Adults simply come forward one by one to claim each child, almost casually. The children are asked, in turn, if they recognize the grownups. Once reunited, the child and adult are given a small kit. The kits are supposed to make it easier for families to absorb new members. In each kit is food, soap, clothes, seeds, and a hoe. And then adult and child simply walk away.

There are no scenes of rejoicing, no tears of happiness, no laughter. I can't understand that. And I ask Carlos Laserda, a Mozambiquan social worker with Save the Children, to explain.

LASERDA: When they meet the parents, they don't believe, because some children are separated from his family about three years and four years. And when they come back to the family, they don't believe. And also it happen with the family. Sometimes when the children disappear, between the family, they have some funeral ceremony. They take the clothes of the children disappeared, they go to the cemetery, and they put the clothes on the grave. And suddenly the kid appear at home, you see, what is the emotion between these people.

CLARK: Soon all the children have been claimed except Manicu. He stands alone, his Save the Children kit on the ground at his feet. His left hand is tucked inside his shirt. He is absolutely silent, his face distant. Suddenly a woman appears, saying she's come for Manicu. There's some confusion. They were expecting an uncle. This woman says she is Manicu's *tia*, his aunt. Manicu walks over and stands by her side.

MANUEL: He said he know her. He's very happy. He's very happy.

CLARK: But Manicu doesn't look happy. In fact, his face is impossible to read. He picks up the kit and, walking beside the woman, he disappears down a path into the village. The Mozambiquans around me seem at ease about Manicu's homecoming, but it's unsettling to me.

Chiringoma seems more cheerful when we return the next morning. Or maybe it's just more familiar. Today the village is full of activity. Men are unloading sacks of corn from a truck. No one bothers to pick up the grain that spills, as they would if hunger were a serious problem. There are other reassuring signs. New desks for the school are being delivered. Kids are playing marbles. Life seems normal here today. An old man has rounded up some kids to sing for us.

Manicu comes to the village center with his aunt. He smiles when he sees us. He's had a bath. His aunt agrees to show me the hut where they live. We set off with a small group of children following behind in single file. On the way, the sandy path curves between huts and small gardens. People wave as we walk through. Manicu's aunt takes us inside her mud hut. It's dark and cool. The dirt floor has been swept clean. There are no possessions, except hanging on one wall is a white, enamel oven door, the kind with a glass window in the middle. It's being used as a picture frame for a wedding photo. There are no chairs in here and no beds.

Can you ask, Manuel, where people sleep in this house?
MANUEL: She say there's two bedrooms, this one and this one. And Manicu is sleeping here. She said she has no blankets for Manicu. She must try to get it.
CLARK: Would you thank her very much for showing us her home?
MANUEL: Manicu, *ciao!*
CLARK: Study hard, we tell Manicu. He has said when he grows up he wants to be a driver. Manicu's life will never be easy, but at least he can get on with it now. It comes down to that. That is what has been accomplished by Save the Children and the Mozambiquan government, by all the people who had a hand in bringing Manicu here. It seems like a modest achievement. But for a child in Mozambique these days, it is a gift just to be able to live with a family, to have enough food, and to go to school. Manicu is one of the lucky ones, one of three, thousand children who have come home. Two hundred thousand more are still waiting.

✦ ✦ ✦ ✦ ✦ ✦ ✦ ✦ ✦

Our struggles in this country to deal with changing family relationships sometimes seem complicated by our options. Many of our listeners wrote to share their own experiences after hearing this essay. Jim Collums is a former airline pilot, now a social worker. He wrote about his father, who was a farmer.

All Things Considered, MAY 24

COLLUMS: The day I brought my dad to the nursing home I stayed with him until visiting hours were over. He was still dressed in his suit and tie and he apprehensively hung onto the hat in his lap as I got up to leave. He stood up with tears in his eyes, and said, "Son, I don't belong here." "You'll get to where you like it, Dad," I lied. "It's best for you." "Well, just stay the night with me then. I'll sleep on the floor and you can have the bed."

I left. My dad spent his last three years there. When I was looking through a cardboard box containing his meager possessions, I came across a tightly folded piece of paper with these words he'd written.

"Too soon, they get us into our tranquil state where objections become mere whispers and humiliation just another itch relieved by an institutional scratch. There's no room here for individuality. We are a collective junk pile of old, discarded shells. Now and again, at birthdays, we're sought out to receive token recognition. But it seems that only one is aware of the event. The rest are immersed in an ongoing cycle of junk pile diversions.

"Bath time is the hardest. If humility be a seed for the tree of godliness, then we are a forest of God oaks flourishing in nursing homes. We are ordered coldly to remove our clothes. New inmates are bashful, shy, reserved, reticent, hesitant, awkward, and desperately trying to hang onto their last shred of pride, having seldom, if ever, done such a thing in the presence of strangers. It was my first realization that, to someone, I was no longer a person. That I was in the same class as Tuesday and Thursday's laundry, just another fabric to be washed. Sheets and towels, floor mats and shirts, have no modesty, no shame, so why should I? I used to think a lot about that, but now I only sleep and wait."

When I finished the letter, I put it back into the box with my father's possessions, a worn-out wallet, a comb, a neatly folded handkerchief, and one gold cuff link. And wished I had spent that first night in the nursing home with my dad.

✦ ✦ ✦ ✦ ✦ ✦ ✦ ✦ ✦ ✦

J ohn Hockenberry was the host of our first call-in show, a program called *Heat*. John wanted it to generate heat as well as light, and he felt strongly that nothing should be off limits. The program lasted for nine months, ending partly because of funding difficulties. Some of its funding came from the National Endowment for the Arts, which ran into trouble with Congress over what public money should and should not pay for.

Heat, JULY 19

HOCKENBERRY: While I'm talking, during this conversation, let's agree on something, OK? So we can communicate. Something like a principle. I mean, if we can't agree on anything, then it's kind of pointless, right? Let's agree that we shall be speaking the English language during this radio program, for this hour, OK? I mean, if we can't agree on that, have a nice day. We'll just leave it.

Now, we could have agreed on something much more narrow, like let's only use words that begin with the letter L. Let's. Listing letters looks lovely. Loud! Last. Linger. Lost. Lonely. Lacks length. Looseness. Less limber. Labor. Language? Uh-uh. It's stifling. After a while there's no communication. If you run out of L words, have a nice day. Can't even say that. The whole thing stinks.

But what if somebody came along with a book of words? A big book filled with words that begin with the letter L. You'd follow the guy. We would call him a leader. Leader! Large love! Lady luck. Listen! You've got their attention. Now what do you say? No problem — just look in my book. Ladies. Listeners. Lend me. Oops. You can't make a mistake. It's tough. People would react. Lacks L's, lewd, they would say. But people would still be thinking with all of the letters. Outside though — L's. Laughter. Laughter. You may like one letter more than the other, but the effect would be on the language. Our language. If leaders control the language, they control us.

The current controversy in Congress over the reauthorization of the National Endowment for the Arts is not about money. Nor is it about obscenity. It's about language controlling the language of art. The NEA is the indication that we as a community have agreed to the principle of supporting artists. People with a common language are free to decide what they like or don't like. There are no rules. They can like certain art. They can hate certain art. No rules. Until now. The NEA has made some rules, something like a license. Oh, there's another L word. License.

Why do I bring all of this up? Because we at *Heat* receive support from the National Endowment for the Arts. We can't just pretend to be objective about all of this and have the pro- and anti-art forces debating on our show once in a while. No, we are in a different position. During the next fiscal year, one hundred fifty thousand dollars from the NEA has been committed to this radio program. We have been asked to sign a document stating what it is not permissible to do or say on this radio program during that fiscal year, which begins this fall. The document came in a book. It came from a leader. Here's what we can't do with our NEA money. "None of the funds authorized to be appropriated for the National Endowment for the Arts may be used to promote, disseminate, or produce materials which in the judgment of the National Endowment for the Arts may be considered obscene, including but not limited to depictions of sadomasochism, homoeroticism, the sexual exploitation of children, or individuals engaged in sex acts, and which, when taken as a whole, do not have serious literary, artistic, political, or scientific value."

We at *Heat* support the full unrestricted reauthorization of the NEA. We think it is a principle worth fighting for and consider art something the institutions of government should encourage and support, whatever the risk. We as a nation take other risks. The right to bear arms — handguns people use to kill each other every day in a country with the highest murder rate in the world. We at *Heat* take this position on the NEA, but we will sign this document even though we oppose the principle. A loss of one hundred fifty thousand dollars would force us off the air. If it came down some time on the air to a choice between what we consider art and the new restrictions, we will make our own choice. We will accept the consequences. Either way, though, voices are silenced. Voices speaking language. Others have not signed and have refused their NEA grant. Some may disagree with our decision, and that is their right. Whether we sign or not, the point has to do with the language and the lucky leader with the book.

You know the crazy part of this, though. Communities can judge art. They do it all the time. But for the government to set limits, control the language of art, this we oppose. We could become a product and enter the marketplace to be bought and sold. There's an idea. Nah. Maybe we should just concentrate on learning those L words. That's something we can agree on. Right? Love it or leave it. Remember that one?

✦ ✦ ✦ ✦ ✦ ✦ ✦ ✦ ✦ ✦

Deborah Amos covered the Gulf War for us. It was a frustrating experience for her because it has always been Deborah's gift to get into the places where the worst things are happening. The tight controls on coverage were frustrating to all the reporters, but to Deborah, who came early and stayed late, they were particularly infuriating. She went to the Gulf as the first soldiers were settling in and filed this story for *Morning Edition* in September as the new American army was making its way into Saudi Arabia.

AMOS: Women soldiers are something new for Saudi Arabia, and it's taken some adjustments. One example is this recreation center for the Saudi military on an air base in the eastern province. When the facility was opened for American male soldiers, it took some negotiating to convince the Saudis to open it for women, too, but the victory was less than complete. The Saudis agreed on condition that the women and men use this place at different times and that the women enter through the back door.

Saudi Arabia is a conservative society, even by Arab standards. Women and men are kept separate in public. There are religious police to enforce the rules, and in keeping with Islamic tradition, most women cover themselves in public with a black cape called an *abaya,* accompanied by a black veil. Theresa Morris and Cathy Gross, flight nurses from North Carolina, say the cultural restrictions have already affected their work.

MORRIS: We're used to going on field exercises, and we're coed in our tents, and we live together, work together, and here we're — we're totally separated from our — the guys that we came over with, and — and so there is a marked distinction, not because we chose it that way.

GROSS: You don't get to develop the teamwork and the cohesiveness that we're used to dealing with in the States because we're usually working side by side with the men and, you know, working with them as a team.

AMOS: Morris and Gross work out in the desert in a field hospital. They've had little contact with Saudis and have only seen women at a distance, covered in their black capes.

MORRIS: It's the most unusual thing I've ever seen in my life. I can't imagine it, personally. Some of our people got some of the *aba* — *abayas,* or whatever you call them, with the veil, and there's only little slits for eyes, and I can't imagine living that way.

AMOS: If the crisis in the Gulf changes Saudi Arabia, the first steps are being taken here at the Girls Health Institute in Dammam, in the eastern province. At about a quarter to four the street in front of this building is jammed with cars, as fathers, chauffeurs, or husbands drop off their black-veiled passengers. It's illegal in Saudi Arabia for women to drive, but for the first time in the country's history, Saudi women have been encouraged to enroll in civil defense classes. Hundreds of women have signed up. This is the first step of an order by the Saudi king. As the country expands its military, Saudi women may be called on to replace men in a variety of jobs. It's a big step in a country where women usually work in fields that put them in contact only with other women.

Mona Bokshide, a thirty-two-year-old housewife, bristles at any questions about her decision to wear an *abaya*. "It's Islamic," she says. She talks about what's ahead through a black gauze veil.

BOKSHIDE: I don't think that I want to work with a man. If I have an ambition in life, that's to be a good citizen, a good Muslim, and a good lady.

AMOS: What do you think about all these American women in the military?

BOKSHIDE: I don't object to it because I understand it. I do respect whatever you are doing because that's your way of doing it, and I want the same respect for what I do because this is the way I do things, you know? This is what I believe in.

AMOS: In the Saudi Arabian desert, Sergeant Adrienne Palatzo is snapping photographs as her husband gets an award. Palatzo had scheduled her wedding for December but moved up the ceremony when her orders came through. She and her new husband were married just two days before they both flew out to join the American forces here, and she jokes about a honeymoon in the desert. Palatzo says this unexpected deployment has raised hard questions among the women in her unit who've had to leave children behind.

PALATZO: Well, it makes me think — it makes me think about what's important in life, you know. Maybe they're not so far off, staying home with the family and stuff, you know, maybe that's the thing, I don't know. We're always preparing for war and always going through de-ployment packets and family care plans, but when push came to shove, I think people had to really relook at what they were going to do with their family. The babysitter's not going to take your child for six months.

AMOS: The question of women's roles is raised every day here because the cultural differences between Saudi Arabia and America forces the issue. One example is driving. Saudi officials waived the no-driving rule for American military women.

PALATZO: I was driving down the road and, you know, lots of women staring at a female driver, and I had a man in the car with me, you know, another one of our soldiers, and one of the women gave me a thumbs-up. It was kind of interesting. I think there's some positive signs over here.

AMOS: The Cleopatra Beauty Salon is crowded again. There are no male hairdressers here. This is strictly for women. Black capes and veils are shed at the door. In the first few tense days of the crisis, Saudi women stayed close to home, working out escape routes with their families if Iraqi tanks rolled south down the long highway that connects occupied Kuwait with this eastern province city of Dhahran. Six weeks later, many here have learned to live with the tensions, but it's raised questions, said Suha al-Bassam, a Western-educated filmmaker in one of Saudi Arabia's biggest oil companies.

BASSAM: It is a crisis that is making us wake up to the fact that we are dependent, we have to be more involved, that we have a role to play. I know a lot of people are saying that seeing American ladies driving here, does that mean that you're going to drive? And I don't think that's going to happen. You know, it's going to happen because our men are going to need to go the field, they're going to need to fight, and there's going to have to be somebody at home who's going to have to take the children, whether it's to school or, or wherever, and if we don't have any foreign labor, there's no one else who's going to do it except the woman.

AMOS: Saudi women seem to have just as many questions about American women soldiers as women soldiers have about them. Donna Garacolli from Hillsborough, Florida, says she joined the air force to get out of a grocery store back home. Her husband is also stationed here. The couple had to leave their two daughters, aged nine and five months, with Donna's mother. Garacolli says that the women in her unit are disappointed in the men here for not fighting for equal treatment for them.

GARACOLLI: A lot of the guys that we came over with are — they do it in fun, but it's, like, "Yeah, you got to sit at the back of the bus. Get back there," and things like "Go iron my shirt, woman," you know. And we — we take this from them, but like I said, it's all in fun right now, but it could wear pretty thin in a couple of months, I'm sure.

AMOS: If you had just talked to a Saudi woman, and she said to you, "It's unimaginable to me that you would leave a five-month-old baby to be in the air force —"

GARACOLLI: I don't think it is worth it, you know. I mean, I'm missing her cut her first tooth, probably her first word, her sitting up, crawling. It's a big price. Like I said, I didn't really have a choice.

AMOS: The Gulf crisis has brought together conflicting images of women: the black veil and the desert camouflage suit, two cultures addressing similar questions at the same time.

◆ ◆ ◆ ◆ ◆ ◆ ◆ ◆ ◆ ◆

That same month, an eighteen-year-old stabbed and killed a young tourist from Utah on a subway platform in New York City. The boy who died had attempted to defend his mother from a mugger. The mugger was charged with the murder. He had a street name, Rock Star, and was part of a "crew," or gang, called FTS. Maria Hinojosa sought out the members of that crew to do a story on gang violence in New York City. She found a very loosely affiliated group of kids, hanging out in a schoolyard, living in a middle-class neighborhood in Queens.

All Things Considered, NOVEMBER 6

HINOJOSA: Coki is a seventeen-year-old Ecuadorian immigrant who's been in the United States ten years.

COKI: This is original FTS, right? It started out in this school right here. It started out as HBO, Home Boys Only, then turned into FTS, all right? It stands for Flushing's Top Society, or Fight to Survive. We fight to survive. FTS was more like a go-out, hang-out-with-the-guys group. That's what it was about. But, I mean, it wasn't about no violence. But once in a while, you know, you do have to defend yourself.

HINOJOSA: Coki is a founding member of the crew FTS and, like its other members, he's a relatively recent immigrant from South America. Coki has just gotten out of school, and he's lighting up a cigarette, a Newport. He has on his backpack and is wearing a hooded sweatshirt pulled up over his head, so I have to strain to see his face. Once I get a glimpse of him, though, I see he doesn't have the look of a hardened street kid. He's coy with a baby face and a cute smirk that comes across every now and then.

COKI: Right now I'm what is known as an intelligent hood, all right? So —

HINOJOSA: What do you mean?

COKI: I mean, I go to school. I dropped out of school, but I realized a lot of things, so I went back. I want my diploma. It's going to mean something. I'm going to need it in the future, OK? I'm trying to do something with myself, but at the same time no one's ever going to step on me.

HINOJOSA: Coki is a good friend of Rock Star's, the kid who's now in jail for allegedly stabbing and killing Brian Watkins, the Utah tourist.

Coki says Rock Star didn't mean to do it. It was a mistake. Charge him for the robbery but drop the murder rap, he says. He looks over to a graffiti memorial he helped paint on the side of the schoolyard. In a rainbow of colors, it says, "For Brian, in memory." I asked Coki whether or not Rock Star's arrest has had an impact on him. He says yes, but he can't spend all of his time worrying about what might happen in the future. "I have to live for today," he says.

About a week later, I had plans to meet the crew on a Friday night to join them for a graffiti tagging session. A tag is when you leave your mark on a wall, a school, a building, or a subway. Coki is about an hour late. I'm getting ready to leave when I see him and a group of about seven friends walking down the street with a gait, an attitude that smacked of a toughness I hadn't seen before. Coki is giddy, nervously excited. So are his friends. I don't understand until finally Shank, another crew member, tells me they've just been released from a police lineup.

SHANK: We were supposed to get picked out if we did the assault, but luckily the guy didn't see who did it, so we got off scot-free.

HINOJOSA: Wait a second. So does that mean you guys did it?

SHANK: Yeah. I mean, we're telling the truth right here. I mean, I don't have nothing to — as long as my face ain't in there, I'll tell you the truth.

HINOJOSA: I became a little nervous as Shank went on to describe what happened the night they decided to, in his words, get paid. "Getting paid" is the street term for acquiring money or goods. He says they saw a guy looking "vic," which in crew language means victim. They decided to go on a mission, which means to assault someone, and then they jumped him. They got enough money for a weekend at the movies and some food.

SHANK: He's high, too. Don't mind him.

HINOJOSA: What are they high on?

SHANK: Beer or weed or — I don't know. I don't — personally I don't do drugs, but —

HINOJOSA: But you do assault people?

SHANK: Yeah, like they're good at doing drugs, I'm good at this. I get my anger out doing that. You know, see.

HINOJOSA: Shank talks about this violence openly in the same tone he might use to talk about school or a baseball game. I'm taken aback at first, but as Shank continues to describe how he feels and why he does what he does, I realize he understands it quite well. He's angry about his own family violence, angry about seeing too few realistic opportunities for his future, and angry at himself for not being strong enough to give up his habit of assault as a means for relieving his tension.

SHANK: I've tried, believe me, I've tried hard. I tried — how do you say it? — constructive things, but I don't know. It just don't give me the same feel of release. Ahh, you know, like that. That's the only thing I can do to express it. Ahh. Like when you fill up a balloon and it's about to pop, and then you just let the air go, you know, without letting it pop. You just go *Sss*, and that's it. And then it all builds up again. It's like a little cycle and stuff.

HINOJOSA: And the cycle goes something like this. The weekend comes around. No one has any money. Shank has built up little pieces of anger throughout the whole week, and the crew decides they want to get paid. Coki, who I've been told is high on a tab of mescaline, has joined us now. I ask him why he did this. "When your father, who's a cabdriver now, was a kid, he would have never thought about jumping someone to get paid," I tell him.

COKI: The difference between now and thirty years ago, times are hard now. Believe me, times are hard. You got no bread on your table, and your parents can't hack it. You've got to do something about it. That's your family and that comes first.

HINOJOSA: These kids seem to fit the standard profile sociologists give to explain youth violence — kids who start out believing they can make money legitimately and then lose hope as they see their own parents' poverty after years of hard work. Like all other teens, they are kids who are going through a stage where they must test their limits. And there are those who come from broken homes where there is a history of family violence. Other sociologists talk about the degree of violence kids are exposed to in movies or on TV. But more and more sociologists are bringing up another form of violence that doesn't receive as much attention but that is just as important: the violence of unemployment, the violence of a poor education, the violence of racism.

Underneath the Triborough Bridge in Queens, there is a park with an incomparable view of Manhattan. Late at night teenagers from all over the city converge here, and just like in the 1950s they spend the night cruising, driving up and down the road for hours as they scope out the scene. Coki and Shank told me to meet them here this Friday night. They say this park is a neutral zone. Crews from all over show up, but there is an unspoken law that no one fights here. This place is beautiful, with its majestic view of the city and the river. It's a safe place they use as an escape from their neighborhoods and the violence. This evening Coki seems tired, not of anything in particular, just tired. He says even though he may feel safe here, there are bigger problems he can't escape from.

COKI: I think the scariest thing for a teenager is being seventeen years old and being scared that your parents have no money for the rent and that you're going to get kicked out of the house soon and you ain't got nowhere to go because you ain't got no family around. I think that's the scariest thing ever in my life. I've been shot at, I've been swung at, I've been everything, I — I've done the same things, but I think that was the scariest thing. That was it.

1991

The United States marched into Kuwait in 1991, but as the year began we were watching another army on the march, the Red Army of the Soviet Union. Lithuania, one of the Baltic countries we used to call the "captive nations," had declared its independence from the Soviet Union in March 1990, beginning the breakup of the empire we had faced across the proxy battlefields of the cold war. Two weeks into the year, the Soviet Union was moving to put down the peaceful revolution of the Lithuanians and their president, Vytautas Landsbergis. Ann Cooper, our correspondent in Moscow, was in Vilnius when the Soviet army took back the radio and television broadcast center using tanks, firing on unarmed civilians. Landsbergis had appeared on television the night before, promising to resist the Soviets "until the last second." Ann watched and we listened with *Weekend Edition* host Liane Hansen, as it was happening.

Weekend Edition, Sunday, JANUARY 13

COOPER: Several of these shots have been fired. People are starting to leave from around the base of the television tower. The tanks are shining their spotlights up on the tower. About one-thirty this morning word went out that a column of tanks and armored personnel carriers was on its way to the Lithuanian television tower. Lithuanian TV for the last few days has been broadcasting twenty-four hours a day, showing what's happening at the Parliament Building, showing the Soviet soldiers as they gradually occupied one building after another in the city. Apparently this was announced on Lithuanian TV. Someone who saw it told me that the announcers are very agitated, very upset obviously, that this convoy was on its way to the TV tower.

We grabbed a car, basically ran into the convoy en route and turned in behind it. Dozens of other Lithuanian cars were on the road, also following the convoy. People had been watching TV, heard it, decided to go out and go and try to join the human barrier that was already there protecting the tower, thousands of people who were keeping an overnight vigil in case, you know, last night was the night that the troops moved.

The convoy was, I would say, twenty, maybe twenty-four vehicles, several tanks and armored personnel carriers. When they got close to the tower, to the bottom of the hill that leads up to the tower, one of the tanks just plowed right over some kind of a vehicle, just, you know, crashed right on top of it. Then some people in the crowd tried to form a barrier to stop that tank, and, after briefly hesitating, the tank kept right on moving, knocking people off and rolling right over people.

They started playing a recording. I'm not sure whose voice it was, but it was a message from the Soviet army, and I'll just read you a little bit of what they were saying. This message was in Russian. It said, "Brother Lithuanians, in the name of the Committee of National Security, I report to you that all power of the republic has transferred to the hands of our committee." What this meant basically was a coup attempt against the popularly elected government of Lithuania. The Committee of National Security is a very shadowy group about which we know almost nothing except that it is connected with the Communist party. This announcement went on to claim that this committee is the power of the simple working people. It said that some of the people in the crowd last night had come under the influence and the deceits, lies, and demagoguery of the Lithuanian government, and then the announcement said, "There's no reason to remain, no reason to have a confrontation. I ask you to go home, where your parents, your mothers, and fathers are waiting for you, your brothers and sisters, your grandfathers and grandmothers. Go home."

At this point, the tanks started shooting. I guess they were blanks because we could never see any damage that was caused by them, but they were huge explosions, very scary, very frightening, and also automatic weapons fire you could begin to hear. Those were not blanks, because there were a number of people shot. Of the fifteen people officially reported dead, most of them were shot, and they were unarmed people.

Inside the television tower, there are about thirty young guards. Their weapons were clubs, some Molotov cocktails, fire hoses, and one hunting rifle. Those guys apparently fled fairly quickly, obviously. There was very little they could do in the face of such force. Hundreds and hundreds of people remained on the spot, refusing to be intimidated into running away completely from the television tower.

I stayed there for about an hour and a half. Most of the Lithuanians also stayed. Some of them went down and, you know, circled around the armored personnel carriers, shouting "Fascists," shouting "Free Lithuania," waving their fists at them, but not doing anything to try and attack the army troops or their machinery. I don't know quite how long all of those people stayed there. I know that by this morning at maybe six o'clock they were basically gone, and the army was in full control of the television tower. I'm told that they hung a hammer-and-sickle symbol, the symbol of the Communist party, from one of the windows of the TV tower.

HANSEN: What is the status now of President Landsbergis's government? And where, indeed, is the president?

COOPER: The president, as far as I know, is still inside the Parliament Building, which I'm very close to. Maybe you can hear the chanting right now. I'm just going to hold the phone up so maybe you can hear some of that. [*Chanting.*] That's the crowd in front of the Parliament Building chanting the Lithuanian word for freedom, waving their fists. Landsbergis and many of the deputies of the Lithuanian Parliament have been inside all day meeting, talking about how they're going to try to defend this building, which obviously they can't do for very long if tanks show up here. At one point, one of the deputies encouraged people to leave. The people refused to leave. They're still out there, still very determined, and still waiting to see what happens next.

HANSEN: Yesterday we were getting reports that Soviet President Mikhail Gorbachev was pledging to end the use of force, and there was some speculation that the army may be acting on its own. Do you think there's any basis to this speculation?

COOPER: You know, it's obviously a very confused situation here, but it's very hard to imagine that this is the army just going off on its own without Gorbachev's blessing, orders, whatever. Right now the crowd is chanting, "Free Lithuania." Let me just hold the phone up one more time. I don't know if you can hear that over this long distance, but it's very loud, very determined sounding from here.

HANSEN: Yes, we can hear it very well here. Martial law has been declared there now?

COOPER: Well, the words "martial law" were not used, but the new commandant of Vilnius came on the radio early this morning, announcing that a curfew is now imposed from ten P.M. to five A.M. All meetings and demonstrations, such as the enormous one that's going on right outside, which you could hear just a minute ago, that's banned supposedly. Strikes are banned. People are not to have cameras or recording equipment like tape recorders. Basically the army has power to check people's documents at will.

HANSEN: At the moment you cannot see any Soviet tanks or any Soviet military. Do you have any idea where they are at this moment?

COOPER: No, I know that they're stationed around the main places like the television tower, but they're not within sight here. Now the crowd's chanting, "Landsbergis," Vytautas Landsbergis, the president of Lithuania.

HANSEN: Where is the prime minister now?

COOPER: We don't know. A few hours ago it was announced that the prime minister and his entire family are missing. Nobody knew what their fate was. The Parliament appointed a new prime minister in an effort to try to carry forward their authority, their power as a government.

HANSEN: I know it's a little bit difficult to speculate what might happen next, but what is your feeling about what you're witnessing, what you've already witnessed and perhaps your own concerns about what might happen next?

COOPER: Well, my own feelings are, I can't believe this happened. I've been to Lithuania many times. I've lived in this country for four years, and, frankly, I still find it hard to accept the idea that such brutal force could have been used against unarmed people here. I expect this will draw a tremendous reaction throughout the country. There are demonstrations scheduled today in Moscow. There are several republics that are also seeking independence from the Soviet Union. Lithuania was just the first to do that. Obviously, this is horrifying and chilling to all of those people because they have to imagine, Are we next?

✦ ✦ ✦ ✦ ✦ ✦ ✦ ✦ ✦

When the Gulf War began, we stayed on the air with *Morning Edition* live until midday and *All Things Considered* during the afternoon and evening. We added a call-in program to the schedule, and invited all sorts of experts, debriefed our own reporters in Saudi Arabia, and took calls from listeners. On February 1, Daniel Schorr and Neal Conan were on deck, and Deborah Amos was on the telephone from Saudi Arabia. Deb had been in the Gulf since Iraq's invasion of Kuwait in August 1990 and was concerned about the restrictions on the press imposed by the American military. Reporters were briefed but, except for escorted visits, kept away from troops and fighting. For the first time, an American war was off-limits to the press.

Special Coverage, FEBRUARY I

SCHORR: In your young years and long career, you've had a lot of violence to cover, including, for example, the invasion of Lebanon. How does this assignment of covering people killing people differ from some of the other ones?

AMOS: It's different in two respects. One, it's different because of the kinds of arms that are being used here. I keep thinking I'm covering world war two and a half. And it makes it different in your calculations when you're out in the field. I don't know how far those weapons can reach. You don't know where to be.

The second thing is a matter of information. In the Israeli invasion of Lebanon, we had what I now realize was the luxury of being able to see Israeli officers on one side of the line and finding out what they had to say about what was going on, and crossing the line and going to talk to Palestinians on the other. And you could make comparisons every single day about what you were seeing.

Information here is so difficult to get. The pool structure makes it very difficult to see what's going on up close. And you can already see contradictions in the kind of information we're getting. The pool reports are well ahead of the information that's coming out of the briefings both in Riyadh and at the Pentagon. So it makes it a very different kind of war to cover.

CONAN: I want to follow that up, Deborah, by asking at this point, what are relations like between that rather large contingent of U.S. and other reporters in Dhahran and the Joint Information Bureau, the military's outpost there?

AMOS: It's becoming more and more acrimonious, and even the briefers here in Dhahran said that they are worried that the "I" is coming out of the Joint Information Bureau. I think that they also feel the pressure from us and the frustration of not being able to get us out there. I think where some of the holdups are are in the field, and some are political considerations. I'll give you one example. The Battle for Khafji is politically being sold as a battle that the Saudis won. Now, the Saudis did very well and so did the troops from Qatar, but the truth is that the marines played a rather large role and it has something to do with the limitations on our access. Today there was enormous frustration, both in the briefing in Riyadh and in a rather large meeting tonight between pool members and some of the military here.

SCHORR: Deborah, on that subject, let me fill you in if you don't already know it, on a story that's appeared here from Cox News Service, dateline outside Khafji. The byline is "Botched Attack Aimed to Save Marine Scouts." This is a totally different version than the official version we've heard and suggests that the marine scouts went into Khafji and were cut off there, and then a lot of time and effort and energy was spent trying to get them out, that there was then a comedy of errors involving Qatari troops, and Qatari tanks and Saudi tanks. They began firing at each other, and there were two six-man marine reconnaissance teams stuck in the middle of Khafji while Iraqi tanks were shooting all around them. It describes a picture a lot different from what was considered to be the brilliant success that the generals have described. Are you aware of some of these different versions of the Khafji battle?

AMOS: Dan, I was with that reporter, about six miles outside of Khafji yesterday. We were standing on a little spit of sand when the first reconnaissance teams came out. There is a lot to that story. There was some exchange of friendly fire inside Khafji. What we have now discovered, according to a pool report that came in today, is that those two reconnaissance teams were prepositioned in Khafji. What they were doing is they were calling in air strikes. We had a long talk with the colonel, who told us yesterday about those two teams. That information wasn't released until today, in Riyadh, and we are just piecing it all together.

There came a moment yesterday in the desert when a marine public affairs officer came when we were talking to the colonel. And he essentially said, I can't order you to get out of here, but if you don't, I will call the Saudis and have you arrested. So we could only get half of the story yesterday because we were not in a media pool. We had gone up unilaterally. In the business, that means working for your own company instead of working for the American media pool. So the problem is you get little bits of these stories as it goes along.

SCHORR: You say that you were with the reporter for the Cox newspapers. The story says the correspondents visiting the two forward marine outposts were without military escort. Were you able to go up without escort, and is that now allowed?

AMOS: It is not allowed. We were acting like reporters. There is one road that goes between Dhahran, the city that I'm in, and Khafji. It's about a four-hour drive. There are Saudis on the road. There are roadblocks, but when they see Americans they tend to pass them through because they think they're military. So we were able to get all the way up and stopped with some marine units. What was interesting was we ran into a colonel who was quite willing to talk to us. He was relieved that his two reconnaissance patrols got out. He wanted us to know that story. He also wanted us to talk to his troops. They like it when reporters come. They have a story to tell and they want to tell that story. So it's not in the field where you find that problem.

SCHORR: But in fairness to the military command, the people in the field may themselves not know the reasons to keep things secret at a certain time, isn't that right?

AMOS: That may be true. I don't think, Dan, we're altogether looking for the secrets of it. I think in some cases we're just looking for the details of it. When there is a battle, such as the one for Khafji, there's just a lot of questions. What happened? Who participated? Why was it that Iraqi troops were able to enter the city? It tells you about the course of the war. So I think everybody's been very sensitive about giving out numbers, which is against the ground rules, giving out information about future operations. You do find out a lot on pools, and there's not anybody I know of so far that's broken any of the ground rules.

SCHORR: OK, let's go now to Mary in Columbus, Ohio. Hello, Mary.

MARY: Hello. I have a request, and then if you have time I'll say something else. She was talking about teasing information from the military about operations, and my request is for our sons and daughters who are over there. Please don't get any information from them that might cause my son to die.

SCHORR: I think you're safe. I think that the military is very careful. They don't let things out that shouldn't be out, I think.

AMOS: And it's not operational. That's not what we're trying to get. We're trying to get the details, we're trying to tell you what is happening with your son. That is the point. We aren't trying to put anybody's life in danger. We know what the ground rules are. We are responsible. But we just want to know what happened.

SCHORR: OK, let's go to Jay in Wichita, Kansas. Hello, Jay.

JAY: Hello, how are you doing today? Deborah, I guess I've got a question for you. I've listened to you say several times that "we know what the ground rules are," and yet earlier you said that you went up to the front. In the same basic conversation you said that the press was not allowed to do those things without military guidance. But yet you and four other reporters snuck up to the front, endangering not only the lives of our boys, but endangering your own lives. And the fact that it may cause our military to take their minds off what they're doing to come find people like you who are up there where you shouldn't be! I personally think that's wrong, and I feel like when you do things like that you should face some type of criminal charges! That's my personal opinion. What do you think about that?

AMOS: Well, I think that what we were doing yesterday was acting like reporters. What we knew is that there was a lot we didn't know. There is nothing that says that what we did was illegal. When we spoke to the colonel, a public affairs marine officer came and said to the colonel, "If you want to talk to them you can, and if you don't want to you don't have to," and he chose to do so. There's nothing in either Saudi law or American law that says we can't do that.

Were we risking our lives? I didn't feel that at the time. We were far enough back from the fighting. We were watching as we were going up the road. Marines who were sitting beside artillery pieces, you are right, we didn't know if they were going to shoot in two minutes, but I felt that we were so limited in our information that it was worth the risk. Reporters do risk their lives, and that's part of the job. I don't claim to be a hero because that wasn't the point. The point was to see if we could find out what was happening.

SCHORR: Very quick question, Deborah. Is there any penalty for going somewhere unescorted, other than being taken back?

AMOS: At the moment, no, Dan. And as a matter of fact, there were some people in the Joint Information Bureau who applauded the effort. I think that some of them are as frustrated as we are. They know this is one way to get the military's attention. There could come a moment when the pool system could break down if we don't get more adequate information.

✦ ✦ ✦ ✦ ✦ ✦ ✦ ✦ ✦

The liberation of Kuwait was accomplished in just a few days. The president and his advisers took more time to decide what ought to happen to Iraq and Saddam Hussein, whether troops should drive deep into Iraq, perhaps to Baghdad. There were reports of uprisings against Saddam Hussein in other Iraqi cities, including Basra. A group of reporters, venturing across lines to cover that story, were captured by Iraqis and held for several days. One of them was NPR's Neal Conan, traveling with Chris Hedges of the *New York Times*. After being released in Jordan, Neal phoned Lynn Neary.

Weekend All Things Considered, MARCH 9

CONAN: An Iraqi jeep pulled us over, and two guys got out and came over. They didn't ask us any questions. They just stuck AK-47s in our faces and jacked us out of the jeep and out of our Land Rover, and put us in the back seat of the jeep. One of them got in the Land Rover and one got in the jeep and drove us quickly into an army camp that was right near there. And we met this army colonel who came up in a Mercedes and stepped out with his field-jacket strap draped around his shoulders and carefully oiled hair and his sidearm, and sat down in a chair and ordered everybody about as if he were some sort of Mafia don. He questioned Chris, obviously, who spoke Arabic, and not me. I was just sitting and trying to not look scared and smile and look intelligent. They were talking about, you know, how we came up, and did we know we were in Iraq, and did we know we had violated the border and this is very serious and that sort of stuff, when another car suddenly pulled into the same camp and out came two Brazilian reporters and a Uruguayan who'd been held in this camp for two days.

NEARY: Neal, what was going on in your mind at that point? I mean, did you have a sense that you were going to be taken into custody for a long time? Did you think you were going to talk yourselves out of this?

CONAN: I always have the sense that I can talk myself out of something. However, there was this minor language problem. And Chris, who's more experienced than I am, told me later that he thought that was the scariest moment of the whole trip because they didn't ask any questions. I mean, they didn't say, "Who are you? What are you doing? Where are you from?" They just grabbed us and threw us in this jeep, and that was that. And he said that was very, very frightening. He's had a lot of experience in Central America, and it seemed to him that, you know, thirty seconds later it could be all over. But then this other car drove up with the other reporters, and six people is a very different proposition than two, it seemed to me. And I thought that maybe we were going to be OK for a little while and that we just might be detained when — then they decided to drive us all to Republican Guards divisional headquarters, which was at Basra University. On the way we could see what was going on around us, the green flags of the Shiite rebels flying on some buildings over the city. And there was a lot of gunfire all over the place, some of it heavy artillery, which was almost certainly Iraqi, and a lot of small-arms fire, but in all directions. And there was smoke rising from some parts of the city.

NEARY: At that point, could you tell that the Iraqi army was in control, or was it still a situation of flux?

CONAN: Monday evening it was really sort of a poignant moment. Our guards — we were in the hands of the Republican Guards by then, and they took us out to this building that had windows so we could see what was going on. And there were all the flares, the green and red flares that the Iraqis were firing. And that was then illuminated by the staccato of the AK-47 fire that was fairly light but almost constant. And then beyond that, the Iraqi soldiers were singing some Arabic music, and our Uruguayan was singing this very plaintive tango. And it was just a marvelous moment. But then the firing got heavier, and we were moved back inside the building.

NEARY: Did you have any sense of what was going on back at home? Were you thinking about that at all?

CONAN: That was interesting, too, we were talking about Jacobo Timerman, the Argentine who wrote that great book *Prisoner without a Name, Cell without a Number* about how the only way he could deal with thinking about his family was to say, "I'm on a different planet, I'm in a different dimension. I'm here and they're there and there's no connection between the two." If you started thinking about your family, you would start, you know, obviously feeling very weepy and this was not going to help you in the situation you were in. So throughout the whole experience, until we crossed the Jordanian border, I did not open my wallet and look at my pictures of my family.

NEARY: I have to say, Neal — and this is very typical of you — but you sound so composed right now. Were you able to maintain that composure during the whole experience?

CONAN: With the help of the other people in our group, I think we did maintain our composure. And also with the help, I have to say, of the Republican Guards, who treated us very, very well. And they kept repeating, "You shouldn't worry, you're our guests. We're going to treat you well. We're going to take you to Baghdad, and then you'll be going back to your country." Even though you know that when you get to Baghdad you're going to be turned over to another group, and that these people really have nothing to say about it, it's pretty reassuring to hear that at least. So that at those moments, we felt pretty safe.

The bond became even greater the next morning when they said, "All right, we're all going to Baghdad." And the whole headquarters company of this division began to move out. And this was Tuesday morning. And we were going to drive to Baghdad. And then we got about sixty miles north of Basra, according to the signs, and we turned off the road and we were told we were heading for a pontoon bridge but that the river was very high. It's in flood stage this time of the year. This is the Euphrates. And it was, the current was too strong for the pontoon bridge, and we had to wait, and we waited in this village all afternoon. And finally what happened was that late in the afternoon, it was just about dusk, we got the word, all right, we're going to go ahead. And they started their motors, and we just started driving. And all of a sudden, gunfire erupted from the front and the back of this armored column. And there were tanks and armored personnel carriers in the column and towed artillery. But all of that stuff was tightly packed in this tiny little village on this narrow street and we were being fired on from ahead and — and from behind and from the side by Shiite guerrillas. And this is where Major Assam — he really was just terrific. We all jumped out of the cars and fell face first in the mud, just to try to keep down from the gunfire. And he stood over us with his AK-47, protecting us and blasting away at the Shiites. I would have to say that he was terrific and the rest of the Republican Guards were not. They were very poorly arranged to stave off this kind of an ambush. They had an advantage in firepower of about a million to one, which they couldn't use because of the way they were deployed. And we were pinned down for about a half hour before they could finally, you know, unlimber some of the tanks to go out and start clearing the road.

NEARY: When did they bring you to Baghdad? When was all this taking place? When did you finally get there?

CONAN: We finally got to Baghdad on Thursday. I mean, after this mess with the convoy and the ambush, we were driven off to an airfield where there were three helicopters, all with UN markings but flown by Iraqi army aviation pilots. Their notebooks said they were from the 214th Squadron. And they were clearly concerned that there were only six of us. I mean, they said, "Where's everybody else?" And we said, you know, "We're the only ones." And then they flew us by helicopter to a base about halfway to Baghdad where they refueled, and we could see the hardened shelters where they had been bombed and blown up. And then we refueled finally and then flew just one helicopter the rest of the way to Baghdad. And we were helicoptered to another helicopter base, also in Baghdad, where we met with everybody else who'd arrived, just as we did.

We were then transferred to the hands of the secret police, who installed us in a sort of a seedy motel on the Tigris for the night, the Hotel Diana. And they locked us in our rooms and we didn't quite know what to make of that, though again they said that we were guests and we were going to be all right. I mean, these guys are some of the nastiest secret police on the face of the earth. And so we didn't know what was going to happen, but we all went to sleep. And then the next morning, they said, "We don't know what's going to happen." And Radio Baghdad, at that point, was still saying they didn't know where we were. And then we were turned over suddenly, again that night, to the International Red Cross, who put us in a pretty good hotel with hot water and a good meal and a beer. And then we got out today.

✦ ✦ ✦ ✦ ✦ ✦ ✦ ✦ ✦

C armen Delzell gets more mail than almost anyone at NPR. Somehow she gets under the skin or in the face or, I often think, into the hearts of our listeners. She complains, she whines, she describes a life barely above bag lady, but it's also the life of a woman who does what she wants. In this essay, she wanted Prozac.

All Things Considered, JUNE 24

DELZELL: When I first began to hear about Prozac, the miracle antidepressant known as the "yuppie upper," I was going through a pretty rough time. I'd lost my business, split up with the cowboy boot salesman, and had been informed that the magazine I'd been writing for had filed for bankruptcy. Not only that, but it was coming on Christmas and my truck broke down to the tune of twelve hundred dollars, just two days before we were supposed to go to Grandma's old folks home for a rollicking good time.

I've heard that depression is genetic, that I was born depressed. So after eight years of therapy and thousands of self-help books, which all contradicted themselves, I decided that antidepressants might be the only answer left for me. To save a little time and money, I hauled out the yellow pages and started calling psychiatrists. "Look," I'd say to the receptionist, "I'm depressed and I want some Prozac. Does your doctor prescribe it?" If she said anything that sounded vaguely as if the answer might be no, such as, "Well, you'll have to come in for an evaluation," or "The doctor doesn't give out information over the telephone," I'd hang up and try another one. Finally, I found the kind of doctor I was looking for. He answered his own phone. That's a good sign. And, yes, he sure did prescribe Prozac, and if I came in right away, he would give me three weeks' supply included in the price of my first office visit. I was out the door and on my way.

As soon as I was ushered into his office, I couldn't help but notice that it was entirely decorated with Prozac promotional gimmicks: a Prozac clock, a Prozac ashtray, a Prozac calendar. This doctor believed in Prozac. He wasn't the slightest bit interested in why I was depressed. As a matter of fact, he spent a good part of the hour telling me about painting his house. But at the end, he gave me three boxes of Prozac, and I gave him eighty dollars cash.

Well, for a while I thought it was working. I was happy, unusually happy. I loved everything, especially cleaning and going to the Laundromat. I stopped writing, I stopped complaining about the government, and I fell in love with an emotionally disturbed handyman who worked at the Goodwill. I began to see the beauty and humor in *Highway to Heaven* with Michael Landon. And I spent hours wandering blissfully through shopping malls, listening to the music. Nothing bothered me. Nothing.

I gained ten pounds. Hey, what the hell? I'm forty-three, after all. My boyfriend began to drink and steal money and stay out all night. The same response: "So what?" Gulf War, flat tire, poverty, piece of cake. I'd just take an extra Prozac in the evening. The doctor said it wouldn't hurt, just as long as I could afford to keep coming in for it. Well, as fate would have it, I began to break out in hives. I itched all over and started getting red welts on my whole body. The doctor said maybe I ought to stop taking Prozac for a couple weeks. "Stop?" I said, "stop?" "Sure," he said. "See if the rash goes away, and if it does, we'll put you on something else." "But I don't want something else," I cried. "I love Prozac. Do you hear me? I love it!" But he wouldn't give me any more.

Three weeks passed. All of a sudden I realized just how bad things had gotten while I was away. We were at war, for God's sakes, why hadn't somebody tried to stop it? I looked in the mirror. I really was fat. My butt looked like a bag of popcorn. What else? Let's see, no money, crazy boyfriend, stacks of cutoff notices and letters beginning with, "We know it's easy to forget, but . . ." How had this happened to me? I mean, I'd been depressed before, but I'd always held it together somehow. What does this drug do? Make you stupid, make you insensitive, or just give you the will to live, no matter what? I don't really care. I've already let everything go to hell, and I can live with the itch. It's reality I'm allergic to.

◆ ◆ ◆ ◆ ◆ ◆ ◆ ◆ ◆ ◆

T his was also the year that the Balkans returned to their old ways. Slovenia and Croatia had declared their independence from the Yugoslav federation, and the stage was set for years of war. Sylvia Poggioli covered the independence movements and wrote this essay on the difficulties of dealing with the Balkan paradox.

Weekend Edition, Sunday, AUGUST 18

POGGIOLI: There's a new spectator sport in the Croatian capital, Zagreb: the changing of the guard outside the presidential office. The ornately costumed guards click their heels while their right arms, elbows cocked at shoulder height, sway in incongruous movements. The new ritual is the brainchild of a choreographer of the Zagreb opera house. Watching it is like seeing a thirties movie about Ruritania, an imaginary central European statelet. Understanding Yugoslavs' sense of history or their need to re-create it is necessary to understand today's events, but choosing the right history book can been tricky. I came with a book on the Balkans published in 1989, just before the collapse of communism in the East. I soon realized it was useless. Another reporter had a battered edition of a book on the Balkan Wars written in 1931. It was eerily up-to-date. But Yugoslavs' perception of their past is often entrusted to legends and songs, which no historian dares challenge.

In one of many paradoxes, the Serbs still celebrate their defeat at the hands of the Turks, but no one really knows what happened in the Battle of Kosovo Polje six hundred years ago. A simple example of how history can transform something as basic as a last name was the tale of a man I met on the Croatian island of Brijuni. Gino belongs to the small Italian minority and speaks in the same lilting dialect heard in Venice. His father was born under the Austro-Hungarian Empire. His last name was Raich. When Gino was born, his part of Croatia was under Italian rule and his last name became Razzi. After World War II, Gino became a Yugoslav. He now goes by the name of Raich.

Yugoslavia bears a heavy burden of never forgotten historical vendettas. The most vicious, in World War II, pitted Serb Chetniks, the anti-Nazi partisans, against the Ustashas, the Croatian fascists. And the horrors of the past are constantly dredged up. A Serbian paper recently reprinted excerpts of the war diary of an Italian writer who visited the Ustasha leader Ante Pavelić, one of the most brutal of Hitler's followers. The Italian complimented Pavelić on a large plate of oysters on his desk. Pavelić is said to have responded, "Those aren't oysters. They're the eyes of Serbs." This is more or less the tone of press coverage in Yugoslavia. Ancient feuds, the lack of democratic traditions, and forty-five years of communism are not the best foundation on which to create an open independent press. A blatant example of intolerance for the press happened to me in the province of Kosovo. The only hotel in the capital, Priština, was packed with reporters, covering anti-Serb demonstrations by the ethnic Albanian opposition. Reporters were not welcome. One night, canisters of particularly potent tear gas were poured into the hotel's air ducts. In the clean air of the lobby, two men, who could have been characters out of Arthur Koestler's *Darkness at Noon*, appeared to enjoy the scene as dozens of sneezing and coughing reporters fled their rooms.

In the conflict raging between Serbs and Croatians, the attitude toward reporters can be described as paranoiac. At many roadblocks, I was told repeatedly by both Croatian militiamen and Serb insurgents that they considered us spies for the other side. But even in urbane Slovenia, treatment of the press can be psychologically brutal. I sat through many press conferences of the information minister, who caressed a P-38 in his hip holster while a dozen militiamen pointed Kalashnikovs at reporters. More often than not, information becomes disinformation and propaganda. But the Croatians' attitude towards information is mystifying. It's very difficult to find out anything at all in Zagreb. It's not a news blackout but an information black hole. Things did improve two weeks ago after a new government was installed. The new Cabinet seems to be more media-wise, and suddenly the first press releases on what was happening in the republic began to appear.

◆ ◆ ◆ ◆ ◆ ◆ ◆ ◆ ◆ ◆

It is not possible to predict which of those events in American public life will change our minds about something, will start us thinking in new ways. One of those events was the Senate hearing to confirm Clarence Thomas as a justice of the United States Supreme Court. A law professor from Oklahoma named Anita Hill testified that he had sexually harassed her. The situation was further complicated by the Senate committee's initial decision not to call Hill as a witness, to ignore her sworn statements alleging harassment. Thomas was confirmed and now serves on the Court, but the controversy started something in all our minds which can be invoked now by naming the woman who testified, Anita Hill. Nina Totenberg broke that story for NPR. We and the New York newspaper *Newsday* both claim credit for going first. Nina went with the story on the morning of the first Sunday in October.

Weekend Edition, Sunday, OCTOBER 6

TOTENBERG: In an affidavit filed with the Senate Judiciary Committee, law professor Anita Hill said she had much in common with Clarence Thomas and that she initially believed that common background was one of the reasons he hired her as his personal assistant ten years ago. Hill was raised in poverty on a farm in Oklahoma, she said, the youngest of thirteen children with strict disciplinarian parents. Like Thomas, she graduated from Yale Law School and, after a brief stint in a law firm, was hired by Thomas as his personal assistant at the Department of Education in 1981.

According to Hill's affidavit, Thomas soon began asking her out socially and refused to accept her explanation that she did not think it appropriate to go out with her boss. The relationship, she said, became even more strained when Thomas, in work situations, began to discuss sex. On these occasions, she said, Thomas would call her into his office to discuss work or, if his schedule was full, would ask her to go to a government cafeteria for lunch to discuss work. According to Hill's affidavit, Thomas, after a brief work discussion, would, "turn conversation to discussions about his sexual interests. His conversations," she said, "were vivid. He spoke about acts he had seen in pornographic films involving such things as women having sex with animals and films involving group sex or rape scenes. He talked about pornographic materials depicting individuals with large penises or breasts involved in various sex acts."

Hill said she repeatedly told Thomas she did not want to discuss those kinds of things but sensed that her apparent disgust only urged him on. "After some months," she said, "the conversations ended." Thomas had a girlfriend, and she thought the episode was over. When Thomas became head of the Equal Employment Opportunity Commission, Hill said, she moved with him, but some months after she went to the EEOC, said Hill, Thomas resumed his advances. He never touched her, she acknowledged in an interview, and he never directly threatened her job. But, she said, she was twenty-five, and she began to worry that she would soon suffer professionally if she did not submit.

HILL: I felt as though I did not have a choice, that I was going to have to submit to the pressure in order to continue getting good assignments, being able to work, and be comfortable in the work environment. If I had submitted to his pressure, I would not have felt comfortable anyway, but I felt that that was part of the bargain that he was trying to make, the message that he was trying to send to me, that if I did not submit, that I was not going to continue to be a good employee.

TOTENBERG: In 1983, after being hospitalized for what she believes was stress-related stomach pain, Hill resigned her job and took a teaching job at Oral Roberts Law School in Oklahoma. She says she will always remember her last conversation with Clarence Thomas at the EEOC.

HILL: Well, he made a statement about his behavior, that if I ever did disclose it, that it would be enough to ruin his career. My response was that I really just wanted to leave the experience behind me. I just wanted to get out.

TOTENBERG: Hill says that back in the early 1980s, she told only one person about what was happening to her, a friend she'd gone to law school with. The friend, now a state judge in the west, agreed to talk to NPR on condition her identity not be revealed. And she said that Hill had, indeed, told her, at the time, of the alleged harassment. When Thomas was nominated to the Supreme Court, Hill said she initially decided not to reveal her experience because she did not want to relive it. But in early September, she changed her mind.

HILL: Here is a person who is in charge of protecting rights of women and other groups in the workplace, and he is using his position of power for personal gain, for one thing. And he did it in a very, just ugly and intimidating way. But he is also really, in spirit and, I believe, in action too, violating the laws that he's there to enforce.

TOTENBERG: The law defines sexual harassment as including a hostile environment. By the time Clarence Thomas was testifying before the Senate Judiciary Committee the week of September 10, Hill had contacted the staff of the Judiciary Committee's chairman, Joseph Biden. She says that while Biden's staff seemed interested, it was not until ten days later, after repeated calls from her, that she was interviewed by the FBI. Her friend, the state judge, was also interviewed, as was Clarence Thomas. Thomas, according to Senate sources, told the FBI he had asked Hill to go out with him, but when she declined, he said, he dropped the matter. According to sources who've seen the FBI report, nothing in it contradicted Hill's story except nominee Thomas, who denied any harassment.

Hill is now a tenured law professor at the University of Oklahoma Law School. The dean of the school and the former dean of Oral Roberts speak highly of her, calling her an outstanding professional, a woman of the highest integrity. Last night the White House, responding to inquiries from NPR, issued a statement saying that it had been informed by the Senate Judiciary Committee on September 23 about the allegation against Thomas and that the president had directed the FBI to conduct an investigation. Two days later, the White House reviewed the report and, "determined that the allegation was unfounded." A White House spokesman said the president continues to believe that Judge Thomas is eminently qualified to serve on the Supreme Court, but several senators contacted by NPR say they are troubled by the Hill allegations and the long delay in investigating them by Chairman Biden.

1992

Michael Sullivan veers between producing and reporting stories for us. At times he's run my daily life, as what we call the line producer of *All Things Considered*. Michael will go anywhere and do anything. But in this case, he was in a peaceful place, the west of England, to see a medieval war engine, a trebuchet, fling a pig. Noah Adams, introducing this story, said with careful emphasis that the animals used were "recently deceased."

All Things Considered, JANUARY 2

SULLIVAN: In a grassy field in the rolling green hills of Shropshire near the Welsh border, Hugh Kennedy stands at the controls of his trebuchet, ready to send a five-hundred-pound pig carcass skyward. A trebuchet is a thirteenth-century siege engine, a sort of supercatapult. This one, built by Kennedy and his neighbor, dominates the horizon. But before today's launch, an explanation from Kennedy as to why the two men decided to shell out nearly twenty thousand dollars to build a trebuchet:

KENNEDY: Well, just for amusement. I mean, you can be pompous about it and say it's a medieval experiment if you like, but it was really just for a laugh. And obviously I'm interested in old weapons. I've always collected armor, and I'm interested in that line of thing.

SULLIVAN: As a young man, Hugh Kennedy's warrior spirit led him to enroll in the army. It was while attending the Sandhurst Military Academy, Britain's West Point, that he first got the idea to build a trebuchet from a sixteenth-century book on weaponry. The idea lay dormant in his mind for more than thirty years but came back, inspired in part by the thought of an Englishman succeeding where the entire French army had failed. Napoleon III commissioned a trebuchet in 1851, but it performed miserably. "In their day," says Kennedy, "that is to say, nearly eight hundred years ago, trebuchets were awesome machines of destruction, used with devastating effect against besieged medieval cities."

KENNEDY: I mean, they're bloody marvelous because, you see, castle walls were very, very thin because they weren't even made against cannon. And a half-a-ton rock landing on them would really do some damage. And of course it was the huge thing which terrified the besieged as well. And that was the lot of warfare in those days, was the old terror business.

SULLIVAN: Back then trebuchets threw captured soldiers, heavy rocks, even the occasional dead horse. All three being in short supply in Shropshire these days, Kennedy and his partner, Richard Barr, have had to improvise. They've thrown pigs, pianos, even a small car.

KENNEDY: What's going to happen? Let's work it out. The pig is going to fly too low, isn't it? No, no, it's going to go straight up in the air, isn't it, if we're not careful? It releases soon. The heavier the missile, the sooner it releases. So if it's set for a piano, and you shoot something that weighs more than a piano, you get the old trouble of it coming out backwards or straight up in the air. Straight up in the air would be very messy with a pig. Its guts would be draped all over this.

SULLIVAN: The trebuchet is more than four stories high and simple in design, working on roughly the same principle as a catapult, but with a much greater range and a heavier payload. A long wooden beam between two wooden posts is fitted with a five-ton weight on one end and a sling on the other. The ammunition goes into the sling, and then the weighted end is hoisted to the top of the structure and cocked by a tractor. Release the pin, and the weight swings down, so fast that it scoops the load up and over the machine and into space. But we're not quite there yet. Downfield a flock of sheep and a few cows keep a watchful eye on the commotion up above. The field is littered with the remains of dead pianos and mounds of dirt where previous cargoes have been buried where they landed.

Spectators are warned to keep a close eye on the pig's carcass, since it doesn't always land where it's supposed to. Then the signal is given, and what follows is the truly amazing spectacle of a pig in flight. The pig flies well, almost the length of two football fields, before bouncing heavily and skipping over a nearby fence. Kennedy is jubilant. It could be a new record. And he proudly examines the perfect pig-shaped imprint in the flattened grass where the animal first landed.

KENNEDY: I've seen a photograph of a thing in Norfolk in the First World War where they shot down a zeppelin, and there's a photograph of the hole where the German commander landed. This little kraut-shaped hole in the turf. This is just like it. Good, isn't it? The trouble is, it's taken that fence out, which is a real bore. It was quite a good throw, eh?

✦ ✦ ✦ ✦ ✦ ✦ ✦ ✦ ✦

Robert Siegel talked with Salman Rushdie in March, when he was in Washington to speak at a conference on freedom of expression. He had by that time been living in hiding for three years, following the publication of *The Satanic Verses*. The late Ayatollah Khomeini of Iran had issued a religious edict, a *fatwa*, declaring the book blasphemous, ordering Rushdie killed. The British equivalent of the Secret Service was protecting him because the edict amounted to state-sponsored terrorism. Rushdie was, at that time, hopeful that the release of hostages held in the Middle East might free the hands of Western countries to resolve his situation. In this conversation, he first talked about the politics, but then he described his personal situation.

All Things Considered, MARCH 25

SIEGEL: What is life like under sentence of this *fatwa*, of this edict? Is it boring?

RUSHDIE: It's not boring, it's never boring. It's extremely un-boring. But I want it to stop, please. I think I would like it to be more boring.

SIEGEL: You're a great comic writer. Do you find any humor in life under these circumstances?

RUSHDIE: Oh, there's been, I mean, one of the reasons why it's very frustrating is that at the moment, for reasons of security, I can tell you very little in the way of significant detail about how life is to answer your question in the way I would wish to answer it. I would really like to be at the other end of this so that I can answer the question properly because it has been, I mean, it has been comic. It has been surrealist. It has been very bizarre. You know, I mean, for example, I'm somebody who has always been in Britain associated with the left, really. Plenty of right-wing writers, journalists, so forth, have pointed out the irony of the fact that I should now be protected by the British secret police, who in many cases in the past I would have criticized. And, I mean, the fact is, the British secret police are perfectly sophisticated politically, and I have quite interesting conversations with them. And they have a kind of delicious fear that one of these days I'm going to write a book which takes the lid off the Special Branch, you see, and I do occasionally threaten them with this. And I pointed out to them once that there aren't a lot of left-wing writers in Britain who had had such an intimate experience of the inside workings of the British secret police, and one of them said to me, "Well, actually, there aren't a lot of right-wing writers either who have had this." So I do think I have — there's some material there.

SIEGEL: For the great book on the British Special Branch security forces.

RUSHDIE: Yeah, yeah. One of these days. I can't, literally, can't begin to tell you how strange it's been. Imagine a situation in which you can't do anything you did before. Well, that's to say you have to reinvent every single process of life. If you want to post a letter, you can't do it. What do you do? If you want to post a letter, it can't be posted anywhere in proximity to where you live. How do you get it posted? Your trousers rip because you've put on weight. How do you buy a pair of trousers? You send a policeman to buy them for you? You want to go for a walk. Well, you can't go for a walk out the front door because if somebody sees you, you can't go home again. So you have to drive three hours in order to have a half-hour walk and then drive three hours back.

I mean, I'm just giving you examples. In fact, even the most minute details of life alter completely. So you live in a situation where you literally have to reinvent the whole of daily life. And then it changes again, so you have to reinvent it again. Well, that's, I mean, in a way, quite educational. You learn a lot about yourself. I've learned a lot about what's essential and what's not essential. For example, I haven't seen the inside of my home in three years. Most of my stuff is there. I've had to learn how to let go of things, how to live with very few things. I've had to learn a completely new technique of writing because I was always a very conservative writer who had to sit at a certain place, you know, at a certain chair, at a certain desk, and have certain things around me. Well, that's a luxury I can't have now if I want to work. So I've had to learn how to write, literally speaking, on the run. So it's been, as they say, real.

SIEGEL: Your family.

RUSHDIE: Well, you know, that's what I'd like back most of all. I think, really, I've missed out, a quarter of my son's life, from the age of nine to the age of twelve, I've lost all that. And I haven't been able to do things that any father would take for granted, like, you know, throwing a ball in a park, or whatever it might be. Well, I've just had enough, frankly, and it seems to me that it's about time it stopped. And we've got to find a way of doing it this year because I'm just not going to live in this box anymore.

SIEGEL: But if there's no resolution, you can't simply decide to jump out of the box?

RUSHDIE: But there has to be. I mean, the point is the world doesn't stay the same. You know, one of the greatest dangers of politics is to believe there can be no change. I mean, just look at what's happened in the world in the last two or three years. Look at the speed of change. Why should we assume this is the only issue which can't change? Everything's changing every week at the moment, and in this particular case there are immensely good, solid reasons for believing that there will, there has to be, a change. In the end, governments act out of their self-interest. And there is a lot of self-interest both in the West and in Iran, and certainly on my part to get this thing fixed.

SIEGEL: Does it ever seem possible to you, despite all your optimism about the current equation and your conviction that it has to end and that things do change, that this could go on for decades?

RUSHDIE: Well, yes of course, it's theoretically possible. But it won't be possible for me because frankly there will come a point at which I won't live like this anyway. Because in the end you have to have some sort of life, and it's better to have some sort of life than none. Let me put it this way, one of the reasons it's been possible for governments to fudge the issue is because I've been invisible. Very high risk strategy is to be visible. What does it say about a government that can't protect its citizens against foreign terrorist attack? You know, at that point it becomes essential to solve the problem.

SIEGEL: If you're visible, then I as your fellow citizen have to empathize with your dilemma. If you hide, I don't.

RUSHDIE: Exactly. That's the problem. One of the double binds of this situation has been the thing that's safest to do has also been the thing that enables people to forget about you. You know, so here I am. One of the reasons for all this, as people have said to me, that clearly what this kind of a process does, this kind of coming out and talking to people and being around, is raise the stakes. And therefore, it raises the risks. And simply the calculation I've made is that that has to be done in order to achieve the solution. Because one of the things I've learned is that even though there are all sorts of people, very eminent people anxious to speak on my behalf and make the case for me, the media frankly, they won't listen to them. They will only listen to me. So if

I'm going to fight the case, I have to do it. And that means coming out and that means taking the risk.

✦ ✦ ✦ ✦ ✦ ✦ ✦ ✦ ✦ ✦

A fter leading police on a high-speed chase across Los Angeles, a black man named Rodney King was brutally beaten by the officers in full view of the nation. The violent arrest of Rodney King was videotaped by someone who happened to be nearby with a camera. The photographer took that tape to a local television station, and the world became a witness to what had happened on a dark California street. The echoes of that event could be heard in the spring of 1992 when a jury refused to convict the police officers, and south-central Los Angeles rioted. Again we saw a brutal beating on television, and another man, Reginald Denny, became a part of our history. Cheryl Devall covered the violence in Los Angeles. This report is about lives changed by those events.

All Things Considered, MAY 7

DEVALL: This past week it seems every conversation in LA has been long and intense. Some of my longest conversations have taken place with Roderick Brown, a security guard at the building housing NPR's Los Angeles bureau. Unlike the reporters traveling *to* South Central, Brown's been commuting *from* the home he's owned there for twenty years, or at least he used to. The night the riots began, Brown moved his wife and three children out to Monrovia, a suburb northeast of the city, where his mother and brothers live. His sons have already transferred into the schools there.
BROWN: I went back by the old house about three A.M. and boarded it up. It's a sad thing to do, you know. I talked to a few people, and they said, "Well, you're running out on the city." I kind of think the city ran out on me.
DEVALL: Brown says his family voted to stay in Monrovia because of what they saw in their LA neighborhood a week ago yesterday.
BROWN: My wife and I were walking outside to go up on Western Boulevard to see, you know, what was going on because there was a lot of smoke and stuff, fires and things, and she's from Belize and she never seen anything like this. Went up there, and a group of kids, couldn't

have been no more than fifteen, sixteen years old, about twenty of them had just ransacked a liquor store and shot up the liquor store window right on the corner. And they were walking up the street and they reached in this church and dragged this guy out of the church and they stood there and they beat him for about fifteen, twenty minutes. And I stood helpless because there were so many of them. They had guns, and I feared for my life if I tried to stop them. I told my wife right then, I looked at her, I said, "Go home, pack the kids up. Let's get them out of here."

DEVALL: Roderick Brown is a tall, sturdy man. He's an army veteran of the Vietnam War. He owns a gun and knows how to use it. But the part of him that works another daytime job as a nurse and coaches his son's Little League team hates the thought of living amid violence.

BROWN: What can you do, you know? I got three kids and I don't want to see them killed because some asshole's riding up and down the street shooting his gun because he's bad, he's got a gun. I don't want to see that, you know? And like I said, Mayor Tom Bradley and Chief Daryl Gates, you guys can have this city. I don't want nothing of it.

DEVALL: Brown is bitterly angry about the verdict in the police beating trial. Indeed, he refers to the LAPD as just one of the many gangs that terrorize the city. But Brown also is angry at his former neighbors, who, to his mind, have neglected the hard day-to-day work of maintaining a community.

BROWN: Your family is the most important thing, it should be the most important thing to you, and I wish so many other fathers would think the same way. Maybe if they did, we wouldn't have all these gangs and deterioration of societies and people wanting to get out.

DEVALL: Well, it's not necessarily a fair question, but I'm going to ask: When everybody like you leaves the city, then what?

BROWN: Until they clean up the city, people like me that want a good life and want to provide and want to be able to get up every morning and go to work. . . . I loved to go around here to Builder's Emporium on Saturday and buy something new for the house and make it look presentable and make my block look presentable. I like to encourage people, my neighbors and stuff, to cut their lawns, and if they can't do it sometimes I go out there and do it for them or something. Anything to make the city work, I'm willing to do. I've been here for twenty years and I've been a productive citizen for twenty years, all right? I feel now that the city has betrayed me. I'm pouring my life into this city, and for what? No more. No more.

DEVALL: The trade-off here involves more than one family and its taxes, more than four bedrooms and two baths, a new roof and two-car garage. Roderick Brown is losing hope. The city is losing a thirty-seven-year-old black man who believes in working hard, educating his children, and striving for something better. The costs of this damage are unlikely to show up in anyone's official assessment of what happened here last week, but the damage is real all the same.

✦ ✦ ✦ ✦ ✦ ✦ ✦ ✦ ✦

This was a curious election year. The sitting president dropped from ratings as high as any president has ever had, to underdog, in a matter of months. The Democrats were preparing to nominate a candidate from a new generation, a small-state governor who had protested the Vietnam War instead of fighting in it, an intense and attractive young man who had admitted to causing rough patches in his own marriage.

And suddenly, a third choice presented himself in the unlikely person of H. Ross Perot, a Texas billionaire. Perot volunteered to run for president on CNN's *Larry King Live* and began to rise in the polls. He was able to finance his own campaign, and voters who were unhappy or mistrustful of their choices liked the idea of Perot's independence. "We've got to put the country back in control of the owners," he said. "In plain Texas talk, it's time to take out the trash and clean out the barn." Ross Perot appealed to voters weary of Washington insiders, but in fact Perot had pulled some government strings himself. I was sitting in the House Ways and Means Committee in 1975 when an amendment was offered, a so-called designer amendment intended to help some unspecified person get a big tax break. I called Ross Perot and asked him about that, and it made him angry.

All Things Considered, MAY 13

WERTHEIMER: In the early seventies, Ross Perot was a young millionaire, not yet forty. He'd made a fortune from the idea that computers could be used to process insurance claims. Perot had contributed to the election of President Richard Nixon, and he told us the tax refund story begins with the president's men asking for his help to, as he put it, "pour a fortune" into an ailing Wall Street brokerage house, du Pont Glore Forgan.

PEROT: I got a call one morning from the White House staff, from the attorney general of the United States, from the secretary of the treasury, just about everybody who was breathing, that if du Pont Glore Forgan went under, the New York Stock Exchange would cease trading because the fund that was set aside in Wall Street to protect the brokerage houses was out of money, and would I go to New York immediately? I met with the who's who of the New York Stock Exchange: Bernard Lasker, Felix Rohatyn, so on and so forth. And the plea was that millions of people's pension funds, et cetera, et cetera, et cetera, would be damaged, all right?

WERTHEIMER: OK.

PEROT: And that I should do this as a civic service. So as I walked out of the room, one of my associates, Mort Meyerson, looked at me. He says, "You know, we ought to do this. You can keep a lot of people from getting hurt." I said, "All right." We talked about it. We agreed to do it.

WERTHEIMER: Did Ross Perot invest millions in a shaky brokerage business because it was a civic service? People we talked to who were familiar with his bailout said he and many other people saw it as an opportunity to make money. Wall Street was buried at that time in paper, unable to deal with paper stock transactions in a timely way, plagued by scandals in which securities were lost or stolen. Perot had solved the paper problems for a large segment of the insurance industry with his company, EDS, and he hoped to lead the way on Wall Street.

Peter Flannigan was a special assistant to President Nixon and reportedly one of the people who enlisted Perot in the bailout. Flannigan says he doesn't remember that, but as the staff person who dealt with influential businesspeople for the White House, he did write a memo about the bailout and Ross Perot.

FLANNIGAN: As the point man, I wrote a memorandum at the time, saying, "We shouldn't thank him because he did this as a commercial venture," not that we weren't happy he did it. And there are other memoranda saying that I, at his suggestion, called the stock exchange, with whom he was trying to get a data processing contract at the time, pointing out to them that they too would be glad if he made this investment and that having this contract would be a good thing.

WERTHEIMER: There was concern among some people in the investment community at the time that a major firm's failure could trigger a financial disaster. We talked to William Simon, then a partner at Salomon Brothers, later to be secretary of the treasury. Perot asked him to head du Pont Glore Forgan. Simon turned him down.

SIMON: The general notion that if du Pont went down that Wall Street wouldn't — would be tremendous, serious — was so ridiculous on the face of it that it wasn't even worthy of comment. Du Pont was a nothing firm, and its disappearance would be nothing, period.

WERTHEIMER: Despite solving many of du Pont Glore Forgan's problems and reorganizing the business, the company ultimately was liquidated because of economic conditions. Then, as Ross Perot explained it, he felt that having lost about sixty million dollars of his own money doing what he called a civic service at the request of government officials, the government should help him get some of that money back. Perot wanted to charge his losses off on taxes he'd already paid and get a rebate of millions of dollars, but the tax laws would have to be changed to make that possible.

PEROT: If you had done this as a corporation, you could have a capital loss carryback, and if you do it as an individual, you can't. OK? So then the question was raised in terms of was this fair to let corporations do this and not let individuals do this? — and raised this issue with the Ways and Means Committee openly, and they took a look at it and decided not to do it.

WERTHEIMER: That's not what happened. In fact, it was not open at all. As the *Wall Street Journal* described it in a front-page story, it was ten-thirty at night on the last day of a tax bill drafting session in the House Ways and Means Committee. An amendment was offered by a congressman from Georgia, Phil Landrum. Although questions were asked about who would benefit, no specifics were offered, debate was perfunctory, and, the *Journal* said, it went unnoticed that the Landrum amendment represents what may be the most gigantic tax break in history for one person. Congressman Pete Stark of California was on the committee. He told us committee members did not know who that late-night tax break was for.

STARK: It's quite likely that only somebody on the staff knew that. Certainly his lawyer, Sheldon Cohen, knew it. He probably drafted the amendment, but we were, for the most part, ignorant. A few of us voted against it anyway. It was a bad amendment on its face, but we weren't aware that I think fifteen million bucks went to one individual.

WERTHEIMER: According to members of the tax-writing staff of the committee, only two people on the staff knew the amendment was for Ross Perot, and they were sworn to secrecy. Treasury officials responsible for tax legislation at the time say they knew nothing about it. Mr. Perot's attorney, former tax commissioner Sheldon Cohen, confirmed for the *Wall Street Journal* that the amendment had been drafted for Perot. The *Journal* also noted fifty-five thousand dollars in campaign contributions given to Ways and Means Committee members after they won their elections. After the *Journal* piece appeared, there were disapproving newspaper editorials about those contributions, and members of Congress hastened to remove the Perot tax break on the House floor. Congressman Stark proposed its removal in debate.

STARK: The amendment dropped out, and Ross Perot, for one of the briefest moments in legislative history, had fifteen million bucks in his pocket one morning, and when he woke up the next morning it was gone again.

WERTHEIMER: We asked in the beginning of our interview with Ross Perot whether his business practices can really be squared with the rhetoric of his presidential campaign. And the other question is, Can Ross Perot get through a campaign where he is asked that kind of question?

PEROT: I assume this is the sole reason for your taped interview. And this is a classic setup. So now that you have — you know, whoever you're trying to do a favor for, you've done it, and I'm sure you had a smirk on your mouth as you got me into this. And since you misstated it totally, and I have given you the facts on it, what else would you like to know?

WERTHEIMER: I would like to pursue it further, but — let me just ask you —

PEROT: What is your show, anyhow?

WERTHEIMER: *All Things Considered.*

PEROT: And is this a radio program?

WERTHEIMER: It is. But let me ask you —

PEROT: It's really a radio program? You're not just somebody calling in?

WERTHEIMER: No, sir. No, sir.

PEROT: Now, do you — well, do you want to know more about it?

WERTHEIMER: I'm just wondering if you think that business practices may be somewhat more difficult —

PEROT: I don't —

WERTHEIMER: — to explain than, say, personal behavior has been to explain for some other candidates?

PEROT: I'm not going to worry about it for a minute, and I just assume that there'll be days when people like you show up, doing a favor for somebody, and you've done it.

✦ ✦ ✦ ✦ ✦ ✦ ✦ ✦ ✦ ✦

In the 1992 elections, the torch had passed to a new generation of reporters who were required to fly around the country on campaign planes, listening to the same speech several times a day, trying to peer through the political fog to find out what the campaign meant to voters. Elizabeth Arnold is now our political correspondent (my old job), and in May she heard some tough talk about President Bush from Californians just before their primary. It is a fact of life that Republicans must carry California to win and, as Elizabeth reported, California was not working for the president.

Morning Edition, MAY 28

ARNOLD: On one point, the White House, the Republican party, veteran political analysts, land developers, and defense industry workers all agree: President Bush has his work cut out for him here in California. The state is in the midst of a punishing recession. Unemployment is higher than the national average with the decline of the state's two key sectors, real estate and aerospace. And the state's Republican party is engaged in a civil war over taxes, abortion, gay rights, and the environment.

Even in 1988, when the state's economy was booming and with then President Ronald Reagan's support, Mr. Bush won only fifty-one percent of the vote against Michael Dukakis. Now, says California Congressman Dana Rohrabacher, Mr. Bush has been dealt a double blow which, combined with his lack of roots in California, severely undermines his reelection effort.

ROHRABACHER: Bush is going to have to fight this notion among conservatives, who basically dominate the party in California, that Bush is not a real conservative but is instead a moderate Republican who leans conservative. And on top of that, he doesn't have the California contacts and the California ties — family ties and background — that Ronald Reagan had. So it's going to be a tough road for the president.

ARNOLD: The Bush campaign is well aware of its problems here. Martin Wilson, statewide director, sits in the midst of unopened boxes, brooding in an empty suite of offices in Sacramento which will soon be filled with campaign workers. He's anxious for the president to "reach out," as he puts it, to California voters hit hard by the recession.

WILSON: And so I think he needs to come out here and, you know, let them know that he understands the anger and the frustration that our people are feeling in this state. People are worried about jobs and the fact that the economy in California — that we're in the worst recession we've had in this state since the 1930s. And frankly, while other parts of the country are beginning to pull out of it, we're not. And, I mean, he has got to acknowledge that.

ARNOLD: A few blocks away, Sal Russo, a long-time Republican consultant in this state, says reaching out isn't enough, especially in the wake of the Los Angeles riots, which he says exacerbated the president's problems.

RUSSO: It fits in with his image that the president's unfortunately got for himself that he's not doing anything, that his interest is foreign policy, not domestic.

ARNOLD: One key group of voters whose support Mr. Bush may have lost is known as the Reagan Democrats, blue-collar workers whose jobs are on the line because of the state's economic problems. Jeff Weir has been campaigning all over the state for Senator John Seymour.

WEIR: This year in California, you'll find this everywhere you go: the economy is the number-one, -two, and -three issue for just about everybody. And you can throw in other subplots, but the economy is it, and that's where the Reagan Democrats live.

ARNOLD: At four o'clock, just outside the putty-colored McDonnell Douglas plant in parking lot 10, workers are heading for their Camaros and pickup trucks. A huge sign says, HOME OF THE U.S. AIR FORCE C-17. This is also home of Reagan Democrats. Of the workers who stopped to talk, the majority had voted for Ronald Reagan and supported George Bush in 1988 but have no intention of backing Mr. Bush a second time. Tom Catching says the president has had his chance.

CATCHING: And he can, you know, whine all day long that it's Congress's fault for not passing legislation. I still see, you know, that it's no different in this company right here. If we can't get anything done, whose fault is that? You get rid of the CEO and you bring someone in, and you give them a shot. Maybe they don't do it either. You bring someone else in.

ARNOLD: Ron Cannick says Mr. Bush went back on his word.

CANNICK: He said he's no wimp. He is a wimp. "Read my lips. No new taxes." We've got new taxes. Saddam Hussein was a bum, yet why didn't he go after him after the — you know, after the war? I just think he's all B.S. There's no substance to it. It's all talk.

ARNOLD: This sense of inaction and betrayal is characteristic of another group of voters, conservative Republicans. California conservatives were furious at Republican Governor Pete Wilson for raising taxes. Wilson, like Bush, ran as a conservative antitax candidate. Assemblyman Tom McClintock, who is described as the most fiscally conservative Republican in the capital, supported both Wilson and Bush. He is now leading the charge against them. He says his constituents are angry.

MCCLINTOCK: I was walking precincts recently and encountered a fellow in his garage — Republican household. I said, "Are you folks Republicans?" And he glares. And usually the response you get is a big smile and a "You bet we are." This time — and his response was fairly typical, the response I've gotten from a lot of folks — was to glare at me, and say, "After George Bush? Hell no." So there are very, very serious divisions. Again, everything that Reagan built has been torn down by the current leadership in Sacramento and in Washington.

ARNOLD: The division within the Republican party is not only over fiscal issues. There are also bitter splits over abortion, gay rights, gun control, and the environment.

Bill Bradley, a columnist and editor of a political newsletter, *New West Notes*, says Republican feuding leaves President Bush in an awkward position.

BRADLEY: President Bush, nice guy, is trying to find middle ground. He's standing on two logs in the middle of a river. The logs are getting further apart, and he's about to do a very embarrassing split.

ARNOLD: The Bush campaign dismisses interparty skirmishes in California, but Ed Rollins, the Reagan-Bush campaign manager in 1984 and a thirty-year veteran of California politics, says the conservative base with all its warring factions can't be ignored.

ROLLINS: So I would argue very strenuously that the president needs to get the conservatives back in the fold. He obviously needs to start talking about things that matter to them. And if he does, then he'll win. If he doesn't, if you lose five or ten percent of your conservative base, it's awful hard to win California.

ARNOLD: That view is shared by California Congressman Dana Rohrabacher.

ROHRABACHER: We're not talking about building an organization. What we're talking about is getting people out of their houses and down to the polls. And people have to be motivated to do that, and there's a lot of cynicism in America today. And President Bush has been the president for four years. So he's going to have to make sure that those people are willing to get out of their house and go and vote.

ARNOLD: Rohrabacher cautions that the Bush campaign shouldn't take for granted the state's inclination toward Republicans in past presidential elections. There's a popular belief that national trends begin in California, and there's growing concern among Republicans that the state that launched the Reagan revolution may lean in some new direction.

✦ ✦ ✦ ✦ ✦ ✦ ✦ ✦ ✦ ✦

The American elections went on against a backdrop of increasing violence in Bosnia, as the parts of the crumbling Yugoslav confederation renewed the ancient battles of the Balkans. Tom Gjelten spent time in Sarajevo with Gordana and Ivan Knežević. He is a philosophy professor, she a newspaper editor. Two of their three children had been sent to stay with friends in Cairo. Their teenaged son, Boris, remained with them. They talked about the separation of their family, about the dangers and privations of Sarajevo, but they also talked about the ethnic warfare from their own perspective.

All Things Considered, JULY 8

GJELTEN: Serb paramilitary forces throughout Bosnia-Hercegovina have for the past two months been engaged in a brutal campaign of what they call ethnic purification. The Serb forces drive Muslims and Croats from their homes, in some cases even killing them, if refugee stories are true. The object is to establish clean Serb enclaves. Sarajevo and other cities with large mixed populations, meanwhile, are simply bombarded day after day in an evident effort to force their surrender to the Serb forces that encircle them. Gordana Knežević has reported on the Serb offensive in Bosnia since the beginning of the war. The experience, she says, has soured her on the Yugoslav peace movement in which she was once active.

GORDANA: I must admit I am not devoted to the peace anymore in spite of all this evil which is going around us. Now I don't want peace at the moment. At the moment, I want for this war to be finished in a justified way. It means that the other side have to be conquered, and without real conquer, there is no good end of it. At the moment, I don't believe in any kind of dialogue, and I don't believe that it's possible to make dialogue with this extreme Serb side.

GJELTEN: What's remarkable about this statement is that Gordana Knežević is herself a Serb, an anti-Serb Serb, she explains. Her whole life, she says, she and her friends have considered their ethnic back-grounds irrelevant and insignificant. Now they find nationalist leaders on all sides encouraging people to think of themselves first as Serb, Croat, or Muslim and to stand against other ethnic groups. Gordana and Ivan are dismayed.

GORDANA: By my parents' origin, I should be a Serb. But if I am one, I'm a bad Serb anyway. My husband is a Croatian.

GJELTEN: Do you feel like a Croat?

IVAN: My biggest disappointment was the fact that I was forced to think about nation at all. And being almost fifty, I just can't pull myself together as a Croat or whatever just because all my relation with other people are not based on their nationality. So we form a family of bad Croat and bad Serb.

GJELTEN: Boris holds up his hand. With his keener hearing, he can tell that an artillery shell is coming. There are explosions a moment after Boris's warning.

GORDANA: Before the war, if you would ask me what I would do in the case of shelling, I will tell you I would hide in the darkest spot of my house, but once it came I was afraid at first moment, but after a few days of shelling, I simply was not afraid anymore. You can be afraid for some time, but you can't be afraid all time.

GJELTEN: Gordana and Ivan and others in Sarajevo who stubbornly continue to go to work in the midst of artillery bombardment and sniper fire say they do so as a form of resistance. The enemy, Gordana says, is determined to bring life in Sarajevo to a halt. So refusing to stop working, in Gordana's case, putting out a newspaper day after day, becomes a way of defying the relentless shooting. There have been days, Gordana says, when the only two things sold on the streets of Sarajevo were bread and her newspaper. But she finds it's becoming more difficult, not because it's any more dangerous to get to work. Rather it's getting harder and harder just to think clearly. Gordana says she is losing the ability to analyze facts, to assess each day's develop-ments, to look back and to look ahead.

GORDANA: I think that the worst part of it, that we lost any sense of time, and every day, I must think ten times a day, Which day is it today? And I can't remember which day in the week it is and which date in the month it is, and I can't even remember which month it is. And if you want me to be very honest, I almost forgot which year is this. We lost any sense of seasons in the year, and we lost any sense of the fu-ture. I don't know when the spring was finished, and I don't know when the summer started. And there are only two seasons now. There is a war season, and somewhere in the world, there is a peace season. Not for us here, no.

GJELTEN: What do you think, Ivan?

GORDANA: He thinks we should turn the lights down.

GJELTEN: At the sound of explosions, we get up from the kitchen table and move to the hallway.

GORDANA: Ivan thinks that the worst part of it is that the normal life is destructed or whatever looks like normal life is absolutely lost. And he miss — he miss the children very much.

IVAN: Yes.

GORDANA: And all situation is humiliating.

♦ ♦ ♦ ♦ ♦ ♦ ♦ ♦ ♦

M ara Liasson became our White House correspondent after this campaign, in part because of her uncompromising coverage of candidate Bill Clinton. In this profile, which ran after the conventions, as the real campaign was getting started, she was positively prophetic.

Morning Edition, OCTOBER 6

LIASSON: When you ask long-time Clinton watchers in Arkansas to describe the way their governor makes decisions, they all love to tell one particular story. It goes like this. At the very last minute Clinton had vetoed a bill that would have given tax credits to contributors, to state colleges and universities. The legislature had gone home for the night, so he slipped the vetoed bill under the house clerk's door. Then, as *Arkansas Times* Editor John Brummett recounts, he called the lobbyists for the colleges to tell them the bad news.

BRUMMETT: And they got him to change his mind. He sent a state trooper out to the house clerk's office, who had to get a coat hanger out of a closet and go under the door to fish out the vetoed bill, take it back to the mansion, where Clinton could take a black pen and mark through the "DIS," leaving the bill approved.

LIASSON: For Brummett, this is an example of how Bill Clinton has trouble making hard decisions and sticking to them.

BRUMMETT: I find him overly conciliatory rather than tough. I find him obsessed with trying to please. Usually he's well intentioned, has some high-minded rhetoric, has some sound ideas, and then, as the opposition begins to develop to some of the specifics, he sometimes too quickly bails out.

LIASSON: Clinton's former chief of staff and top campaign aide, Betsey Wright, agrees that the story of the unvetoed bill is an extraordinary anecdote, but she insists this example of his governing style is the exception, not the rule.

WRIGHT: For reasons I don't completely understand, he recognized the valid points that both sides were making on it and recognized them as valid. You know, there isn't anybody who regrets all of the developments on that veto and unveto more than Bill Clinton does.

LIASSON: No one denies that Bill Clinton has a gift for recognizing the valid points on both sides of an issue, but whether that's a strength or a weakness depends on who you talk to. To his supporters, Clinton is a great conciliator, someone who has used his talent for consensus building to pass a good deal of substantial legislation. To his detractors, he's too flexible, too quick to cave in to special interests. It wasn't always this way. During his first term in office, when he was just thirty-two, Clinton had an ambitious agenda. He tangled with Arkansas's powerful interests. He took on the timber industry and the power companies and he raised taxes for a highway program. Then he got beat. Thrown out of office in 1980, he spent two years reexamining the way he governed, and he changed. Even unabashed Clinton boosters, like state legislator Jodi Mahoney, say when Clinton made it back to office, he was more cautious.

MAHONEY: He came back then, and I think that maybe he went a little bit too far the other way, where he did want to listen too much, accommodate too much.

WRIGHT: Those people think that it's fine just to make speeches about what you want the world to be and not ever do anything about getting it there. Bill Clinton didn't become more cautious. He did not become less idealistic. He became smarter about how to make progress.

LIASSON: Beginning in his second term, Clinton put far more importance on building a consensus before moving. A policy wonk, he studies the issues exhaustively, searching for options that have the best chances of bringing as many points of view as possible together. He often relies on blue-ribbon panels and commissions. He spends lots of time explaining his proposals to the public, holding meetings all over the state, never getting too far ahead of what the voters want.

Professor Ernie Dumas, a former editorial writer for the *Arkansas Gazette*, says that if Clinton thinks he's going to lose, he'd rather not make the fight, but when he decides to fight, he does it the same way he campaigns, relentlessly and personally, with lots of one-on-one contact.

DUMAS: He had an unusual style here that we hadn't seen before in which he would come down from the third floor and hang around the hallways along with all the other cigar-smoking lobbyists and button-holing legislators, going into committee rooms and holding up his hand and asking to testify.

LIASSON: Clinton seems to have a natural salesman's belief in his own ability to convince and persuade. He's described as a sympathetic listener, but sometimes, says John Brummett, the energy Clinton invests in convincing people he's open to all points of view backfires.

BRUMMETT: I can provide testimony. I mean, as a reporter and columnist, I have sat in his reception area and seen opposing legislators or lobbyists go into his office, come out, and they both think he's on their side. It has happened many, many times.

MAHONEY: I've been in those meetings that you're talking about. The governor simply did not make the commitments that people thought they heard. And it's not that he's being tricky or anything. It's just that he's talking about the issue, talking about the different sides.

LIASSON: More than anything else, this is what earned Clinton his derogatory nickname, Slick Willie. On the campaign trail he's been accused of pandering, tailoring his answers to be the least offensive to his particular audience. In the Midwest recently, he slammed President Bush's proposal to cut the capital gains tax as he spoke to a working-class audience in Michigan. The next day he touted his own targeted capital gains tax cut to a business audience in Chicago. He's given carefully worded answers to questions about personal matters, like the draft, marijuana, and Gennifer Flowers, and he's danced around thorny issues, like the North American Free Trade Agreement. He likes to tell voters that he is pro-labor, pro-business, pro-environment, and pro-growth. In Arkansas, this desire to please meant spending lots of energy winning over opponents. Supporters and critics of Clinton's joke that it's better to be his enemy than his friend.

BRUMMETT: You want something from Bill Clinton, history would suggest over the years that you be against him. He just thinks, One of these days, if I could talk to everybody, I'm going to get a hundred percent of the vote. So naturally if you're motivated by that sort of thing, the people you're most interested in are the ones that you haven't gotten to vote for you yet.

LIASSON: If Bill Clinton becomes president, his supporters say he would use his prodigious powers of persuasion and consensus building to find solutions to the problems he cares about: education, health care, job training, and the economy. His critics say he would be unable to confront the powerful interest groups who will fight against him. Ernie Dumas says he thinks Clinton has the skills and ability to lead the country, but he cautions that one thing would be very different. In a poor state like Arkansas, when Clinton raised taxes he was always able to offer voters something tangible in return: better highways, more teachers, or smaller classes, something a president is in less of a position to do.

DUMAS: Well, it's a different equation altogether. He's not going to be raising money to expand services but to reduce the deficit, ultimately, is what he'll have to do. I'm anxious to see what he'll do. I'm not sure whether he'll make the tough decisions that he has to, the things that Ross Perot, for example, is talking about. But liberated from a race two years hence, maybe he can make those tough decisions.

LIASSON: If the achievement of his lifelong goal helps him overcome some of his deep-seated caution, it probably won't change other hallmarks of Clinton's style. Clinton has told voters that if he's elected he'll continue to hold forth in his favorite format, answering questions from voters in televised town meetings, and his aides predict there'll be a lot of 800 numbers installed in the White House.

✦ ✦ ✦ ✦ ✦ ✦ ✦ ✦ ✦

Liane Hansen, the host of *All Things Considered* on Sunday, offered a cautious view of the next president, one colored by personal history and past tragedy but one that was shared by many Americans in the fall and winter of that election year. It ran on the anniversary of President Kennedy's death.

Weekend Edition, Sunday, NOVEMBER 22

HANSEN: I was an eighth-grader at Woodland Prep, a public junior high, just behind Robert Goddard's lab in Worcester, Massachusetts. The school day ended at noon, so my friends and I often would while away the hours over ten-cent Cokes at the counter at Woolworth's. The store sold TVs, which were turned on for the customer's enjoyment. That's where I heard the news twenty-nine years ago today. Not much thought was given to the fact that a president had been assassinated. No, I considered it murder of a husband, a father, and a man from my state. There'd been no school on inauguration day. My mother knew someone who knew someone who had been invited. John F. Kennedy was practically family.

Later that weekend we were sitting around the kitchen, where we had wheeled in the big black-and-white to watch Lee Harvey Oswald. I saw my first man die for real on television. The high school years flew by like calendar pages in a cheesy movie. My friends and I studied history, talked about civil rights, and engaged in political debate, our arguments tinged with the sort of optimism that is only possible in the rarefied air of an all-girls Catholic academy.

Then Martin was taken out. Bobby was almost too much to bear, and optimism trickled away with his blood on the hotel kitchen floor. By the time John Lennon was gunned down, the era of creeping cynicism was in full swing — Vietnam, Watergate, Squeaky Fromm, John Hinckley. Then there were the hostages and questions: Will the job last past the next rent payment? Why does the subway fare card machine give better interest than the bank?

But something happened when the Berlin Wall came down. We began to talk about democracy and the nature of a democratic society. This past summer we defined it. Three men ran for president, and we talked about who we are and what we stand for and what we want to get done. We voted in greater numbers than before. So did a new generation.

On election day, I remembered the video the Democrats showed at their convention of the contender as a young man gazing intently at the face of his president. Now, Bill Clinton is no Jack Kennedy, and it will take more than a few newly painted set pieces to transform this shining city on a hill into Camelot. After all, this is the kind of town where people put Clinton-Gore bumper stickers on their cars after the election.

When Mr. Clinton came to Washington this past week, I watched the face of a twelve-year-old girl light up when, while walking up Georgia Avenue, her new president promised her an invitation to the inauguration. I heard his airline pilot's voice reassure everyone that things were going to get better. And I thought maybe, just maybe, there is a place in the hearts and minds of the next generation for a thing called hope.

✦ ✦ ✦ ✦ ✦ ✦ ✦ ✦ ✦

Bailey White is not an eccentric little old lady, but she does live on the edge of a great swamp. Until her mother died in 1994, the two of them lived there together. Bailey has written a great deal about her mother and food, including their treaty on potential meals made from pheasants and other creatures found dead by the side of the road. The road-kill agreement involved times, locations, and license plates, and was strictly enforced by Bailey. But there were dangers everywhere.

All Things Considered, DECEMBER 16

WHITE: It was a blustery, damp fall evening when I came home to find my mother in the middle of one of her ongoing experiments with lethal and nonlethal foods. Last time it had been the big floppy leaves of the deadly poison pokeberry bush.

"If you boil them up five times and pour off the water each time, you get rid of the poison. Then you boil them up a sixth time and they're safe to eat. Have a taste." She held out a forkful of green slime.

"But what's the point?" I asked. "You've poured out all the nutrition with the poison."

"Nutrition, nutrition," she snapped as she sat down to a steaming bowl of poke leaves. "Are the French thinking about nutrition when they make *pâté de foie gras*? Are the Mexicans thinking about nutrition when they grow jalapeño peppers?"

She shook a tablespoonful of Louisiana hot sauce on her poke leaves and dug in.

"But my question is, Mama, what are you thinking about when you cook poison for food?" I asked.

She savored the poke leaves for a second, waved her hand in the air, and said, "Delicious."

But on this fall day, she has collected mushrooms. She is deep in her favorite field guide among the mushrooms and the kitchen table is littered with fungi. There's the grayish black trumpet of death with its hollow stem, and the sticky red cap of *Boletus frostii*, and beside it a cluster of something ghastly white with fleshy tatters and frills drooping over a single stalk like the bouquet of a witch-bride.

Mama has carefully arranged several mushrooms on sheets of white paper to collect their spore deposits for identification. The spores drift down onto the paper from between the gills of the mushrooms and leave a telltale dusting that can mean the difference between life and death. From two similar-appearing mushrooms, a black spore deposit means edible and choice while a dusting of lilac says instant death.

"Supper?" I ask.

She licks her fingers and flips the pages in her book. "Not quite yet," she says. "I had the cream sauce in the double boiler, but I just want to check one thing first."

"Don't tell me we're eating the one where you have to parboil until no more yellow scum floats to the surface?" I say.

"No," she says. "That's *Amanita muscaria.* This one" — and she twirls a big white mushroom by the stem and reads to me from her book — "'edibility not known,' but other books say 'taste — marked but pleasant.'"

They recommend if you're unsure of an identification, feed it to chickens. If the chickens don't die within twenty-four hours, you're safe to eat it. We don't have any chickens, but our old canary bird, Howard, gives out a shrill squawk and cowers in the back of his cage. I get out the box of Cheerios and the one-percent milk. Mama cuts up the white mushroom and stirs it into the sauce. We make room among the mushrooms on the kitchen table to eat our supper. I keep imagining that airborne lilac-colored spores are wafting into my Cheerios. That night, I check on Mama several times. Each time, she is still alive and sleeping peacefully. After twenty-four hours, I relax. And soon it will be winter. With the cold, dryer weather, the mushrooms will not emerge. But in the spring, I know, out she'll go again with her knife and basket among the mushrooms to play her little culinary games with death.

1993

Bob Mondello reviews movies for *All Things Considered*, but this piece is more a memory than a movie review. It started with the film *Matinee* with John Goodman, loosely based on the career of William Castle. Castle is best known for promoting his film *The Tingler* by wiring theater seats to give viewers a small electrical shock. The movie took Bob back to the days of B movies, when radiation had remarkable properties.

All Things Considered, JANUARY 29

MONDELLO: I saw my life flash before me in *Matinee*. I was an impressionable thirteen-year-old who ducked and covered during the Cuban missile crisis, an event that is just taking place as this film begins. I knew as well as any kid my age that the atomic radiation coming from those missiles could cause tiny bugs and lizards to mutate into fifty-foot monsters. Every Saturday at horror matinees, I heard dialogue exactly like the dialogue in *Mant, Matinee*'s film within a film:

WOMAN: How could such a thing happen, Dr. Gavall?

DOCTOR: The ant's saliva must have gotten into Bill's bloodstream and gone straight to his brain, just as the radiation, which is measured in units roentgens, was released.

WOMAN: And that's how he became a —

DOCTOR: Mant.

MONDELLO: But watching *Matinee*, I wasn't just identifying with the young hero who attends these movies. Before I became a critic, I was a movie publicist for a chain of suburban movie theaters in the Washington area, doing much the same things that John Goodman's character does when he promotes *Mant*. The owner of the theaters was Paul Roth, a showman's showman who's still in the business and who taught me the art of Hollywood ballyhoo, an art which, as a bona fide hippie when I went to work for him in 1971, I wasn't entirely attuned to.

My idea of a great movie promotion was to get the fire department to bring a hook and ladder truck to an opening of *The Towering Inferno* or to organize a martial arts demonstration in the lobby for *The Karate Kid*. I was pretty proud of those, actually, but Roth was from the old school. He cut his teeth on movie promoting in the 1950s, when theaters would do anything to combat TV. Some offered dinner plates with every movie ticket. You could collect the whole set if you went often enough. Roth liked to stage fifteen-hour dusk-to-dawn horror-thons at his drive-ins, complete with mandatory consent forms at the door, just like the ones in *Matinee*. Every Halloween, we had our refreshment stands put red food coloring in whatever that butter-flavored stuff is they squirt on popcorn so we could call the result a bucket of blood. When we opened a doctor drama called *Coma*, all our employees had to wear surgical gowns. For *Friday the Thirteenth*, we sent an usher rushing through the theater in a hockey mask to shock people during the end credits. This was what we termed "scaring the yell out of patrons," and there was no question it worked. So did more benign efforts. When a picture called *The Bride* came along, Roth's first instinct was to find a justice of the peace and a couple who wanted to get married, and stage a wedding in the theater's center aisle on opening night. A local bakery donated the wedding cake and, to my astonishment, we got coverage in the *Washington Post* for that one.

My crowning glory, as I recall, was the day I came back from a search of rural Pennsylvania junkyards with the tail section of a one-engine plane. I had bought it for about two hundred dollars, and, with the help of a projectionist, a manager, and two ushers, we managed to hang it off the front of our theater right above the marquee. The idea was that it would seem to have crashed into the title, *Airplane II*. We knew it looked right when, while we were roping it into place, a motorist screeched to a halt on the busy street below, leaped out of his car, and yelled to us not to worry, that he was going to call an ambulance.

I can't prove that any of this actually sold tickets, but my gut tells me it had to. It made going to the movies an experience you couldn't get elsewhere, certainly not at home watching the tube. These days, when I go to glistening nationally owned multiplexes, everything from the ticket booth to the projection booth is run by computer. The food selection is better, the stereo sound wraps around you, the floors aren't as sticky, and none of it matters. I miss the showmanship.

Matinee, though it's primarily aimed at teenagers who think of the sixties as ancient history, made me nostalgic for what they now miss, and I suspect it will do the same for pretty much anyone who once believed as fervently as I did that radiation could make ants fifty feet tall.

◆ ◆ ◆ ◆ ◆ ◆ ◆ ◆ ◆

Daniel Pinkwater's favorite topics are dogs and food. He's written wonderful essays for us on both subjects, funny and touching accounts of dogs he has known and loved and food he loves almost as much.

All Things Considered, APRIL 16

PINKWATER: "With rue my heart is laden / For golden fries I had, / For many a Polish sausage, / When I was a Chicago lad."

The Hudson River valley, where I live, is a beautiful place. There are gentle, rolling meadows, picture-book farms, and pleasant forests. From any hilltop you can see the blue Catskills in the distance. Hawks circle overhead, sometimes an eagle, and I often see deer on my morning walk. Too bad these things mean nothing to me. Well, they don't mean nothing. They just aren't as important as some other things. I didn't know this until last week. If you had asked me, I would have said I was happy and fulfilled. I had forgotten who I was and what was what, where I'd come from and in general what is the meaning of life. Now I know. I'm a man in touch with his inner reality.

This is what happened. Jill and I were driving down Route 9 toward the southern part of Dutchess County. We don't go down there very often. It's your typical suburban commercial blight, mall after mall, traffic and congestion. There was formerly a city there, Poughkeepsie, but feeble-minded planning cut the heart out of it in the seventies, and now there's nothing but the edges, with no center. In the midst of this hopelessness, in a tatty strip mall, we found a little enterprise we hadn't noticed before, Hershel's Chicago Hot Dogs. "Shall we give it a try?" Jill asked. Now, I am from Chicago. I know what a Chicago hot dog is. It bears only the most general resemblance to the New York street frank, the sphere of influence of which extends as far as Boston, to Baltimore, and all up and down the eastern seaboard. "Sure, let's try it," I said, but only out of desperation. I knew the best we could hope for would be something less than a complete disaster.

For those unfortunate to have never had one, I will attempt to describe a Chicago hot dog. Words aren't adequate to the task, but I will try. First, it's on a poppy seed bun, which is doughy and substantial but not heavy. The bun is lightly steamed at the point of serving. The hot dog is all beef, spicier than the New York variety. It is steamed and has a natural casing. It snaps when you bite into it and squirts hot deliciousness. A variant is the Polish sausage, which the gods ate on Olympus. This is what goes on it: yellow mustard, bright green pickle relish, chopped onion, a kosher pickle spear, two slices of tomato, two tiny but devastating peppers, and, all-important, celery salt. All of this is fitted together with fiendish cleverness, enabling the eater to get most of it in his mouth and only a little on his shirt. If there are fries, they are hand-cut, skinny, and glorious.

The chance of encountering a genuine Chicago dog in this part of the state — where even the New York City dog is relatively unknown and the natives delude themselves with those pink, skinless things on supermarket rolls — seemed vanishingly small. But so lonely and desperate and miserable and starved for some vestige of culture were we that we marched in and ordered one apiece. They looked right. They smelled right. We carried them to a little table and made ready to address them. I cautioned myself not to be a sucker yet one more time. Repeated experience has taught me to hold back a little enthusiasm, to tide me over the inevitable disappointment that lurks behind most experiences. I took my first bite. It was completely authentic.

It turns out that Hershel is a guy who retired from a big job in the recording industry and created a Chicago hot dog stand by way of a hobby, business, and work of art. The hot dogs, the buns — everything — even the mustard, is imported from Chicago. As I munched, thirty-five or forty years rolled back, compressed, extended, and realigned. A flood of clear and distinct memories that had been locked away suddenly became immediate and accessible. The meaningless suburban highway transformed, became a street with streetcars. The next errant breeze might carry the sound of distant cheering at Wrigley Field or the redolence of the stockyards.

I let on that the tears in my eyes were because of the peppers, but it was not so. Only the ringing in my ears and the itching of my scalp was because of the peppers. The tears were about something else. The next day we were back. As can easily happen, we went to the wrong strip mall, and in the spot that should have been Hershel's was a vacant store.

"I knew it," I said. "It's gone." "Like Brigadoon," Jill said. But we soon realized our mistake. In the next little retail outcropping, there was Hershel's, dispensing the genuine article. And the experience was not diminished when repeated. More little rents in the fabric of memory were closed up while I filled up.

I've been back several times now. It's working like a high-speed, deluxe psychoanalysis — with the option of grilled onions. The days of my childhood and adolescence, those critical moments which set the course for the rest of my life, are all linking up like Vienna sausages. I think I have the makings of a novel here. Marcel Proust, eat your heart out.

◆ ◆ ◆ ◆ ◆ ◆ ◆ ◆ ◆

O ur newly elected president had already begun work on the major initiative of his campaign, health care reform. During this year he presided over the beginnings of peace in the Middle East, the famous handshake between Israel's Prime Minister Yitzhak Rabin and the leader of the PLO, Yasir Arafat. But President Clinton also faced difficult decisions on social issues, particularly on abortion and gays in the military. New laws were under consideration in the spring of 1993 to guarantee access to abortion clinics when Kathy Lohr went to a training session in Florida for opponents of abortion. The training was done by Operation Rescue, an organization that blocked clinic entrances. Protesters were preparing to face an administration with a different attitude toward abortion.

Morning Edition, APRIL 12

LOHR: The twenty-two recruits at Operation Rescue's training camp stand at the back of an abortion clinic in Port Saint Lucie, Florida, where they've come on a bus to practice part of what they've learned over the past twelve weeks. They sing, pray, picket, and do whatever they can outside clinics to try to convince women to change their minds about abortion. Seventeen-year-old Jessica Uchtman has tears in her eyes as she tries to communicate with women inside the clinic.

UCHTMAN: It's not worth it. Think about it! This is serious. You will be hurt, but your baby will be ripped apart.

LOHR: Jessica is shouting to them through closed windows. She's learned that some women could change their minds about abortion even after they've entered a clinic. It's evening now and the second time in a single day that the group has come to stand here. Tonight no one attempts to block the doors to the clinic, the action that has made Operation Rescue famous.

Being visible on the street is just part of what the students learn in school. Much of the time is spent in classrooms at a couple of local churches and in a kind of basic training designed to teach recruits how to be effective leaders. Keith Tucci is the executive director of Operation Rescue National and one of the trainers here. Focusing on the Bible, knowing the Scripture and quoting from it to support the anti-abortion position, is a big part of the training. Tucci seems at home handing out suggestions during a course on preaching.

TUCCI: And don't be afraid to use adjectives. "We see God's response here": no. "We see God's definite, without contradiction, response to this." OK? Just put some adjectives in there.

What I ask the class every day is, "Where are you going to be ten years from now? Are you going to be in the battle ten years from now?" And we're trying to teach them this is a long-term struggle, and it takes people that are educated, it takes people that are well spoken, it takes people that can interpret the issues, but most of all it takes people that are persistent and aren't going to be intimidated and aren't going to be driven off by some other situation.

LOHR: The issue of intimidation comes up a lot here. Tucci says those who don't agree with them try to intimidate antiabortion activists to make them stop protesting. Abortion rights activists, on the other hand, have long called Operation Rescue's tactics intimidation and harassment.

Tucci is teaching the class to trace license plates and social security numbers, search court records, and locate the home addresses of people who work at the clinics, but he denies that protesters stalk, follow, or harass clinic doctors or staff.

TUCCI: We've got to identify every practicing abortionist in the community, OK? We've got to identify them by their real name, and then we have to try to find out their last residence.

LOHR: What has heightened tension surrounding Operation Rescue's training school is the murder of a doctor last month in Pensacola, Florida, about five hundred miles away. Some abortion rights advocates say that the antiabortion movement, including this group, didn't condemn the shooting strongly enough and that this movement attracts the radical and the violent. Operation Rescue's official statement opposes the murder, saying the group stands for all life, born and unborn.

Student Mark Gabriel was a civil engineer before he decided to join the antiabortion movement. He paid six hundred dollars to attend this training session. Mark says it's not right for anyone to take justice into their own hands. Yet he has little sympathy for the doctor.

GABRIEL: This was a murder of a mass murderer, and just as, you know, we didn't mourn Hitler's death or someone who's, you know, raped and killed women, a mass murderer, you know, we don't mourn those people's death. I don't believe it was appropriate to mourn. I believe it was a tragedy as all deaths are tragedies.

LOHR: Michelle Cramer protests regularly outside Minneapolis clinics.

CRAMER: I'm always afraid that it'd happen to their side first, that someone has been killed.

LOHR: If there's violence, Michelle says, it comes from the other side, the abortion rights activists. She says she's been pushed down into the street and sprayed with Mace. She's not surprised by the murder, but she, too, believes it was wrong. Michelle had an abortion six years ago. She's here in part because she now believes abortion is wrong, evil. And Michelle intends to translate her beliefs and her training here into action.

CRAMER: What we're doing is normal Christianity, is what everybody should be doing. I am not a radical and I'm not pro-life. I'm a Christian.

LOHR: Michelle, Mark, and the others at this Operation Rescue training ground say they're devoted to nonviolent civil disobedience. They say the furthest they will go to stop abortion is to sit in front of clinic doors and risk arrest. They blame the heightened tension in this battle over abortion on the Clinton administration. The president's promised reversal of antiabortion policies, Cramer says, is frustrating some who she calls extremists. For Michelle and Keith Tucci, there's no question that this is war.

TUCCI: We can generate the ground troops, and that, ultimately, I believe, is what is going to turn the tide in America.

LOHR: In one of the few strategy sessions open to the media, Tucci told the class that at times rescuers have been fooled by so-called plants, women who are only pretending they're going to have an abortion. Protesters blocking a clinic end up getting arrested before the real patients get there. To avoid this, Tucci described what he called "the wave rescue," sending in protesters a few at a time.

TUCCI: Five people go and sit in front of the door. They get arrested. They get dragged away. The paddy wagon comes. Big commotion.

The police lines go up. OK? Everything's stalemated. Another woman tries to come. The whole scenario starts over again. All day long this place looks like a war zone.

LOHR: This weekend the clinics in Melbourne and Fort Pierce became the latest battlefields, a kind of graduation for the Operation Rescue class. Most of the recruits were arrested, some twice. Michelle Cramer and fifty others refused to obey an injunction and stay thirty-six feet away from the Melbourne clinic. She was arrested Saturday as she read from the Bible.

CRAMER: "Anyone who does not love remains in death. Anyone who hates his brother is a murderer."

LOHR: Michelle's training is over. She's in a Florida jail, but when she is released, Michelle Cramer will go back home to prepare for her leadership role in this summer's battle. Operation Rescue's next training ground is set for Minneapolis beginning in June.

✦ ✦ ✦ ✦ ✦ ✦ ✦ ✦ ✦ ✦

G ays in the military was the most politically damaging and difficult issue the new president faced, partly because it came early and created an impression of confusion, partly because he attempted a middle ground that satisfied no one. While Bill Clinton was in the process of arriving at a policy, gay veterans took a bus tour to make their case: they had served with distinction; they and other gays and lesbians should be allowed military careers. They called the trip Tour of Duty. Ina Jaffe, from our Los Angeles bureau, went along for the ride.

Morning Edition, APRIL 14

JAFFE: It's sunset, midway through the longest haul of the tour, 350 miles from Miami to Jacksonville, city number twenty-two. This journey began in Minneapolis and will end in Washington on April 23, just before the gay rights march. On this leg of the trip, the bus is rolling through mile after identical mile of flat, wet, green scrub, punctuated by the occasional orange grove. The army and navy veterans on this trip decide it's a good chance for a nap. The visit to Miami was brief and busy, starting with the previous evening's cocktail reception for local gay and lesbian activists. Tanya Domi is a retired army captain and now the captain, so to speak, of the Tour of Duty.

DOMI: Even within our own community, we have to impress upon them the importance that they too write and call their members of Congress, and just because one is gay or lesbian does not translate necessarily into their understanding that this is a very important issue.

JAFFE: Attorney Greg Baldwin has helped raise twenty-five thousand dollars to support the bus tour. He was an army lieutenant and served in Vietnam.

BALDWIN: I fought for this country and I fought hard and I got shot and I get a disability check every month and, you know, I've got a knee that I can't use, and I've always been proud of that. From what I remember of combat, what you're worried about is, is the guy next to you reliable, is he trained, is he gonna break and run under fire or is he gonna stay? Sexual orientation has no more to do with it than race or sex.

JAFFE: The next morning, the men and women on the bus tour try to demonstrate that point to members of the media and their readers, viewers, and listeners in Miami. The news conference is held in front of a war memorial near the beach.

DOMI: We are here today to tell our stories about how we have served our country in a very distinguished way in both war and in peace.

JAFFE: Opinion polls show that people who know gay men or lesbians are much more likely to support lifting the ban, so there is an event like this in every city. One by one, the veterans stand at the microphone and tell their personal stories: why they joined the military, why they left, their contributions and decorations. Former Lieutenant Karen Stupsky served in the navy for two years after completing ROTC at Harvard.

STUPSKY: It appeared that I could look forward to a promising career as a naval officer, but then one morning, in a moment of emotion, I told my boss that I was a lesbian. I explained that I had not yet had a sexual relationship with a woman but that I had gained an understanding of my sexual orientation through a process of inner growth and change. I was immediately removed from my ship and informed that I had only two options: resign or be discharged.

JAFFE: Sometimes, there are crowds of supporters at these events, but not in Miami. In fact, the speakers at the conference outnumber the reporters, and the rest of the day is no improvement. It's filled with visits to the offices of both of Florida's senators and a newly elected Miami congressman. All are Republicans, and if they are not already outspoken opponents of allowing gays and lesbians to serve in the armed forces, none are considered likely to become supporters of lifting the ban.

DOMI: It is kind of enjoyable to walk in there, and say, "I'm a lesbian. I served in the army for fifteen years." And I think it's shocking to them. You give them a human being, three feet across the table from them, dispelling all the myths. It's fun.

JAFFE: There are usually about a half a dozen former soldiers and sailors on the bus. Some are just there for a couple of days, or a week, but a few, like former army lieutenant Alan Stevens, have signed on for the whole six weeks.

STEVENS: Lately I've been waking up, and I try to remember what city I'm in, and they all run together.

JAFFE: Stevens is a native of Alabama, and he played football for legendary coach "Bear" Bryant of the university there. He says the high point of the trip so far was in his native South, on the steps of the state capitol in the neighboring state of Mississippi.

STEVENS: It was high noon, media everywhere, and it was particularly empowering for me because the South fed me all of these stereotypes and myths that wouldn't allow me to identify myself as gay, so it was very therapeutic standing on the state capitol of Mississippi while all these ol' boys were walkin' out of the Mississippi state capitol, you know, smokin' their cigarettes and chewin' their tobacco, and some of them even stopped and listened.

JAFFE: The day before that, in Little Rock, was the tour's low point. That was the day President Clinton said he would consider allowing the armed services to separate gays and straights in living quarters and on the job.

STEVENS: I just felt like someone just kicked me in the teeth because Tanya and I both, we worked for Bill Clinton's campaign, and we really believed in him. You know, we're out here, we're busting our tail, and then Bill Clinton with, you know, two paragraphs, just completely destroys everything I've been working for.

JAFFE: The bus arrives in Jacksonville around midnight. A little after eight the next morning, Tanya Domi and Alan Stevens are on their way to do yet another talk radio show. For the next ninety minutes, the phones ring off the hook. All but one of the callers are men. Jacksonville is a conservative town in a conservative state, and home to several naval bases. This proves to be a long morning for Alan and Tanya.

CALLER: And similarly, there are certain underlying moral, ethical, and, yes, even religious reasons why society approaches dealing with various issues —

DOMI: Well, the reason that —

CALLER: And, y'all, as a minority, can think that you're gonna educate the rest of us to believe that heterosexuality is not normal, and that possibly homosexuality is, but you're gonna have a tough time —

DOMI: We're not suggesting that —

CALLER: You're gonna have a tough row to hoe.

JAFFE: Later, they can take some comfort from the crowd that's turned out for the Jacksonville news conference. The news conference goes well. There is coffee and cake and fellowship offered afterwards. Alan Stevens still can't get the callers on that morning's radio show off his mind.

STEVENS: It bothered me that we had a lot of men calling in, and they didn't know what kind of question they wanted to ask. All they knew is they were against it, and that's really tough to fight that. Here's a group of people who grew up hating gays, thinking being gay was wrong. They can't justify their discrimination, but they're gonna be a bigot anyway, and that's frustrating to me because it's almost like you're gonna have to write those people off and you have to try to address an audience that's a little bit more tolerant and at least willing to listen with an open mind.

JAFFE: In the morning, the bus will leave for Charleston, South Carolina, one more stop on what all the passengers know will be a very long road, indeed.

✦ ✦ ✦ ✦ ✦ ✦ ✦ ✦ ✦

Katie Davis drove down the Blue Ridge to Charlottesville, Virginia, to interview Rita Mae Brown. They talked about Brown's newest book, *Venus Envy*, but not before Katie met and spoke with many of the author's animals. The introductions included detailed descriptions of their characters. Katie noted that there were six dogs, eight cats, and twenty-one horses. Then she and Brown talked about reading. Brown said she started at the library as a child, beginning with the shelf she could reach, which happened to hold books on mythology. They also talked about writing.

Weekend All Things Considered, APRIL 24

DAVIS: When did you actually sit down and start writing? Did you keep a journal?

BROWN: I used to write plays. When I was about five, I started writing. I remember I used a crayon — that's all there was — and butcher paper. I did. I started very, very early, and then, by the time I actually had some facility with the language, I was always the kid that would write the little speeches for other kids. I was the kid that would write the class plays, just all straight through.

DAVIS: Did that make you different?

BROWN: No, it just made me busy.

DAVIS: Made you popular, too?

BROWN: I guess. I think what made me unpopular as well is that I tend to be forthright, and I had to learn to temper my opinions. I mean, I think a little bit of discretion goes a long way. You don't always have to say everything that you think, but when I was young I didn't know that.

DAVIS: Hmm. You do tackle that subject a lot, the idea of being honest and direct with people. It's something that comes up over and over, I've noticed, in your books. Of course, in *Rubyfruit Jungle* there's the idea of being honest with people about who you are. In so many of your books, it's a key subtext that you're tackling: Be honest. Otherwise, you're spiritually dead.

BROWN: Well, of course, it's the whole core of *Venus Envy*. This woman thinks she is dying, she's told she's dying, and she writes letters. She believes this is her last communication with people, and she tells them the truth about themselves as she perceives it, and then the truth about herself. It turns out, of course, that she's not dying, and the letters have gone out, so she has to live with this. I chose that theme because I feel all of us, to a greater or lesser degree, aren't being our authentic selves. There's a line between being authentic and being brutal, but if you aren't who you are, number one, you do kill yourself eventually. It's a form of slow suicide. You're so busy pleasing other people, you don't please yourself. Number two, how can you really be pleasing them, because they don't know who you are? It's like continually playing this role, this empty role, in a pretty boring play, and the easiest symbol for lying is the gay person. Because of all the people in America, they are rewarded very heavily for lying and they're punished severely for telling the truth. So that had to be Frazier's emblem for how she had to find herself.

DAVIS: Frazier is the main character in *Venus Envy*. Your philosophy of being honest, how does that translate into your writing? You, when you're sitting down looking at a page that you've written?

BROWN: The first choice I have to make that involves honesty is the style. Every book has a chord. Is it E minor? Is it C major? That's your stylistic choice. The second choice you have to make is your characters. A character can be narrating a book in the first person and lying to you the reader, and you the reader have to figure that out. That's a very interesting choice for a writer to make, how truthful are their characters, because if you just present everything as flat reality, meaning everything these characters say is the truth, that's not the way life is and your reader is going to get bored. So you have to give your reader an awful lot to do. They've got to pick through this the same way they would if they were in a room full of new people.

DAVIS: And find the truth?

BROWN: Yeah. And that's what makes reading a novel so terribly interesting. If you're writing a nonfiction book, you have to tell the truth. It's literal. A nonfiction book, no matter how beautifully written, is, in essence, a very large term paper, but a work of fiction comes from the heart. It's about the emotional truth. So people will be duplicitous, situations will be confusing. There are no easy answers.

DAVIS: You said once that "I'm a funny person, and that makes me dangerous."

BROWN: Oh, I think humor is always dangerous. It's the comedian that tells you the emperor has no clothes. It's the comedian that laughs. And I think anybody who is in power, or who's pompous in any sense of the word, and a pompous person just aspires to power — perhaps it's social power — can't bear the laughter. 'Cause it's usually directed at himself.

DAVIS: Did you set out to be funny when you were little?

BROWN: No. I think I just am, by nature. I mean, I don't know if I've displayed much of it today, but if you get to know me for a long period of time, I'm pretty silly. I mean in the good sense of the word. I'm just silly. I have a good time, and I don't feel compelled to always address weighty matters. You've heard this line before, but life is a comedy to those who think, and a tragedy to those who feel. I think the more you think, the funnier it is, truly.

DAVIS: Do you think that humor is a better path to the honesty that you care about so much?

BROWN: I don't know if there is any better path, but it's my path. I just naturally see things as tilted. I mean, my consciousness isn't raised, my consciousness is tilted. That's probably why I was never elected to high feminist office. I don't have the necessary . . .

DAVIS: Diplomacy?

BROWN: No, it isn't even diplomacy. I don't necessarily believe everything those folks say either, although, of course, I'm a feminist, but, you know, when people start to get self-righteous, I just want to say, "Come on, Mary. Get a life." Nothing is so awful that you can't laugh at yourself.

DAVIS: And Rita Mae Brown is perhaps best when she's laughing at herself and others. This note was included at the beginning of her novel, *Southern Discomfort:* "If you don't like my book, write your own. If you don't think you can write a novel, that ought to tell you something. If you think you can, do. No excuses. If you still don't like my novels, find a book you do like. Life is too short to be miserable. If you like my novels, I commend your good taste."

✦ ✦ ✦ ✦ ✦ ✦ ✦ ✦ ✦

For more than seven weeks, David Koresh and his followers, a religious sect called the Branch Davidians, were barricaded in a compound called Ranch Apocalypse, outside Waco, Texas. Reporters watched the buildings for weeks, while federal authorities tried to talk the Davidians out of the compound. Finally, armed officers from the FBI and the Bureau of Alcohol, Tobacco and Firearms went in. A fight followed, the buildings began to burn, and most of the Davidians died. But a small group who did not live at the ranch were left behind. John Burnett found two women who remained committed to their dead leader.

Morning Edition, MAY 12

BURNETT: Janet Kendrick and Janet McBean are reluctant survivors. As devotees of David Koresh, they were taught that the Branch Davidians were God's chosen people, whom he would lift up to heaven at the appropriate time. But these two women, along with six others, mostly elderly, were left behind. They now face a bewildering future. Their prophet is gone, their home is in ashes, all their men are either dead or in jail, and the community at large reviles them.

Do both of you regret not being inside the compound when it went up in flames?

MCBEAN: I wouldn't use the word "regret." I would have liked to have been there February the twenty-eighth, but in all my experience with God, many times what we would like, God has not chosen that path for us. My path was to be outside. So, no, I don't regret it.

KENDRICK: I feel the same way, but we don't spend time dwelling on it because we accept the fact that we weren't there because God had something else for us to do.

BURNETT: Do you wish that you had died with the group?

KENDRICK: Well, I wish it was all over for me right now, yes. In that respect, yes, because I wouldn't be here having to think about what's going to happen about the sentences and the people that hate us and all that. That would be all over.

BURNETT: Talking to these two women is like stepping into a time warp and speaking to members of an early Christian community nineteen hundred years ago. They find themselves alone in a world that neither understands them nor wants anything to do with them. The death of their messiah has redoubled their faith. Janet Kendrick has been "a Branch," as she puts it, for more than thirty years.

KENDRICK: What happened to the disciples? After Christ died, weren't they all killed? Did people love them? Did they follow them? Sure, a certain number, but every one of them was killed, tortured. The world hated them. It says in the Bible, "The world hates you. You're going to be despised." So we accept this. It doesn't matter.

BURNETT: On a recent overcast day, the two women have come to the original Davidian camp, twenty acres of red clay and slash pine forest outside of Palestine in East Texas. Here in Palestine, Koresh had not yet begun to stockpile assault rifles or take other men's wives for himself.

Life was primitive and pious. They slept in tiny plywood cabins, hauled water in plastic jugs, relieved themselves in the woods, and studied the Scriptures by the light of kerosene lamps. Kendrick stayed behind as a caretaker of the property after the group moved to Mount Carmel, near Waco, in 1987.

KENDRICK: When everybody lived here, the grounds were real clean. Even David, sometimes, he got a lawnmower and he would just mow all this stuff down.

BURNETT: With the Waco compound demolished, the Palestine camp is the last visible evidence of the Davidians' reclusive God-fearing lifestyle.

KENDRICK: Well, you can smell mold and mildew. The creatures have been in here. You see this?

BURNETT: Kendrick opens the door to a two-room log cabin that housed the communal kitchen and indoor worship area. The inside of the building is decorated like a Sunday school classroom. Bible quotes are thumbtacked around the room, bookshelves are filled with religious texts. On the walls, the Davidians have hung handmade tributes, not to Jesus, but to Koresh.

Janet McBean and Janet Kendrick have a version of the standoff and the fire that differs dramatically from the official story. They maintain that Koresh is not the monster the government is portraying him as, that the ATF provoked the standoff, and that the FBI started the fire accidentally.

McBean is a thirty-seven-year-old registered nurse, born in Jamaica. She was the head of a small group of Davidians in La Verne, California, which the police raided shortly after the standoff began. Like other surviving cult members, McBean denies they had a suicide pact. As to the bodies found with bullet holes in their heads, she can only speculate.

MCBEAN: I know that if I was in there and I saw the fire start, and I had a gun beside me, I wouldn't see it as being suicidal or wrong. It's just taking the gun and finishing myself off.

BURNETT: Rather than being burned or dying from the smoke?

MCBEAN: Burned alive, right, because I would not be coming out to go to these wicked people who have just destroyed my place and set fire to it and so on.

BURNETT: In discussing the fire with these two followers of Koresh, it's remarkable how matter-of-factly they can talk about an event that killed their leader and many of their closest friends. Kendrick lost her son-in-law in the blaze; McBean had an even closer relative inside, her brother.

Did that traumatize you?

MCBEAN: No, not in the sense that the world uses "traumatize." You know, I just hope he didn't suffer. So I wasn't sad, I didn't cry or anything. I know the news reporter said we showed no emotions. No. He's gone up, and that's it, OK?

BURNETT: What about the seventeen children?

MCBEAN: Oh, I see them the same as my brother.

BURNETT: Christians profess to believe in an afterlife, just as the Davidians do, but most people were horrified just the same when they watched the flames consume the compound, knowing the children were inside. So steeped are the Davidians in the theology of Koresh, that, according to Kendrick, they simply did not react this way.

KENDRICK: No, I don't view it as a tragedy, like some people. "Oh, those poor people," you know?

MCBEAN: We're gonna see them again.

KENDRICK: We're gonna see them again. Every one of them survived. There's going to be a Kingdom in Israel. They're the people that's going to be there. We're going to be there. It's not the end of it.

♦ ♦ ♦ ♦ ♦ ♦ ♦ ♦ ♦

There was a royal wedding in June. Crown Prince Naruhito of Japan married a diplomat's daughter, Masako Owada, in a series of ceremonies involving many courtesies and costumes. Three foreign journalists were invited to attend, including T. R. Reid of the *Washington Post*, who regularly shares his observations on Japan with Bob Edwards. He called during the festivities.

Morning Edition, JUNE 9

REID: You know, the most striking thing about it was the silence. This was done in complete silence — no music, no cheering, no banzai, not a word said, no songs. It seemed strange, but it added a certain dignity to it. The only sound you could hear was these ushers in tuxedos sort of crunching across the gravel. It was really a stunning thing to see. Beautiful, strange in some ways, but really extremely dignified and moving, I felt.

EDWARDS: And tasteful. There's no official cola of the royal wedding, anything like that?

REID: [*Laughs.*] They're not into that kind of thing. But, you know, they really hoped that this would sell a lot of products like, particularly, high-definition television, and one TV executive said of the bride, Masako Owada, "She's not just photogenic, she's high-vision photogenic."

EDWARDS: I see.

REID: Other than that, not much, no.

EDWARDS: You're along the parade route now?

REID: Yeah, would you please ask me what kind of phone I'm talking to you from?

EDWARDS: Tom, what kind of phone do you have there?

REID: I am talking to you from a gleaming golden public phone right on the parade route because they changed all the plain green public phones in for gold ones. There are these nine-story-tall posters hanging from every building, flags, bands. This is a marvelous scene.

EDWARDS: Do they have any security on the phones? Somebody might want a souvenir.

REID: Well, if, you know, if you want to really be honest about it, it's a plastic green phone that was painted gold, but, from a distance it looks gold. You probably want to ask me what kind of ice cream I'm eating at the moment.

EDWARDS: Uh, what kind of ice cream would you be eating at the moment?

REID: I'm eating Baskin-Robbins Flavor of the Month, which is Princess Owada Wedding, while I'm talking on the gold phone. I mean, I'm really living this up. This is the way to go to the wedding. It was a rotten day, as you know. This is the middle of the rainy season, which is a stupid time to set the wedding. It rained like crazy, and then, just in time for the parade and the convertible Rolls-Royce, the sun goddess came through, the rain stopped, it turned into a beautiful day, and the parade was lovely.

EDWARDS: You were wondering about the tie, what color tie you were going to wear?

REID: I finally went with the whitest thing I have, but I really was underdressed. These people had the most beautiful formal kimonos on, and the men who didn't wear kimonos wore, you know, white tie and tails. So those of us in business suits and a plain white tie really were not up to par.

EDWARDS: Now, has the royal couple passed by yet on the parade route?

REID: Yeah, they went by, and Masako-san, she looks great. I mean, this poor woman, you know, she had to go from 1993 back to the year 1000 in this costume she wore, back up to 1993. She handled it all with total aplomb. She had this serene look of confidence on her face. She was never nervous. This is a woman who can do anything.

EDWARDS: So now what happens? She does photo ops the rest of her life?

REID: Tonight, for the next three nights, she has to do this fruitful womb ceremony, where they pray for her to have a male child real quick. But, after that, maybe this is the woman who can bring this monarchy more into the world.

EDWARDS: This is the beginning of a number of days of celebration.

REID: About a week from now, they're going to start having two banquets a day for a few days, and, finally, at the last banquet is when the foreigners get to go. She has many friends in America, but none of them have gotten close to this thing so far.

EDWARDS: Well, enjoy it.

REID: I'm having a great time.

1994

The Golden State still has its coastal mountains and beautiful beaches, but it seems to be slowly turning from the place Americans dream of going to a place where the American dream is going wrong. In 1994, California began the year with an earthquake in Los Angeles, and our commentator Karen Grigsby Bates saw it as an awful blessing for the city.

All Things Considered, JANUARY 20

BATES: We Californians, both native and adopted, live with a seismic equivalent of Damocles' sword hanging above us. On Monday, the hair that suspends the sword became a bit more frayed as the earth groaned, rocked, and buckled beneath us once again. We are all too keenly aware that we pay a price for where we live and that the inevitable bill is coming due, maybe sooner than we thought. The 6.6 temblor that hit us in the dark lasted less than half a minute, but faint daylight a few hours later began to illuminate exactly how much devastation could be wreaked in such a short time. Like Andrew, the hurricane that leveled much of south Florida, or the ravages left behind the swollen Mississippi this past summer, or the holocaust that destroyed huge chunks of Oakland two falls ago, this natural disaster too will have tragic consequences. But these horrors are also the glue that binds communities together. Usually in Los Angeles, it feels as if we are daily, hungrily surveying each other's jugulars as we dance a frenzied pavane at social Darwinism's rhythms, the urban equivalent of musical chairs. The haves sit. The have-nots watch as the economically fortunate perch anxiously on their expensive seats. But Monday's quake brought out myriad instances of personal generosity that transcend race and class.

I watch as a local news station zeroes in on a young black man in hip-hop clothes gently guiding a weeping elderly woman with an Eastern European accent into a hospital parking lot that has been fashioned into a makeshift emergency room. "It's OK, lady," he soothes her. "Really. It's over now. You're going to be all right." She leans heavily into him and grips his brown hand so hard that his flesh beneath her fingers is nearly white. Two tough-looking white kids who look as if they could be skinheads work furiously to free a dazed and bleeding Latino man from his crumpled car. Strangers offer other strangers sips of precious water and stop to comfort shaking children they don't know and probably will never see again.

It is a vastly different atmosphere than the one that electrified this region after the civil unrest in 1992. Then we regarded each other with barely concealed suspicion. Are you for King or for Gates? Is this a riot or an uprising? Here the only questions are, Are you all right? And, Wasn't that something? For a few days, weeks maybe, this fractured city will pull together and work as its founding fathers, who were a mosaic of different races and cultures bound by the same vision, hoped it would. The irony, of course, is that it took the near destruction of the city to make us behave toward each other as we should have all along.

✦ ✦ ✦ ✦ ✦ ✦ ✦ ✦ ✦

I ra Glass has made schools his special interest for several years. He roamed the halls of Taft High School in Chicago long enough to become familiar to students and teachers, and he listened long enough to get their stories on tape. At Taft, forty-three percent of the students were failing when Ira did a series of stories on the efforts of a principal and his staff to motivate their kids.

One of the hard lessons learned in our series of reports on Taft was that the threatened cutbacks in support for Chicago schools had teachers worried about their own careers. At the end of the school year, several talented teachers, including Jerry Patt, left Taft.

All Things Considered, MARCH 3

GLASS: Kids who don't like many teachers or pass many classes say good things about Jerry Patt. He's a math teacher. They say he takes the time to explain things until you understand them. They say they like his class. Mr. Patt is friendly and upbeat, a youthful thirty-three, dressed most days in a tie and blue jeans. When I ask him how to motivate students, he says what most teachers at Taft say.

PATT: I don't know how to motivate kids, I don't think. Some get motivated by what I do and some don't. If I knew how to do it, I would motivate them all.

GLASS: Between a third and a half of his students don't do the homework on any given day. Another fifteen or twenty percent simply don't show up. All of this is typical for Taft and not unusual for a Chicago high school or a high school in any big American city. Jerry Patt tries whatever he can think of to get the students involved and interested. He tutors and encourages them one-on-one. He tries to play up the parts of the curriculum that classes find the most interesting. He has them and their parents sign contracts agreeing to come to class prepared. He has them work together in groups, which in educational circles is now called cooperative learning. And he says that every time a class finishes a unit and reviews for a test, he gets a certain feeling.

PATT: Every test, they're going to do good this time. They really are. They're going to do well. I know it. They're doing it. Then the test comes and half the class fails the first one. And you're, like, Oh, man, what am I doing?

GLASS: Teachers say the traditional tool for motivating students, the threat of bad grades, simply doesn't work with large portions of their classes. Lots of students don't study. Lots of students don't do much work at all outside of class. And so teachers instead send them on a forced march through the curriculum during class time. In English and history classes, many teachers read aloud to their students, knowing they won't read on their own. In Jerry Patt's math classes, students who don't study simply take and retake the unit exams until they become familiar with the material that way. Even the most basic classroom activity, taking notes, is something teachers have to coach and coerce students into doing. In Mr. Patt's classes, as in many Taft classes, students turn in their notes for a grade.

PATT: You know what I'm saying? If they write it down, maybe just by the fact of writing it down something will go inside their head, you know. I mean, even if they copy someone else's homework, I don't like that, but that's better than doing nothing.

GLASS: In his geometry class he tried everything to get his students to simply take notes. When all else failed, he told them that if they took notes they could use them on the test. Many still didn't pass.

PATT: I have given a test where I know the day before, or that week, anyways, I have given them the entire test in their notes, I mean. And I get kids that miss fifteen out of twenty. I'm at a loss to explain that, you know. I have done things where I've left a problem on the board worked out, put the same problem on the test with the same numbers, left it on the board knowing that I did that. Kids still miss it.

GLASS: James is one of the students who missed this particular problem. He says, sure, it may sound bad, but there was a simple reason he didn't see the problem on the board.

JAMES: Because I was busy concentrating on the test, and I wasn't even looking on the board. I'm like, How am I going to get all these answers? and stuff like that. Then he's like, "Well, the problem was on the board." I'm like, you know, "Thanks for telling us."

GLASS: James is a junior taking geometry a second time and not quite passing. He's failing history also. He's blond and stocky and blushes when I press for details about his work habits. He says he does his homework maybe half the time, forgets when the tests are sometimes, and prepares for tests by glancing over his notes for maybe fifteen minutes beforehand. He thinks Mr. Patt is a good teacher.

What else could he do if he wanted to get you to, you know, pass the test the first time around and do more work?

JAMES: Seriously, I have no clue. Probably nothing else because he makes it as easy as possible. It's not what he could do, it's what I could do because I'm lazy when it comes to school, real lazy. That's about it though, just school, not outside of school.

GLASS: Outside of school, James holds down a job at Elliott's Dairy and practices a few times a week with a heavy metal group he's in. He's responsible and apparently capable. His parents aren't totally out of the picture. When he gets a bad report card, he isn't allowed to use the family car for weeks. But none of this makes a difference.

JAMES: I kind of get bored with school.

GLASS: Do you have a class you really like?

JAMES: Yeah, probably third period, history.

GLASS: You're failing that class.

JAMES: Yeah, but it's a class I like going to.

PATT: Now here's a kid maybe you'd want to talk to.

GLASS: Math teacher Jerry Patt pulls an embarrassed teenager over to my microphone.

PATT: Pablo is — now, tell me when I'm wrong, Pablo.

PABLO: OK.

PATT: Pablo is exceedingly lazy in math. However, if I lean on him constantly, he does well and he does his work. His father is up here a couple of times talking to me already. I don't know how many times with the other teachers. This is a kid that if we push him and motivate him any way we know how, he'll do the work. If we don't, he won't.

GLASS: Pablo then launches into a description of the speeches that Mr. Patt made first semester to warn him he was going down the tubes.

PABLO: Yeah, Mr. Patt tells me, "You're looking at Burger King in front of you," like he's looking at the future.

GLASS: Like you'll be working at a Burger King.

PABLO: Yeah.

PATT: And then we do this, huh, Pablo? This is the gesture of flipping hamburgers. But let's see, you got your makeup work there?

GLASS: And at that moment, by handing in makeup work for two units, Pablo successfully completed the first semester of geometry. Just two months before, he was failing the class. But victories like this can be fragile and short-lived. On Friday of last week, Pablo stopped coming to school. By Tuesday of this week, Mr. Patt was worried and headed down to the office to call Pablo's house.

PATT: I tell you, you know, I hadn't seen him in, like, three or four days so I started asking the kids. And they said he had transferred out or he's going to leave because he was threatened to be beat up. I don't know the first thing about it.

They stole the phone out of here. You know that, right?

GLASS: No.

PATT: Yeah. Fourth period. Everyone was in the office. Somebody just kind of got in the crowd and swiped our phone.

GLASS: Someone lets us in the office, and Jerry Patt dials one of the remaining telephones.

PATT: Yeah, Pablo? This is Mr. Patt. What's going on? Yeah. What's happening? Why haven't you been in school?

GLASS: His story went like this. Some students decided they wanted to keep their clothes and shoes in Pablo's gym locker. Pablo said they were gang members. He didn't want them there. And after a while, he took his stuff and the combination lock to another locker. Then they came looking for him, saying their stuff had vanished, demanding he pay for it all. They told him people get killed for this kind of thing.

PATT: So what are you going to do? Are you going to come back to school?

GLASS: Pablo told him he was too scared to come back to Taft.

In a teacher's daily work, trying to motivate students means inventing lessons that will engage them. In other words, the basic craft of education. John Bennett's third-period class is a work co-op. All of his students get real-world jobs as part of the class. When he teaches them about business principles like markup and profit margins, he uses examples from their jobs.

BENNETT: This is a good one, by the way, Little Caesar's, because they have deals that sound so bizarre to me I don't how the hell they do it. How about you buy one pizza, you get another one free? And if you spend a buck, you get a third one. How the hell do they do this? What is this, cardboard pizza? Jesus!

GLASS: He calls on a teenager who works at Little Caesar's.

BENNETT: OK, hold on. We're going to ask Mr. Pizza how they do this. Billy.

GLASS: Billy explains that the ingredients for three pizzas cost Little Caesar's a total of three dollars and seventy-five cents, meaning the markup is over nine dollars. Mr. Bennett has the class compute the markup for White Castle hamburgers and Nike gym shoes. He makes wisecracks. The class makes wisecracks. The degree of involvement is especially impressive when you consider that these are some of the hardest students to teach. They include learning-disabled and special-ed students, who have notoriously low attention spans. To motivate them to show up to class and do their assignments, Mr. Bennett is strictly old school. If they miss three assignments, they fail. If they miss ten classes, they fail. Every Friday, he reviews the rules and tells each kid where he stands.

BENNETT: As you all know, when you hit the magic number of ten, that's the end. Every week we're going over this. Every week we're going to count. We're going to keep count.

GLASS: John Bennett has been a teacher for twenty-five years and, like a number of the veteran teachers at Taft, he resents the notion that the only good teacher is an innovative teacher. He says all these so-called innovations are just old ideas with fancy new labels on them promoted by hucksters out to make a dollar. He himself would never use jargon like "active learning," except to make fun of it. But in fact there's as much active learning in his classroom, as much student engagement, as in any classroom at Taft.

✦ ✦ ✦ ✦ ✦ ✦ ✦ ✦ ✦ ✦

In April, former President Richard Nixon died. He was, I believe, the dominant political figure of my generation. Nixon came early to the idea of engaging communism at home and abroad. His use of television to campaign and communicate set a pattern. His understanding of how elections are won in this country still shapes politics. Even without

Watergate it would be hard to overestimate his influence. NPR's news analyst Daniel Schorr was on President Nixon's famous enemies list.

Weekend Edition, Sunday, APRIL 24

SCHORR: In the end, one is left to wonder how a man so creative could be so self-destructive, as though the architect of stunning victories had to be also the author of his own downfall. I'm thinking not only of the Watergate cover-up and the missteps that led Nixon to hang himself politically with his own Oval Office tape. I'm thinking also and more personally of the idiotic enemies lists and wiretap lists, and, in my case, the FBI investigation that ended up as an item in the bill of impeachment.

Nixon did seem, at times, to thrive on adversity and to be uncomfortable with success. I remember covering his campaign headquarters the night of his big 1972 landslide and noting how strangely grim he looked before the wild cheers of his supporters. Next day, we subsequently learned, he called together his Cabinet and, without any time out for self-congratulation, asked for resignations and announced a shakeup of his government. He wanted to create a super-Cabinet to bring the government more effectively under his control, with White House commissars watching the bureaucrats.

Control seemed the key to Nixon. He needed to control everything around him, from public opinion to dinner menus. And that led him to divide his world into enemies and supporters, and that produced a need to know what opponents were planning in order to do him in. In 1971, preparing for his reelection campaign, he told his aides they must see to it there were no surprises. And that led to the break-in into Democratic headquarters to learn what surprises might be lurking there.

Nixon was himself tightly controlled most of the time. He was awkward, his gestures sometimes out of sync with his words. He was nervous about small talk, telling off-color stories to make him seem like a regular guy and inappropriately talking about money to make him seem like just folks. During the photo opportunity chat with Israeli Prime Minister Golda Meir, he asked whether she had flown to Washington on an Israeli air force plane, and, when told, "no, on El Al," the Israeli airliner, all he could think to say was, "Are they making money?"

Comebacks were his specialty, and the most amazing campaign he waged was a twenty-year campaign for ex-president. It was carefully orchestrated from his first public appearance on a California golf course thirteen months after his resignation. Then he plunged back into foreign affairs, visiting Moscow and Beijing, where he'd always been treated like a hero and made comfortable. He had always displayed a greater interest in America's global condition than America's human condition. It seemed easier for him to deal with maps than with persons. It was because he was so uncomfortable with persons that he preferred memos to briefings. That was why his presidency and Watergate were so richly documented.

But in his twenty-year campaign for elder statesman, he forced himself to deal with people, even journalists, in a friendly manner. And so he contrived a reconciliation with me, having me invited to dinners where he gave briefings on Russia, giving me an interview for NPR, and, a few weeks ago, inviting me to participate in the Richard Nixon Foreign Policy Institute that he was planning to create. That was to have culminated his long march back to Washington — that and having been received by President Clinton at the White House.

He didn't live to see his own think tank in the nation's capital, but he left his monument in ten books, the last of them titled *Beyond Peace*, completed shortly before his death. A brilliant, restless, brooding man with a rage to dominate and a rage to fail. For half a century, his presence hovered over America, and, for those of the Nixon generation, a presence it's hard to believe is gone.

◆ ◆ ◆ ◆ ◆ ◆ ◆ ◆ ◆ ◆

A s the elections approached in South Africa, we sent Ray Suarez and the telephone talk program *Talk of the Nation* to Johannesburg. Ray took calls from the U.S. and from South Africa, and the program was broadcast in both places. At the end of election week, Ray wrote this essay.

Talk of the Nation, APRIL 29

SUAREZ: I can say one thing without hesitation as *Talk of the Nation* prepares to pack up and take the program back to Washington. I leave this country far more optimistic about its future than I was when I arrived two weeks ago. We've seen armored personnel carriers stuffed with bored soldiers parked outside the townships of the east Rand. We've seen the teeming shantytowns of Soweto and Alexandra without plumbing, without electricity, without gas for heating. On the warmer days, the slightest breeze picks up the stench of the outhouses and the buckets that carry the wastes of too many people packed into too small a space. These people would have every reason to be bitter after forty-five years of apartheid, but maybe they're too busy, working too hard just to get by every day, to nurse the grievance, too burdened to spend much time keeping their wounds open and fresh. They were moved by their chance to vote. They paused to remember all the people they knew who died before this day came and they did their long-postponed duty.

How did it happen? How was all the violence not met with violence? How did the evil supposedly done in the name of Western Christian values not provoke an uprising, a vengeance? The cynic might answer that black South Africans know how their bread is buttered, they don't want to kill the goose that lays the golden eggs. But answers like that underestimate what the black majority here has done. By not setting aside one bullet for every settler and then making sure that each bullet found its mark, millions of South Africans took their birthright into their hands with their moral authority intact, and with those hands still clean.

All during this week, white callers talked of a burden being lifted from their shoulders too, in many cases a burden the weight of which they never really understood until now. Though it was not the first time voting for many of them, it was the first time that carried any real meaning. Something new, something that is going to play a big part in the success or failure of this country in the coming years, was kindled in all kinds of hearts this week.

Earlier this week a promised lowering of the old South African flag and a raising of the new banner at the union buildings in Pretoria never happened. Soldiers at this national landmark told the crowd to go away. Since there was no spotlight for the top of the flagpole, the raising of the new flag would have to wait until morning. About a hundred and fifty people gathered around the flagpole anyway, a rowdy group of young whites sang "Die Stem," the Afrikaans national anthem, at the top of their lungs and then followed with a lusty rendition of the Transvaal Republic's Dutch national song, the mood more than a little ugly at that moment. Then a group led a more solemn version of "Die Stem" at night, the last moment of the old order, the old constitution, the old country. At midnight, "Nkosi Sikeleli Afrika," God bless Africa, was to be the new national anthem. No one in Pretoria sang that. "We don't know the words yet," laughed one young law student. She worked as an election monitor and said she would learn the lyrics soon. She's a part of this story too. She knew the country she had grown

up in was gone and could not be retrieved and she was getting on with
it. She said she was going to learn the words to "Nkosi Sikeleli Afrika,"
and I believed her. Like the song says, God bless Africa.

✦ ✦ ✦ ✦ ✦ ✦ ✦ ✦ ✦ ✦

O nly a few days after Nelson Mandela was elected president of
South Africa, Rwanda's people began to kill each other. After a
plane carrying the Rwandan president, an ethnic Hutu, crashed, massacres began. Hundreds of thousands of ethnic Tutsis were slaughtered,
even as a rebel force dominated by Tutsis raced across the country to
overthrow the government and stop the killing. Michael Skoler, who'd
been a reporter on our science desk before being reassigned to Africa,
went into Rwanda with the rebels, and described what he saw.

In all his conversations, with Tutsi and Hutu, he asked if they could
ever be reconciled. A nurse in the town of Gahini told him, "We are
going to like each other again because we don't know politics. We lived
together, we liked each other before, and now we are going to live
together and like each other again. We are going to forgive them
because they didn't know it wasn't necessary to kill. Those people were
taught badly, but they are not wicked."

This is only one of the terrible scenes we heard about. It happened
in a village church about thirty miles from the capital.

All Things Considered, JUNE 13

SKOLER: As I drove up to a set of orange brick church buildings, I had
to clamp a bandanna tightly over my nose and mouth. The stench was
unbearable. Outside the church, there are maybe two or three dozen
bodies, and in the heat here in Rwanda, many of the bodies are already
almost fully decomposed. You can see some skulls, some backbones.
There are what seem to be women in brightly colored clothing, as well
as children, lying about. This is amidst what is a very beautiful area of
eucalyptus trees and pine trees. There are bodies scattered all over the
church. The blood on the floor is so thick it's dried to kind of a muddy
brown dust that may be in some places a quarter of an inch thick. Most
of the bodies are blackened and decomposing. Some lie on mattresses,
some on the floor, some are covered with blankets. By the altar, there
are probably about thirty bodies clustered around. One is the body of
an infant with parents, it seems, on either side. There's a suitcase that is

open and kind of torn apart in front of the altar. On the floor of the church, you can see baskets, plastic water cans, pails, combs, brushes, sandals, sneakers, tins of food, a bottle of talcum powder.

The windows, stained-glass windows on either side, are broken. There are wooden pews that have been thrown against them. Above the whole scene, above the altar, is a small wooden statue of Christ with one hand raised. In one of the church offices in the back, the bodies are piled, one on top of the other, crowded into a room, some still sitting in chairs. Windows broken, the plaster inside is cratered. It looks like, perhaps, bullets came in through the windows.

A few hundred yards away, I find Emmanuel Mutsinzi. He came to help dig graves to bury the bodies, one or two thousand, he says, maybe more. When I ask if he knows what happened here, he nods. He tells me he is Tutsi, and he had been hiding in the church, too. He is a tall, thin man, and tells his story slowly, with an empty face, as if the feelings behind what he is saying had long since drained out. There is no reason for him to exaggerate, since my two rebel escorts are back in the car and out of sight. Mutsinzi says the massacres began in his area on April 6, the same night the Rwandan president was killed in an apparent attack on his plane. He knows that because the next day, Thursday, frightened Tutsis poured into his town on the run, telling how government soldiers and armed citizens' militias had attacked them and anyone suspected of opposing the government. Mutsinzi and several thousand others ran to the church buildings in Karubamba. All weekend, they stayed bolted inside as roving mobs killed anyone who ventured out.

The local mayor came to the church, and they asked him for protection, and Monday evening the mayor returned, but not to help. He came with some soldiers and a mob of more than one hundred militiamen. They were local people, neighbors, trained and armed by the government over many months. They splashed gasoline into the church buildings and threw in hand grenades. That's when so many people got burned. The attacks continued Tuesday and Wednesday, killing hundreds. Mutsinzi says he climbed into the rafters to get away from the fire and the grenades. Each night when the *interahamwe*, the civilian militias, grew tired and left, he helped drag out the dead so the others, he says, could breathe.

Then, says Mutsinzi, on Thursday, they broke down the doors of the church buildings with axes. They shot and speared, hacked and clubbed, those inside for hours. Mutsinzi climbed under a pile of dead bodies to hide. Two girls I met later said they had been taken away and raped. On Friday, he says, the rebels, who had been advancing steadily from the north for several days, were getting close, and those in the church heard their guns in the distance. But the militiamen came back to kill any survivors, hacking them to death with machetes.

Finally, the *interahamwe* ran off as the Rwandan Patriotic Front reached the church on Saturday morning. But Mutsinzi had already lost his parents, grandfather, nieces and nephews. He knows the killers, he says. They included teachers at the local school, the town constable, storekeepers, and other neighbors. When I ask if Mutsinzi thinks he can ever go back to living with his Hutu neighbors again, he answers quickly. "Yes, of course," he says. His wife is a Hutu.

✦ ✦ ✦ ✦ ✦ ✦ ✦ ✦ ✦ ✦

M ike Shuster covered the Soviet Union through the difficult years of adjustment, in the wake of the cold war, through the dissolution of the empire. He wrote about economic chaos and the uneven leadership of Boris Yeltsin. On his way home, he wrote this piece comparing Russia to the Weimar Republic, to the brief period between the wars when Germany attempted democracy and ended in fascist dictatorship.

Morning Edition, JUNE 23

SHUSTER: The Weimar Republic in Germany was named after the small town where, in 1919, Germany's first democratic constitution was written. And it is from that very first step that the astonishing parallels between Weimar Germany and present-day Russia begin. That constitution created a German republic with a president, a parliament, and a democratic separation of powers, somewhat like the constitution written and adopted last year in Russia.

By 1920, German voters had already rejected the very Democrats who had written the constitution, much as Russian voters rejected reformers in last December's parliamentary elections here. For thirteen years, Germany lived with political instability, economic crisis, crime, political violence. It could be a description of Russia today. Finally, in 1933, the German people welcomed Adolf Hitler to power. Many in Russia today dream of the day when a strong hand could take hold of Russia, clean up the mess, and restore it to its former glory. The most obvious parallels are in the realm of the economy. Russia has been shocked by more than two years of near hyperinflation. In 1923, hyperinflation was so enormous in Germany that money became literally worthless. In the late twenties, the Great Depression hit Germany. The collapse in production in Russia today means that this country is living through its depression, along with the pain of inflation.

Germans blamed Weimar for the economic crisis. According to historian Dmitri Gudamenko, the similarity with Russia today is obvious.

GUDAMENKO: For Russia, the great danger is that the public, or a part of it, will promptly associate the unfavorable situation in the economy with the establishment of a democratic, or quasi-democratic, government, that which we have right now.

SHUSTER: Germany had little experience of democracy before Weimar. Its traditions were monarchical. It was an empire ruled by a king, its government run by strong leaders. Its people had little say in their nation's affairs. Before the Soviet Union collapsed, Russians never had any say as a matter of course in their nation's affairs.

GUDAMENKO: In both cases we are dealing with a democracy that was born not from the deep wishes of the people, but which was established more or less by accident. And, in both cases, we are dealing with a situation where most of the population is either not psychologically ready for the democratic process or does not see a need for it. That's, of course, what's most tragic.

SHUSTER: This is where the parallel takes on such great significance, the issue of whether Russia will remain committed to democracy. Using Weimar Germany as a guide, historian Vladimir Jerusalimiski has grave doubts.

JERUSALIMISKI: The young Weimar Republic and Russia's democracy were not the result of a gradual maturing of liberal democracy, or of serious and profound step-by-step reforms, that is, of the natural and organic growth of civil society. To a large extent, they were the results of catastrophic developments.

SHUSTER: That is, for Germany its defeat in the First World War, for Russia its defeat in the cold war. There are arguments, of course, over whether the cold war was really a war and whether, therefore, Russia really lost it. But in Russia, people in increasing numbers do feel that they have been defeated, just as the growing wave of German nationalists blamed Weimar's weak democratic government for the humiliation of defeat in the First World War, and for the humiliating conditions of the Versailles Treaty and the peace that followed. So do Russian nationalists and more and more ordinary citizens blame Russia's nascent democracy for similar national humiliations. "Everything was better under the kaiser," was the refrain in Weimar. "Everything was better under Brezhnev, or even Stalin," is not an uncommon remark here today. Historian Leonid Istyagin is alarmed at how rapidly this view has emerged in Russia.

ISTYAGIN: Here we are also seeing a longing for the past, a feeling that we have been wronged and even the replication of what was peculiar to the Weimar period: a belief that we were stabbed in the back, that someone prevented us from victory, that we were betrayed. Maybe it was Gorbachev or Shevardnadze who withdrew our troops from Europe. They betrayed us. And now, as one of the leaders of the opposition wrote, our soldiers are turning in their graves. All of this resembles, more than a little, Weimar Germany.

SHUSTER: So in Weimar, Germany, the hunt began for the betrayers, led by the ultranationalists and, in particular, by Adolf Hitler. Hitler found his scapegoat in the Jews. Here too the hunt is on for scapegoats, and there are many. This can be seen in the disillusion with the West, and with the United States in particular, with the vilification of Boris Yeltsin, and the sneer with which many now refer to the democratic criminals who run Russia. And, again, the Jews are also counted among the betrayers. Within the radical nationalist opposition here, there is an astounding degree of anti-Semitism. Caricatures of Jews are common in nationalist fringe newspapers. Jewish stars are always scrawled over Yeltsin's face on signs that the nationalists carry at their numerous demonstrations. Many Russians believe that Jews are conspiring to take over the world, just as Germans were susceptible to such views in the 1920s. This is not just a phenomenon on the political fringe, though. Professor Jerusalimiski points out the response, or lack of it, to the recent desecration of the Jewish cemetery in Saint Petersburg, where more than 150 graves were smashed or defaced.

JERUSALIMISKI: Had this happened in France or Germany, we could expect the government to condemn it. The mayor of the capital and the leaders of the main parties would declare their indignation, and in the streets of, let's say, Moscow and Saint Petersburg, there would be impressive antinationalist demonstrations. Here we cannot imagine anything of the sort, just as we cannot imagine that our police will catch these hooligans, and there might be a trial that would have wide public resonance.

SHUSTER: Of course, there are differences between Weimar Germany and Russia. As all of these historians have pointed out, Russia is not Germany. It has its specific cultural characteristics far different from

Germany's. It has a different history. And, in fact, it has already lived through a long period of totalitarianism, making it less likely — some say impossible — that the Russian people would permit such rule again. And many here point out how different the world is now than it was in the 1920s and the 1930s. Then the victorious powers in World War I imposed a harsh peace on Germany, exacting punishing reparations, expelling it from the world community. In the process, the West helped to undermine the very democracy in Germany that it professed to support. For political analyst Alexander Konavalov, that is precisely the choice the West is confronted with now in relation to Russia.

KONAVALOV: See, after the First World War, Germany was isolated, disarmed, and left alone to settle her problems. And very quickly it led to the massive wave of radical nationalism and, finally, to Hitler. And after the Second World War, Germany was engaged in the family of the democratic nations and assisted to overcome the consequences of the war, and now Germany is a member of the family of the democratic nations and at least doesn't possess any military threat. Some parallels could be drawn. How to deal with Russia? Either to isolate and to live alone with your uncertainties and difficulties, or to actively participate in the process?

SHUSTER: Given all the other troubling parallels between Weimar Germany and Russia, Konavalov and his colleagues among the historians would argue that there is really no choice for the West but, as he says, to stay actively involved in the process.

♦ ♦ ♦ ♦ ♦ ♦ ♦ ♦ ♦

The political campaign in the fall of 1994 began a process of political change for this country. Republicans running for the House of Representatives made a public ceremony of signing a "Contract with America," a ten-part promise to bring specific changes before the Congress for a vote. They rallied behind the number-two man in the Republican leadership, Congressman Newt Gingrich of Georgia, and posed for a photograph on the steps of the Capitol, members and challengers, campaigning on change. It was the same theme, Mara Liasson pointed out, that had elected a president in 1992. She also provided a label for this election year.

LIASSON: This is the year of the angry voter. Poll after poll shows that the electorate is crabby and cynical and not in a mood to give anyone in power the benefit of the doubt. President Clinton himself has wondered out loud what this is all about.

CLINTON: This is a good time and we are plainly moving in the right direction. So what is the beef? Why is there this anxiety, this tension, in the country?

LIASSON: The president and his advisers have offered lots of answers to that question. Despite a growing economy, they point out that family income continues to decline. Americans are still working harder for less. Voters feel their families, schools, communities, and values are under assault. The public thinks government, instead of helping, is making things worse. And White House officials admit President Clinton's inability to meet the expectations he raised has also left voters disappointed. But White House officials, such as domestic policy aide Bill Galston, maintain that voters' anger this year is generic. It's an indiscriminate disgust with everyone in Washington.

GALSTON: I don't think it has to do with one man, or one branch of government, or one political party. I think it's much broader than that. The people are saying, "We want a change in the way the public business is done." And we have to take that very seriously.

LIASSON: At one time, Galston's analysis may have been correct, but, as Election Day draws closer, voter anger is taking on a decidedly partisan edge. In Senate races, for instance, Democratic incumbents are struggling for survival. No Republican Senate incumbent is behind in the polls. And President Clinton himself has become the biggest symbol of voters' antigovernment pique. It wasn't always like this. Clinton's presidential campaign capitalized on public disgust with politics as usual. The hope that he could change things helped put him over the top. In his first address to Congress, he promised policies to change the way Washington worked.

CLINTON: I believe lobby reform and campaign finance reform are a sure path to increase popularity for Republicans and Democrats alike because it says to the voters back home, "This is your House, this is your Senate. We are your hired hands, and every penny we draw is your money."

LIASSON: Pollster Frank Luntz is a specialist on voter anger. He's working for the Republican party now, but in 1992 he polled for Ross Perot, studying the views of the nineteen percent of voters who were the advance guard of today's surly electorate. Luntz says Clinton's first State of the Union speech spoke right to them.

LUNTZ: I watched his State of the Union speech in 1993, and I thought it had been written by Ross Perot's speechwriters. It was so good. It had all the right words, it had all the right intonation. He communicated with that nineteen percent better than anyone except for Ross Perot, and, at that brief shining moment, Clinton had an opportunity to create a new majority that would last at least a decade, if not more.

LIASSON: But President Clinton never followed through. Early on, his pollsters cranked out strategy memos on how to appeal to the Perot vote, and White House officials talked about how important it was to prove to the public that government was reforming itself before asking voters to support any big new government initiatives, such as health care reform. But issues like cutting the federal work force, reforming welfare, campaign finance, and lobbying, issues that could have sent voters a signal that President Clinton was fixing the mess in Washington, got lost in the shuffle. Senior White House adviser George Stephanopoulos says that's because there was just too much else to do.

STEPHANOPOULOS: We had a lot to get done, and the president brought it up at every leadership meeting. It did get bogged down. We had a lot of important initiatives in the lifeboat. You can only speak to so many issues at a time.

LIASSON: Other White House officials say the president did bring up campaign finance reform and lobby reform in private meetings with congressional leaders, but, beyond a line or two in a few speeches, he rarely spoke about the reform agenda in public. White House Chief of Staff Leon Panetta says that was a mistake.

PANETTA: In hindsight, knowing what I know now, knowing what we know now, in terms of what we faced, obviously it would have been better had we probably taken on welfare reform and the other reform issues, and pushed those forward, laying the base for then going on and then dealing with health care.

LIASSON: In the administration, Panetta was an advocate for the so-called Perot agenda. As director of the president's budget office, he pushed hard for deficit reduction during the budget battle of 1993. But early this fall, when some of the president's outside strategists argued belatedly that Mr. Clinton should give political reform a higher profile, Panetta didn't go along. He deferred to Democratic leaders in Congress. The congressional leadership in the House had long argued that since the White House was asking them to cast so many tough votes, it wasn't smart for the president to take on his own party over its reluctance to change the campaign finance system. And by this fall, too many things were falling apart. The crime bill was in trouble, and a congressional vote that would have undercut the president's military action in Haiti was likely. That made the White House even more beholden to the congressional leaders. As one official said, "Gephardt and Foley and the Black Caucus were saving us on Haiti. We couldn't go out and bash them on campaign finance reform."

Stanley Greenberg is the president's pollster.

GREENBERG: You've got to, at the same time, position yourself relative to Congress. Congress isn't a popular institution, and it's one of the things people want changed. On the other hand, Congress also has to test things. And sometimes you just don't have the freedom to, you know, speak out on the issues you'd most like to speak out on because you also have to move your agenda through the Congress.

LIASSON: The decision not to push the congressional leadership on political reform had consequences. Reform issues were left until late in the session when they became easy prey to across-the-board Republican filibusters. And, as one White House official explains, "The president lost his chance to show the public he was fighting to change the way Washington worked." When asked which party is more closely tied to special interests, voters now tell pollsters they see no difference at all. Pushing harder on the reform agenda may not have changed the outcome of the midterm elections, but some embattled Democratic incumbents believe it could have helped.

Freshman Eric Fingerhut of Ohio ran on political reform in 1992. Now, as he fights for survival in a close race for reelection, he has little to show for his efforts to pass campaign finance reform and lobby reform. He says President Clinton deserves some of the blame.

FINGERHUT: I think that he meant to be active on these issues, but I think that he followed the advice of the Democratic leadership, particularly in the House, that these issues should be put off because they would hurt their efforts at the substantive agenda items. I think he took, frankly, some bad advice. I wish he had rejected that advice, and, had he done so, I think we might have had a more successful two-year term.

LIASSON: Even beyond the strategic mistake on political reform, some White House officials now admit they fundamentally misread the public's mood. "We didn't read the result of the ninety-two election accurately enough," said one source. "We felt empowered to a greater extent than we were. We thought Bill Clinton had made the sale." Because they underestimated the intensity of voter anger at government, White House officials failed to address it, and now pollster Frank Luntz says the wave is reaching tsunami proportions.

LUNTZ: We're now right in the middle of a tornado that's gonna sweep out a lot of Democrats that people would have expected to survive in this town for years, and it may even sweep out a president who argued for change more strongly than any other in the last twenty years.

✦ ✦ ✦ ✦ ✦ ✦ ✦ ✦ ✦

The day after Republicans won a majority in the House and the Senate, I carried on with the themes of uncontrollable natural forces on *All Things Considered.* I was at the Capitol, standing in the old House chamber, which is now called Statuary Hall. This room contains a famous whispering gallery and the legend that one party overheard the other's secrets as murmured conversations slipped along the arch and dropped to the other side of the chamber. But the Republican party wasn't whispering on November 11. After forty years, the Grand Old Party was taking over again, the party of Lincoln reborn with its base of suppport and its leaders coming from the South. This was an election that could change the country. Certainly it changed everything for the president and the thousands of people who worked in the six office buildings within sight of the tall dome of the Capitol. It was a political earthquake that shook the buildings named for the old leaders of Congress, Cannon and Longworth, Dirksen and Hart, Russell and Rayburn, spilling representatives and clerks, senators and staff, onto the streets.

The "Speaker presumptive," Newt Gingrich of Georgia, fascinated the country from the first. Like other leaders before him, Gingrich seemed startled to see his casual comments analyzed, his financial arrangements scrutinized, and his private life made public. But there was a strong sense that he and the Republican revolution he headed had turned a dismal, gridlocked Congress into a place where anything could happen. Martha Raddatz reported on the triumphant return to Washington of about-to-be-Speaker Gingrich.

All Things Considered, NOVEMBER 11

GINGRICH: I am very prepared to cooperate with the Clinton administration. I am not prepared to compromise. The two words are very different. On everything on which we can find agreement, I will cooperate. On those things that are at the core of our contract, and those things which are the core of our philosophy, and on those things where we believe we represent the vast majority of Americans, there will be no compromise.

RADDATZ: The core of the philosophy of which Congressman Gingrich speaks is what he and other Republicans call the "Contract with America," something which Congress and the nation will be hearing even more about, come January.

GINGRICH: It was printed in the *TV Guide*. We will read the contract as the opening item of business every day for the first one hundred days and, at the end of the first one hundred days, the American people at Easter will be able to say they saw a group of people who actually said what they were going to do and then kept their word.

RADDATZ: At the end of the opening day, said Gingrich, they will introduce the ten bills described in the "Contract with America."

GINGRICH: Some of these are very controversial. Litigation reform, including malpractice, product liability, and strike law firms, is one item; a balanced budget amendment to the Constitution; a vote on term limits; an effective, enforceable death penalty with a one-time unified appeal; beginning to phase out the marriage penalty in the tax code; allowing senior citizens to earn up to thirty-nine thousand dollars a year without penalty from Social Security; a capital gains cut; and indexing.

RADDATZ: Gingrich cautioned that he's making no promises all ten will pass. The Republicans will try, he said. In addition to what he mentioned, the Republicans want to change the welfare system, beginning with a clean slate, and get a line-item veto. Gingrich has also promised to cut the number of congressional committee staffs by a third, and some of the benefits that go with those jobs. Gingrich also sent a letter to House Speaker Thomas Foley, who lost his own reelection bid, asking that no key documents or official records be destroyed during the transition. Helping Gingrich with the transition is Congressman John Linder from Georgia.

LINDER: We're going to find out where the payrolls are padded in the patronage jobs, how many former members and former staffers still have reserved parking in the garages, and we're just going to open up to the public. We'll not come picking at anybody. What we're going to say is, in a positive way, that the American people have voted us in to change how things work and we're going to change how things work.

RADDATZ: And in the committees, the incoming chairmen are promising big changes as well. Representative Bill Archer of Texas, in line to be the chair of the House Ways and Means Committee, said that he wants to cut the capital gains tax and give tax breaks to married couples.

The military may be big winners with the Republicans coming into power. The man likely to chair the House Armed Services Committee, Representative Floyd Spence, issued a statement saying he will try to reverse the past two years of neglect. And the tobacco industry may be big winners, as well. Representative Thomas Bliley, Jr., likely next chair of the House Energy and Commerce subcommittee on health and environment, told the Associated Press this week, "I don't think we need any more legislation regarding tobacco." As for their Democratic colleagues on the Hill, Republican Linder said, "I think we should treat them the same way they treated us."

LINDER: Part of the reason there's so much meanspiritedness here is the condescension and arrogance by which we were treated. And so it was time for us to swing back. If we were satisfied just taking the crumbs off the table and putting up with this condescension and having no authority over a thing, allowing them to continue to write all their bills behind locked doors that we weren't even a part of, having them decide that Republicans were going to prove to be irrelevant before this administration took office, that we're not even going to include them in the discussions — that's what created the meanspiritedness here.

RADDATZ: All the Republicans agreed there is an enormous amount of work to do, with Gingrich repeating his promise that they will be open to working with everyone, cooperating with anyone, and compromising with no one. "That," said Gingrich, "is where we're going, and that's what we believe this election is all about."

✦ ✦ ✦ ✦ ✦ ✦ ✦ ✦ ✦

The story that closes this chapter will also open the next one. We will spend a great deal of time now following the progress of a political change which some people see as a righteous revolution and others see as a calamity. And now we bring twenty-five years of experience to the enterprise. In these years, National Public Radio has grown considerably. We have more news programs, more people working to gather and shape the stories we cover, and now we send our reporters all over the world. We have grown with public radio stations, which have spread our programs across the country, bringing us to an audience many times the size we ever hoped to reach. But I am fascinated to think that we begin our next quarter century as we began the first one, listening to the American people debate about the future and the character of our own country.

INDEX